Award of the Silver Star Medal, 19 March 1945

James Megellas, First Lieutenant, 504th Parachute Infantry. For gallantry in action on 28 January 1945 near Herresbach, Belgium. After breaking a trail across country for twelve hours in deep, dry snow, First Lieutenant Megellas, a platoon leader, was ordered to advance with his platoon and two supporting tanks along the main road leading into Herresbach. About one mile from the town, his platoon was fired upon by about 200 Germans forming for a defense. Quickly grasping the situation, he led a frontal assault on the startled enemy who attempted to fight back. First lieutenant Megellas's direction and leadership of his men was so superb that within ten minutes the entire force of enemy was either killed, captured, or fled into the town. He then reorganized his platoon and, with the two supporting tanks, followed the enemy into the town. Braving heavy enemy sniper and rifle fire, he personally took a leading part in flushing the enemy out of their houses, killing eight and capturing five enemy. As a result of the First Lieutenant's fearless leadership and skillful handling of his men, over 100 enemy were killed, 180 captured, and large amounts of valuable equipment fell into our hands. This feat was accomplished without the loss of a single man wounded or killed. First Lieutenant Megellas demonstrated a remarkable degree of tactical skill and a brand of courageous leadership which reflects highly upon himself and the Airborne Forces. Entered military service from Fond du Lac, Wisconsin.

— signed James M. Gavin,
Major General,
U.S. Army, Commanding

ALL THE WAY TO BERLIN

A Paratrooper at War in Europe

JAMES MEGELLAS

PRESIDIO
PRESS

BALLANTINE BOOKS • NEW YORK

A Presidio Press Book
Published by The Random House Publishing Group
Copyright © 2003 by James Megellas

www.presidiopress.com

ISBN 0-89141-836-9

Maps © the Aegis Consulting Group
All photos from the author's collection

Manufactured in the United States of America

First Edition: March 2003
First Mass Market Edition: March 2004

OPM   10   9   8   7   6   5   4   3   2   1

To Carole and our two sons, James and Stephen

This book is also dedicated to the memory of my buddy 1st Lt. Richard G. LaRiviere—or Rivers, as we called him—whose World War II experience was a mirror image of my own. We first met in 1943 at Fort Benning, Georgia, where we went through parachute school together. From that point on, we were with each other, from Africa to Italy and through Europe, until May 1945, when the Germans surrendered.

We were assigned in December 1943 as platoon leaders in H Company, 504th Parachute Infantry Regiment, located in the mountains of Italy. When the war ended, we were still combat platoon leaders. Although we had both been wounded in action, we managed to survive and continued together in H Company. An incredible bond developed between us that was stronger than brotherhood. In December 1967, while Cornelius Ryan was researching his book *A Bridge Too Far,* I responded to a questionnaire from him asking whom in the operation I would recommend he contact. My answer: "Rivers was perhaps the most daring and courageous soldier in the entire 82d Airborne Division. He was a fearless leader who received and commanded considerable respect from all the men who served with him. As an inseparable team, our two platoons fought side-by-side on a number of occasions."

I am also dedicating this book to those paratroopers with whom I served and to the thousands more in frontline units who came face-to-face with the enemy in World War II. These paratroopers endured the rigors and hardships of combat, often under the most miserable conditions imaginable. They asked no quarter and gave none. Many who survived have vanished, taking with them the memories of their closely held exploits. Thousands never made it back, and many more still carry physical scars of combat. Collectively, they swelled the numbers of American casualties in World War II, each becoming a number in the statistical game. These countless noncommissioned officers and junior commissioned officers led the soldiers in battle, bore the brunt of the fighting, and paid the highest price. This is their story as I saw it through the sights of my gun.

Contents

Preface

For the past twenty years, I contemplated writing my memoirs of World War II from the perspective of the combat soldier. I was not inclined to write a book about the war as such but rather about the men who fought it, focusing on their fears, emotions, needs, and hopes.

The young soldiers who manned the ramparts for our nation in World War II were a special breed. They came from all walks of life: farms, factories, professions, and colleges. They were teenagers just out of high school and high school dropouts. They had one common purpose—to serve their nation in a time of crisis and to defend those principles we hold dear. They were stout of heart and spirit, the finest our nation had to offer. The title I had in mind for such a book was "What Manner of Men."

After I became immersed in writing, it seemed that a more encompassing title for what I had in mind would be "Through the Sights of My Gun." It gave me latitude to write not only about the human aspects of war and the men who fought it, but space to express how I saw it from a foxhole. In the process I could tell it as it actually was, and let the chips fall where they may.

I have not contrived or concocted any of the experiences or opinions related in the book. What I have written in all instances is a true and accurate reflection of what I saw and felt at the time and frequently expressed in letters I wrote home. All the barbs, arrow stings, and piques are exclusively mine, and they are as valid today as they were fifty-five years ago.

Introduction

After the victory parade in New York City in January 1946, I left the army and the 82d Airborne Division and returned to private life in Fond du Lac, Wisconsin, where I had entered military service in 1942. When I mustered out at Fort McCoy, Wisconsin, in 1946, I remained in the U.S. Army Reserve. At the time I was a captain, of which I was proud. I reasoned that by joining the reserves, if hostilities broke out again I could be recalled to active duty.

As a civilian, I was attracted to the political arena largely because I felt that it was the best avenue for the expression of my ideals for further service to my country. The first attempt for public office was in November 1946, when I ran for the Wisconsin state legislature in a predominantly conservative, agrarian district. When I had been awarded my first Silver Star for gallantry in action in 1944, my closest friend, 1st Lt. Richard G. LaRiviere—we called him Rivers—congratulated me, then said: "With that Silver Star and ten cents you can get a cup of coffee, if you're lucky enough to get back home alive." As it turned out, Rivers was prophetic; you could get a cup of coffee, but first you had to have the dime. Nor did the second Silver Star, the Distinguished Service Cross, two Bronze Stars, two Purple Hearts, and two years in combat make the price of a cup of coffee less than a dime. Applying Rivers's comment to a political campaign, all my combat decorations did not change one conservative voter's mind. But if at the time I'd had a sizable campaign war chest, the outcome would probably have been different. Rivers was right; combat medals accounted for little if you did not have the "dime."

However, it counted with Sen. John F. Kennedy, to whom combat experience was defining and distinguishing. I came to know him well when we were both campaigning in Wisconsin in 1960, he for the Democratic nomination for president and I to be representative for the state's sixth congressional district. For three continuous days we campaigned together, sharing the same podium, shaking hands in shopping centers and at factory gates first thing in the morning. Most of the time we were alone in my car, with Secret Service agents and Kennedy's political entourage enveloping us as we rode from city to city. He talked about his combat experiences as a PT boat commander and I talked about mine as a paratrooper in the 82d Airborne Division. In the April 1960 presidential primary, Kennedy carried my district and narrowly won the state of Wisconsin in a hotly contested primary. It made him the front-runner and gave him a big boost on the road to the Democratic presidential nomination. I did not see him again until he was president, but he kept tabs on my congressional campaign. At a critical time when I needed outside help, Kennedy sent his brother Robert into my district to campaign with me. In spite of a determined effort, as Rivers would have put it, "I came up a dime short."

In 1961, the first year of the Kennedy presidency, I was offered an opportunity to join the new administration in some capacity. After considerable thought and soul-searching, I expressed a preference for the foreign service. My military experience had taken me to Africa and across Europe, and the lure of going abroad in a peacetime situation was tempting. In November 1961, I received an appointment to the U.S. Agency for International Development (USAID), with the highest grade, FSR-1, and a commitment to an overseas assignment as a USAID mission director.

In May 1962, I married a young lady from Fond du Lac, Wisconsin, whom I had courted for four years. Carole Laehn and I packed our bags and headed for Yemen in June 1962, stopping en route in Europe to enjoy several days of a "honeymoon abroad." It was the beginning of a new chapter in my life that I would find both demanding and challenging. Before I concluded my career in the foreign service, I served, in addition to Yemen, in Panama and Colombia and two years in Vietnam during the height of the war. My tour in Vietnam was unaccompanied; my wife and two sons, ages five and two, lived in "safe haven" in Manila. It was not until I retired from the foreign service and established my residence in Florida that I had the first impulse to set in writing what I had experienced and observed in World War II.

After the war, my preoccupation with civilian pursuits, my new career, and my family responsibilities in helping to raise two boys were foremost in my mind. Although many of my combat experiences were still vivid, they were closely held. Most of my service in AID was abroad, and I had little contact with my war buddies. After I retired and returned to the United States, I resumed old acquaintances, attended reunions, and rehashed combat experiences with them. Many of the observations and thoughts that had lain dormant began to emerge. In the process, a number of my former comrades in arms encouraged me to write a book and "tell it like it actually was." I gave the idea serious consideration, because I felt I had a story to tell about the young American boys who had fought it. Although 16 million men had been mobilized to respond to the threat to our nation, less than 5 percent of that number endured the hardships and risks of combat or ever came face-to-face with our enemies. Many of these men never returned, losing their lives in combat or carrying the scars of enemy onslaughts. As one who shared those experiences, I had a strong compulsion, bordering at times on obsession, to tell their story.

I would not have attempted this writing if I'd had to rely entirely on my memory of events that took place more than fifty years ago, vivid though those memories remain. In the intervening period, I had accumulated copies of correspondence and inquiries from authors, historians, and students writing theses on World War II. Most I ignored for a variety of reasons, mainly for lack of time, but I did respond to several in some depth if the purpose seemed valid. On 27 October 1967, I received a query from Cornelius Ryan, who was writing *A Bridge Too Far*, containing twenty-five questions—some personal, but mostly regarding my recollections of the events of 1944 during the Holland campaign. I did not know Ryan personally, nor had I read his two previous war books, but I decided to respond to his query in considerable detail. In 1991, at the request of the 504th Parachute Infantry Regiment Association, I wrote an account of our epic battle in Anzio, Italy, during the first ten days of February 1944. It was for that action that my battalion, the 3d of the 504th, had received the Presidential Unit Citation for its stand against a determined enemy assault, which may well have saved the beachhead from being overrun. A group from the association was going to Anzio to dedicate the battle site. For them I again went into considerable detail. That account forms the basis for a large part of the chapter on Anzio (Chapter IV).

I was fortunate to receive a copy of Cpl. George D. Graves Jr.'s narrative of the Battle of the Bulge from its inception, 17 December 1944, until 18 February 1945, when we were relieved of frontline duty and returned to France. George was originally assigned to H Company but was transferred to the 504th Regimental headquarters, where he spent most of his service in the regimental S-1 section. In addition to his other duties, he maintained the official S-1 journal of daily activities. His detailed account, written on a daily basis, was a valuable historical source regarding dates, times, and places of combat actions.

Several years ago I found a box of letters in a corner of my attic that I had written home after I left for the army, many from the European theater of operations (ETO) and some while I was on the front lines. I had never kept a diary, but these old letters revealed how I had felt about the war and battles and conditions on the front lines. Reading them brought me back to the days when I was a combat platoon leader called "Maggie" by my peers. It was as if I were looking in a mirror. Mail censorship restricted what I was permitted to write concerning units, places, dates, et cetera, but I was able to make personal observations and comments on some of the most notable battles in which I'd been involved. These letters have been an important source of information to which I refer frequently in the book. I consider letters written shortly after the heat of battle to be the most authentic record of disputed issues, such as the number of enemy killed in battle.

The fiftieth anniversary of the end of World War II, celebrated in 1995, revived national interest in the war. A number of books were written and movies produced that attempted to cover the brutality of the war rather than the glory of victory. After reviewing this portrayal of World War II, I was convinced I had a story to tell in a way that had not yet been written. I believed I could add another, more focused dimension on the level where wars are actually fought: in the rifle squads and platoons. I had been in combat almost continuously as a lieutenant leading my platoon on patrols and in defense and attacks. This book deals with the micro aspects of war, wars as fought by young teenage GIs in squads and platoons led by noncommissioned officers and junior grade officers. Anyone interested in the macro aspects, the grand strategies, the political intrigues, and the relationships among the Allies can look elsewhere. This is my story of the way it was in the foxholes.

Writing this book some fifty years after the war presented many difficulties with respect to names, time, places, and personal experiences. On the other hand, writing in retrospect gave me the advantage of perspective, history, time, and maturity, which have been instrumental in placing my combat experience and those of my buddies in a broader context. I don't believe that "Maggie," fresh out of the army in 1946, with vivid and stark memories of the details in combat, could have written this book. In looking back on this experience, history and perspective are important factors in attempting to analyze the true meaning of young men killing one another.

82nd Airborne Division
Major Battles in Italy, 1943-44

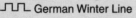 Battles of the 82nd Airborne Division

 Battles of the 504th PIR when detached from the 82nd

German Winter Line

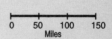

ADRIATIC SEA

ITALY

Rome

Anzio

Venafro

Naples
Salerno

TYRRHENIAN SEA

IONIAN SEA

Major Battles of the 82nd Airborne Division

⭐ Major Battle

0   150   300
Miles

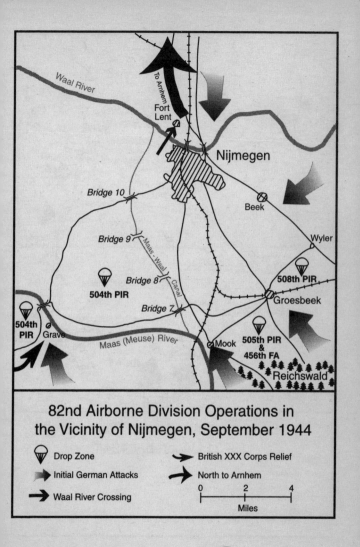

Waal River

To Arnhem

Fort Lent

Nijmegen

Bridge 10

Beek

Wyler

Bridge 9

Maas - Waal Canal

Bridge 8

508th PIR

504th PIR

Groesbeek

Bridge 7

504th PIR
Grave

Maas (Meuse) River

Mook

505th PIR
& 456th FA

Reichswald

82nd Airborne Division Operations in the Vicinity of Nijmegen, September 1944

🪂 Drop Zone

British XXX Corps Relief

Initial German Attacks

North to Arnhem

Waal River Crossing

0   2   4
Miles

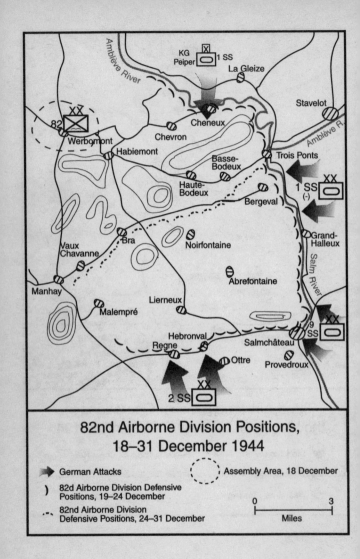

82nd Airborne Division Positions, 18–31 December 1944

➤ German Attacks

◯ Assembly Area, 18 December

❱ 82d Airborne Division Defensive
Positions, 19–24 December

--- 82nd Airborne Division
Defensive Positions, 24–31 December

0   3

Miles

Map labels:

KG Peiper — 1 SS
La Gleize
Stavelot
Amblève River
Cheneux
Chevron
Werbomont
82
Habiemont
Basse-Bodeux
Trois Ponts
Amblève R.
Haute-Bodeux
1 SS (-)
Bergeval
Grand-Halleux
Vaux Chavanne
Bra
Noirfontaine
Salm River
Abrefontaine
Manhay
Lierneux
9 SS
Malempré
Hebronval
Regne
Salmchâteau
Ottre
Provedroux
2 SS

82nd Airborne Division Major Battles in Germany: The Siegfried Line and Beyond

☆ Breaching the Siegfried Line

⭐ The Huertgen Forest

★ Crossing the Elbe River

0   50   100
Miles

I

At War

On 7 December 1941, when the Japanese attacked Pearl Harbor, I was a senior at Ripon College, in Ripon, Wisconsin, expecting to complete my bachelor of arts studies and looking forward to graduating the following June. At the time, the future was uncertain. The country had suffered through the Great Depression of the 1930s, and prospects of a liberal arts graduate finding a suitable niche in the workplace appeared bleak. War clouds were gathering in Europe and the Pacific, and German submarines were prowling off the Atlantic coast, attacking U.S. shipping destined for Great Britain. A military buildup was going on in the United States, and fervor to enter the war on the side of the Allies was growing. I also was in my final year of reserve officer training at Ripon College and, upon graduation, would receive a second lieutenant's commission in the U.S. Army. Given the situation, even before Pearl Harbor, it was almost certain that the new crop of Ripon officers would be ordered to active duty. The universal draft was instituted in 1940, so there was a growing need for officers to lead newly recruited enlisted men.

The Japanese attack on Pearl Harbor ended all the uncertainties I might have had concerning my future, at least for the short term. The United States was at war. This was stunning, and my knee-jerk reaction was to drop out of school (even though graduation was only about six months away) and enlist in the army. This reaction was soon dispelled when an accelerated schedule for graduation was announced. The best course of action would be for me to stay in school and receive a commission, then go on active duty. Graduation was set a month earlier than scheduled, at which time we would also receive our commissions and active duty orders. In the meantime, our Reserve Officers' Training Corps (ROTC) instruction became more intense and took on greater significance. The only questions remaining were where and how soon we would be on duty. Everything else became mundane. Academic studies, homework, and term papers began to suffer from lack of priority. Although it was still important to complete school and receive a degree—an officer's commission depended upon completion of studies—for the next six months, concentration on anything but the war was difficult.

The nation responded vigorously to the mobilization, with young men forming long lines at recruiting offices, volunteering for service. Factories turning out the sinews of war worked overtime. Women were replacing men who had answered the call to serve. Legislation establishing priorities for the use of essential resources was quickly approved. Victory gardens replaced lawns; sewing and knitting were in vogue. Patriotism knew no bounds as the nation mobilized for war. It was the defining moment for my generation.

On the day of graduation—28 May 1942—when I walked across the stage dressed in a black cap and gown, I was given a diploma in my left hand and an officer's commission in my right. I was a second lieutenant of infantry in the U.S. Army. Only moments later, I received orders assigning me, along with six others, to report for duty on 8 June 1942 at Fort Knox, Kentucky. I was twenty-five years old.

Eight years earlier, I had graduated from high school. In 1934, during the throes of the Great Depression, continuing the education of the third born in an immigrant family of seven children had not been an option. Struggling to provide the basic necessities of life, my father was laid off more than he worked at the local leather-tanning factory. My brother George, nine years my elder, had dropped out of school after the eighth grade. He had found a job setting pins in a bowling alley. We were, by any economic definition, a poor family, but we were rich in love and tradition. Adversity had brought us even closer. With a high school diploma in hand, I would take my turn helping to put food on the table. Every morning I made the rounds of local factory employment offices. The answer was always the same. In 1934, a high school graduate could not beg, borrow, or steal a job.

In August 1934 I heard that the Civilian Conservation Corps (CCC) provided clean outdoor work. I applied, was accepted, and in October found myself in the north woods of Wisconsin. The CCC transformed me from a seventeen-year-old kid to a working man. I ate three wholesome meals a day, kept regular hours, and worked outdoors in all kinds of weather in a healthy environment. More importantly, the CCC taught me discipline, self-reliance, organization, and how to work and live as part of a unit. Every morning we stood reveille and answered roll call; in the evening, it was retreat and lowering the flag. At ten o'clock, it was lights out in the barracks. We wore surplus army khakis, slept on army cots with army blankets, and on Saturdays we stood at barracks and personal inspection. Two reserve officers—a captain and a lieutenant—ran the camp. They received officer's pay and benefits much greater than our "dollar a day."

This experience was one of the reasons I sought a reserve officer's commission when I entered Ripon College in 1937. In a tight labor market, a reserve officer's commission could be a big plus and might open the door to a job not available otherwise. Also, in the event I was called to active duty, I would enter as an officer. The CCC was not in the true sense military duty, but it was the closest thing to it at the time.

After leaving the CCC, I worked for a local construction company; the pay was good and I was able to put away some money. I entered Ripon College, some twenty miles from home, encouraged by its football coach, and with two job offers that would pay my room and board. I would repay tuition and other costs with monthly pay deductions after I went on active duty.

At the start of my junior year at Ripon, a notice appeared on our ROTC bulletin board that the U.S. Army Air Corps was accepting applications for pilot training. To qualify as a cadet, an applicant had to have a private pilot's license or had to have successfully completed two years of college and be able to pass a rigid physical examination. Although I had never been in an airplane, the thought of becoming an officer and a pilot in what was a fledgling branch of the army was too strong to resist. I applied, passed the physical examination, and was accepted. In December 1939, I dropped out of college and proceeded to Tulsa, Oklahoma, to begin the first phase of intensive training. The planes used for training were of World War I vintage—biwing Wright Whirlwind Jennys with dual open cockpits and stick controls.

I gave it my best effort, but my career in the Air Corps was short-lived. I did not qualify to advance to the second phase of training. I'd had my heart set on becoming a pilot, and the failure had a demoralizing effect on me. After knocking around the Southwest for a while, I decided to return to Ripon College.

In my senior year, I took advantage of a new U.S. government program designed for college students to receive civilian flight training. The training was held at the nearest civilian airport, and the trainers were small single-engine airplanes. Compared to my previous flight training in the army, I found flying a small Cessna a snap. I completed my ground school course and flight training and was granted a private pilot's license.

All this was behind me as I packed my bags and prepared to report to Fort Knox in June 1942. It is said that the past is a prologue. My experience of hard work, adversity, and challenges prepared me for what lay ahead when later I found myself in combat.

II

The Call to Arms

On 8 June 1942, just ten days after graduating and receiving my commission, I reported for duty at Fort Knox, Kentucky, assigned to the armored forces training center.

On 10 June I wrote my first letter home:

This place is really huge. It is expanding very rapidly. Armored Forces is a comparatively new branch of the Army and offers a good opportunity for advancement.

Starting this Saturday, we will go through eight weeks of Armored Force School. In this course, we will review everything we've had so far, plus what we do not know about Armored Force. We will have school from morning until night. We will cover a lot of ground and we will have a lot of studying and hard work ahead. The Army really means business now.

In the school course we will pursue, we will study and fire many automatic weapons, besides driving a two and a half ton truck, a light tank, and a medium tank.

We eat in the officers' mess. The food costs us a dollar a day, but is very good. We live in barracks and have an orderly who cleans out our rooms and shines our shoes. We pay him three dollars a month. We also have officers' clubs to which we belong and we pay three-dollar monthly dues for this privilege. Our laundry comes to about five dollars a month. All this is paid out of our wages of $168 a month. So you see, an officer isn't as well off as some people might think.

This letter, one of the many I would write home, pretty well summed up my initial reaction to my first days of active duty. I was happy to be in the armored forces. It was one of the combat arms, and, as a tanker, I was looking forward to seeing combat. I was thankful that I was not assigned to one of the support branches of the army, where the likelihood of seeing combat was next to nothing. Also, being assigned to a relatively new branch would provide an opportunity for advancement up the officers' ranks. I viewed the war as meaning combat and looked forward to extended service as a tanker.

But that was not to be the case. In the army, nothing is for certain or forever. On 15 June, just one week after I reported for duty at Fort Knox, I was called out of the morning formation and told to report to the adjutant's office. I was being transferred immediately, although I didn't know at the time that I would be going into the signal corps. The next day I sent the following telegram home: "I'm being transferred to Fort Monmouth, New Jersey, tomorrow. Will send address when I arrive." I had no choice but to proceed directly to Fort Monmouth. I was disappointed with my new assignment for three reasons: I did not feel I had the technical background for service in the field of communications; I was leaving my Ripon College colleagues; and, most importantly, I was being transferred from a combat arm to a service arm, where seeing combat was not likely. I could not envision myself killing an enemy soldier with a pair of pliers. The signal corps was given priority in identifying and recruiting officers who it felt were qualified to meet the corps' rapidly expanding needs.

On 20 June I reported for duty at Fort Monmouth to begin an intensive twelve-week course focusing primarily on signal communications, circuit diagrams, line route maps, overlays, and field orders. On 2 July I wrote my brother Louis: "The Signal Corps right now is taking officers who have had any physics or math out of all branches of the service. The Signal Corps needs officers so badly that they will not let anyone transfer to something else."

On 21 July I wrote to Louis again: "It's all classroom work, no getting outside. We have school six days a week from 7:30 a.m. until 5 p.m., and sometimes at night. Besides this they give us homework to do. Boy, this sure is getting me down."

I never doubted that the signal corps was an important branch of the service, and in combat has a vital job to do; it just was not for me.

Shortly after I arrived at Fort Monmouth, I read in the *Army Times* that another new branch of the army, the glider pilot corps, was seeking volunteers. It was given top priority for officer recruitment. Among the several qualifications was a valid current private pilot's license. Happy day! I immediately applied, then waited. I was hopeful that I might still see action if I became a glider pilot.

On 2 July I wrote to my sister Catherine: "This school [signal corps] will last 12 weeks, if I'm here that long. When we finish that course, we will probably be sent out as Division Signal officers. I'd like to get into some other branch of service. I have asked for glider pilot and am even trying to get in the Commandos."

I was pursuing every possible avenue that might get me into a combat unit. But nothing developed, so I continued in the signal corps school. On 13 October I graduated and received my diploma. I was a full-fledged signal corps officer. On that date, I also received orders assigning me to the 64th Signal Battalion, located at Fort Meade, Maryland, fifteen miles north of Washington. So for the third time since 8 June, I packed my bags and headed for another post.

I was just getting settled down as a signal officer when I was notified that my application for transfer to the glider pilot corps was approved. The battalion commander was upset with the news, telling me how much the signal corps had spent training me and how badly it needed signal officers. He implied that the least I was guilty of was disloyalty. I was undeterred; my mind was set on being in a branch where combat action was possible.

On 5 November my brief tour of duty as a signal officer ended. I was bound for Lubbock, Texas, assigned to the Lubbock Army Flying School (LAFS) in what would be the first stop in my quest to be a glider pilot. I reported for duty on the morning of 9 November. I was now in the United States Army Air Corps. In less than six months, I was wearing my fourth different service insignia: Infantry, Armored Force, Signal Corps, and Air Corps.

On the day the first American troops went ashore in Casablanca, Africa, the first American teenager was killed in combat in the European theater of operations. I was eating Texas beef and living the life of Riley. Such are the fortunes of war.

I didn't realize it at the time, but my stay in the Air Corps would be temporary. In the next few months, I would be in and out of a number of air bases. I was able to retrace my footsteps and revisit those fields from letters I had written home. On 12 November, shortly after my arrival at Lubbock, I wrote to my brother Louis: "I haven't been near a glider. This is not a glider field, and we will be here only a couple of days more . . . and then will be sent out to start training. . . . I sure am anxious to get going."

On 24 November I reported for duty at the Army Air Navigation School, in Hondo, Texas—my fifth post in less than six months. Just as with Lubbock, Hondo was not a glider-training base, so my stay here would be short. On 26 November I wrote home: "I should be down here a little while yet, at least another month anyway. I've got a hunch I may spend part of my winter in Oklahoma or Kansas."

In the meantime, more U.S. infantry and armored units were joining the fight in Africa against Rommel and the Afrika Korps. The war effort was intensifying, and all my efforts to get into combat notwithstanding, I was still biding my time in Texas, with frequent visits to San Antonio and across the border into Mexico, weekends at dude ranches, and no responsibilities. What did Sherman mean when he said, "War is hell"?

Finally, on 10 January 1943, I received orders to report to the 24th Army Air Force Glider Training Detachment (AAFGTD) at Okmulgee, Oklahoma. En route, I detoured through Little Rock, Arkansas. Without prior notice, I surprised my oldest brother, SSgt. George Megellas, at Camp Robinson by walking into the kitchen of his mess hall. What a surprise for him and a treat for me.

On 15 January I reported for duty with 24th AAFGTD. The next day I wrote to my sister Catherine: "There are two hundred enlisted men and six officers in training here. The men go through training just like cadets, only they all live together in downtown hotels and eat in restaurants. They have bed checks, reveille, and strict regulations. The officers . . . live separately. All we have to do is attend classes and fly when we are scheduled. I am staying in the Belmont Hotel and have my own room with bath, telephone, big double bed and porter services. . . . This phase of training lasts four weeks."

The flight training was conducted in light, single-engine planes similar to those used by the artillery for identifying targets in range adjustment. Our course was referred to as "dead-stick landing" training. A student would take off with an instructor and climb to about 2,000 feet at some distance from the airstrip. At that point, the instructor would turn off the ignition and the student would make an approach to the field and glide the plane in for a landing. The purpose was to simulate the landing of a powerless glider. This routine was repeated every day for four weeks, weather permitting. All the while, I qualified for Army Air Corps flight pay of $75 per month, which, in addition to my second lieutenant's pay of $168, increased the officer's pay to $244 per month.

At the successful completion of the dead-stick landing course, I expected to be transferred to advanced glider pilot school and fly actual gliders. Instead, I received orders to return to Lubbock AFS. On 10 February I wrote to my sister

Catherine: "In two days I will be leaving here for Lubbock, Texas, again. . . . I understand it is a glider pilot pool . . . where we will be stationed for a short while until an advanced glider school can accommodate another group of students. Right now, they have more glider pilots than schools."

So once again I packed bags, loaded them into the trunk of my beat-up 1936 Chevrolet, and headed back to Lubbock and an uncertain future. Meanwhile, U.S. and British forces were pushing Rommel back into Africa, and a major battle was fought at Kasserine Pass on 10 February. While American GIs were dying in battle, I was heading for my seventh post in nine months since being ordered to active duty. I was becoming increasingly frustrated and questioned whether I would ever be assigned to a combat unit.

On 10 March I wrote to my youngest brother, Louis, who had volunteered for the service after graduating from high school and was stationed at Camp Roberts, California: "I sure had some bad news when I got back to Lubbock. The glider-training program has been discontinued. Most of the schools have closed and no more men will be trained. At this point, there are 35 officers and 600 enlisted men who are waiting to go on to the advanced glider school. Next Monday a board of officers will be here to interview us for something else."

So, after four months in the Air Corps seeking to become a glider pilot, it was back to square one.

On 13 March a board of officers arrived from Washington to interview the officers and men in the glider pilot pool and reassign them to appropriate branches of the service. I was at a crossroads in my life and my military career. As a college graduate, I could name the branch, assignment, and location of my next post. Even the Pentagon was an option, but I would have no part of that. At the conclusion of my interview, I asked one question of the board: "What is the quickest way I can get into combat?" The answer was: "Go to the parachute training school in Fort Benning, Georgia." That was it, and the sooner the better. I went through the formality of making a transfer application. The board took it back to Washington, and I was told I would be hearing from the adjutant general. I expected my orders momentarily. But much to my consternation, I learned that the Washington bureaucracy does not move that fast.

I continued to bide my time at Lubbock AFS. On 1 April I wrote to my brother Louis: "I still don't know what's going to happen to me. I've written two letters to Washington volunteering for the paratroopers, but I haven't had an answer yet. There's a lot of red tape in the Army and it generally takes quite a while for anything to come through Washington. You have to write a military letter and send it through channels."

Once again, for several months I was unassigned, unattended, and uncertain about my situation. I wrote to Louis: "I haven't got too much to do here now. I have two officer calls to make, one at 8:30 a.m. and one at 7 p.m. My job is Athletic Officer of the glider pilots (500 men). I give them PT once a day, sometimes for two hours. That's all I've got to do. The rest of the time, I'm at the gym working out or lying in the sun."

Although we were no longer in the glider pilot corps and soon would be transferred out, we were kept on flying status. I managed to fly enough time in small planes (Cubs) to qualify for the additional $75 a month in pay. However, that would end and the flying status would terminate when I received my new orders.

On 17 May, after two months of waiting and uncertainty, I received orders transferring me to the Parachute Training School at Fort Benning, Georgia. That same day I wrote to my sister Catherine: "I just received my orders today. I'll be leaving here Wednesday. I have seven days to drive there, a distance of 1,400 miles. Intend to go through Little Rock and surprise brother George again."

Just one year after I entered active duty, I reported for duty at the Parachute Training School. I was assigned to Company T, 1st Parachute Training Regiment. After passing

another physical examination, I began training. On 27 May
I wrote to my brother George, who was still stationed at
Camp Robinson, in Arkansas: "You've probably heard what
a tough outfit this is. Well, it's no rumor. My class is due to
start this Monday. In the meantime, we're getting some
hardening up to get in shape for it. The course lasts four
weeks. . . . The first week is devoted entirely to strenuous
physical training. From morning until night, everything is
done on the 'double.' At the end of the first week, you are
required to run eight miles without stopping. I'll do it if it
kills me. The third week is devoted to jumping from the
towers and the fourth week from planes. You must make
five jumps in order to qualify. . . . A friend of mine from
Ripon College is here in his third week. There were 85 officers in this class when he started; now there are 45. The
rest have either dropped out or are in the hospital. The hospital is full of paratroopers with broken legs or arms. I
never saw so many cripples in my life."

After having lived off the fat of the land in Lubbock for
more than two months, I was not in the best physical condition. The first week was grueling physical exertion and
exhaustion. The ninety-degree-plus heat did not help. I
sweated like a butcher. On 6 June I wrote my sister Catherine: "I just finished the toughest week I have ever spent in
my life. It's the toughest physical test that is given in the
Army. Yesterday, we ran eight miles. I was in an officer's section and they make it tougher for us than they do for the enlisted men. On our runs we would all run in formation and
in step. On yesterday's run, an officer in front of me, a captain, collapsed and fell over after a few minutes. When I
made a move to pick him up, an instructor yelled at me, 'Let
him lay; someone will be along to pick him up.' And so it
was along the way. They dropped out like flies. They say that
the only thing that gets one through is sheer guts and determination. During this week they find out how much you
want to be a paratrooper. . . . Tomorrow I start a stage, which
isn't as tough physically. One half of the day is devoted to

chute packing and the other half to jumping out of mock doors, landing trainers, etc. We must pack our own chutes for every jump. . . ."

The four weeks of training at parachute school were intense and physically demanding, but fortunately I was not injured and was up to the ordeal physically and mentally. I had to qualify as a paratrooper; otherwise, it was back to the treadmill I had been on for more than a year. If determination was the key ingredient, there was no way I could fail. Qualifying as a paratrooper was my ticket overseas and to combat. Failure was unthinkable.

Here are excerpts from some of the letters I wrote home during my three-plus months at Fort Benning.

On 13 June I wrote to my sister Mary: "Well, I've got two weeks yet to go, if I don't get injured. I just finished two tough weeks. Last week we had training towers and mock-up towers. This week we will be working off of 250-foot towers. We will be released off the towers, open chutes, float to the ground, and land. Next week we will also learn to pack a parachute. Next Friday, we will pack our own chutes for our first jump from a plane, a week from tomorrow. . . . We had 90 officers in our section when we started, now we have 55. After two weeks, the rest have been 'washed out,' quit, or injured. The heat down here is terrific."

On 20 June I wrote to my sister Catherine:

I just finished three tough weeks of training and tomorrow morning comes the real thing—my first jump from a plane in flight, or should I say "plane in fright." We packed our main chute and reserve chute on Friday. We pack our own chutes for every jump, so if it fails you have no one to blame but yourself. . . . Yesterday afternoon we drew our plastic jump helmets and got our final jump instructions. We will jump from 1,200 feet. Tomorrow will be the first of the six jumps we will make this week in order to qualify and receive our paratrooper wings. So, by next Saturday and barring any accident, I hope to be a full-fledged paratrooper.

Last week was spent on jump training off of 250-foot towers. The towers are equipped with a pulley system that pulls you off the ground rigged to a parachute already inflated. You are then released from 250 feet and the rest is exactly identical to a plane jump. I made four such jumps last week, including one night drop. On another tower, we are rigged up in a shock harness and pulled up to the top suspended by a cable and fastened in a harness horizontal to the ground. You can imagine the feeling you receive being 250 feet off the ground and lying with your arms and legs horizontal to the ground. At a command from below, you pull the ripcord, which opens the harness and lets you fall about thirty feet before your fall is broken, then you bounce and swing all over like a jumping jack. This is supposed to simulate the initial shock received by the opening of your chute.

In the barracks there are five of us in a row who will make our first jump tomorrow. The boys are all polishing their jump boots and kidding one another, but they are all "sweating it out." We've got from now until tomorrow to sweat, it's only natural, it happens to everyone. No phase of the training has frightened me yet, and I'm not thinking of tomorrow's jump, but I know about the time the plane takes off the ground, butterflies will be running around in my stomach. There will be a bunch of scared boys tomorrow until the jump is over.

While we were spending the weekend preparing mentally for the first jump, it did not help to have officers in the same barracks who had already qualified recounting some of the earlier horror stories. It was all in fun but questions such as, "when you packed your chute, did you remember to take out the shot bags?" That did not ease the "sweating out" process. Then there was a story of the first-time jumper. He was told that when he exited, his chute would open automatically. "Count to three and if your main chute hasn't opened, pull the ripcord on your reserve chute. When you hit the ground there will be a truck waiting to pick up you and your chute and bring you back to the hanger." The first timer exited the door and when the main chute did not open he pulled the ripcord on his reserve chute. That didn't open either. As he was descending from 1,200 feet, the first timer, bemoaning his bad luck, said, "And I suppose that when I hit the ground the truck to pick me up won't be there either."

I wrote to Catherine again on 23 June:

I made my third jump today and I walked away from every landing and that's doing good in this outfit. I still have one jump to make tomorrow and two on Friday before I finish my training. If I don't have any tough luck, I'll be wearing paratrooper wings this Saturday.

When the plane took off just before I made the first jump, I experienced a feeling I will never forget. I don't know if it was in anticipation of what I was about to go through, if it was fear, or just a feeling of anxiety, but whatever it was, I had a sick feeling in my stomach and I was sweating freely. I remember standing in the door and getting the command to "go," but I don't remember anything until the chute opened. What a great feeling—suspended in air and it's so peaceful and quiet. In my second and third jumps, I was aware of everything that happened. I saw the tail of the ship as I was falling through space. Then there is that glorious feeling—the opening of the chute. Today, when I hit the ground, I came down pretty hard. I came in on a backward oscillation and landed hard on my feet, then butt, and smacked my head hard, but luckily I had on my helmet so I didn't hurt my head. My butt is so sore that I have trouble sitting down tonight, but I know I'll be ready to jump again tomorrow morning.

It's a tough racket, but the thrills you get and the glorious feeling of descent more than make up for the risks you take.

Completing a tough and potentially risky course where only one-third of the officers make it in the scheduled four weeks leaves one with a sense of accomplishment and pride. This was true with all who qualified. That same sense of pride in being a paratrooper carried over into combat. No mission was too dangerous or impossible. The shiny paratrooper boots and wings created a bond among those who wore them. These men were not ordinary soldiers. This sense of pride was expressed in a letter I wrote to my brother George at Camp Robinson on 27 June:

I got my parachute wings last Friday. I made my fifth jump Friday morning and my sixth on Friday afternoon. The General pinned our paratrooper's wings on us Friday night. Of the original 86 who started in our class, 27 finished last Friday. The rest, well, suffered an assortment of fates. Some were disqualified, some had to repeat some weeks, but the majority of them were injured and we had one death.

I was fortunate not to get hurt bad enough on any of my jumps to have to go on sick call, but I sure took a beating on some of them. The last four jumps I landed on a rear oscillation and hit on my butt and head. I had a headache for days, but it went away and my butt is still sore so that standing is a pleasure.

However, I'm happy to be a paratrooper and to have qualified in four weeks, which is something to be proud of down here. The class of men found here is strictly the finest in the Army. The boys with the "boots and wings" are looked up to and respected by all the Infantry here.

On all my six jumps, I jumped as number one man and led a "stick" of 11 enlisted men out the door. We jump 12 men in eight seconds. It sure is a pretty thing to watch those boys bail out, not a fraction of a second's hesitation from anyone. If one man should hesitate or freeze in the door, the entire jump would be ruined. The enlisted men will follow you anywhere without question. It is the officer's job to stand in the door while the plane is in flight, pick out the jump field and time the jump commands so that all your "stick" of men gets in the field.

When you approach your field, you stick your head back in the plane and give the command, "Are you ready?" to your sweating "stick" of men and in reply you get a blood curdling "Yeah!" This command is a psychological one. Then you give the command "Let's go" and out you go with your men behind you.

There's no question but that this is a rugged outfit and you take a lot of risks, but I would not trade this outfit for any in the world.

On 28 June, after completion of parachute school, I was assigned to Company H, 515th Parachute Regiment, located in the frying pan area of Fort Benning, some eight miles from the barracks we had occupied during training. The 515th served as a pool for paratroopers awaiting assignment to airborne units. The most likely was the 82d Airborne Division, which had been activated in May 1942 at Fort Bragg, North Carolina. On 29 April 1943, it sailed from New York on the troop ship George Washington; it arrived in Casablanca, Africa, on 10 May. A combat mission for the 82d appeared imminent, with Italy or perhaps Sicily being the target. In the meantime, we were kept busy training and preparing for what most likely would be an overseas assignment.

Fort Benning was a beehive of activity. In addition to the parachute school, it housed the Infantry School, Infantry Officer Candidate School (OCS), and a number of regular army units. It was the largest post in the country, home to at least 125,000 enlisted men and 15,000 to 20,000 officers. There was plenty to do after training hours: swimming pools at the officers' club; dances on the patio; quick trips into Columbus, Georgia; and weekends in Atlanta. Atlanta, particularly, was a paratrooper's heaven; with their shiny boots, bloused trousers, and silver wings, they were the "cocks of the roost."

The officers' club at Fort Benning was a favorite watering hole for junior officers. After a long, grueling day in the hot Georgia sun, a pitcher or two of cold beer was eagerly anticipated. I recall one of those days when four of us, all lieutenants just out of jump school, were enjoying a cold beer on the patio of the officers' club. It would have been just another night at the club except for one memorable fact: Jane Russell happened to be there. Every officer in the room was aware of her presence. Jane Russell was a national celebrity and one of Hollywood's sexiest and most glamorous stars. She was a red-blooded paratrooper's type of pinup gal. She happened to be at Fort Benning because her husband, Bob Waterfield, was there in officer candidate school. He had been an All-American quarterback at the University of Southern California, then was drafted by the Los Angeles Rams. He was a top professional quarterback, but he was not yet an officer or a member of the officers' club.

Jane Russell was enjoying the hospitality of the post. She had been escorted to the officers' club that evening by the top brass. Although she was the center of attention, we did not see her on the dance floor. As young lieutenants and brash paratroopers, we agreed that something should be done about that. So we dared one another to ask her to dance. We were not inebriated, but neither were we feeling any pain. Dancing with Jane Russell was something you could brag about to your grandchildren, but we were reticent to accept the dare. After several more beers had raised our courage levels a notch, we narrowed the choice to two of us. We decided to flip a coin, and I won.

There I was, a lowly second lieutenant, asking generals for permission to dance with Miss Russell. They nodded and she agreed. That evening at the officers' club is the only thing I remember of my three months at Fort Benning. Dancing with Jane Russell was the crowning achievement of my fledgling military career.

After that evening, it was back to reality. The much-anticipated invasion of Hitler's European fortress was taking place. The 82d Airborne Division, in support of the sea invasion, jumped in Sicily on the nights of 9 and 11 July 1943. It was one of the first uses of airborne troops in the history of the U.S. Army. The news of the Sicily jump left me with an empty feeling. I was a qualified paratrooper, eager to see action, but I found myself still at Fort Benning going through what I considered menial training exercises involving more jumps. Due to strict censorship of the news, it was days before we knew what had happened in Sicily. There were varying reports as to the extent of casualties. But one thing was certain: The 82d would soon be in need of replacements. I expected that shortly we would be receiving a sailing date, but for one reason or another we encountered delays.

On 8 August, almost a month after the 82d jumped in Sicily, I was still at Fort Benning when I wrote to my brother George: "I got all my equipment issued last Friday and yesterday we took a physical and got some inoculations. I was all packed and ready to go on Tuesday, but today we got some bad news. We are not leaving until the end of the month. Something like this lowers your morale but, of course, as you know that's the old Army game—hurry up and wait. I won't feel happy until I'm on the boat. . . . I'm not sure of where we are going, but it's going to be a temperate climate. I am going in a big shipment and we will all be replacements, so I'm guessing North Africa or Sicily."

That same day I wrote to my sister Catherine, saying I was afraid that "something might come up and the order to ship out canceled altogether." I said we'd been busy marking every piece of equipment and undergoing showdown inspections. We had been issued all our overseas equipment: two jumpsuits, leather flying jacket, a bedroll, and all our field equipment.

On 15 August I wrote home: "Last week we had a three-day tactical problem and it included one night jump. I was really loaded down when I jumped. I wore a musette bag with a shelter half, blanket, clean change of clothes, toilet articles, one-day's K rations, canteen and cup, first-aid kit, compass, dispatch case, steel helmet, 30 foot jump rope, and a jump knife. I carried all that besides my main and reserve chute and a rifle. I hit the ground so hard I thought I jarred my teeth loose, but I walked away from it and that's what counts."

On 16 August I wrote to my brother Louis, who was stationed at Camp Roberts, in California: "I suppose you've heard by now—I'm going overseas soon . . . where to, I do not know. All I know is we received clothes for a temperate climate and we're going as replacements, so I guess that means Sicily. We were supposed to have left last Tuesday, but it was postponed because we did not have men enough to fill the order. They need 1,500 paratroopers and all going as replacements so that gives you an idea of what happened in Sicily. There are 67 officers also on the shipment."

On 20–21 August the 82d Airborne Division returned by air shuttle to Africa, the place of departure for Sicily, thus ending its mission. In Africa the men refitted, received replacements, and planned the next operation, probably a jump soon somewhere in Italy. In the meantime, I was growing impatient to get going. I couldn't understand the reason for the delay, but then as a second lieutenant, how could I? In retrospect, however, I realize that the vast movement of men and arms across the ocean was no small undertaking. The nation entered the war short of the means of transportation, so freighters with a 10,000-ton capacity were being converted to troop carriers. Convoys leaving the East Coast required naval warship escorts to protect against attacks from German submarines. The ports of embarkation (POE) were jammed to the saturation point. All these factors, not to mention the logistics involved, caused delays in shipping schedules. In the meantime, we kept in a state of readiness and alert. On 24 August I wrote my sister Catherine: "I expect to be leaving within a week. For the past week, we have been training the men who will be going with us. We get up every morning at 5:30 a.m. and start the day off with a half-hour run. I'm getting so now that I can run about as easily as I walk. . . . When we leave here to board our trains, we will not be allowed to wear any clothing which will distinguish us as 'paratroopers.' We cannot wear any boots, shoulder insignia, or cap insignia. We will wear regular G.I. shoes and leggings and all Infantry clothes. They don't want anyone to know we're paratroopers while we're still in the country."

Finally, after more than three months since my arrival at Fort Benning and a little more than two months after I finished jump school, we got our orders to move out for shipment overseas.

On 29 August I wrote to my sister Catherine: "I'm spending my last day at Fort Benning. Tomorrow we will board our trains for the P.O.E. I don't know where our P.O.E. is, but it will be on the East Coast someplace. It will be a 24-hour train ride from here, probably New York. We may spend a few days at the P.O.E. before sailing. This weekend, we were restricted to the area and we can't get away tonight either. . . . I am pretty anxious to go. I wish you wouldn't worry about me but feel as though I am one of the many across and we all have a job to do. As for myself, I am glad to be able to go and I hope I will get a chance to do my share. I know I would have felt awful if I didn't get to see any action. I know one thing and that is that the outfit I'm with is plenty rugged and if we see action it will be the toughest of assignments, but that's what we want. I wish you at home would feel the same way and be proud of the fact that I'm going."

On 30 August we boarded a troop train heading north from Fort Benning, not for New York as I had surmised but for Newport News, Virginia. On 4 September I wrote my last letter home from the United States and stated that it would probably be the last one for a couple of months. The following day we boarded a liberty ship, a 10,000-ton freighter converted into a troop carrier. The freighter was outfitted with a larger galley and triple-decked bunk beds. We were jammed into every nook and cranny on the ship. On the ship with me was 1st Lt. Richard G. LaRiviere, from Chicopee Falls, Massachusetts. We called him Rivers. He and I had become close friends during the four weeks of parachute training and readying for our assignment. We were destined to be together until the end of the war and to become true friends.

We set out from Virginia in a convoy of eighty ships, which included, in addition to the troop-carrying liberty ships, an escort of naval combat vessels, one of them a battleship. It was an awesome sight from the deck of our liberty ship as we headed east across the Atlantic to a destination unknown to most of its human cargo. We would be navigating waters where German submarines had been exacting a heavy toll on U.S. shipping. The pace was slow as the convoy employed evasive action, zigzagging to keep German subs from getting a precise fix on our course.

A converted freighter, crammed to capacity with troops, could hardly be likened to a luxury cruise liner sailing the Atlantic. The food was palatable at best, but we ate it or went hungry. It was adequate if one had a cast-iron stomach. We encountered a lot of stormy and rough weather, and bounced around in heavy seas. The combination of the weather and the food caused seasickness in most of the men, and many did not recover until we landed. Fortunately, I was one of those with a cast-iron stomach. In a letter I wrote home, I stated: "The trip was monotonous and long but I didn't mind it. We had some pretty rough days, but I didn't get seasick. However, I was certainly glad to hit land again!"

The ship carried daily newscasts from the Armed Forces Radio Network, and we listened eagerly for news about the 82d and the progress of the war. We would soon be in it. On 13 September 1943, the radio blared out the news of the invasion of Italy. For the first time, American troops had landed on European soil. The 82d had jumped in Salerno in support of the U.S. Fifth Army. Earlier, on 11 September,

the 3d Battalion of the 504th, less H Company, had joined
the Rangers, transported in LSIs (landing ships, infantry),
and made a landing on Salerno Beach. Two days before,
H Company of the 504th and a group of Rangers had left
the convoy and made the first landings on the Italian coast
at Maiori, during daylight hours. News from the front was
tightly controlled, and it was difficult to follow the progress
of the 82d. I lamented the fact that while this action was
taking place, I was somewhere in the Atlantic. We speculated what the jump at Salerno might mean to our final destination, how soon we would be joining the 82d, and, more
importantly, where we would be joining it.

On 25 September we spotted land for the first time in three
weeks. We had entered the Port of Oran, French Morocco, on
the North African coast. Just the feeling of standing on the
deck of a ship that was stationary and not rocking back and
forth was a tremendous relief, especially for the men who
had been seasick.

Africa

The men were not impressed with Oran. The sun was stifling;
the streets were unkempt and dirty. Arab children were working the streets begging for a chance to earn a few francs.
Street vendors were everywhere, eager to sell anything from
leather goods to postcards and haggling down to the last
franc to make a sale. Most women were veiled, and for the
first time we were exposed to a different culture, language,
dress, and behavior. All of the immorality that accompanies
the savagery of war in the war zone was prevalent. Pimps and
prostitutes were hawking their wares, looking for prospective
clients. As squalid as it was, Oran was still a bustling city
with modern buildings and streets. The outskirts of the city
stood in stark contrast, with poverty in all its miserable
forms.

I wrote home from my new address: Company A, 3d

Battalion, 1st Replacement Depot. It was in a tent city outside Oran:

> There's not much that I can tell you due to the strict censorship, but I can say I am in North Africa, well and safe. Things are sure a lot tougher here than being in a camp back in the States. We're living in tents with a hard wood bunk that has neither springs nor mattress. We also eat in the field out of mess kits.
>
> I have talked with a number of men back from the front and for once I realize the grim reality of what is really happening.
>
> I've been in town a few times and it's very interesting and educational. The people are mostly French and Arab but they all understand Spanish, which enables me, with my two years of college Spanish, and my buddies to get around and be understood. The Army, however, has control of the town, which was occupied by the Germans until May 1943. Public stores are open a few hours a day. All bars and restaurants close at 6 o'clock every night and the town is blacked out. There are not too many cafes because they have nothing to sell. The bars sell wine, cognac, or brandy, but no beer or whiskey. Coca-Cola or sodas are unheard of. The Army is in charge of foodstuffs and even feed the people. I gather from the natives that the Nazis were very strict and gave the populace very little to eat.

After a short stay in the Oran area, we packed up again and headed for the airborne training center in Oujda, located in northeast French Morocco close to the Algerian border. We were loaded onto old, creaky 40 & 8 boxcars, so named for the conveying capacity—forty men or eight horses. These were the same boxcars that had been used to transport our World War I comrades in France. At our frequent stops, Arab panhandlers met us with an incredible array of merchandise from a variety of sources. The Arabs had maintained a neutral status and during the war in

Africa had learned to do business with both sides as a matter of survival. If something in tents was not nailed down, it had a way of disappearing in the night. If the Arabs favored the Allies over the Axis or vice versa, you would never have known it. It was said that in a pitched battle between the opposing forces, the Arabs would walk between them selling oranges and tangerines to both sides without partiality.

We soon learned that of all our equipment and clothing, the Arabs coveted our mattress covers the most and would pay up to twenty dollars in French francs for one. If one thing here irritated us about the Arabs, it was being out-haggled and overcharged. So on this snail's-pace trip to Oujda, we plotted our strategy to beat them at their own game. In our boxcar, Rivers and I had a mattress cover we managed to requisition in Oran for trade bait or sale on the trip. We tied one end of the mattress cover to the inside of the boxcar; the other end lay in the door of the boxcar in plain sight of any prospective buyers. Invariably at every stop, most of which were only a matter of minutes, we found several interested buyers with money in hand. We had a fixed price of twenty dollars and would not come down a franc with our haggling friends. Once the deal was struck, I advised the Arab that we couldn't make the transaction until the train started pulling out of the station. My college Spanish was good enough to tell them that we were not permitted by our commanding officer to sell any of our equipment. However, he should have his money ready, and as soon as the train started we would have a simultaneous exchange. As the train began to accelerate, we got the twenty dollars and tossed him the end of the mattress cover. Then the tugging began. We were trying to pull it away and the buyer was trying to claim his purchase. I'll say one thing for the Arabs; they did not give up easily. They would hang onto their end of the mattress cover until they could no longer run fast enough to keep up with the train. For those who wouldn't let go and were dragged alongside the train, we reached out of the boxcar with a long pole and whacked them next to the head. That generally concluded the transaction. Before we reached Oujda, our final destination, we had "sold" the cover at least half a dozen times, and we still had our inventory for future sales. As for the money, Rivers and I split it. After we pulled into the railroad station in Oujda, we boarded U.S. Army two-and-a-half-ton trucks that had been awaiting our arrival to transport us to the airborne training center.

Oujda, a backwater town, didn't have much to offer in the way of recreation or places of interest. The few bars in town had little to sell except for bilgewater in a wine bottle. Horse-drawn carriages lined the streets; there were no cabs or other motorized vehicles. Oran was situated between contrasting areas. To the north, approaching the Mediterranean, grass, flowers, and palm and other trees graced the landscape. To the south, the landscape changed drastically. The airborne training center, which would be our home for the next several months, was located to the south of Oran in a veritable dust bowl—one of the worst in Africa. On 9 October I wrote to Catherine: "My outfit is now in combat training and it's pretty rough. . . . We sleep in tents with no cots so we use the hard ground, no lights, and for water we walk about two city blocks for a helmet full of water in the morning to wash, shave, and brush our teeth. If people back home think they are doing without or are being put to hardships, they should be here in some of these boys' boots so they could realize how lucky they are back home. . . . At present I am leading a platoon (45 men) and am the mail censor for the company (500 men). . . . All the men miss the USA. They all ask for candy, cigarettes, and other sweets. All wish that this war was over. I feel sorry for those who are married and are expectant fathers. . . ."

In the meantime, the 82d had broken out of the Salerno beachhead and was moving north at a rapid pace. On 1 October 1943, the 504th Regiment had entered Naples, Italy, the first American unit to do so. From Naples, the 82d resumed its northward advance to the Volturno River and the mountains that lay ahead. I found it difficult to concentrate on training or anything else that occupied our time and attention while the 82d was engaged in combat and suffering casualties. I felt my place ought to be in Italy with them and not here in Oujda. I didn't believe I needed any more training or to make any more jumps. However, previous trainees had been deployed as replacements, and the 82d had been at Oujda for two months of intensive training prior to the Sicily job. So it could well have been that my impatience to join the 82d was unwarranted, but I failed to see it that way at the time.

The training center at Oujda consisted of rows of tents in a barren, desolate area devoid of vegetation or shade. The days were hot and dirty, and winds that blew up to thirty miles an hour kept the air filled with dust. We did most of our training after sunset: nighttime compass marches, tactical jobs, digging foxholes, and preparing defenses. Rivers and I were platoon leaders in Company G and were generally together on field exercises. Once on one of our night jumps, we were to assemble our platoons, then meet and move out together on our target. There was a fairly stiff breeze that night that caused a wide separation of our men on the ground after exiting the C-47. We had field phones—EE8A—which supposedly had a range of about a mile. We continually tried to reach each other, but with no success. Either the phones did not have the specified range, or Rivers and his platoon were more than a mile away. Finally, in frustration, I had quit trying when out of the still African night came a clear, distinct call: "Greek." Rivers, with his gravelly voice and a powerful set of lungs, had a vocal range greater than the army's new field phones. This was true of communications throughout the war. Battery-operated field phones and walkie-talkies used at squad and platoon level were not reliable. Whenever the time and the situation permitted, we strung wire from the platoons to the company command post (CP); those phones were reliable. Lines were run as soon as command posts were established.

When we trained at night, it was difficult to keep up our energy level; we got little sleep because it was hot in the tents during the day. Our food was canned; it was heated and served out of large garbage pails and slopped into mess kits. On 13 October I wrote to my sister Catherine: "Things are pretty rugged over here and the training is rough, but it's not getting the best of me. I just came back from making a jump, the second I have made since leaving the States. . . . We jump very low to the ground here, it's only a few seconds after leaving the plane and I'm on the ground. I've now got quite a number of jumps to my credit, and so far Lady Luck has been with me. . . . We're working seven days a week and going through the toughest of training. If there is a tougher outfit anywhere, I want to see it!"

In our free time, if we had money, we played poker or shot craps. Money had little other value; there was nothing to buy. However, we were able to send it home if we didn't lose it gambling.

We tried to track the advances of the 82d in Italy. Rumors circulated daily that our departure for the war zone in Italy was imminent, but until that time our grueling training continued.

There were some lighter moments, as I noted in a letter home on 30 October: "After dinner, the French Foreign Legion band played several numbers for us. They have an 85-piece band and it is just as good as any I have ever heard of. They played the 'Star Spangled Banner' as well as I ever heard it. . . . I was able to take an outdoor shower and change clothes, so my morale is really high. Generally things are so rough that you don't care whether you live or not, but it's funny how just a few little things can pick you up."

No matter how rough the going got or how adverse the situation became, the one thing that could pick us up was mail from home. While living and fighting in a strange land, receiving good news from home was the best morale booster a combat soldier could have. Although bad news and "Dear John" letters had the opposite effect, combat soldiers found solace in their buddies and grew stronger in adversity. My three brothers and I were in the U.S. Army, three of us in combat: one in the Pacific and two in the ETO. My younger brother, also a paratrooper, and I were both wounded in action (WIA). We communicated frequently with each another and with our three sisters at home. Given the circumstances we found ourselves in and the distances between us, mail became the most important thing in our lives.

As an officer I read, censored, and signed the outgoing mail of men in my platoon. Accordingly, I learned a lot about their feelings, needs, morale, and state of mind. Without exception, mail from home was first on their list of priorities. During the war the U.S. Army, in the interest of the shipping space and weight, developed V-mail, a one-page letter with room for about a hundred words; it was censored, microfilmed, and sent in a three- by four-inch envelope. V-mail was sponsored as a free mail service by the war and navy departments (regular mail required a six-cent airmail stamp). Although V-mail provided a medium for a soldier to let his family know that he was all right, that was about all. When a soldier had mail from home, he looked for much more than he found in V-mail; it was a poor substitute for a long letter from home.

After Naples was secured and firmly under the control of the Allied forces, the 82d Airborne Division, less the 504th Regiment, departed Naples for Northern Ireland. At the request of the U.S. Fifth Army commander, Gen. Mark Clark, the 504th was left behind under Fifth Army. Also remaining behind were Company C, 307th Airborne Engineers, and one battery of the 376th Field Artillery Battalion, forming a regimental combat team (RCT) under the command of Col. Reuben Tucker. In the meantime, the 504th was pushing north through the mountains of central Italy and was twenty-two miles ahead of the Fifth Army, on its left. It crossed the Volturno River and had entered the road center of Isernia. On 13 November 1943, the 504th was relieved by the 133d Infantry and went into reserve to refit and await replacements. Back in the training center in Oujda, we were alerted for a move to Ciorlano to join the 504th. On 13 November I wrote my last letter home from Oujda: "I'd like to be able to tell you where I've been, where I'm at now, where I'm going, and what I've done, but censorship does not allow it. So you see, I don't have much to write about. We can't even say what kind of training we're doing or what outfit we're in. . . . I have been doing quite a bit of what I did in Fort Benning. I am Officer of the Day and in a few minutes I'm going out to check the guard again. It's pretty cold tonight, but I'm bundled up pretty warm. I don't imagine I'll get any sleep tonight; the Officer of the Day seldom does."

My next letter home would be from "somewhere in Italy" from Company H, 504th Parachute Regiment.

III
Italy

After the 82d Airborne Division left for England, the 504th pursued the German forces in the rugged Apennine Mountains. Resistance was sporadic from the Germans, who were pulling back to defend from higher ground and were booby-trapping and mining the mountain trails. The going was slow and treacherous in the mountains, and German S mines were taking a toll. One of the first casualties from a mine was the H Company commander, Capt. Fred E. Thomas, who had part of his heel ripped open. He never returned to H Company, so I never met him. First Lieutenant Carl Kappel, a platoon leader, assumed command and shortly thereafter broke his leg in the mountains. Kappel recovered, was promoted to captain, and returned to H Company in Anzio after the successful assault landing. That left only two officers in H Company: 2d Lt. Edward J. Sims and 2d Lt. Payton Elliott. Sims was the senior; he took command of the company and continued the attack, narrowly averting disaster on three occasions from German S mines. The first mine he stepped on bounced up under a mule, tearing apart the mule's rear end. The second mine went off but didn't bounce up; it exploded on the ground. The third mine bounced up but didn't explode. It was an early sign of the charmed life that Sims was to lead from that point until the end of the war.

Lieutenant Sims, from Hamilton, Ohio, had enlisted in the army on 14 October 1940 at age twenty. As a sergeant with the 37th Infantry Division, he exhibited signs of leadership and infantry savvy. He was quickly identified as officer material; he applied for officer candidate school, was accepted, and successfully completed the course. On 25 June 1942 he was commissioned as a second lieutenant. Intrigued by the formation of new paratrooper forces and the challenge this presented, he volunteered for paratrooper training. The parachute school was still in its infancy; there were risks involved and the training was grueling, but Sims prevailed. On 7 August 1942, he earned his paratrooper wings. When I first met him, he was already a combat veteran of the Sicily jump, the assault landing at Salerno, with the Rangers at Maiori, Naples, and northward to the Apennine Mountains of Italy.

On 23 November 1943, the 133d Infantry relieved the 504th of frontline duty. The 504th pulled back to the rear near Ciorlano as the Fifth Army reserve. The 504th had suffered heavy casualties, and all units were below combat strength. They lost many of the officers, so sergeants were leading most of the rifle platoons. The men needed a rest period to recuperate from the grueling pace they had endured. The three battalions had to refit and resupply.

It was after Thanksgiving Day that the 504th received badly needed replacements. Rivers and I were in that group. I will always remember the night that we reported for duty to the 504th regimental headquarters, just to the rear of the mountains in a small blacked-out house with a deep cellar. We reported to the regimental commander, Col. Reuben Tucker, who was seated behind a desk in a dimly lit room. He was an impressive-looking man who had a deep voice and wasn't given to small talk. As he welcomed us, he talked about what we would be up against: rugged terrain and a determined enemy giving up ground only grudgingly and at a high price. The sounds of incoming and outgoing artillery permeating the air made the briefing short. For me, I had found a home with the 504th; it would be my final destination after eighteen months of frustration trying to become part of a combat unit. I would not be reassigned again, nor would I be with any other unit for the balance of my nearly four years of active duty. I could not have been assigned to a better fighting unit than the 504th Parachute Regiment.

Lieutenants Richard G. LaRiviere (Rivers), Peter Gerle, and I were sent to H Company along with a number of enlisted men, including James Musa, John Granado, and Valentine Maliborski. From that point until the end of the war, H Company, 504th, would be the mailing address for Rivers and me. When we reported, staff sergeants had taken over platoons when the platoon officers became casualties. Staff Sergeant Tom Harmon had the platoon to which Rivers was assigned. Harmon was later given a battlefield commission. I was sent to the 3d Platoon, then being led by SSgt. Michael "Mike" Kogut, who reverted to platoon sergeant. Mike was an original member of the 504th, a combat veteran of the jump in Sicily; the landings at Salerno, Maiori, Chunzi Pass, and Naples; and the crossing of the Volturno River. It was my good fortune to be with him during my baptism of fire. I learned from him some of the tricks of staying alive and how to lead men, not command them. At six foot three, Mike was an impressive figure, but his stature was based on the respect his men had for him more than his physique. As a replacement officer in combat for the first time with a lot to learn, I relied heavily on Mike's advice and assistance. Being an officer and a platoon leader did not automatically command the respect of the men. It had to be earned, and that could be done only by leading.

After receiving replacements, H Company and the rest of 3d Battalion moved out of the bivouac area to relieve the 3d Ranger Battalion, which had taken and was holding Hill 950 (950 meters). As we moved forward, we encountered heavy German automatic and small-arms fire. I Company was hit hardest; by noon of the next day, it had suffered more than forty casualties, some of them replacements who had just arrived with me. The following morning, the 2d Battalion, after a perilous climb, reached Mount Sammucro (1,205 meters) and took over positions formerly occupied by the U.S. 143d Infantry.

The 1st Battalion, advancing on our left, had to overcome enemy resistance and contend with ever-present mines and German artillery, causing the pace of advance to be slow and tedious. Staff Sergeant Ernest P. Murphy, B Company, 1st Battalion, had taken over a platoon when the officers had become casualties. While leading his platoon up Hill 950, Murphy had an experience with a mine similar to that of Lieutenant Sims. He stepped on a German S mine (which we called "bouncing Betsy") that had been embedded in a narrow mountain pass. The mine hit Murphy in the buttocks but did not explode. Someone later remarked that the malfunctioning mines must have been assembled in German slave labor camps.

On 11 December, after beating back several German counterattacks, H Company took up positions on Hill 950. My first night is one that will forever remain in my memory. The Apennine Mountains in the area occupied by the 504th consisted of a number of mountain peaks ranging from 610 to 1,205 meters in height. They could be reached only by climbing narrow, rocky paths. This terrain was more suited for goats and donkeys than men, and extensive use was made of donkeys to carry supplies, food, water, and ammunition and to bring back those killed in action (KIA). The Apennines run in all directions and do not follow any semblance of a pattern. On Hill 950 as well as on Hill 1205, we were exposed to German snipers who had taken up concealed positions in the ridges and saddles around us. It was impossible to dig a foxhole in the rocky terrain for protection from German artillery. Instead we took cover behind large boulders and ridges that faced in the direction of enemy fire. German artillery fire was intensive and continuous, restricting our movement during the day. At night small groups of German snipers would position themselves in the saddles and ridges around us where they could observe our movement. They were difficult to deal with, and they were taking a toll. G Company, 2d Battalion, on our left on Hill 1205, was being harassed by enemy snipers concealed in a saddle between G and H Companies. Lieutenant James Breathwit, G Company, took a patrol from Hill 1205 to clear out the snipers who had been firing on them. He and his patrol proceeded cautiously over the rugged terrain, advancing in single file toward the suspected location of the snipers. As they neared the saddle, they moved in to a skirmish line. The Germans remained concealed until the patrol was within range of their rifles. They then raised up and opened fire, killing Breathwit and scattering the rest of the patrol. The word from G Company was that Breathwit was wearing his second lieutenant gold bars on his shoulders and the gold stripe on his helmet, making him a special target.

Several days later, German snipers from other concealed positions were able to observe Hill 950 and created a problem for H Company. Lieutenant Peter Gerle, who, with Rivers and me, had just joined H Company, became a target for snipers. He was shot and killed. We directed artillery and mortar fire at the suspected location of the snipers, neutralizing the location, but the damage had been done. Gerle had also worn gold bars and binoculars hanging from his neck. Trained snipers looked for signs of officers and noncommissioned officers as primary targets. In combat you learn fast. From that day until the end of the war, neither Rivers, Murphy, nor I wore insignia or anything else that would identify us as officers when we were on the front lines and within sight of enemy gunners.

Private Lawrence Dunlop was a machine gunner with H Company and, like Lieutenant Sims and Mike Kogut, was one of the originals in the 504th. He had been drafted in October 1941, at age twenty-one, and sent to Keesler Field, in Mississippi, for medical training. He told me, however, "This was not for me, so I volunteered for the paratroopers. I had to borrow money from the Red Cross in order to get to Fort Benning. I got my paratrooper wings in early July 1942."

Dunlop had jumped in Sicily and fought with H Company through Italy, all the while toting a light machine gun. He was with me in H Company as we were moving up to occupy Hill 950. He recalled that advance: "Around December 8th, I was on guard duty at night. There was an artillery blast from a self-propelled 90-mm gun that the Germans had brought up only two hundred yards or so from me. Cripes, I jumped a foot high. The next morning, just after the sun came up, Private Sylvester Larkin, Private Robert Anglemeyer, and I were all together eating our C rations when a German plane came diving at us. The pilot was probably looking for U.S. tanks of the Fifth Army who were to attack San Pietro. Anglemeyer was hit and died of wounds. . . . Larkin and I were not scratched. We hurriedly started our climb up the mountain and along a ridge. This was our position. Larkin and I found a little shelter between some boulders. I was told to set up my machine gun on the ridge, covering another draw. It was miserable up there, rainy and cold."

Sergeant Donald Zimmerman, H Company, recalled that morning of 8 December when a German Stuka plane came in low with the sun at his back over a group of H Company men. The men had built fires to warm up, dry out, and heat rations. Apparently, the German pilot spotted the smoke: "The plane came in low over the area and dropped a bomb that landed about 60 feet from me. Bomb fragments hit a number of men, including Anglemeyer, who was with Dunlop and Larkin. Others suffered from the concussion, one of whom landed on top of me. Anglemeyer got up and walked over to show me where he had been hit. He had a small round hole just above his belly button. He was helped into an ambulance and died on the way to a hospital."

Zimmerman, who was an original member of the 504th and had jumped in Sicily and fought all the way to Hill 950, was not wounded or injured.

We reached the top of Hill 950 shortly after dark, and Mike Kogut and I staked out our platoon position and set up our command post behind large boulders. It had been a long, trying day, and everyone was tired. For dinner that night, the men broke open and heated K rations. Each squad in the platoon had a canteen cup and a small single Coleman burner capable of heating a ration or boiling water for coffee. One man in the squad had the stove fastened to his web belt when we were on the move. Fuel for the stove was carried in a canteen that also hung off the web belt. At mealtime the burner was passed around the squad so everyone could use it. K rations came in a box small enough to fit in the pocket of a jumpsuit or combat pants. The daily ration of three meals contained enough calories to sustain a soldier in combat, but not much more. A steady diet of three K rations per day for days and weeks on end with nothing else to go with it left little to savor. Fresh fruits, vegetables, bread, and the normal diet staples were a distant memory on the mountaintops of Italy.

I had just finished my evening K rations and needed a drink of water. I grabbed a canteen that was lying nearby. I took two big swallows before I realized that the canteen contained not water but gasoline for the squad burner. Both water and gasoline were carried in identical containers, but I should have known better. It was a rookie mistake that could have made me a casualty before I ever saw a live German soldier or fired a shot. There was little that anyone could do for me. Nothing in the first-aid manuals dealt with "drinking gasoline." For the next twenty-four hours, I lay behind a big boulder moaning and groaning. I could see my headstone in some nearby Italian cemetery, "Lieutenant Megellas, American gasoline got him." Fortunately my cast-iron stomach worked it out of my system and I recovered.

With the 504th Parachute Regiment now holding Hills 1205, 950, 954, 700, and 687, the war became one of attrition. The Germans had fallen back to higher ground and were solidifying defenses. At night I could hear them drilling into the hard rock mountains with something that sounded like an air hammer. German artillery increased in intensity to the highest levels thus far in the Italian campaign. Both sides made extensive use of mines. Company C, 307th Airborne Engineers, laid minefields in the valley between Hills 1205 and 950, denying its use to German snipers.

Along with the artillery the Germans were throwing at us, they made extensive use of mortars. Accurate at close range with a high, arching trajectory, mortars could land on concealed targets, behind hills, and in openings shielded from artillery shrapnel.

On 16 December, during an enemy mortar barrage on the 2d Battalion, a shell hit Capt. Robert Johnson, commander of Headquarters Company, 2d Battalion. He died from his wounds.

Our Protestant chaplain, Capt. Delbert Kuehl, was actively assisting the wounded on Hills 1205 and 950. He recalled those hectic days: "I stayed up there when battalions changed so one could go to the rear. I helped wounded down and brought up replacements. That was pure misery up there. We will never forget those long days and nights, week after week, in the rain and snow, not enough to eat and the constant shelling in the Italian mountains. One day during that terrible winter fighting in the mountains of Italy, I was standing by a rocky trail and a sergeant came by with no boots on, as his feet were too swollen. He had his feet bound up with cloth and rags. I said, 'Sergeant, you can't go up this rugged trail like this, you need medical attention.' He replied, 'Chaplain, I can't go back [down], my men need me.'"

Chaplain Kuehl and the Catholic priest, Father Kozak, had volunteered for the paratroopers knowing the risks involved serving with paratroopers in combat. Armed only with a cross and a prayer, they would go wherever the men were sent. They had jumped with the 504th in Sicily and had accompanied the combat forces through Italy and onto Hills 950 and 1205, on which we were now perched. More often than not, they could be found near the front lines exposed to enemy fire.

In addition to spiritual guidance, the chaplains assisted the combat troops in myriad ways, helping the wounded and comforting the tired and bedraggled GIs, many still in their teens. It was not beneath their calling to help bring food, water, and supplies to the fighting men in the mountains. The chaplains were everywhere they could help—with the wounded at battalion medical stations and ministering to the men in the evacuation hospitals. Neither Kuehl nor Kozak were of my religious persuasion. The religion I adhered to when I was in combat was my faith in the might of my Thompson submachine gun. I had the greatest respect, however, for chaplains who risked their lives with combat units and for the work they did.

The Germans had intermittently occupied Hill 610 some three hundred yards to our immediate front on Hill 950. From Hill 610 they were able to observe and direct artillery fire on Hill 950 and send out patrols and snipers. When I was sufficiently recovered from my binge with gasoline, my platoon was ordered to seize and hold Hill 610. For several days we had not seen or detected any enemy activity on 610, but we were prepared to fight for it if the Germans were there and resisted. We proceeded down Hill 950 on a narrow, rocky path in a single column. The path led to a draw at the bottom of the hill, wound around the base of Hill 1205 and across a mountain pass from which we could be exposed to German artillery, and ascended Hill 610. The distance as the crow flies was about three hundred yards, but the actual distance was at least three times that. The going was slow and treacherous. As paratroopers we were trained to jump and fight behind enemy lines; climbing mountains more suitable for goats was something we did not know. It was undoubtedly the worst terrain in which we were ever to fight. As was always the case when moving into no-man's-land, the column was well spaced so that an enemy artillery shell or bouncing Betsy would not produce multiple casualties.

We reached the base of Hill 610 and started climbing to the crest. At about the halfway point, an explosion and a flash appeared in the center of the column. The call went out: "mines," then "Scannell is hit!" The platoon froze in place. More than half the men had passed over the bouncing Betsy before Scannell stepped on it. An S mine, when activated, would bounce up about head high, explode, and send pellets about the size of marbles scattering in all directions. Several pellets had penetrated Scannell's helmet, killing him instantly. I remember the date, 18 December 1943, and the place where he died, Hill 610, which we called the "pimple" because of its shape. I had joined the company only a short while before and was not familiar with most of the men, but I will always remember Private Scannell, the first man killed in a platoon I led. He would not be the last.

From that point we proceeded cautiously and slowly, looking for any signs of mines or trip wires. Fortunately, the Germans had withdrawn from the "pimple" the night before, but not before planting mines in the approaches and on the crest itself. I say fortunately because if they had still occupied the "pimple," they would have been looking down our throats when we were held up by the S mine.

We reached the crest of Hill 610 without activating or stepping on any more mines and encountering no German resistance. Scannell's body was left where he fell. After dark, the mules coming up with water and rations would take his body back to graves registration. Before we took up defensive positions, we made a fine-toothed-comb search for enemy mines left behind. I learned to look for and trace a trip wire, often concealed, to an armed and activated mine, but more importantly I learned how to disarm and render it ineffective. On Hill 610 I developed a healthy respect for German antipersonnel mines, the silent killers.

Mines of all types were deployed extensively by both sides against personnel, tanks, and vehicles. The Germans used them effectively as they pulled back from one defensive position to another in the mountains. Taking advantage of the rugged terrain, and with the use of mines, snipers, patrols, and artillery, the Germans were able to hold off and inflict heavy casualties on the Allied advance.

Combat engineers would lay larger minefields when it appeared that units would remain in defensive positions for protracted periods. In those cases, antipersonnel mines were laid in patterns and could be disarmed and recovered by those engineers if need be. An attacking unit was unaware of how the mines were sown, however, so engineers would clear and mark paths for their advancing forces. As a battlefield moved forward, the minefields, unless they were cleared, remained armed and active. In World War II, mines were part of the arsenal available to combat forces as another weapon to kill or maim the enemy; however, when left in place after the war was over, the mines became civilian time bombs. Countless innocent men, women, and children have since fallen victims to abandoned mines.

Technological advances in weapons of destruction should obviate the future use of mines. We tout our advances in guided missiles and "smart bombs"—which reportedly can be dropped in a smokestack—to damage only military targets. On the other hand, a "dumb" mine cannot differentiate among its victims. Be they friend or foe, combatants or noncombatants, soldiers or women and children, a mine once armed and activated remains lethal until it claims a victim. The world community has been making an effort to find and disarm active mines and ban their future use in warfare, an effort I applaud.

On 20 December, the 504th RCT was holding Hills 1205, 950, 954, 710, 687, and 610 and had settled into a static situation, with neither side able to advance. Combat was restricted to small, confined engagements between patrols, generally not larger than a squad.

In our advance from Hill 950 to Hill 610, we had strung lines connecting the "pimple" with the H Company CP. Laying wire to maintain telephone contact between the units of the regiment seemed to be an endless task, because German artillery kept knocking out the lines. Finding and repairing breaks in connecting wires was a hazardous job but one that had to be done.

From our position on Hill 610, we could see Mount Cassino in the distance to our left front. San Pietro lay in a valley below Hill 1205 and to our left. We couldn't see it, but at the time we were aware of a major attack that the 36th (Texas) Division was making to capture San Pietro. We also heard the rumble of tanks supporting the attack, but the rugged terrain made them ineffective. The 36th captured San Pietro, but not without heavy losses.

My platoon settled into our new quarters, taking cover behind boulders or making barriers out of smaller rocks for protection from incoming shells. German artillery was incessant around the clock, firing at our positions, and on schedule interdicting the passes and draws, restricting our movement in daylight hours. Artillery on both sides fired counterbattery, and most of those shells, incoming and outgoing, whistled over our heads. Occasionally, the Germans left their calling cards with us on Hill 610, but as long as we kept under cover they inflicted no casualties. We were not ordered to advance or attack, but we sent frequent patrols to probe enemy positions, draw fire, and gauge enemy strength.

My so-called baptism of fire was nothing like I had expected. In the first two weeks of combat in the mountains, I had seen dead German bodies, but I had yet to see a live German, let alone kill one. However, that would soon change. I found myself in a protracted war with neither side able to advance in the rugged mountains.

We suffered from the elements and a shortage of food, water, and medical supplies. It was cold at night, and we were still dressed in our summer jumpsuits. Winter was the rainy season in the Apennine Mountains, and the rain turned to snow.

One night on Hill 950, Lt. Thomas A. Murphy, I Company, awoke with an upset stomach. His evening K ration hadn't set well, and he went behind a rock and vomited. In the process a fitted upper dental plate fell out, and rather than feel around for it in the dark he decided to wait until daylight to find it. That night it snowed, and a white blanket covered the hill. The following morning, Lt. Harry "Pappy" Busby, also in I Company and Murphy's close friend, went down the mountain to relieve himself. His urine melted the snow around the rock, uncovering Murphy's plate. Busby called for Murphy, and he came running. He picked up the plate, wiped it off on his jumpsuit, and stuck it back in his mouth.

Just behind Hill 950 were several wells, the source of our fresh water. It was also the farthermost point that ration trucks would bring supplies from the valley. From there the supplies came up the mountains into our forward positions on Hill 610 on the backs of mules led by hired Italian mule skinners. Men from whatever unit of the 504th happened to be in reserve were detailed to assist in the handling and loading of supplies. Apparently the Germans were aware of the location of the wells and may have used them before pulling back, so they would frequently send artillery rounds in that direction. Sergeant Dunlop wrote: "One day Sergeant Mike Kogut picked a half dozen of us to go down to the well to pick up some combat jackets. The Germans would send a few high and low 88 shells down over the wells every so many minutes, very punctual. So you had to gauge the time the last barrage came in and get down and back up in between. I got back almost to our area and lost my balance. Down went the bundle of jackets. Now I'm worried the 88s would get me this time, so down to the well I go, pick up the large bundle, and start back up the trail. I was pooped."

The mules came every day after dark to go to the "pimple" (although in other mountainous areas occupied by the 504th, because of the treacherous terrain and steep climbs, supplies from there had to be carried by the men). It was tough going for the mules; they were limited in the weight they could carry over the rough ground. They carried crated boxes of K rations and water in five-gallon metal containers. Each man on the "pimple" got three boxes of K rations and one canteen of water. The K ration, also called a combat ration, was designed for paratroopers. More appropriate than the C ration, which came in cans, the K ration was lighter in weight and came in a box that fit in the side pocket of a jumpsuit. It was packaged to withstand the rigors of combat. The packages were distinctly marked as breakfast, dinner, and supper. All three contained a small tin of compressed egg or meat product, hard biscuits, processed cheese product, a pack of four cigarettes, chewing gum, candy bar or caramels, and a wooden spoon. The breakfast included a package of coffee with sugar, water purification tablet, and toilet paper. The dinner included a juice powder, sugar, and salt tablets. The supper included a bouillon cube and coffee with sugar.

The meals, designed to sustain a man for one day in combat, never varied. The egg or meat product could be heated, but generally in a foxhole it was eaten cold. That was the daily fare on the "pimple" for ten days. One canteen of water was available for brushing teeth, heating soluble coffee, and drinking. For other purposes, rainwater was caught in helmets or snow was melted.

When I arrived on the "pimple," I carried only a toothbrush, which I used to keep my gun free of dirt and sand. I had no need for soap or shaving cream, because I did not carry a razor. Personal hygiene was a matter of low priority when you barely had enough water to drink. You felt miserable on the inside; there was no reason to look different on the outside. The small pack of cigarettes in the K ration was eagerly awaited.

When I was at Ripon College, I played football and was on the boxing team. I never counted smoking as one of my vices. So in Italy I passed around my daily ration of cigarettes, until one day I thought I'd try one. I found that it eased the stress, monotony, and misery of dealing with the conditions on Hill 610. Thereafter, until I returned home in January 1946, I kept my daily ration and continued smoking.

Our ten days on top of Hill 610 were largely uneventful. The Germans did not attempt to dislodge us, content on engaging us with their artillery. Meanwhile, they were busy strengthening their defensive positions, improving their security, and mining the paths and approaches to their positions. One day toward dusk we had a visitor, an Italian goat herder who came into our area from the direction of the enemy. The way he bounced along the rocky path, he seemed part goat. Fortunately, our outpost had identified him as an unarmed civilian, so he was escorted back to my CP, behind a big boulder. He couldn't tell us anything we didn't already know about the location of the Germans, but he had come from that direction without running into mines. The path he used in no-man's-land was useful information to us. We would use that same approach in frequent patrols we sent out to probe enemy positions. We hoped to capture a German prisoner on patrols, but we always came back empty handed. Their fortified positions were a tough nut to crack with our small, lightly armed patrols.

Late one afternoon an unarmed German soldier, arms raised and carrying a white handkerchief, came up the "pimple" and surrendered. He had been alone on outpost, and the first chance he had without being observed he decided to surrender to us. As he approached, he called out "Polski," identifying himself as a Polish national. He had been recruited by the Germans after the conquest of Poland and sent to the German army in Italy. He said that other Polish soldiers in the ranks with him would also surrender if given the opportunity. Had he been seen leaving his post by his German noncommissioned officer (NCO), he undoubtedly would have been shot. When he identified himself as a Polish national, he quickly found that he was in a group of American soldiers who could speak Polish. The men in my platoon of Polish descent included Mike Kogut, Sgt. Stephen A. Tokarczyk, and Valentine Maliborski; there were also others who spoke Polish. The man was beside himself and asked, "Is this the Polish army?" He had expected to be mistreated as a prisoner by the enemy, but instead found himself communicating with the enemy in his native tongue. He talked freely about his duty with the Germans, but beyond speaking about his squad, he had no information of value to us. We kept a guard on him, and that evening he was taken back with the returning mules as a prisoner of war. He wanted to enlist in the U.S. Army, join my platoon, and fight against the Germans. That was the story he told me, but I questioned how many of the foreign nationals fighting with the Germans had joined voluntarily and how many were recruited under duress.

It was the holiday season on Hill 610, and Christmas, the holiest of days, was soon approaching. Thoughts of the men in my platoon were about Christmases past, family get-togethers, Christmas trees, presents, and a scrumptious Christmas Day dinner. We knew where we would be spending Christmas Day and what our Christmas dinner would be:

another day in the rain, snow, and cold on top of Hill 610 with another K ration.

Christmas Eve night was calm, cold, and serene. The battlefield had been relatively quiet that day—no patrols, no enemy contact—but the normal amount of artillery fire had been coming in and going out passing over our heads. Back in the valley the support troops were attending church services. In between the crackling of shells over our heads, we could hear the Christmas carolers. The strains of "Silent Night" were echoing through the valley and drifting to the mountaintops. As I strained to hear the voices between artillery shells, I clearly recognized the carols "Silent Night" and "Oh Come, All Ye Faithful." They left me with an empty and eerie feeling. Christmas services were behind us proclaiming the birth of the Savior, and Germans were in front of us; like us, they had one purpose—kill their fellow man, the enemy in front of them.

Back on Hill 950, Sgt. Donald Zimmerman, H Company, also heard strains of the Christmas carols resonating from the valley. He recalled: "It brought tears to my eyes and my mind wandered back home and what Christmas Eve was like there. But on Hill 950, it was just another miserable night on a cold barren slope."

For the 3d Platoon, H Company, Christmas Day was like all others on Hill 610. The weather was cold, wet, and miserable, and the incessant volleys of artillery shells went their unabated way. It had been almost two weeks since I'd had my boots off, washed, brushed my teeth, or changed clothes. The menu was the same except for one small change. Apparently, someone in the valley had scrounged up loaves of Italian bread—enough for one piece of bread each—placed them in burlap bags, and loaded them onto a mule to be brought up the mountain with our regular quota of K rations and water. But there was one problem. The mule on his long and difficult climb had sweated profusely, dampening the bread right through the burlap bag. So we heated it over our small Coleman burner and devoured it. The meal was a far cry from the traditional Christmas dinner we had known at home, but we still had a lot to be thankful for on that Christmas Day: our lives.

Bogged down as we were in the inhospitable mountains of Italy, the prospect of breaking through the Germans' impregnable mountain defenses seemed unlikely. The present stalemate could prove to be permanent. It also seemed that our efforts, despite the terrible price in blood, were of low priority in terms of the grand strategy for winning the war in Europe. The main emphasis in men and materiel was elsewhere. Italy was just a detour on the map intended to keep the Germans busy. Of the millions of men in the service and about a hundred activated U.S. infantry divisions, only a handful of us were in Italy fighting the only war in the ETO that U.S. forces were engaged in. It was a frustrating situation, and efforts in Italy appeared to be thankless. Yet there were no complaints, no question of "why us," no desire to change places with noncombatants. We had volunteered for the paratroopers, expecting to be in combat, and this was our little war. Our efforts, however, to dislodge and push back the Germans were proceeding at a snail's pace, and no one would suggest that the end of the war was anywhere near. We were in for the duration, and the end loomed far in the distance. We were stopped cold in the mountains, and we paid dearly for our hard-fought advances.

On 27 December 1943, the 504th was relieved of front-line duty by the U.S. Rangers and pulled back into the valley out of range of German artillery to refit, rest, recuperate, and receive replacements. On that day, a Ranger lieutenant came forward to look over the positions his platoon would soon take up to relieve us. I laid out a map of the area to orient him on our position and the suspected enemy locations. I was prepared to brief him on the situation, but neither the map nor a briefing interested him. He had just one concern: He moved forward on the "pimple" overlooking the mountainous terrain in front of us and said, "Just point to where the Germans are." He wasn't interested in anything else. Shortly after dark, the lieutenant returned with his platoon and the relief was effected.

The platoon and I returned to Hill 950, rejoined H Company, and proceeded to our rear in the vicinity of Pignatory, where we were to bivouac. It was later in the evening when we arrived in an olive grove lined with pyramidal tents and what would be our home for the next seven days. Our nineteen days on Mount Sammucro were over, but at a terrible price for the 504th: 54 KIA, 226 WIA, and 2 missing in action (MIA). This did not include the casualties suffered by the 376th Airborne Artillery Battery and the 307th Combat Engineer Company, the two units attached to the 504th.

Our new home wasn't exactly the Ritz; but compared to our last one on Hill 610, it was heavenly. Tents kept out the rain and snow, no artillery shells constantly whistled over our heads, no bouncing Betsys awaited the next victim, and no evening mule trains carried our food. For the first time in three weeks, I showered, shaved, shampooed, and shed dirty clothes for clean ones. Shower stalls were set up some distance from the tents, but the brisk walk in the cold was worth it. We had water enough for coffee, brushing teeth, and drinking—a far cry from Hill 610. The renewal of some of the things we had always taken for granted as part of our daily lives again made us feel part of the human race.

Although we didn't have to rely on mules for our daily sustenance, the food was still terrible, but of a different label. The daily fare changed from cold K rations to large cans of C rations; there were three varieties, all served hot from large garbage can–like containers and slopped into our mess kits. At the end of the chow line was another large garbage can for dumping our leftovers. At every serving, a line of Italian women with little children would form; they carried an empty C-ration can begging for the leftovers. They were a scraggly lot, dirty and ragged children, and victims of a war that left many homeless. I will never forget the words of one mother: *"Cinque bambini, no mangiare, Roosevelt buon, Mussolini no buon."* She was standing at the end of the line with five kids in tow. In Italy, as in the United States, everyone loves a winner, and I wondered what refrain the Italians were singing when Il Duce was riding high. I have never found it in me to have compassion for either the Italians or the Germans who became turncoats when their cause was lost. The memory of my buddies killed in combat against the Italians and Germans erased any feelings of compassion I might have had for the victims of a war that was not of our making. I'm certain not all Americans felt as I did at the time, particularly those for whom the war was something they listened to every day on Armed Forces Radio.

All the while we were in the front lines, I neither received nor sent out letters; but when we returned to a rest area, all accumulated mail and packages were delivered. We had been on the line during Christmas, so we had a backlog of letters, Yuletide greetings, and Christmas packages. Most packages included things we didn't need: socks, underwear, lotions, and even a necktie. What we really wanted were things we couldn't get—sweets, fruitcakes, cookies, candy bars, and, more than anything else, booze—but the latter was not a permitted shipping item through the army post office (APO). Rivers had a letter from home that mentioned his cousin. "Get this, Maggie," he said to me. "My cousin [who was of military age but not in the service] is always complaining about how tough things are at home. Can't get enough gasoline to go anywhere, everything is rationed and meat is hard to get." That letter drew a laugh, and many times later when the going was tough, I'd remind Rivers about how bad his cousin had it. But that raised a broader question that I often thought about. If his cousin couldn't get meat at home, and we certainly saw little if any on the front line, who was getting it?

Along with first-class mail, we would get back issues of newspapers and magazines. A good number of small-town papers would send copies gratis to hometown soldiers overseas. Also we would get copies of the U.S. Army newspaper *Stars & Stripes*. Due to the strict censorship of information that might be of value to the enemy, the paper was limited in what it could print. However, it did carry news of general interest to the troops. Lieutenant Sims did not have a high regard for *Stars & Stripes;* he noted in a letter, "*Stars & Stripes* was a rear echelon paper and had little coverage of small unit actions."

Only infrequently did I have a chance to read the army newspaper, but back in the olive grove nearer Pignatory, Italy, I read an issue that had a big impact on me. The issue carried Christmas messages from the Supreme Allied Commander in England to the troops in Europe and folks back in the States. The message to the troops was about what you would expect: "Ours is a righteous cause; we will prevail," et cetera. But it was the message to folks back home that surprised me. It referred to "your sons in the front lines, . . . they are the best fed and cared for in the ETO." Then the blockbuster: "Every American soldier had a turkey dinner with all the trimmings for Christmas." I looked at Rivers and asked, "Did you get yours on Hill 950?" Of course he did not, and neither did any other combat soldier on 1205 or on any other mountaintop in the Fifth Army front.

My irritation was not that we didn't get turkey for Christmas on the front—because it was not possible and we never expected it, nor was it waiting for us in the rear—but that our great leader in England was unaware of what it was like fighting in the mountains, or he was misinformed by his aides, or the politician in him was showing, or, worse yet, he was just terribly naive. My little world with my platoon on Christmas Day feasting on a slice of bread flavored with the sweat of a mule, and General Eisenhower's world in a palatial headquarters in England, were miles apart, not just in distance but in every other respect where combat soldiers were concerned. My sentiments did not reflect disrespect or preconceived notions about anything; it was what I saw through the sights of my gun. And I would not have traded places with those in the rear who undoubtedly did enjoy turkey for Christmas.

On 31 December 1943, I wrote home for the first time in almost a month: "The reason for the long delay was that I have been fighting on the front line and have seen quite a bit of action. At present we are some miles back of the lines in a rest camp. I'm spending New Year's Eve in my tent listening to a heavy rainfall. Happy New Year to you all and may God bless you."

On this New Year's Eve, there wasn't much to do or celebrate or anything to drink, but we waited up to see the New Year in. Exactly at midnight we were all out in front of the tents firing our weapons in the air and wishing each other a Happy New Year.

After we arrived at Pignatory, we were given all our back pay. We were never paid when we were on the front, so sometimes when we were in a rest area we would receive as much as two months' pay. On 3 January I wrote to my sister Catherine: "You know, Sis, I've been saving quite a bit of money lately. A lot more than I ever expected to get together. I want you to let mother know that she is free to use any or all of it at any time. It will be nice coming home and having money in the bank. But there is a good chance of not coming home to it. I don't want to be scaring you with such talk but in case I don't, I would like to have a couple of things done with it and my insurance money since you have my power of attorney. See that Mom gets a nice big house and send Louie to college. Nothing would make me happier— promise. P.S. Yesterday, January 2, 1944, Mr. and Mrs. Humphrey Bogart put on a show for us in nearby town. I got his autograph on a 50 lire note. You can have it."

During the week that we were bivouacked in Pignatory, rumors regarding our next mission ran rampant. One thing was certain: We were not going to be sent home, although rumors had that as a possibility. One rumor gaining currency was that we were going to England to rejoin the 82d Airborne Division. Others had the 504th making another jump somewhere in Italy, perhaps in Rome. A parachute drop on Rome was seriously considered, but the plan was deleted as not being tactically feasible. The possibility of returning to the Apennine Mountains never arose. We were bogged down in a defensive situation, and if we were to advance on Rome—the grand prize—we would have to get around the mountains, or, as the Americans put it, make an end run.

On 4 January 1944, the 504th moved once again, this time to the suburbs of Naples. It now became obvious that we were not leaving for England or anywhere else but staying put in Italy.

The men of the 504th were happy to be in Naples, a city that they and the Allies had captured from the Germans on 1 October 1943. After sporadic fighting the city was cleared and the 504th undertook police duties before moving out to pursue the German Wehrmacht in the rugged Apennine Mountains. During the intervening four months, Naples had changed. It had become an international city much on the order of other large cities the Allies had wrested control of from the Germans. City streets were bustling with sailors and soldiers from at least a dozen countries, including a battalion of Greeks, some of whom I met. Support troops of Fifth Army had established their headquarters in Naples; an elaborate enlisted men's club, rivaling anything in the States, was flourishing. Electrical power and water were restored, movie houses reopened, and the Naples opera house was once again playing to large crowds. Italian restaurants were serving pasta to soldiers and sailors who waited in line for tables. Italian wine, although not of high quality, was available everywhere. Clubs for officers, NCOs, and enlisted men were doing a land-office business. The wreckage of the earlier battle for Naples and of the post office the Germans had blown up was cleared and the city readied for an invasion of another sort—Allied sailors and soldiers seeking not war but love and fun.

Returning to Naples four months after taking the city from the Germans, the troopers of the 504th looked forward to the wine, women, and song of the city. But that was not to be. The men who had taken the city and driven out the Germans were welcomed not by the Italian *signorinas* but by American military police (MP). Peninsula Base Section (PBS) had placed Naples off-limits to the 504th RCT. This really ticked us off. Hadn't the 504th taken the city, and for whom? Had this now become a haven for lovers with no fighting men allowed? It didn't set well with any of us.

On high ground overlooking the city of Naples and the Adriatic Sea was an Allied officers' club, the "Orange Garden Club." Ignoring the PBS off-limits order, Rivers and I and other 3d Battalion officers made frequent visits to the Orange Garden, where a low-grade wine flowed freely. One night after imbibing heavily, Rivers got into an argument with an English officer who also wasn't feeling any pain. Rivers was not a small man, but this Limey was huge. Rivers apparently struck a sensitive chord with him. Fisticuffs ensued. When Rivers was getting the worst of it, I intervened and pulled the Limey off him. A good thing I did. I dragged Rivers screaming, swearing, and kicking out of the Orange Garden and got him into a jeep just ahead of the irate Brit, who still hadn't got his full pound of flesh. The next morning Rivers woke up with a man-sized hangover, little recall of the events of the prior night, and a doozy of a shiner. "Rivers," I said, "you owe me one. If it wasn't for me, that Limey would have wiped you out."

The enlisted men ignoring the PBS order would sneak into town devoid of any 504th or combat identification and leave their imprint on Naples. A number of men ran afoul of the MPs who were protecting their turf from the 504th. But the saving grace for the fighting men was another combat mission that appeared imminent. We were not about to leave any of our buddies behind. The PBS would be happy to see us leave for the front, where combat soldiers belonged.

On one of my sojourns into Naples, I met some soldiers from Greece. They had fought the Italians in the northern mountains and had the upper hand when the Germans came to the Italians' rescue. Advancing infantry and panzer units supported by the Luftwaffe drove the Greeks out of their mountain defenses and overcame what little resistance they could muster. Greece was then occupied by German and Italian forces. This battalion fled Greece to safe haven, vowing to continue to fight the enemy. After Italy surrendered, the Greek battalion came to Naples to join the U.S. Fifth Army. The Greeks had an intense dislike for the Italians. They recounted atrocities committed against Greek civilians and the violation of women by Italian soldiers. One day they offered to take me to their bivouac area. Communicating was not a problem for me, because I spoke fluent Greek, my first language. The Greeks drove a British lorry down crowded, narrow streets where military vehicles vied for right-of-way with Italian cyclists. I sat in the middle of the front seat, and as we approached an Italian cyclist, the Greek on my right would holler out, "There's one." The driver would pass close to the cycle while the other Greek would reach out with a large club and whack the Italian over the head, toppling him off the bike and onto the curb. Then they would have a hearty laugh and move on, looking for the next target. For these two Greek soldiers, it was payback time for a former enemy they would never forgive.

However, all was not fun and games in Naples and with PBS. We were veteran combat troops awaiting word of our next mission. It was time to go back to the serious business of a war that had no end in sight. Training exercises, physical conditioning, fitting replacements into the combat squads, and care and cleaning of our individual and crew-served weapons kept us focused on the job at hand. All the while rumors were making the rounds through the ranks until word came down of our next mission. Rumors had a way of vanishing once the men were told of their next mission. It would be another parachute jump in an area north of the stalemated front of the German Gustave line and twenty-eight miles south of Rome. The mission was to jump behind German lines in the vicinity of Nettuno/Anzio and support the assault landing of the Fifth Army. Intelligence estimates of enemy strength in the area varied but was considered strong enough to impede a sea landing and justify the need for paratroopers to soften up the Germans. Preparation began in earnest. Sand tables were constructed depicting the drop zones, enemy dispositions, and suspected strength, and the 504th's initial objective. Briefings filtered down from regiment all the way to the men in the rifle squads. The initial invasion force would consist of several U.S. infantry and armored divisions and one British division, the 1st Guards.

In a joint operation with our British allies, there was always a concern of troop recognition and coordination. To address the recognition factors, I was ordered, along with two sergeants and two privates, to effect liaison with the 1st Guards Division. They were bivouacked in the same area of Salerno, about twenty miles down the coast from Naples, and like the 504th had received alert orders for the assault landing on Anzio.

We arrived in the division area dressed in paratrooper combat jumpsuits and wearing full combat regalia, so the British could see what American paratroopers looked like. I briefed British commanders on our modus operandi—how we assembled on the ground, moved out on our objectives, and linked up with friendly forces. It would be probably only a couple of days before we would be going through the real thing.

Only a little more than a month before, Salerno had been the site of intense fighting. On 8 September 1943, units of the U.S. Fifth Army had invaded the mainland of Italy, storming across the beaches and pushing inland in the face of determined German resistance. The Germans counterattacked with panzers, threatening to drive the Allies back to the sea.

On 9 September 1943, H Company (which at that time was a rifle company), along with a unit of Rangers, made the initial landing on the Italian coast at Maiori, about nine miles from Salerno. Shortly after midnight on 13 September, the 3d Battalion jumped into the Salerno beachhead to bolster friendly forces in the vicinity of a threatened German penetration. Two days later, on 15 September, the 3d Battalion, less H Company, landed on the bloody Salerno Beach and rejoined the 504th Regiment at Altavilla, Italy. After coming ashore with the Rangers, H Company moved inland and seized high ground near Chunzi Pass. For their part in the action, the company was awarded the Presidential Unit

Citation, making it one of the first units of the 82d Airborne Division to be so cited.

The war had now passed Salerno, which, like Naples, had become an important base for Allied units. American rear-echelon units had established a base of operations from where they could support combat units fighting in the Apennine Mountains near Monte Cassino. Once the rear-echelon units settled in, they set up NCO clubs and an officers' mess, and Red Cross clubs followed.

That evening I found my way into an officers' mess for dinner. It was a real treat to sit down for dinner and be served hot food on real tableware. But what I remember most about that evening was not the food and how it was served, but the company. I was seated with three other officers, two of whom were majors. In the course of the meal, the evening news came on Armed Forces Radio in an adjoining sitting room. The three officers left their meal on the table and crowded around the radio to hear news of the war in Italy. It reminded me of how we used to gather around the radio to hear who was winning the World Series. These officers who let me eat in their mess had a job to do, just as I had mine. They were part of the U.S. Army team, the 95 percent who were backing the 5 percent who did the fighting. What rear-echelon units did was important to the war effort, but their living conditions and exposure to risks were in stark contrast to ours. I had no quarrel or even took issue with those in the rear echelon who diligently did their jobs and understood the purpose of their mission. They were essential. But I was where I wanted to be, in combat with the 504th Parachute Regiment, one of the finest regiments, if not the finest regiment, of fighting men in the entire U.S. Army.

As was often the case, estimates of German strength in the landing area were unsubstantiated and revised downward. There was no tactical need to drop paratroopers behind enemy lines. On 20 January 1944, the planned airborne mission was canceled, and instead the 504th would board LCIs (landing craft, infantry) and come ashore with the initial assault forces. It was back to the sand tables. In place of a C-47 flight manifest, the men of the 504th were given craft boarding lists. Movement orders were issued, and the following morning the 504th was loading on LCIs at a tiny port north of Naples, then heading for the open seas and the beaches of Anzio. The invasion was under way in what would turn out to be one of the bloodiest battles of the war.

IV
Anzio

On the afternoon of 21 January 1944, the convoy of LCIs set out from port to join the huge northbound invasion fleet. The weather was ideal, the sun was shining, and it was a quiet, peaceful afternoon. No German aircraft were spotted and no enemy reconnaissance aircraft were in evidence. Heavy bombing of German airfields in central Italy had focused the Germans' attention away from the Anzio/Nettuno coastline. To the men of H Company, the vast Allied armada that was assembling was an impressive sight. In the convoy, in addition to the tanks and troop carriers, was an Allied naval escort of cruisers, destroyers, minesweepers, gunboats, and submarines as well as hospital ships, headquarters ships, scout craft, and motor launches. Ships strung out in both directions as far as the eye could see. Of the 374 craft in the convoy, 210 were British, 157 American, 4 Greek, 2 Dutch, and 1 Polish.

Three landing sites had been selected. The British were to come ashore four miles south of Anzio, and the 504th and three battalions of American Rangers would land in the Anzio/Nettuno area. At about 0200 the rocket ships would send more than 2,000 five-inch rockets onto the beaches to soften up any enemy resistance that might be developing, and to clear the beaches of minefields.

Dawn on the morning of 22 January found H Company and the 504th poised to come ashore. The thirteen LCIs carrying the 504th were ordered to land on Red Beach. Enemy opposition was strangely nonexistent, with only sporadic artillery from the distant Alban Hills breaking the silence. The lead LCIs had grounded in the sands of the beaches and slammed the exit ramps in the water, and the men had begun wading toward shore when without warning the silence was shattered. Straight out of the east with the sun at their backs, six Messerschmitt dive-bombers came in low with guns blazing, dropping bombs over the Allied landing areas. The landing craft continued unloading their human cargo while enemy planes kept strafing the beaches, unchallenged by Allied aircraft. Men of H Company were scrambling down the ramp and jumping into the water to evade the fire from German planes.

One LCI carrying paratroopers from G Company, 504th, was hit by a bomb. The nose of the craft settled in the water and the stern billowed black smoke. Its rear was a mass of battered metal, and men could be seen enmeshed in twisted steel. Captain Hyman Shapiro, 3d Battalion medical officer, was one of the men wounded in the blast. He managed to get to the beachhead, where he treated the wounded before leaving for the field hospital. For his gallantry he was awarded the Silver Star. The blast served to hasten the exit of the paratroopers from the other LCIs. Men were jumping into the water, some over their heads, others up to their waist. There was a mad scramble to get off the LCIs, hit the beaches, and seek cover. Private Dunlop recalled the moment: "Suddenly, a German plane dived down on us. I hit the deck facing G Company's LCI. Boom! Black smoke and steel were flying through the air. It was only 50 yards away from H Company. We all got the hell off now in a hurry. I jumped with my machine gun held over my head. The water was up to my shoulders. I lost a good friend on the G Company boat, PFC Henry E. Ferrari of H Company. . . . He was on G Company's LCI as an interpreter. He died of wounds from that bomb."

Private Jim Musa recalled his frantic effort to get off the LCI: "I jumped into the water up to my waist, holding my rifle over my head. I quickly waded onto shore and charged inland . . . with 3 other men from H Company. I remember a German machine gunner firing . . ."

The H Company LCI backed off the sandbar it had hit and moved to the right, near the damaged G Company LCI, then toward shore seeking shallow water to unload the rest of H Company. Sergeant Zimmerman recalled: "When the LCI made its second landing, it was on a sand bar. It appeared to be in shallow water but instead it was deeper just behind the sand bar. I jumped in the water and it was over my head. I was a good swimmer and I managed to get to the sand bar. . . . I lost my helmet and my rifle, but when I got ashore I picked up a discarded rifle. I remember the German planes strafing over us. They made three passes before they left."

Sergeant Clement Haas, H Company, one of the 504th originals who had jumped in Sicily, wrote his account of the landing: "We were about 50 yards from the G Company LCI that was hit. The H Company LCI backed off from a sand bar and moved closer to the hit LCI and beached on a sand bar. I jumped into the water up to my chest holding my rifle above my head. I remember Cpl. Andrew Kendrot and one other man jumped into water over their heads. Staff Sergeant William Kossman jumped in after them and helped them make it to the sand bar. Bill Kossman saved their lives."

After regrouping, we quickly moved inland. There were a number of bridges over the Mussolini Canal. Bridge No. 2 was the objective of H Company. Private Musa recalled a strange incident: "As we approached the bridge, I noticed an American soldier, probably a Ranger, propped up at the approach with an M-1 rifle on his legs. He had a bullet hole in his head. Why he was left there dead and by whom I never knew."

Sergeant Zimmerman remembered the advance: "It was after dark when we approached a crossroad on the way to the Mussolini Canal. There were Germans in a house and they fired at us, then swam the canal to get away. German artillery opened up on us. I was near Lt. Harmon who had just gotten a battlefield commission. He was hit badly. I went over to him and called for the medics. About 10 minutes later an artillery shell hit near my foxhole and the concussion shook me up. I didn't know where I was [and didn't remember] anything after that. I was sent back to the evacuation hospital and then to a hospital in Naples."

Zimmerman was treated for shock and a concussion. He did not return to action at Anzio but rejoined H Company at Naples just prior to the 504th leaving for England. Zimmerman had been wounded in Sicily and evacuated to a hospital in Oran but returned to H Company in Italy.

H Company attacked and seized Bridge No. 2 over the Mussolini Canal. In that action we lost our new company commander, Captain Nitz. His time with H Company had been short, and he never returned. Lieutenant Sims took command and continued the attack. For the first time we were up against German paratroopers. They were a tough, determined enemy, but after several hours of heavy fighting and many casualties, they withdrew and we seized the bridge.

As we were attacking, the naval ships in the harbor were supporting our advance with a rolling artillery barrage, but something went awry. Either we were advancing too fast or there was a wrong computation, but a round fell short, hitting one of my squad leaders, Sergeant Tokarczyk. I rushed over to him, but he had died instantly. I felt a certain kinship with him, because he was a fellow Wisconsinite. After I returned to the rear, I wrote to his mother: "He was a gallant, courageous soldier who died fighting for his country. He died instantly after artillery shells hit him and I was with him when he died." That was about it, nothing more, nothing about who fired the artillery. He was killed in action; by whose artillery really didn't matter.

For the next several days, all three battalions of the 504th were engaged in action across the Mussolini Canal. We were supported by the navy. German resistance was fierce at times, because they used tanks and flak wagons. They counterattacked to regain lost ground. The 504th was successful in holding outpost positions, but after one week the main line of resistance (MLR) was still the Mussolini Canal. All along the 504th front, squads and platoons of riflemen were making contact with the German forces. Each small unit had its mission or objective, whether it was a patrol at night to secure prisoners or a daytime attack on an enemy outpost. Although the battle comprised small-unit actions, taken collectively from the sights of the guns of the individual soldiers, it formed the big picture as seen in the higher commands. Shortly after the war ended, Ross S. Carter, Company C, 1st Battalion, wrote and published *Those Devils in Baggy Pants*. Carter's description of the nature of war and the feelings of the men who fought it (page 114 of his book) so closely parallels mine based on my own combat experiences that I feel it bears repeating.

The average soldier, much less a civilian, can form little concept of the scope of a battle. For us it was the part we were mixed up in. Over a large area little scraps are taking place with men suffering, fearing and dying in them, and the loosely connected little scraps constitute a battle. The war, to the dogface dodging mortar shells, is concentrated on him. He judges the nature of combat by his own relation to it. Thus battle becomes a very personal thing. If he gets killed, the war is over; if he lives, the war goes on. It becomes personally important therefore to the front line infantryman that the war for him continue! He will not cease to be in it until he is either dead or seriously incapacitated. War gets to be the one permanent value to his being. After one or two battles time comes to mean nothing. A day may seem longer than a week, a month even a year. He divides time into two parts: before entering the war and after engaging in battle. The only time-point that has meaning exists in the brief intermissions between battles. I think I aged as much in ten days on Hill 1205 as I would in ten years in civilian life. Any veteran who fought six or seven campaigns in the infantry will know what I mean.

Since the Anzio campaign, the 504th Parachute Regiment has been known as the "devils in baggy pants" or just plain "devils." A diary that was found on the body of a dead German soldier on the Anzio beachhead noted: "Devils in Baggy Pants are less than 100 meters from the outpost line. I can't sleep at night, they pop up from nowhere and we never know when or how they will strike next. It seems like the black-hearted devils are everywhere."

The 179th Infantry then relieved the 504th and assumed our position on the Mussolini Canal. The 3d Battalion, including H Company, was detached from the regiment and ordered to deploy to the northern sector of the beachhead to secure the right flank of the British 1st Guards Division. H Company took up defensive positions to the right of the British and anchored our right flank to the left of the main road in what was known as the "factory area" in Aprilia, near the little village of Carroceto. Aprilia was a red brick settlement built by the Fascists on reclaimed land. It consisted of houses, apartments, shops, offices, a church, and a community center, but to us it looked like a factory. It was on the main road leading to Rome within sight of Campoleone and the dominating Alban Hills. The factory area was the scene of some of the most bitter fighting on the Anzio beachhead. The Allies had held it; then the Germans took it in their offensive to drive us back to the sea and almost succeeded before counterattacking Allied forces pushed them back and regained control of the factory area. The blood of countless men—British, American, and German—had saturated the soil around Aprilia.

While the Allied forces were consolidating and expanding their hold on the beachhead, the Germans were busy bringing up reinforcements of men, tanks, and artillery and preparing to counterattack. They occupied the Alban Hills, the high ground to the north of us on the road leading to Rome, and were looking down our throats. When we made the initial landing, enemy resistance was nonexistent except for a few Luftwaffe sorties. We could have easily occupied the Alban Hills, which was the dominating terrain feature on the road to Rome. For that matter, I felt at the time that given the supplies and support we needed we could have gone on to Rome. I believed that Rome, only twenty-eight miles away, was ours for the taking.

We were dug in in open, barren terrain below the German positions on the high ground and were well within range of their mortars and artillery. For several days we led a ground-hog's life, coming out of our foxholes only at night when the enemy could not observe us.

H Company was spread thin trying to cover a wide area on the right flank of the British 1st Division. Sergeant Haas was ordered to take three men and fill the gap between the British right flank and H Company's left flank. This is his account of the action: "After it was dark, I took Cpl. Bill Eberhart, Pvt. Louis Holt, and PFC Harvey Seitz to a position on a small knoll to the left and front of H Company. As soon as we started digging in we came under German artillery and small ammo fire. While we were digging, Seitz, who was between Eberhardt and me, was hit by fire from a German automatic weapon. He was hit badly in the stomach and chest. Eberhardt and I pulled him behind the knoll and laid him on a blanket and managed to carry him back to H Company and from there to the Battalion aid station. The Battalion doctor said that Seitz would be sent back to the evacuation hospital and then to Naples. He told me he thought Seitz would make it. We later learned that Seitz died of complications from his wounds on February 20, 1944."

Movement in the day was perilous and would draw fire from the Germans on the high ground. I recall on one of those days that Lieutenant Sims, who had just been promoted on 20 January and had taken over command of H Company a few days ago, called me to report to the company command post on a matter of some urgency. The CP was to the rear of my foxhole and near the factory area. I was apprehensive about coming out of my foxhole and exposing myself to enemy observation, but Sims said the matter could not be discussed over the field phones. I jumped out of my foxhole and took off like a scared rabbit, running as fast as my legs could churn. Sims was in a foxhole about a hundred yards from mine. About halfway there I took cover behind a large haystack in an open field to catch my breath and prepare for the final dash. A few seconds after I started running again, the haystack was shattered by a German 88mm round. The concussion from the exploding round impacted to my front and right and knocked me to the ground. It dislodged my helmet, but shell fragments did not hit me. I got up, put my helmet back on, and made a mad dash for Sims's foxhole. When I dove into his hole, my first comment was, "What the hell are you trying to do, get me killed?" I had heard that the Germans were deadly accurate with their 88mm guns, but it was the first time to my knowledge that they had fired at an individual soldier.

The weather in Italy in February was fine for ducks but little else. It was next to impossible to keep dry in a foxhole, and once wet there was no way for us to dry out in our present position. One night I covered the top of my hole with a canvas shelter half to keep out the rain. It kept me fairly dry, until the weight of the accumulating rain caused the stakes on the canvas to let go and a deluge of water came in on me.

On the nights of 4 and 5 February, as a prelude to an attack in force, the Germans began a deafening, intense artillery barrage. They were hitting the northern sector of the beachhead to soften up the British division and the 3d Battalion, which were blocking their path to Anzio and the beaches. The Germans had amassed considerable ground forces for a frontal assault, including the elite Hermann Goering Division, with whom the 504th had already been through numerous confrontations. The Germans threw everything they had at us: 88mm guns, tanks, flak wagons, and artillery pieces of all calibers. Our own artillery on the beachhead responded with a concentrated counterbattery barrage. The noise was deafening; a shell of some caliber was incoming or outgoing every ten seconds throughout the night. In addition, the Germans brought up a 180mm railway gun, which we called Anzio Annie and was known to the Germans as Slim Bertha. It was one of World War II's most potent weapons. The ninety-six-foot-long gun could fire a 561-pound shell up to thirty-eight miles, so it was capable of reaching anywhere on the beachhead, including ships in the harbor. When the gun was not firing, its firing crew of ten kept it hidden in a tunnel. It was, without a doubt, the most massive artillery barrage—in terms of intensity and duration—faced by any unit of the 82d Airborne Division during the war and perhaps by any U.S. unit during World War II.

Lieutenant Sims was relocating the company CP just south of Carroceto in an old house just east of a railroad overpass when the Germans started shelling. He distinctly remembered the German shelling: "I jumped into a long slit trench next to the house and two men followed me in. Then a direct hit on the edge of the roof over the slit trench and fragments en masse came into the trench killing the two men with me and I was hit in the right shoulder. The trench partially buried us and after being removed we were sent to the aid station. I was given a shot and then transported to the 95th Evacuation Hospital. The next day after I regained my senses, the hospital area came under heavy artillery fire and air attack. So, I located my clothes and equipment and hitched a ride back to the front and H Company, where I again resumed command. That was after Lt. Megellas had been wounded and was sent back to the hospital."

The two men who dove into the trench with Sims were SSgt. William C. Kossman and Pfc. John A. Bahan, both of H Company. Private Lawrence Dunlop and Sgt. Clement Haas were both back at the CP when the shell hit the edge of the house. Private Dunlop recalled the occasion: "A shell hit the edge of the roof. I was standing in the doorway and it blew me back into the room. I think two-thirds of that shell went down into that trench. Chaplain Kuehl was there; he was always around the 3rd Battalion. I helped get Sgt. Kossman inside. I sat down on the dirt floor with Sgt. Kossman on my lap. He whispered, 'water.' I didn't know whether I should give it to him or not so I looked at Chaplain Kuehl and said, 'He wants water.' He nodded his head and said, 'OK.' I got my canteen out, poured some water into his mouth and it came out his stomach. With some help we got him outside 40 feet or so. The only one alive was Lt. Sims."

Sergeant Haas also recalled the German shelling of the H Company CP: "When the shelling started I scrambled out the back door of the CP and dove into a foxhole. I was about 10 yards away from the slit trench that Lt. Sims, Sgt. Kossman and Bahan were in. About a minute or two later a German artillery shell hit the corner of the roof and sent shell fragments into the slit trench. I was not hit. I ran over to the slit trench to get them out. I went with them in a jeep to the Battalion aid station. Not long after we got to the aid station Kossman died. Bahan died the next day. . . . Kossman was my best friend throughout our Army life and I had known Bahan since the 504 Regiment was activated. I was really in bad shape. Dr. Kitchen injected me with a sedative that put me out for about eight hours. When I came to, I went back to my squad in H Company and within an hour I was sent out on patrol."

After Sergeant Haas returned to the States, he went to see Sergeant Kossman's mother and family, who resided in Old Bridge, New Jersey. He wrote to me about that occasion: "Bill's mother was very appreciative of my visit. I told her how he had died fighting for his country and what a courageous soldier he was. While I was there the American Legion in Brunswick was dedicating the Post in honor of Kossman and one other soldier, who was KIA in WWII. I shall never forget how proud I was to deliver a eulogy in Bill's name. There is a bond between paratroopers that is as strong as a brother's love, a bond that lasts until eternity. I never forgot Bill Kossman. I still remember him in my prayers every night."

Just recently Haas and Dunlop returned to Italy and visited the cemetery at Nettuno. Bill Kossman and John Bahan and others KIA at Anzio are still interred there.

During the day, planes of the German Luftwaffe would swoop in low, strafing our dug-in positions, head for the beachhead to unload their bombs, then give us another going-over on their way back. We kept in our holes until they were overhead; then we would rise up and fire at them out of frustration. The odds of an infantryman shooting down a plane with a rifle were infinitesimal, but then again we could get lucky.

Chaplain Kuehl, who was with 3d Battalion when we were on the British flank in the northern sector of the beachhead, wrote: "I was with four other men by one of the old stone houses on the front when four German fighter bombers which evidently dropped their bombs near the beach and then two came just above treetops on both sides of the road—there were two on each side. The fellows with me jumped in their foxholes as the planes were spitting out machine gun fire along both sides of the main road. I grabbed one of the M1s the fellows had there and got three shots into one plane as he passed—it was stupid. I should have jumped into my foxhole because the machine gun cut a path right beside me and up the house. One fellow who was on the other side of the old house said later that whoever fired at one of the planes hit it and it was smoking badly. I never spoke about that then, as Chaplains are not supposed to be firing at the enemy. I still don't know why I did all that. It was the only time I fired a gun at the enemy."

In the 504th, like all parachute infantry regiments, the chaplain and medical doctors and corpsmen jumped into battle with the GI riflemen and had stormed ashore in the landing at Anzio. Chaplain Kuehl, who never carried a weapon or fired a shot except at Anzio, jumped with the men in Sicily, Palermo, and Holland and was at Hill 1205 in Italy and on the beachhead at Anzio when the 3d Battalion received the Presidential Citation for saving the beachhead from being overtaken by the Germans. He was in the flimsy canvas boat with Maj. Julian Cook, the 3d Battalion commander, in the first wave crossing the Waal River in broad daylight to assault and capture the bridge at Nijmegen. While the men frantically attempted to navigate the mighty Waal in the face of murderous and withering enemy fire with paddles and rifle butts, Major Cook, acting as an impromptu boatswain, attempted to maintain some rowing order by continually reciting, "Hail Mary, full of grace; Hail Mary, full of grace." These men who laid their lives on the line to be with the combat soldiers of their unit were the real heroes of World War II. Their "big picture" was like mine. What they saw was the struggle for life and death, with the outcome of the war hanging in the balance.

On the night of 5 February, the Germans sent out patrols to locate our positions and probe our defenses. They were active in the British sector, which as it turned out was the main focus of their thrust. A German reconnaissance vehicle approaching H Company's position from the north was knocked out and set afire and its crew was killed by a forward outpost. The vehicle continued to burn and smolder through much of the night, illuminating the road approaching our position. Shortly after dark the Germans lit up the sky with flares searching for targets for their artillery and mortars. This continued well into the night and was so intense that I could have read a newspaper in my foxhole from the glare of the flares.

The combination of the enemy flares and the drone of the artillery shells in the air provided a spectacular, unforgettable event for those who experienced it. Hollywood with its latest technology and resources would find it hard to duplicate those two nights on the battlefield. This scene, however, was not produced for Hollywood's benefit; its mission was deadly serious. It was, to say the least, a most terrifying experience for the few who were there and lived to tell about it. It ranks along with the 3d Battalion assault in broad daylight across the Waal River at Nijmegen, Holland, as my two most memorable experiences of the war.

The following day, the Wehrmacht launched the attack they had been preparing for. They made a frontal assault along the entire northern front, hitting the British the hardest. I do not know any of the details of the penetration of the division, nor was I aware at the time that the Germans had broken through. I always said that my "big picture" was what I saw through the sights of my gun. The flanks and rear were someone else's worry. It was the enemy to the front of me that stood in the way of my mission. However, as we were soon to learn, the Germans had broken through the

British lines, overrun the brigade headquarters, and routed the troops. The British were hastily beating a path to the rear in utter chaos. I'm certain now, as I reflect on the actions of the next several days, that the Germans would have pushed all the way into Anzio had it not been for the heroics of H Company and the 3d Battalion.

It was early in the evening of 6 February that H Company was pulled out of its position next to the Rome/Anzio road to counter the German threat. The entire northern sector of the beachhead was under heavy enemy fire. The echo of machine guns and pistols permeated the whole front. The German counteroffensive was under way. As H Company was pulling back from the lines to the south, we were told that the Germans had broken through and were threatening the beachhead. Our mission was to find their lead elements and stop them. After proceeding south, then east, we turned to the north in the direction of the German advance, expecting to make contact with the beleaguered British forces.

It was a dark evening. The terrain was unfamiliar and the size and location of the enemy forces were uncertain, but we pushed forward seeking to make contact. At the time, H Company's strength consisted of two officers, Rivers and me, and about twenty-five men. Lieutenant Sims, the commander, was still back in the evacuation hospital. The tables of organization and equipment (TO&E) of a parachute rifle company called for 8 officers and 135 men, but we were never anywhere near that strength in combat.

H Company, like the rest of the 504th, suffered heavy casualties, but we were going to have to stop the Germans with what we had. Although on the overlay of the battle area we were listed as H Company, in reality we had the strength of a platoon.

While Rivers and I and the able-bodied men who made up the remnants of H Company were slogging in the direction of the attacking Wehrmacht, Chaplain Kuehl was busy just to the rear of us. He wrote: "If ever we had a chance to see the caliber of our paratroopers it was during that time. Almost completely depleted of men, H Company and the others would not give in. I knew you were hurting for men so I got hold of a Jeep and went around the area trying to find some men, some stragglers etc. to give you help. The Jerrys spotted me and an 88 zeroed in on the Jeep. I was moving pretty fast. The 88 hit just under the Jeep, lifted it up in the air, broke the windshield and bent some metal but I didn't get hit. Fortunately, the shell hit in some soft ground so that cushioned the explosion. I still can't believe how H Company held in attack after attack."

The first contact we made as we were moving forward was not with the advancing Germans but with retreating elements of the British. Given the chaotic situation we were in, it was difficult to determine the extent of the British retreat, but from my vantage point it appeared to be in full force. While we were moving forward I stopped a British soldier, hoping I could get some information from him concerning the situation. He was of no help. He had long since discarded his weapon and appeared to be panic-stricken as he struggled to break the grip I held on his arm. The only information he gave me was, "The bloody Jerries are everywhere." In terms of our mission to stop the German breakthrough, it became evident to me that the British were not going to be of any help. We pushed ahead down the forward slope of the hill until we reached what must have been an old railroad embankment, where we held up and took cover. We still had not made contact with either the Germans or organized friendly forces. Rivers ordered the men of H Company to take a position behind the embankment and dig in while he and I, the only remaining officers, went forward alone to reconnoiter the high ground in front of us.

According to the *Infantry Manual on Tactics*, Rivers and I going forward at night in a fluid, confused situation and leaving the company in control of a sergeant was hardly an appropriate tactic. In reality, however, this was indicative of the leadership qualities of the officers of the 504th. They led by example and never asked the men to do anything they would not do themselves. Rivers and I proceeded up the high ground in front of the embankment, taking advantage of available cover. We soon found ourselves in the midst of German soldiers moving in the direction of the H Company position behind the embankment. The Germans had broken through and were moving quickly to exploit their initial gains and reorganize their units. They were calling out to one another to determine their locations; from the sound of their voices, they appeared to be in high spirits. We could hear them clearly; they were flushed with their initial success. I often remarked later that on that night I received my first lesson in conversational German, which was to hold me in good stead later in the war. Continuing to move forward at this point would serve no further purpose, because Rivers and I had found out all we needed to know: The Germans were everywhere, and the British were nowhere to be found.

Following our same path of advance, we beat a hasty retreat back to the embankment where we had left H Company. The company was already engaged in a firefight with the advancing Germans to our front. It was obvious that we were in a tough situation: no contact with the British forces and only Germans to our front. We still needed to determine if there were friendly forces on our flanks—to the left and right of our position behind the embankment. We decided that this was the spot where we would make our stand. Rivers, the ranking officer, ordered me to take a small patrol to reconnoiter the high ground to our left. I took the entire 1st Platoon with me, which at that point consisted of just six men (the full complement of a 504th rifle platoon called for two officers and thirty-five enlisted men). I was the lead man in the patrol as we headed up the high ground to our left while the platoon sergeant, Sgt. Thomas Radika, brought up the rear, keeping the patrol together. When we reached the crest of the hill, I noticed a sharp drop on the other side: a cliff steep enough to protect our immediate left flank from an enemy attack. At that point a German machine gun opened fire from high ground across the roadbed on the silhouetted targets we presented. It was almost point-blank fire. We hit the dirt and I gave the command to turn around and crawl back down the hill to the company position behind the embankment.

Because I had started out leading the patrol, when we turned around and started going back downhill I found myself bringing up the rear. I soon caught up with Sergeant Radika going downhill. He lay motionless, his arms and legs still in a crawling position. I crawled alongside, exhorting him to get going: "Radika, that's machine gun fire." As I shook him I noticed that the left side of his body had been ripped open by enemy bullets. He had been killed instantly. There was nothing anyone could do for him. I could not rise up to expose myself to the machine gunner, so I crawled back. I determined that our left flank was secure but at the cost of a life that was important to us.

One of the men in my platoon was Pvt. James J. Musa. He had been with me at the airborne training center in Oujda and in Venafro, Italy, when we joined the 504th as replacements. He recalled this patrol: "The machine gun opened up on us at almost point blank range. I hit the ground and started crawling for cover. When I got downhill another man and I turned and threw grenades at the machine gun."

Private Musa was missed by that machine gun and made it through Anzio, but he was severely wounded in Holland about eight months later and evacuated to a hospital in the States.

Having determined that an impassible terrain obstacle secured our left flank, our attention turned to the right flank. I took another patrol of six men, followed the cover of the embankment to its farthest point, crossed over the road, and proceeded to our right (east), following a contour in the terrain at the bottom of the hill. Having proceeded in an easterly direction for about a hundred yards without incident, we heard Germans talking behind the hill on our left. They were apparently regrouping to continue their advance to the south and Anzio. I deployed my small patrol at the foot of the hill, taking advantage of available cover, and waited for the Germans to charge downhill. As soon as we were set, the Germans, in what I estimated was a platoon-sized force, stormed over the top of the hill and straight toward us, not knowing we were positioned just below them. In the patrol, I was armed with a Thompson submachine gun; one soldier had a Browning automatic rifle and the other five carried M1 rifles. We held our fire until the Germans were within close range, then we opened up with rapid fire. A large number fell with the first outburst before they could take cover and attempt to fire back. Confused and not knowing the strength and location of the force that had hit them, they retreated and took cover behind the hill. We reloaded and waited, expecting they would come back at us, but they did not. I do not know for certain how many casualties we inflicted on them, but I would guess they were substantial. We could hear the anguished cries of the wounded while their buddies were attempting to retrieve them. I might add that the Germans we fought at Anzio were highly trained, combat hardened, disciplined, and well led, unlike the forces we were to encounter later in the war, particularly after the Battle of the Bulge, when the German cause was lost. The Germans at Anzio, like the troopers of the 504th, would risk their lives if need be to retrieve their dead and wounded, a mark of good troops. After a brief period of time, the battlefield became quiet, so we continued our mission, moving east along the same terrain we had been following, still seeking to make contact with any friendly forces that might be on our right. My patrol did not suffer any casualties in the firefight we'd just had. The following morning we scanned that area with field glasses looking for dead bodies, but the Germans had been careful to police the battlefield.

After moving farther west for about another hundred yards and still following a contour at the bottom of the hill, we again heard Germans behind the hill calling out to make contact with elements of the unit. We could hear them plainly. Again we held up, took cover, and deployed at the bottom of the hill. After a brief period, another German force, about platoon sized, probably from the same company, stormed over the crest of the hill, not knowing that they would be running directly into a hail of small-arms fire.

We were ready for them. We were in a position we often dreamed of: looking down their throats. When they got into a good killing range, I gave the order to fire, and we unloaded our weapons at everything in sight.

This firefight was also brief, similar to the earlier one about a hundred yards back. We inflicted heavy casualties on the enemy, and the survivors retreated behind the hill for cover. We did not suffer any casualties. The Germans then shot up flares attempting to locate our positions and dropped mortars in our direction, but they were off the mark.

We stayed concealed until the flares stopped and the battlefield quieted, then we got up and proceeded with our mission, heading east and looking for friendly forces. After moving east for about another quarter of a mile without making contact, I concluded the obvious: There were no friendly forces on line with H Company, only Germans to the front of us. All this time we did not see any British soldiers, and I had no idea where they might be. We crossed back over the roadbed and headed west to rejoin the company dug in behind the embankment. It had also been engaged in frontal assaults by the enemy but had been able to repulse each attack. We must have been gone for more than two hours; it was well past midnight when we returned. Because we found no friendly units on our right, our flank was vulnerable. I placed the Browning automatic rifle (BAR) man, Cpl. John Granado, on the high ground to our right with orders to dig in and shoot anything that approached from the direction of the enemy.

The roadbed that we were dug into became the main line of resistance. The Germans continued an attempt to dislodge H Company from its entrenched positions with mortars and automatic fire. A few Germans were able to penetrate to the other side of the embankment from us and were lobbing grenades over the road and into our position. We placed Privates Dunlop and Larkin with their machine gun in the draw to our left, with the field of fire being the roadbed, in the event that the Germans attempted to storm over the road to engage us in hand-to-hand combat. Meanwhile, we were lobbing grenades back at the Germans on the other side of the embankment. It was during this engagement that I suffered a flesh wound that would immobilize my left arm. Several days later I would be taken to the evacuation hospital in Anzio and from there to the 45th General Hospital in Naples.

We came through the night without further casualties while repelling every German effort to overrun our position. The break of dawn found a small force of two officers and about twenty-four men still entrenched behind the roadbed and determined to hold the position against any odds. During the night the Germans evacuated their wounded and recovered most of their dead. However, several dead Germans still dotted the hillside to our front. I remember zeroing in our weapons that morning by firing at the helmets of the dead Germans as targets less than two hundred yards in front of our position. On the high ground to our left lay the motionless body of Sergeant Radika. We could not risk trying to recover his body during daylight hours because of the machine gun across the road that had fired on my patrol the night before. The sight of his body lying on the barren hill haunted us, but for the time being there was nothing we could do without risking additional lives.

We spent the day in the cover of our foxholes, with incoming and outgoing artillery whistling overhead, waiting for the enemy to make his next move. We were in a precarious position, surrounded by Germans and still having no contact or communication with the remainder of our battalion or any other friendly forces. We were running low on ammunition with no prospect for resupply, at least during daylight hours. We would be hard pressed to repulse another concentrated German attack with our remaining resources.

Although we were practically surrounded and cut off from our battalion and other friendly forces, surrender was never an option. The Germans knew where we were, and if they wanted us they would have to come and get us. But before they did, we would take a lot of them with us. We kept down in our foxholes, with our weapons, remaining ammunition, and grenades at the ready. We were short of water and had been without K rations for two days, but that was the least of our worries. Our chances of surviving another attack in force by the Germans with the few men we had looked bleak.

Rivers and I had promised each other that if either of us made it back, we would see our respective mothers and relate what had happened. We were in a lull before the expected storm. It was time to clear our minds of the feelings we had harbored and get them off our chest. Rivers said, "Maggie . . . if we ever make it back, our reward will be, we will be able to live with ourselves. We will have no trouble sleeping at night; our consciences will be clear."

How true and prophetic those words turned out to be. Neither the small group of men we were with nor Rivers or I complained about our predicament. It was a matter of our own choosing, and if we didn't make it out, so be it. Nobody lives forever. We were prepared for any eventuality.

We kept concealed and waited for the next German assault, which did not materialize during the remaining daylight hours. When darkness fell, Rivers and I crawled up the high ground to our left to recover Sergeant Radika's body. With Rivers lying on one side of the body and me on the other, we dragged it facedown by the harness straps to our position behind the embankment. As the two remaining officers in the company, we took it upon ourselves to crawl up the hill at night practically under the barrel of an enemy machine gun to recover the body rather than ordering two of our enlisted men to assume the risk. In the absence of a body, unless a competent medical authority certified the death, the man would be listed as MIA rather than KIA. Any insurance claims the next of kin might be entitled to would be held until the status of the dead soldier could be resolved. His remains would probably never be found or returned home for a decent burial. His next of kin would agonize over the uncertainty of his fate. Often, particularly during night patrols behind enemy lines, it would be difficult to bring back our casualties. But in the 504th it was not impossible.

The thought of being a casualty and your body being left to the enemy could have a demoralizing effect on the men. The paratroopers would make superhuman efforts to ensure that this did not happen.

In addition to the long-range guns the Germans brought up and deployed against us, they threw a barrage of words at the Allies on the Anzio beachhead. Sir Arthur Ponsonby bitterly declared in a volume on Falsehood in Wartime, "When war is declared, truth is the first casualty, and every country uses it quite deliberately to deceive its own people, to attract neutrals, and mislead the enemy." The Nazis had elevated the use of propaganda to an art form. Propaganda was used effectively in uniting the German public and creating a national fervor. It turned the Germans against the Jews and led to the Holocaust. It helped subjugate and control the populace in the occupied countries. In the Italian campaign it was introduced in an attempt to create a rift between the Allies and sow seeds of discontent in the minds of the soldiers.

Propaganda was disseminated in Italy in two ways: radio broadcasts and leaflets fired by German artillery in canisters at frontline positions. Radio broadcasts beaming from Rome, directed at the British, tried to undermine British confidence in the Americans. Between the playing of popular music, Sally—or the "Berlin Bitch," as we called her— would relate to the soldiers how their wives and girlfriends were getting on with other men while they were on the front lines. Leaflets scattered among British soldiers portrayed well-paid American soldiers seducing every British girl they could get their hands on. The Germans scattered leaflets in the area of the 3d Battalion coinciding with their offensive when H Company was surrounded and holding out with a handful of men. One directed at us showed President Roosevelt with a scythe in his hands and the caption, "'I assure you again and again and again that no American boys will be sacrificed on foreign battlefields.' Franklin D. Roosevelt, Oct. 31, 1940."

I, like the rest of the men I was with, found the German propaganda amusing and even silly, but to other Allied sol-

diers it may have been provocative and even as disjointing as
the Germans had intended. Anzio was the only battle in the
war where the Germans fired artillery at me containing
leaflets. Not only did I find them amusing, I preferred them
to their 88s.

Meanwhile, the remainder of the badly battered 3d Battalion was regrouping to establish a defensive line on the
high ground behind H Company. All the companies of the
battalion were reduced to fewer than twenty-five men, and
the entire battalion to fewer than a hundred men. First Lieutenant Roy Hanna, who had landed at Anzio as the leader of
the machine-gun platoon, was sent down to command I
Company after it had lost all its officers. Hanna was ordered
to launch a diversionary attack to relieve the pressure on
H Company, but he was shot and knocked down; he was
dazed and suffering from oxygen deprivation. Later he
learned that his right lung had collapsed. Although he was
dazed, he got up and continued to lead the attack. After he
got word that H Company was able to pull back and join the
rest of the battalion on the high ground, he was taken on a
stretcher back to the evacuation hospital and from there to
Naples, where he was a hospital patient for sixty-two days.
After he was released, he rejoined the 504th in England. For
his extraordinary heroism, he was awarded the Distinguished Service Cross.

While Rivers and I and the remnants of H Company
braced for the next German assault, which we felt certain
was to come, a runner from I Company made contact with
us just after darkness fell. It was the first contact we'd had
with any friendly forces since our initial contact with the
Germans. The remainder of the 3d Battalion was now in
place on the high ground behind us, and we were ordered to
fall back in line while they provided overhead fire. We
passed the word along to get ready to pull back to the high
ground. I went to the position on our right flank where I had
placed Corporal Granado and two men to tell them to rejoin
the company, but they were nowhere to be found. I made a
hurried search of the immediate area but to no avail. The

Germans had attempted to penetrate on our right, and I assumed they had become casualties defending our right flank. But because I could not find any bodies, we listed them as MIA. I later recommended Granado for, and he received, the Distinguished Service Cross. At the conclusion of the war, I learned that he and the other two men, Pvt. Richard Ranney and Pvt. William Riley, had been taken prisoner that night by the Germans and had survived. Corporal Granado, also a prisoner of war (POW), who had come to the 504th with me on Hill 950, related: "I was on an outpost on a small knoll detached from the rest of H Company. The Germans appeared to be everywhere, infiltrating all around us. We had no contact with the Company and were unaware that we were pulling back. We never got the word. The Germans overran the outpost and took us prisoners. We were taken back through the attacking forces and the German lines. We passed through what had been the British lines where we saw a lot of dead British soldiers. A lot of them were killed in their foxholes. The Germans took us back to a big farmhouse and from there to a POW camp. Sometime in May 1945 American forces liberated us."

After failing to find any signs of Granado's outpost, I hurried back to the company and we began to fall back as the Germans were preparing to assault our position again. Rivers ordered the company medic, Cpl. Seymour Flox, to help me get back to the battalion aid station. On that night the full moon was frequently obscured by patches of heavy clouds. Flox and I headed up the hill for the aid station, but we were unable to keep pace with Rivers and the rest of the company. The Germans had started another attack and were not far behind us. They shot up flares to illuminate the battlefield. As the flares were going up, Corporal Flox and I hit the muddy ground facedown to keep from being seen and waited until the flares burned out, then we started out again. This happened about every twenty yards, which greatly slowed our pace. Artillery and mortar shells supporting the German attack were impacting all around us. My arm felt numb, and I was weak from loss of blood. We had all been through a grueling physical ordeal and had been without rations for several days. I most likely would not have made it had it not been for the medic who stayed with me all the way.

If I had died on the battlefield that day, anyone—however well intentioned—who said that I gave my life for my country would have dishonored my memory. Although I accepted the dangers and risks of losing my life in combat, I would never have given it. The Germans would have to snuff it out.

After what seemed an eternity, we reached the aid station in an abandoned, badly shelled house not far behind our defensive positions but within easy range of German artillery and mortars. The entrance was covered by two staggered canvas tarps to conceal the dimly lit interior. The house was full of paratroopers, many more seriously wounded than I. Captain Kitchen, the medical officer, was doing his best to provide assistance to the wounded, but the numbers were overwhelming him. He was short of medical supplies and facilities to meet the immediate demands. The situation was chaotic. The Germans had advanced to the immediate area, and it appeared that Doctor Kitchen and his aid station would have to pull back to keep from being overrun. Kitchen took one look at my arm and said, "Maggie, there is nothing I can do for you here. I'm going to send you back to the evacuation hospital at Anzio."

An ambulance clearly marked with Red Cross insignia pulled up in front of the aid station to evacuate the wounded. The ambulance was full when it started its trip to the 95th Evacuation Hospital some eight or so miles south and near the beach.

The German attack on the northern sector of the beachhead was in full force. Attacking German infantry were being supported by intense artillery and mortar fire. German long-range guns firing from the Alban Hills were covering the entire beachhead. Flares lit up the sky showing the way for advancing infantry and spotting targets for artillery. All roads from the northern sector leading south to Anzio, including the one we were traversing, were being interdicted by continuous fire. The ambulance drove at breakneck speed, dodging shell craters in the road while artillery shells were dropping all around us. It was an unforgettable night for those of us in the ambulance, but the driver, by sheer luck and determination, got us to the hospital in one piece.

I was rushed into a large tent and placed on an operating slab. Instead of trying to take off my damp, muddy combat clothes, an orderly cut them off and threw them into a garbage heap. I objected to my paratrooper boots being cut off, but I was in no position to resist. I had a special attachment to my boots because they were a distinguishing feature and a source of pride.

I was injected with an anaesthetic and told to start counting. I remember making it to a hundred before I dozed off. When I awoke I found myself on a small canvas army cot in a large tent serving as a post-surgery recovery area. I was served breakfast in bed, my first food in more than three days. The army nurse told me that I had been out for thirty-six hours under the anaesthetic.

There must have been at least fifty wounded men in that tent, none of them ambulatory. I remember a badly wounded captain from the 3d Infantry Division lying on the cot next to me. A German 88mm had ripped through the house he was using as his company CP. He had lost part of an arm and a foot, besides multiple body wounds. He was conscious, but irrational, and kept saying he wanted to die. A Red Cross worker was trying to console him by writing to his wife for him, but he was in a state of shock. I understood he was a professional football player with a bright future ahead of him—before a German 88 put an end to that career.

The stay in the hospital was intended to be brief, preparing the wounded for evacuation to a permanent hospital in Naples, pending the availability of space in the hold of an LST (landing ship, tank) and the weather conditions. Heavy winds and rough seas delayed our departure to Naples for several days. While I was in the 95th, long-range German guns shelled the hospital. An air-raid siren was sounded, and the medical corpsmen and nurses turned us over on the ground with the cots on top of us. Captain Shapiro, who was there at the time, recalled that one of the tents had been hit and was burning, and a doctor in surgery and two nurses were killed before the shelling stopped. The evacuation hospital in Anzio was not a healthy place to be.

The Germans continued the attack that night against H Company and the remnants of the 3d Battalion. Lieutenant Sims had returned from the evacuation hospital to resume command of H Company, which was now down to about twenty men and two other officers, Lieutenants Rivers and Elliot. The rest of the 3d Battalion was in the same depleted condition, with I Company reportedly down to sixteen men. Fighting was intense throughout the northern sector of the beachhead, with a major thrust directed at the factory area, where the U.S. 45th Division and the 1st Armored Division were holding out. In spite of the enormous casualties suffered, the Allies withstood the Germans' heaviest blows and restored order to the battlefield. The German offensive, which had threatened to drive U.S. forces off the beachhead and came close to doing so, was contained at a high cost to the Germans. It was for this gallant and determined effort, during the period 8 to 13 February, that the 3d Battalion was cited and awarded the Presidential Unit Citation; one of the first to be awarded to a ground unit in the ETO.

On 13 February the 504th was relieved on the front line by elements of the 56th (London) British Division, which had just been brought up from the southern front to relieve the British 1st Division, so badly battered that it could no longer be considered a fighting unit. Its remnants were relocated to the rear of the northern sector to reorganize, await replacements, and constitute a reserve force. The 3d Battalion, now consisting of fewer than a hundred men, having lost more than 80 percent of its original strength, returned to the 504th Regiment, joining the 2d and 3d Battalions on the line at the Mussolini Canal.

On 4 March, while I was still in the hospital at Anzio, the 504th Regiment received an infusion of a large number of replacements. One of these was Sgt. Albert Tarbell, from Nedrow, New York. He wrote about their arrival: "We had unloaded from the LSTs to the docks of Anzio by DUCKS. At the time 'Anzio Annie' would occasionally fire and the shells would land in the bay or the dock area. That evening we were transported by truck about three miles deep to the front lines. We unloaded from the trucks in alphabetical order; one trooper would get off on the left to one Company and the next trooper would get off on the right to a different Company. All through jump school we had gotten to know each fellow very well because of the setup. As we traveled from Fort Benning to North Africa to Italy and now Anzio beachhead, Pvt. Delbert W. Swellander was always in front of me. As he got off the truck on the right-hand side to go to I Company, I got off on the left side to go to H Company. Pvt. Swellander, following the guide for I Company, stepped on a mine and was killed. That was my introduction to warfare in Anzio."

On that night, H Company received some thirty to forty replacements, almost tripling the strength of the Company. Tarbell recalled only some of those men who had come with him to H Company: Simon Renner, John Schultz, Jimmy Shields, Tommy Smiley, Richard Riordan, William Hannigan, Dominic Moecia, John Rigapoulos, James L. Ward, Charles Thompson, Ray Walker, Robert Harris, and David E. Ward. Not all replacements suffered the immediate fate of Private Swellander. Some were killed later, including Rigapoulos in Holland and Smiley in Germany, but the others remained with us in H Company to see the termination of the war.

Some of the replacements to the other companies soon became casualties also. Sergeant Tarbell wrote: "On March 14, 1944, the German artillery hit a haystack where the mortar platoon was with their ammunition stored inside. It blew the whole squad up. There were six troopers in there from my jump school class and I knew them very well."

While the 3d Battalion was moving out from the northern sector of the beachhead to rejoin the 504th at the Mussolini Canal, I was being placed in an ambulance for evacuation to Naples. The weather cleared and the seas calmed, permitting the wounded to be loaded on LSTs waiting in the harbor. I was carried on a stretcher by two medical corpsmen from the ambulance over the sandy beach to the LST, a distance of about a hundred yards, when suddenly and without warning a German fighter plane came in low over the beach with guns blazing. About halfway to the LST, the two corpsmen dropped the stretcher and me and scurried for cover. As I watched that plane make a pass over the beach, I wondered whether my time had come or the law of averages was catching up with me. The answer was none of the above.

The corpsmen returned, picked me up, and carried me into the hold of an LST. The stretchers were jammed in tightly to accommodate all the wounded. While waiting for the LST to take off, I broke open a pack of cigarettes, compliments of the Red Cross. I glanced over at the stretcher next to me. It was occupied by a young blond soldier in hospital garb whom I couldn't identify. I reached over with my good arm and offered him a cigarette, which he accepted. His response was *"Danke schoen."* I was stunned. I was lying next to a wounded German soldier from the ilk of those with whom I had just been engaged in mortal combat. My first impulse was to grab him by the throat and change his status from WIA to KIA, but my better judgment prevailed. He and I were both in the same boat: survivors of a bloody battle. There was a difference, however; the war was over for him, but I would return to the battlefield when I recovered. For me, the war had just begun.

In the 45th General Hospital at Naples, Italy, I found real hospital beds, real sheets, warm cooked food, wonderful nurses, Red Cross ladies, hot water, and bathing. No wonder combat men called my wound "one you dream about." Several beds from me was the 3d Division captain who had been on a cot next to mine at the evacuation hospital. He was no longer in a state of shock. He had come to terms with his fate. He even managed on occasion to display a sense of humor. The nurse had just finished his morning bath when he said, "Nurse, you wash up as far as possible and then you wash down as far as possible; when is poor possible going to get washed?"

On 18 February I wrote home on Red Cross stationery from the hospital in Naples, my first letter home in more than a month.

I was wounded twice in action on the new beachhead but only slightly on both occasions, so it really is nothing to become alarmed over. I only mention that to you because you will probably be notified by the War Department soon if you haven't been already. If you have, I hope this letter eases your mind.

The last letter I wrote was from the 118th Station Hospital just two days before I left for the front. Almost all my time now in Italy has been spent either fighting or in the hospital.

I've never seen such a hell as we experienced in our last battle. To most people back home the war is over and life is already returning to normal, but most of us who have to face it already feel that we're living on borrowed time. I could write a book on the many narrow escapes from death I've had, but I don't care to ever mention any. I must say I'm very fortunate to be alive with two wounds. Both are slight and I expect to be ready for duty in a couple of weeks more. I'm not certain as to how many Germans I killed first, but in my mind the minimum is at least 10.

Last night I got a Christmas package, my first. I must say, although maybe I should be nice about the matter and forget about it, that I was really disappointed with the package. I received 3 pairs of summer underwear, a sewing kit, and imagine—shoe polish. What did you think I was doing over here? Making a tour with the U.S.O. Clubs? My boots have had two inches of mud on them ever since I've been over here and as for clothes Uncle Sam gives us all the heavy wool clothes we need for combat. Outside of that all you worry about is your hide. At present all the earthly possessions I have is one pair of boots, everything else was cut off of me at the evacuation hospital but when I leave here I'll get another outfit. You never worry about clean clothes and I can't remember when I last took a bath. In combat, we go for weeks at a time without shaving or washing. We barely get enough water to drink.

I hope I haven't offended you or the spirit in which the presents were sent. I'm sure you didn't know because you've been reading the papers too much. They have a wonderful way of making war seem glorified but they should be over here and find out. Over here money is worthless. There is nothing to buy. All you can do is shoot crap or play poker. So far I've been mighty lucky, also lucky in combat. If it holds out I may get to see the states again but I'm getting leery. I had too much luck on the last mission.

Oh yes, I've received a Purple Heart and an Oak Leaf cluster for wounds received in action. I'll send the Purple Heart award home soon. I hope you are able to read my writing. I'm lying in bed and my left arm is in a splint so it's no easy job.

Reference to such hell as we experienced in our last battle (Anzio) was more aptly stated by General Sherman in 1879 when he wrote: "It is only those who have neither fired a shot nor heard the shrieks and groans of the wounded who cry aloud for blood, more vengeance, more desolation. War is hell."

Yes, war is hell for those who are caught in the path of its fury, who do the killing and dying. But for those who have neither fired a shot in anger nor experienced an enemy gunner firing at them, war can be an exhilarating experience of adventure and travel. And there will always be those who will ignore the suffering and dying to glorify it. In war there are no winners, only losers. War is the most brutal form of human endeavor, and those who choose to view it as a glorious national venture dishonor the memory of those young men who suffered and died in combat.

War has the tendency to bring man's worst instincts to bear, turning young men from peaceful sons of loving families to hardened, avowed killers if they survive. But at the same time, engaging in mortal combat with another human being intent on killing you can bring out the best qualities in a man: devotion to duty, loyalty to his buddies, daring, courage, and endurance of body and spirit. In combat, the line between life and death can often be measured in inches, using an old football cliche referring to the margin between victory and defeat. Why some combat soldiers survive and fight on to the final outcome whereas others within arm's length in fierce combat are hit and die, I have never been able to fathom. To find a logical answer to an illogical question has eluded me all these years.

After a week or so confined in bed, I was allowed to walk around the grounds and visit other patients. I saw a number of 504th officers hospitalized in Naples: Lieutenants Sims, Hanna, and Wisniewski, among others. My platoon machine gunner, Pvt. Lawrence Dunlop, was there, having been wounded on 15 March and evacuated to Naples. Before the 4 March arrival of replacements on the line at Mussolini Canal, there were almost as many of us in the hospital as there were on the line with the 504th. Yet we were the lucky ones; many of our buddies weren't as fortunate.

While recovering in the hospital, I had an opportunity to get caught up on my letter writing. When we were on the line, we would often go for weeks and even months without writing home. I was fortunate to recover some of those letters after I returned home. In some respects it was like keeping a diary, except that my observations were not as frequent as daily accounts. They have been important because they jog my memory and authenticate my recollection of those moments. Here are some relevant excerpts from those letters. On 20 February 1944, I wrote to my youngest sister, Helen: "Today I received another batch of mail and two papers, but no packages. Generally mail addressed to the 504th reaches me in about two weeks. Some take anywhere from three weeks to a month if sent to the wrong APO. When I'm in combat, of course, I don't get any until we are relieved and sent back to the rear. . . . I'm getting along very well and should be out of here in a week or two. I still have one hole in my arm and I can't bend my elbow yet, but in another week it will be just like new. 'What then?' is what worries me."

In other letters I wrote about the weather, life in the hospital, and always about how I was feeling, which was most important to my loved ones. On 26 February I wrote to my oldest sister, Catherine: "So they call this country 'Sunny Italy.' When I first arrived here last fall it was raining every day. Everyone said it was their rainy season. Inquiring from the natives, I learned that the rainy season would end in January. Now February is almost gone and instead of raining every day it now rains every three days out of four. . . . I'm feeling fine and getting along very well. Yesterday in the hospital theater, where movies are shown occasionally, I saw the Ritz Brothers in 'Never A Dull Moment.' All I do is eat, read, write letters and sleep, not a bad life, eh?"

On 29 February I again wrote home: "Just a few lines to let you know that I'm feeling fine and intend to stay that way. When I was back in the states I moved a lot and always left my friends behind. I have lost most of my best friends in this outfit, but in this case, a permanent loss. It is a feeling that is much different than just leaving a friend behind. . . . I came here [the hospital] three weeks ago and I'll be leaving this week. So I've had a pretty good rest and a chance to write some letters."

On 6 March I was released from the hospital, almost four weeks after I had been wounded, and reported to the 504th Regiment rear headquarters just outside Naples, awaiting further orders. From that date until the end of the war, more than fourteen months later, I was not wounded or hospitalized again. From May 1945 to January 1946, while the 504th was on occupation duty in Berlin, I would not miss another day of combat as a platoon leader, H Company, 504th Regiment. Referring to a term I used in my pugilistic days, "The Krauts never again laid a glove on me."

On 7 March I wrote my first letter home after being released from the hospital: "I got out of the hospital yesterday and I'm feeling very well. I'm back in the rear so don't worry. It will be about another week before my arm will be ready for duty again. . . . Sometime ago, I had an opportunity to visit Naples. I saw where preparations had been made for the World's Fair of 1944. Most of the buildings had been completed and some had been bombed and destroyed. . . . How these people could have been preparing for the Fair in 1944, while they were planning a war, is beyond me. . . ."

In many of my letters home I mentioned the weather in the combat areas. Of the many factors a combat soldier couldn't control, weather and terrain affected him most. The men of the 504th spent 371 days in combat in all types of terrain and often under the most miserable weather conditions. In combat, men would lose track of the days; surviving to see the light of a new dawn was all that mattered. The combat soldier was exposed to the elements 365 days a year, living in an open hole, shielded only from enemy fire. No wonder we came to be known as "dogfaces." When it rained the combat soldier got soaked; when it snowed he was cold; when the thermometer read zero he froze. Always outside, he fought the elements as well as the enemy. Battles cannot be postponed because of rain and rescheduled later as a doubleheader under more favorable weather conditions.

While I was recuperating from my wound and awaiting the return to H Company and the 504th, I managed to visit Naples for an occasional R and R. In the evenings the Allied officers' favorite watering hole was the Orange Gardens. While there, I met some young pilots from a B-25 squadron located at a nearby airfield near the base of Mount Vesuvius. I went out to their air base, spent the night, and early the next morning went on a bombing mission with them to northern Italy.

The target was a railroad center and marshalling yards north of Rome. I sat in a small seat between and just to the rear of the pilot and copilot. I was enjoying the flight until we approached the target area and German antiaircraft bat-

teries on the ground opened fire on us. All around us I could
see puffs of black smoke, but I heard no sound of explo-
sions, such as the artillery and screaming-meemies I was accustomed to hearing on the ground. The B-25s started their
bomb runs, released over their targets, and started for home;
all planes accounted for and intact. In a matter of minutes, it
was over and we were not challenged again by the enemy.
Once the planes landed, the pilots and crews would await the
next one. They had done their job and had done it well. They
all returned safely from their mission, but that was not always the case. For the pilots the landing was routine, but for
me landing with the same plane I had taken off on was a
strange experience. The last thirty to thirty-five takeoffs I
had made on a C-47, I jumped out the door in midair and the
plane returned without me. But the best was still to come.
Just as we exited the plane, we were welcomed back by a
quart of bourbon and a stiff shot of booze. Then it was on to
the mess hall and a breakfast of bacon and eggs. I'll say one
thing for the air force; they had a tough job, they accepted
the hazards and took their lumps, but they knew how to live.

I saw my pilot friends once more before we departed
Italy. Mother Nature had done to them what the Germans
had been unable to do. Mount Vesuvius had erupted, spewing lava over the base and destroying some of the squadron's
planes before anyone could get them in the air. They were relocating the base, but the pilots were still open for business.

On 23 March the 504th Regiment was relieved of frontline duty on the Mussolini Canal. The men boarded LSTs in
the harbor at Anzio, and the following morning they disembarked at the small port of Pozzuoli, where we had departed
for Anzio on 20 January. The regiment's bivouac area was
Bagnoli, about fifteen minutes from the center of Naples.
Sixty-two days on the Anzio beachhead was a grueling experience for the battle-hardened paratroopers, who had paid
a high cost in men: 120 killed, 410 wounded, and 60 missing in action. Anzio was now behind us, but we had a long
way to go before the end of the war. The question now was,

where next? We would not be in Bagnoli long before that question was answered.

It was a happy day seeing Rivers again and rejoining H Company and taking over my platoon. Many of the men who had made the landing at Anzio had not returned. The majority of my platoon now consisted of new men who had come up as replacements after I was wounded. I was fortunate to have them; they proved to be great combat soldiers.

The rumor gaining most prominence was that we would soon be leaving Italy to rejoin the 82d Airborne Division in England. One rumor had us returning to the States, but that was more wishful thinking than probability. Another mission that would keep us in Italy was not even a good latrine rumor. In the meantime we undertook light training and remained in a state of readiness. On 20 March I wrote what was probably my last letter from Italy: "At the present time I am back in a rest area in the rear, something like the time I came off the mountains. The beachhead was hell. The Germans tried to push us back into the sea, but paratroopers don't push very easily. There's not an outfit in the world as tough as this one. . . ."

Before departing Italy, the regiment held a review for the Fifth Army commander, Gen. Mark Clark, who lavished praise on the 504th as an outstanding fighting unit. He cited the 3d Battalion's heroic action on the northern sector for what he said "saved the beachhead from being overrun." For this action, during the period 8 to 13 February, the 3d Battalion received the Presidential Unit Citation, the Battalion's Colors, and, for the four companies G, H, I, and Headquarters, guidons adorned with the emblematic ribbon. But for all the heroics on the battlefield, that was about it. I received a Bronze Star, and Rivers a Silver Star.

On 10 April we began our departure from Italy for our new "home" in England. We climbed aboard railroad cars for Naples, marched through the center of that town to the waterfront, then boarded a British liner, the *Capetown Castle*. There weren't any tears shed by the men of the 504th when we boarded, but sadness, yes. Many of our comrades in arms weren't on that ship with us. The 504th had more men killed in sixty-two days in combat on the Anzio beachhead than in any other campaign we fought, including the parachute jumps in Holland and the Battle of the Bulge. The Anzio beachhead has been recorded as one of the bloodiest battles of World War II; more than 30,000 Allied soldiers were killed. German casualties were as high if not higher. In no other battle fought by U.S. troops during the war were so many men killed in such a small, enclosed area.

On 25 April I wrote a letter home to my oldest brother, George. Staff Sergeant George Megellas had received a medical discharge from the army but was hoping he could enlist in the Coast Guard. With his three younger brothers still in the army and in combat, he found returning to civilian life hard to swallow. I wrote the letter shortly after arriving in England, but it had a lot to say about how I felt about our rear-echelon troops in Naples:

> I don't imagine you are too happy about being home while all the boys are gone, but George, don't let it bother you. I know that we are all happy that you are home. It's so much easier for Mom and the girls. You don't have to worry about our family not doing their share. George, you can do more by being home and I'd feel very disappointed if you left. You've no reason to feel bad, you served 18 months and you did more than 90% of the people I've seen overseas. I saw more guys with a racket back in Italy. They run the towns, live good, never heard a shot fired and then make it miserable for a combat outfit, besides. A combat man is at home only on the line. All this crap about the cokes, beer, etc. being sent to the front line never got past Naples and the "Bedroom Commandos." Some of these jerks are living better overseas than they ever did in their life.

Just before leaving Italy, our Battalion received the Presidential Citation for outstanding gallantry in action at the Anzio beachhead. This is the only outfit in this theatre to have received it. We are going to be presented with ribbons. At the time we earned the citation my company had 17 men in it. This was the action in which I was hit and evacuated. That was also the time I knocked off at least ten Jerries.

These were not my sentiments alone. When Naples was placed off-limits to the fighting men of the 504th, who had been part of the force that liberated Naples, it left a bad taste in our mouths. Sometimes it was hard to tell your friends from the enemy.

I had an opportunity to return to the site of the Anzio beachhead landing in 1962 during a stopover in Rome. My wife and I rented a car and drove around the area. The beaches where we landed were bristling with motels, cabanas, and bikini-clad damsels completely oblivious of the hell and fury of battle that had taken place eighteen years ago. Although I could picture the location of the railroad bed where I had been wounded and where H Company, surrounded and cut off, dug in and made its last-ditch stand, I was unable to find the exact location. I experienced a strange feeling that I had been there once, but that was the extent of it.

We visited the U.S. cemetery at Nettuno where 144 men from the 504th are still interred. The grounds were immaculately kept. The crosses and the Stars of David on the grave sites were in perfect alignment, as were the names of the soldiers inscribed on the tombstones. I said to my wife, "There but for the grace of God go I."

When we were preparing to go overseas in 1943, I made my last will and testament and a burial request for the U.S. Army. I had three choices of what I wanted done with my remains in the event I died in combat: (1) my body returned to my family for interment, (2) burial in a national cemetery of my choice, or (3) burial in the field of battle where I fell.

The 144 paratroopers interred at Nettuno had felt as I did. If I were to die in battle I wanted to be buried where I fell and with the buddies with whom I fought. To return my body home for a second burial to a family that had already been overcome with grief I felt would only open old wounds.

Shortly after I returned to the States, the mother of Sgt. Stephen A. Tokarczyk requested that the body of her son be returned to Wabeno, Wisconsin, for burial. Sergeant Tokarczyk, one of the squad leaders in my platoon, was killed on the Anzio beachhead in January. I attended the funeral and delivered the eulogy. I was treated like one of the family, the beginning of a long friendship. Although they mourned the loss of a loved one, they were happy I had made it back safely.

V

England

On 24 April 1944, twelve days after departing Naples, the *Capetown Castle* landed at Liverpool, England. It was hello England, our home for the next five months. The days on the high seas had been uneventful, although Sally and George, the Nazi propagandists, were with us on the radio. They predicted we would never make it through the Straits of Gibraltar, that German submarines would get us first. One thing was certain: The Germans knew we had left Italy bound for England. The Wehrmacht would not have to contend with us in Italy any longer, and German speculation now centered around where next for the 504th Regiment and the 82d Airborne Division. They couldn't get the answer from us, because we were asking the same question.

After Africa and war-torn Italy, England was another world. No more Arabs panhandling goods and haggling over prices, no tattered kids pimping and hustling, no Italian women at the end of the chow line with little tykes begging for leftovers. England was civilization as we knew it. It could be said that we in the 504th, like our rear-echelon comrades in England, had traveled abroad at government expense. But unlike our rear-echelon comrades, we had only a short-stay visa.

We were seeing England for the first time in our young lives. In contrast to the wreckage and destruction of Italy, the lawns were green and well kept; everything was neat and orderly. The fortunes of war had taken a 180-degree turn for the men of the 504th, although that would not last. We were in England for a purpose, and as combat soldiers we would inevitably be undergoing the hell and fury of mortal combat, probably soon.

After disembarking at Liverpool, toting our equipment and barracks bags of personal effects, we marched to the railroad station. There we all boarded trains except for Lieutenant Sims, who was taken to the 303d Station Hospital near Leicester. (He would be discharged on 13 June and return to the company.) After an all-night ride, the train pulled up to Thurnby, just outside Leicester. A welcoming committee met us at the station, and the 82d Airborne Division band played what they knew so well, "We're All Americans." For the first time since leaving Fort Benning, we were welcomed at our destination. Combat troops were appreciated.

It was a short ride to the bivouac area, where everything was ready for us. Pyramidal tents were pitched, each containing five canvas army cots with two blankets. And there were latrines, not slit trenches. A large tent housed the mess hall, where cooks prepared hot food. Company streets were graveled and well laid out. After Africa, Mount Sammucro in Italy, and the damp foxholes of Anzio, it seemed like the Ritz.

However, in spite of the improved scenery and living conditions, I wasn't ready to accept the quiet life of England. I was a combat platoon leader and there was a war to be fought. I expressed my disdain for garrison life in a letter to my sister Catherine: "I'm not as happy in England as I was in Italy where we were always on the front. . . ."

The men had no difficulty getting passes into Leicester, and weekends in London were available if you had the sterling. Except for the blackouts and frequent wailing of air-raid sirens, a night on the town in Leicester was reminiscent of back home. There was hardly a street downtown that didn't have at least one pub. Although whiskey was rationed and hard to come by, beer, albeit flat and warm, was always on tap. Leicester had something to suit everyone's interest. There were big movie houses, dance halls, jitterbug palaces, and, best of all, no shortage of girls to dance with. For the sports aficionados, there was the Leicester Golf Club or the

Leicester Racquet Club, bicycling through the unspoiled countryside, and even boxing matches between U.S. and British paratroopers. Those who chose to spend a night in camp found the dayrooms well stocked. At Louise's Doughnut Dugout, there were tea parties and even two-minute shampoos. The 504th and division artillery swing bands provided big band music for paratroopers and their girlfriends doing all the latest steps. When Sherman said war was hell, he failed to qualify for whom.

Meanwhile, the men took turns standing guard duty, carrying out the routine, and doing mundane camp duties generally associated with stateside camps. There was no sense of urgency yet. Although combat soldiers were still fighting and dying at Anzio, that seemed of little consequence in England. Italy was just a sideshow to the British and Supreme Headquarters, Allied Expeditionary Force (SHAEF).

My general impressions were expressed in letters to friends and family, such as this one to my sister Mary on 1 May 1944:

> I am Battalion Officer Of The Day today and I just finished checking the guard and guard posts. I used a bicycle to get around. Transportation is scarce in this outfit since a parachute outfit is not authorized any vehicles so over here a lot of the fellows have bought bikes. I bought one this morning for seven pounds and ten shillings ($30.00). Most of the people here ride bikes. There are very few civilian cars.
>
> We're stationed on the outskirts of a town near the residential district. . . . The people are very hospitable, unlike the Italians who were either stealing or begging from us. I recall how surprised I was when a little English boy said, "Mister, do you have a piece of gum?" I gave him a whole package. Gum is one thing they will ask you for.
>
> The town is very neat and orderly. The pubs (bars) are open from 6 p.m. to 10 p.m. but most of them run out of beer before that. Whiskey is just about unobtainable and

the beer is not very good. They serve beer without any air in it and not cooled. I sure could go for some American whiskey.

They have a very strict rationing system here. Everything is rationed. I have received quite a few of the small boxes you have been sending. They are nice but, honest, Mary, you shouldn't go to all the trouble. I'd just as soon you didn't send anymore. As for my Christmas packages, two were all that I got. One with the clothes in it and the other with the spoiled fruit cake. I imagine the sharks got the rest.

We have received word that we will get a few days leave. God knows that we've earned it. When I get mine, I'm going to try and locate John. I think by now he knows that I am in England.

I'm really enjoying the peace and quiet here. I only hope that it will last for a few weeks. For the first few days here I couldn't get used to it, especially after all the combat days I spent. Our soldiers who have been stationed here for a while have been leading the "good life." I don't want to hear any of them complaining about being overseas. If so, they should have been in Italy on the front. Many of the German prisoners we took claimed that the fighting was harder in Italy against us than it was on the Russian front. . . .

There was little speculation about our next mission, but one thing was obvious: Hitler's European fortress would have to be penetrated if we were to bring an end to the war. Security was so tight that there was not even a good latrine rumor making the rounds as to where or when the invasion of Europe might be. We were certain that those questions were being addressed and the planning had been under way for some time regarding an invasion across the English Channel, but we were not privy to any such information. Planning was tightly held and of the utmost secrecy.

My concern was how to keep a sharp edge on veteran combat troops and prepare them for the next mission while living the life of Riley. One thing was certain—keeping in top physical shape was necessary for survival. That much we had learned from combat in Italy when we were climbing mountains and sloshing through mud. Every morning in England, I would take my platoon for a ten-mile run in the countryside. At the halfway point, if the men appeared to be tiring, I quickened the pace, then turned around and ran backward the rest of the way. That dispelled any thoughts of dropping out or not keeping up, because no proud, self-respecting paratrooper was about to be shown up by his platoon leader, an "old man" of twenty-seven years.

One of the men in my platoon—Sgt. Charles Crowder, who was with H Company, 504th Parachute Regiment, for two years during the war—recalled those early-morning runs in England: "We were all in top physical condition. You had to be able to do double-time six miles with a pack on your back without coming to a walk. Otherwise, you were washed out and disqualified to serve in a parachute company. In H Company we had a Lt. Megellas, known as 'Maggie,' who was in top physical condition and would take the Company on a run just to see how far we could double-time it. He ran us 10 miles without coming to a walk, but we never had a man drop out. I can remember all the men had a big smile on their faces."

Running ten miles every morning in the countryside, especially during the summer months in England, was not exactly a picnic, but the combat veterans of the Italian campaign did not complain. They had earned their parachute wings after completion of six qualifying jumps and four weeks of intense, grueling physical training. Those faint of heart or body who had not been able to keep pace were either disqualified or delayed in completion of the course until they were able to meet the requirements. And because as "light" infantrymen we had not been authorized vehicles to transport us, unlike others who flew or rode into combat, we walked through all kinds of terrain and weather to make contact with the enemy. Living in foxholes, surviving on meager rations, battling endless bad weather, and being subject to long forced marches as well as the enemy required not only courage but physical stamina and endurance. There was no place or tolerance for stragglers in a combat unit.

In England, in spite of the ten-mile runs, and even though the 504th was in continuous training and readiness for the next mission, the first several months of training seemed light. Back in Africa and Italy, training simulated combat conditions: long marches with full field equipment, obstacle courses, night jumps, and forced marches. But in England, forced marches were replaced with close order drill: keeping in step and in precise alignment in preparation for parades. Although in three campaigns in Italy, the 504th had been in combat for 151 days and in all kinds of weather tromping through mud and snow and up and down rocky mountain paths in pursuit of Germans, the top brass felt that in England we had to demonstrate that we knew our left foot from the right and could drill as well as we could fight. I was never able to understand how hours and hours on end of close order drill contributed anything to combat readiness except perhaps to irritate the men.

So it was back to uniforms clean and neatly pressed, trousers creased, jump boots and brass polished so well you could see yourself in the glare, stripes sewn on, and hair neatly trimmed, all for standing inspections. It was time to parade. Jointly with the British 1st Parachute Division we paraded in Leicester with the lord mayor on the reviewing stand and, of course, before visiting dignitaries.

But the main event was yet to come. General Dwight D. "Ike" Eisenhower, Supreme Allied Commander, would review the reunited 82d Airborne Division soon after the return of the 504th Regiment from Italy. Of places and events with the 504th, parades seldom left a lasting impression on me, but I never forgot the division review for Ike, not because of the parade itself but for the remarks he made to the troops from the reviewing stand. Most of what he said I would categorize as boilerplate from a commander to the troops, except for a brief remark. This is almost verbatim:

"You men have accomplished great things and I have greater things in store for you."

Down the ranks of paratroopers standing in formation, 10,000 Adam's apples went up and down in unison. "Greater things in store for you" had a different meaning for us than it did for him. For us it meant that after the next "greater things," one-half to three-fourths of us standing in the ranks would not be returning. That was our experience from the invasion of Anzio, and there was no reason to believe that an invasion somewhere else in Europe would be any different. For Eisenhower, "greater things" meant victories over the Nazis, albeit in a human toll of lives and blood. On this point we were in accord: Great things in combat are achieved at a high price in lives. As combat troops, we accepted that as fact. Eisenhower, however, never alluded to the cost paid for the great things accomplished or for the price we would pay for the greater things yet to come. His great things were realized in the war room and measured in distances and locations on maps. Our great things were realized on the battlefield and measured in yards, hills, or cities captured or rivers crossed. In the war rooms, American casualties were recorded as daily statistics. On the battlefield, casualties were personal, the lives of our buddies. In the war rooms, casualties were highly impersonal and faceless. If the war was won, the commanders were portrayed by historians as the conquering heroes. If the war was lost, the commanders passed into oblivion. Eisenhower's remarks remained with me as an example of how warfare is viewed from the highest levels of command to the lowest. It was the private who did the fighting, killing, and dying.

Combat casualties were publicly reported weekly, if not daily. When the latest tally on casualties was reported in *Stars & Stripes*, I remarked to Rivers, "I've got my name in the paper again, actually twice. If it wasn't for me the cumulative total report of wounded in action of, say 95,735 would have only been 95,733." But for those mothers who receive telegrams from the War Department "regretfully informing you that your son has been wounded in action," it was more than just a statistic. Worse yet, for those who received a telegram "regretfully informing you that your son was killed an action," it opened a wound that never completely healed.

Among the many pleasantries we encountered in England was the Red Cross clubmobile that served us coffee and doughnuts. Clubmobile K and the three lovely ladies who operated it—Mary, Charlotte, and Marianne (the "doughnut dollies")—seemed to always be in the vicinity of the 504th. We enjoyed not only the coffee and doughnuts but on occasion the pleasure of their company as well. Captain Carl Kappel, Rivers, and I escorted them to dances and social functions and occasionally on the rounds in Leicester.

Although whiskey was rationed and hard to come by, I managed a deal with a local pub owner to buy his weekly ration. He sold me on the sly his weekly quota of three bottles of scotch at a premium above what he would receive selling it over the bar in one-ounce shots. It was one of the few things I could spend money on.

With the big buildup of men and materiel taking place in England, there was considerable speculation in the States about when and where D day would take place. Families were concerned about what might happen to loved ones in combat units. The letters I was receiving from home upset me because of the anxiety being felt about my well-being. When I wrote home, I always tried to ease their minds. On 26 April 1944, I wrote to my sister Catherine: "I feel as though this war is a lot tougher on you than on any of us. Combat isn't the most pleasant thing I know of, but I'm getting used to it and it don't worry me too much. . . . I don't have the worries you do at home. I wish there was more I could do to keep you from worrying. I try to write whenever possible, but there have been times when I was unable to. I'm hoping that this will be over soon and we can be together again."

In my last letter from home, I learned that John, my younger brother, was somewhere in England. His unit was not far from Leicester, so I had no problem locating him. He was doing MP duty and living in a private home. Several weeks later, John got a weekend pass and came to see me in Leicester. I introduced him to the men in H Company, and Rivers and I showed him Leicester and all the bright spots. It was a great feeling seeing your brother in the theater of operations, thousands of miles from home. After D day he left England and was assigned to the 8th Infantry Division somewhere on the Continent. I did not see him again until May 1945 in Germany, when German resistance was collapsing and we were in hot pursuit.

During May 1944 there was an air of anticipation throughout Great Britain. British and American forces were accelerating training programs and increasing their state of readiness. The question on everyone's mind was when the invasion of Europe would begin. Those in the 504th Parachute Regiment felt we would play a major role, because we had the most combat experience of any parachute regiment in the theater. We had been in England for almost two months, and although we had not yet received replacements for our losses in Anzio and were still understrength, we were ready to go back to combat. I felt certain that being understrength was the reason we were pulled out of Anzio to rejoin the 82d Airborne Division. Being understrength in the 504th was nothing new. That was always the case in Italy and at Anzio, where we had held off the Germans while we were at less than 25 percent of authorized strength.

When we got word that the 504th would not jump on D day and would be held in reserve, many of us were greatly disappointed. In place of the 504th, two new regiments were attached to the division, the 507th and 508th Parachute Infantry.

A number of reasons have been advanced as to why a veteran combat regiment such as the 504th was not initially committed and held back in reserve. One had the 504th so badly beaten up in Italy and Anzio that we were not yet ready for another mission. Another had the 504th so understrength that it could not be effective as a full regiment, whereas the 507th and 508th, fresh from the States, were at or near full strength. Another held that the 504th, which the Germans had been tracking since leaving Anzio, was held back to deceive the Germans into believing that the main assault would be farther up the French coast. For whatever reasons, the decision was made to leave the 504th in England, at least for the time being.

The 504th was not left out completely. Volunteers were requested from the 504th to man the pathfinder teams, which would jump ahead of the main forces to guide the aircraft to the designated landing fields. Rivers and I heard about the need for pathfinders, so we immediately went to Maj. Julian A. Cook, the 3d Battalion commander, and volunteered our services. Actually we requested permission to join the pathfinders. Our request was denied.

On the night of 5 June 1944, the pathfinder aircraft, of the IX Troop Carrier Command, took off from Witham airfield, and shortly thereafter troop carriers carrying the three parachute regiments took off from airfields scattered around England. The pathfinders from the 504th Parachute Regiment were the first to land on French soil. After ten days on the ground, they were relieved and returned to the regiment, but not before seven troopers from the 504th were killed. The long-awaited invasion of Hitler's European fortress was under way. I remember standing in the company street on that memorable night of 5 June and seeing the sky full of C-47s flying over Leicester. I had an empty feeling in my stomach as I watched those planes heading for France without me. I felt like a bride left at the altar.

On 8 July the 82d Airborne returned to England after thirty-three days of combat without relief or replacements. During that time, the four regiments of the 82d successfully completed every assigned mission. Paratroopers of the 505th liberated Ste. Mere Eglise, the first city to be taken from the Germans in France, four hours before the beach landing on D day.

By dawn, the 82d had captured the strategic bridges over the Merderet River. In less than forty-eight hours, paratroopers of the 82d had driven the Germans out of a hundred square miles between the Merderet and Douve Rivers. During the fighting, the 82d had destroyed sixty-two German tanks and forty-four antitank and artillery guns, while sustaining 46 percent casualties.

The three parachute regiments, the 505th, 507th, and 508th, along with the 325th Glider Regiment, fought gallantly and with distinction. The same was true of the paratroopers and glider men of the 101st Parachute Division. It was a baptism by fire for five parachute regiments, although the 505th had previous combat experience. We envied their accomplishments, mourned the loss of our fellow paratroopers, and were proud to be in the same division with them. We were, after all, paratroopers "cut from the same cloth."

Shortly after the return of the 82d from Normandy, speculation as to the next mission intensified. No one expected that we would remain in England much longer now that the Allied forces had left the beaches and were on the move. Several missions into France, Belgium, or Holland were planned, then canceled. On one occasion, we were isolated for days at a British airfield waiting for favorable weather to jump ahead of advancing American armored forces. This mission also was canceled at the last minute, and we returned to Leicester and the monotony of garrison life.

One thing was certain: Another combat mission was imminent. Exactly when that might be was of little concern, because we would obviously be somewhere ahead of advancing Allied forces on the Continent and there would be no shortage of Germans to contend with. We had been through several alerts and dry runs, so we were ready to go at any time.

In the meantime, we kept close to camp, whiling away our evenings playing cards or shooting craps. The same Lady Luck that had smiled on me in combat was by my side when I was playing cards or shooting dice. Rivers and I partnered up playing bridge and did well. I had my best results, however, playing two-hand casino. First Lieutenant Charles "Hoss" Drew, one of my best buddies in the 3d Battalion, went broke playing casino and ended up giving me an IOU for $300. When Hoss was asked why he went into debt, he replied, "I wasn't gambling; I was taking out insurance with Maggie." Jokingly, the word got around, "If you want to increase your chances of making it back from the next mission, play cards with Maggie and give him an IOU; he won't let anyone who owes him money not return safely." One IOU that I held as a memento of that time was from Lt. Tom Murphy. It read, "Dear Mom, if anything happens to me, pay this Greek SOB $100.00. Your loving son, Tom." Murphy jumped with the pathfinders, and I never saw him again. Needless to say, I never tried to collect his IOU.

Occasionally, when we were around a crap table we would look up and see the regimental commander, Col. Reuben Tucker, join us and try his luck. One night just before we left England, he came to the officers' lounge and joined a game in progress. I had a hot hand that night, and Tucker had the misfortune of covering me. After each pass I let the bet double, and Tucker kept covering me. After the third pass, I let the bet ride and Tucker once again said, "You're covered." Only this time I didn't see the color of his money on the table. I kept shaking the dice and yelling, "Two hundred dollars open," and Tucker kept saying, "You're covered." I was hoping someone with cash would cover the bet, but no junior officer would take a piece of the bet as long as his regimental commander kept insisting, "I've got you covered." I would have liked to withdraw my bet and shoot $5 instead, but I couldn't do that either. Finally, Tucker pulled his wallet out of his back pocket, placed it on top of my $200 bet, and said, "Shoot." I still didn't see any money, but at that point I had no choice but to roll the dice. It was another natural. Tucker picked up his empty wallet, put it back in his pocket, and left, saying, "Maggie, I owe you two hundred dollars." Later the word got around among the junior officers that he had taken out $200 worth of insurance with Maggie.

On and off for about a week, we had been isolated in airports preparing to take off on missions that were later aborted. On 15 September we moved to the airfield at Spanhoe, one of a large number of airfields in England where a vast armada of airplanes and gliders would take off for the largest airborne invasion in history. It was during our staging at Spanhoe that I received my first indication of our mission, although in our alert it was known that we were about to embark on another combat mission. During the week we spent in the airport, the atmosphere was rife with rumors, prognostications, and speculations. However, this was all eventually cleared up when the invasion briefings reached down to the squad level.

Sand tables were set up depicting landing areas and location of our initial objectives. We would jump fifty-seven miles behind the established German lines. The drop zone for my platoon and H Company was between the two largest single-span bridges in Europe, the Maas River at Grave and the Waal River at Nijmegen. The designated drop zone and the assembly area for my platoon were firmly fixed in our minds. As the jumpmaster in my plane, I had no difficulty identifying the drop zone on our approach to the field. It was exactly as I had envisioned it from our sand table briefings. We were all issued a small sum of invasion currency (in Dutch guilders), but I couldn't imagine for what purpose. I was also given two maps of Holland and the invasion area, printed not on paper but on silk cloth; the maps fitted nicely in a pocket of my jumpsuit. We were all given orange armbands, which would identify us as allies of the Dutch House of Orange to the Dutch underground. On 16 September, one of the uncontrolled factors that a combat soldier had to contend with—the weather—caused a delay in our departure. A heavy fog enveloped most of England, and a light rain made takeoff difficult, so we returned to our tents. However, it would be a "go" tomorrow regardless of weather conditions.

One of Cornelius Ryan's questions in researching his book *A Bridge Too Far* was, "How did you feel about a daylight operation?" I replied as follows:

When we first received information that the Holland jump would be a daylight operation, we had mixed feelings. We knew Holland was completely occupied by enemy forces and that our rumbling C-47s would present an easy target from ground small arms fire. My initial reaction was that a daylight operation could not be planned unless the flight area was either secure or unoccupied by the enemy forces. We recognized that we were counting on the element of surprise although it was hard to imagine that German intelligence would not trace our departure from England. On the other hand, although we had never previously made a daylight combat jump, we recognized certain advantages in a daylight operation. It would be much easier to assemble, reorganize, and strike quickly at the initial objectives. I reasoned that there were certain calculated risks involved in a daylight operation, but the advantages of a bold, daring move of this kind would offset those risks. In retrospect, I believe that this calculation turned out to be correct. While initial casualties were suffered, the disadvantages were quickly overcome by the rapidity with which the initial objectives were seized. The initial objective—the bridge at Eindhoven—was seized in a matter of hours by the 101st Airborne Division.

The night of 16 September in the tents at Spanhoe airfield was a quiet, sober time of reflection. It was now definite that we would be loading onto C-47s in the morning for a daylight jump into Holland. We had moved past the rumor stage; everything now was in readiness. Letters were being written home and personal matters discussed with buddies. Most men went to bed early; few slept soundly.

On the morning of Sunday, 17 September, most men woke up early. I remember waking up that morning hearing Lt. Robert "Boobytrap" Blankenship, I Company, singing the song "Down in the Valley." It was a song we often sang during lighter moments, but on that morning it had a moving effect on me. There was a certain air of sadness and farewell expressed in the refrain that seemed to suit the moment.

In contrast to the previous day, 17 September turned out to be clear, sunny, and fairly warm. We began the morning with a big breakfast of pancakes, chicken, and pie, which was not our normal, everyday fare. It was as if the condemned were being served a hearty meal.

After breakfast we loaded onto trucks and headed for the tarmac and the waiting C-47s. My platoon assembled around two aircraft. In my stick there were sixteen men; I was the jumpmaster and would give the jump commands and go out the door first over the drop zone. Sergeant William V. Rice was at the rear of the stick and would make certain that no one delayed in exiting the plane. In the equipment bundles, fastened to the belly of the plane, which I would release when I jumped, we carried bazookas and ammo, M1 ammo, hand and rifle grenades, and 81mm mortar ammo. We again checked our equipment and chutes, then boarded the plane, each man sitting according to his place in the stick. When the aircraft started to move on the tarmac, the noise was deafening. Each man was deep in his own thoughts. I expressed mine when I wrote to Cornelius Ryan: "I personally was happy and anxious to return to action. I know this may sound rather horrible today, but I believe my feeling typified the general spirit of the paratroopers in my company, battalion, and regiment. We recognized that a job had to be done. We accepted the fact that this was a fight to the finish and we were eager to get on with the job. It would be interesting to note at this point that as the war progressed and my experience accumulated I found the business of killing and destruction an agreeable accomplishment. I suppose this comes with the transformation that is necessary to make killers out of soldiers. Also I was anxious to return to combat since I had been out of action since I was wounded at Anzio. I missed the rest of the Anzio campaign in which my regiment participated as a combat team apart from the rest of the Division."

Beginning at 1025 on Sunday, 17 September, the first planes, twelve British and six American, took off with the Pathfinders, who were scheduled to jump forty minutes ahead of the main force. Shortly thereafter, 2,023 troop transport planes and 478 gliders took off from twenty-four separate airfields in England. My plane taxied down the tarmac to the airstrip, got the green light to go, and with minimal delay was airborne. We headed for an established rendezvous point, joined with other C-47s, and headed east in a vee of vees formation. In addition to the C-47s, the invasion fleet was joined by 1,131 Allied fighter planes flying escort for the vulnerable troop carriers. British and American spotter planes, which would find detached planes and gliders, also joined us. During the course of Operation Market Garden, the code name for the Allied invasion, 205 men would be picked up from the sea. As we looked out the windows of our C-47, we saw a sky darkened with aircraft, all heading in one direction toward Holland. Approximately two and a half hours after takeoff, forty-five minutes of which was over enemy-held territory, we would be over our drop zone and jumping out the single door of our C-47s. It was good-bye, England. Holland, here we come.

VI
Market Garden

Our planes climbed to an altitude of 1,500 feet, then leveled off. As we were flying over the English coast, I could see crowds who had gathered in the streets waving flags. They were witnessing history in the making, the largest airborne fleet ever assembled, taking off for the greatest airborne invasion ever conceived. Looking out of my plane at this vast armada left me with a feeling of insignificance, except for the fact that I was part of a historical occasion.

The men in my stick knew they were part of something big, but the combat-hardened veterans of the Italian campaign took it in stride. For the most part they showed no emotion, just waited in somber anticipation. As I sat in the first seat next to the door, I thought about hitting the drop zone and organizing and assembling the platoon. We would have to recover and unpack the equipment bundles and move out to the battalion assembly point. I was concerned about how we would deploy on the ground if we met enemy resistance and how we would join up with the rest of H Company. Nothing else seemed to matter at the moment.

As we approached the coast of Holland, I could see black puffs from exploding German antiaircraft fire. As the muzzle flashes were spotted, escorting fighter planes dove toward them with guns blazing. Fortunately in all of this, we encountered no signs of the Luftwaffe. Although our fighter escorts silenced most of the antiaircraft batteries, they did not get them all. As we approached the Walcheren Islands, off the coast of Holland, enemy ground fire hit one of the H Company planes, setting the belly of the plane on fire. The plane was carrying sixteen men from the platoon led by Lt. Isadore Rynkiewicz of H Company.

The sight of one of our planes burning had a terrible effect on me and my stick of men. We had just approached the coast of Holland and still had about forty-five minutes of flying time over enemy-held territory before we reached the drop zone. At the altitude and speed the lumbering C-47s were flying, they were easy targets. I eyeballed the descent of the crippled plane and saw the camouflage parachutes of the exiting paratroopers open one after the other. The pilot of the smoking plane kept a steady course until the human cargo got out, then the plane crashed in flames in a flooded area of Schouwen Island.

First Lieutenant Virgil Carmichael, S2, 3d Battalion, watched as paratroopers jumped from the stricken aircraft: "I was able to count them as they left and saw that all escaped safely. The pilot, although the aircraft was involved in flames, somehow kept the plane steady until the paratroopers jumped. . . . The Air Corps used white chutes, so I figured it had to be the crew chief. He was the last man out. Almost immediately the blazing plane nose-dived and, at full throttle, plowed into a flooded area of Schouwen Island below. On impact, a white chute billowed from the plane, probably ejected by the force of the crash."

The C-47 we were flying in was part of the 315th Troop Carrier Group. This is their report:

The flying routes selected for the operation were the ones which the planners hoped would avoid most anti-aircraft fire. It was known, however, that both heavy and light anti-aircraft guns were in the Arnhem and Nijmegen areas and at the landfall point at Schouwen Island.

On 14 September, troops of the 504th PIR, 82nd Airborne Division moved on the base and the usual security precautions were taken. At the first briefing, it was learned that the 315th's first destination was drop zone "O," located between Nijmegen and the Maas River. Two serials of 45 aircraft each were to be used to carry 1240 troops and 473 para-packs. The route from the Grantham area was to the English Coast at Aldeborough, then 94 miles across the North Sea to Schouwen Island. From that checkpoint, it was approximately 90 miles to the drop area.

Shortly after passing the Dutch coast, the C-47 piloted by Capt. Bohannon, 34th Squadron was hit by flak. The left engine and one of the underslung para-packs were burning as it went down in a flooded area near Dintellooro Harbor. Capt. Bohannon, Lieutenants Felber and Martinson, Sergeants Epperson and Carter were all killed.

Ground fire increased as the formation neared the DZ and seven C-47s were hit, even though American and British fighters in the area suppressed much fire from enemy ground positions.

Seventy-eight of the planes dropped their troops near the target, but most of the 11 "sticks" of paratroopers whose jump area was south of the Maas River landed 500 to 1200 yards beyond their zone, possibly because the pilots were concerned the men might land in the river.

Second Lieutenant Robert L. Cloer, 315th Troop Carrier Command, was the copilot of the C-47 flying on Captain Bohannon's right wing. This is his account of that fateful occasion: "Clarence E. Stubblefield was the pilot flying on Bohannon's left wing. As I remember it, his plane was shot up so bad that he could not remain in formation, but did get to the DZ and drop his troops. Capt. Bohannon's plane got hit in the belly where the para-packs were. These carried mines and ammunition and they caught fire. We were not supposed to break radio silence, but I called them and told them he was burning and to salvo his para-packs. By then the plane was burning and the paratroopers started to bail out. He held the plane level until all were out that could bail out and then started to dive for the water. I think that he was trying to get down to where he could land in the water and put the fire out. The plane was burning by now in the belly and I think the control cables which were located there just burned in two and he was not able to pull out of the dive."

In addition to 1st Lt. Isadore J. Rynkiewicz, the jump-master, there were fourteen men from H Company and the crew chief of the C-47 in the cabin of the plane. This is Private Reardon's account of the tragic event as he wrote it in 1983: "The reason for the rapid burning and intense heat of the fire, I've always attributed to the fact that we had one para-pack composed completely of composition C [now called C-4, in the terrorist lingo 'plastique']. It required a blasting cap to detonate and could be hit with rifle fire without detonating. As I recall, our para-pack of composition C was in the number one para-pack, left side, and first row. I've always believed that the ground fire ignited this pack and caused the intense fire and heat. . . . As to the question of the two white parachutes, the crew chief left the plane early. He was one of the very few who actually jumped, the rest of us dropped through the burning floor. The second white chute was that of Everett Rideout. He and Leginski were hidden by the Dutch Underground and never taken prisoners by the Germans."

George Willoughby, who was only eighteen years old at the time and the youngest trooper in the plane, wrote an account of this event and what happened to the fifteen paratroopers of H Company. By using devious means, he had been able to enlist in the army before Pearl Harbor at the age of fifteen. He volunteered for the paratroopers and certain combat when he joined H Company, 504th, on the front line at Anzio at age eighteen. He observed his nineteenth birthday in a German POW camp. He gave me a compelling story of a young, daring, courageous paratrooper shot down over enemy territory. He exemplifies the perseverance and will to overcome adversity. This is a common situation experienced by paratroopers, glider men, and airmen shot down over hostile territory. Willoughby:

On September 17, 1944, after visiting buddies at their plane and taking a picture with them, I told them I would see them on the ground. (Little did I know that the Germans had other plans for our plane.)

After we got airborne and headed for the coast, I was so uncomfortable with all the equipment on, that I got down on the floor of the plane and told a trooper next in line to let me know when we crossed the Channel and reached land. (I believe it was Rideout.) I carried a land mine in my left leg jump suit pocket and a Gammon grenade in my right leg pocket; two fragmentation grenades in my jump jacket pockets, K rations, sniper rifle, an ammo bag with 200 plus rounds of ammo, gas mask, pack and other items.

I fell asleep and when we reached the coast across the channel I was awakened and immediately got off the floor of the plane and sat in my seat across from the Lieutenant and the door of the plane. I could see out. It was only a short time before I could hear the crack of small arms fire and hear and see puffs of anti-aircraft gunfire. Shortly after, the plane started filling with smoke. As I looked across the plane I noticed that Lt. Rynkiewicz had been hit in the left knee and Hatfield, the BAR man, was hit on the back of his hand. To my right, a trooper was on the floor of the plane, again, I think it was Rideout. I remember saying, "let's get the hell out of here," and we started standing up. The Air Force Sergeant dove out the door of the plane. Within seconds, the plane was so full of smoke you could not see anything. Some men near the cockpit of the plane started coughing and pushing for the door. At that time, others and I fell through the floor of the plane. We were hooked up and when my chute opened, I could smell flesh and see the skin hanging from my face and hand. I had released my rifle when the flames burned my hands.

I looked down and saw that there was only a small strip of land along the road that was not flooded. I started working my chute to land near the road. When I landed I rolled over and pulled my .45 caliber pistol from its holster and pointed it in the direction of a man near me. He put up his hands and shouted "Hollander." I realized he was friendly, so I put my pistol back in the holster, got out of my chute, and crossed the road to see if I could help any of the other men that had landed in the water.

I saw Donald Woodstock had landed in water about waist deep. As he walked in the direction of the bank where I was standing, he stepped off into a deep trench about four to six feet wide that was around the flooded area. He came up shouting a few choice words and I helped him to dry land. We took our packs off and placed them behind a small house that was empty. We then started checking on the others. Everyone had done a good job landing on dry ground or near the edge of the flooded area.

We assembled in the small house. Lieutenant Rynkiewicz and Hatfield were in the house next door. The Air Force Sergeant and others went upstairs to keep a lookout for Germans while the Dutch people took care of our burns. Both of my hands and my face were wrapped with gauze and I looked like a mummy. I could only see out of my right eye. I held my hands up along my chest because it was painful when they were lowered to my side.

It wasn't long before a truck came down the road with some German soldiers in it. They stopped between the house that Rynkiewicz and Hatfield were in and the house we were in. They dismounted and some came in the direction of our house. One of the Germans threw a potato masher type grenade at the window. It bounced off and struck the one in charge on the leg. He jumped around like he had a broken foot. Someone waved a white piece of cloth out the window and we were taken out of the house. We were loaded on the truck and driven to a small town where we were herded into a building and questioned by a German officer. I was hurting so bad I moved to the side of the room and lay down on the floor. I don't remember how long we were there. It was getting late in the afternoon by the time the questioning was over.

We were loaded onto an old school type bus and traveled all night, arriving in Utrecht the following day. Mark Kaplan and I were sent to a field hospital located in a big church in town. In the hospital, we met up with two troopers from the 101st Airborne Division. There was Stanley P. Hunt from Philadelphia, PA, who had gotten a bad ankle sprain when he landed. The other young trooper had lost his second, third, and little fingers on his right hand. I do not remember his name. There was also a British trooper who had been blinded by a mortar round from German fire at Arnhem.

Three days later the five of us were put aboard a boxcar with straw on the floor along with German wounded and transported into Germany to a hospital in Munster. We stayed there until the 23rd of October. We were in pretty good shape by then. Hunt was still wearing a shower type wooden shoe and still carrying his number ten jump boot in his hand. The British Red Devil trooper had regained his eyesight by then and we were turned over to a German soldier that took us by civilian passenger train to Stalag 12-A at Limburg. There we were processed into the POW system. My POW number was 92789.

After we arrived in Utrecht on September 18, 1944, I never saw any members of my plane again except Kaplan, who was with me in the hospital, and Woodstock, whom we met when we arrived at Stalag 12-A in Limburg on October 23rd. On October 25, 1944, I had my 19th birthday. (No celebration or party!)

On the morning of October 28, 1944, we were taken from our tents and marched to a rail siding and loaded— 48 men in each car. Two five-gallon cans were placed in the middle of the car to be used as latrine facilities (no paper). It was so crowded one could hardly get to the pails near the door from the end of the rail car.

After approximately 28 to 30 hours we arrived at the rail station in Hammerstien, Germany, and marched 1 1/2 miles to Stalag IIB.

On January 28, 1945, we were told to be ready to leave camp by 0800 hours the next day. We had only been given one Red Cross food box to every two men each week in the past. On the morning of January 29, 1945, about 1200 POWs started out in the snow up to our knees and bitter cold. We stayed overnight in a large barn.

The following morning, Willoughby fell to the rear of the column and attempted his first escape from the Germans. He managed to elude his captors, but four days later he was recaptured and returned to Stalag IIB, where he stayed until 18 February 1945.

The following day, he was loaded on a boxcar with forty-eight other men. After twelve hours the train pulled into a rail siding at Stargard. That morning, a Russian plane bombed the railroad yard, scattering the POWs. Willoughby then made his second attempt to escape. Three days later, he and three other POWs were rounded up by the Germans and sent to a jail in Stettin, located northeast of Berlin on the Oder River.

Early the next day, Willoughby, fifteen Americans and two British, all of whom had been captured at Dunkirk, and two Russians were moved again. They left Stettin and marched northwest through Pasewalk and Anklam and arrived at a small camp at Greifswald.

Willoughby was at Greifswald until 26 April, when he was moved again—this time to the town of Barth, the location of Stalag Luft I. There he heard that the Americans and Russians had met on the Elbe River at Wittenberge.

From Greifswald, Willoughby made his third escape from the Germans. This time he would not be recaptured. After a harrowing experience of hitchhiking with the Russians, commandeering a bicycle, and eventually meeting a unit of the 84th U.S. Infantry Division, he located the 82d Airborne Division near Ludwigslust, Germany. From there, he located H Company, 504th, and remained with us until the end of May.

The Dutch underground watched as this vast armada of

planes and gliders crossed over the coast of Holland. Huib van Dis, a member of Netherlands Interior Forces (NIF), was in the area and recorded the following: "Sunday, September 17, 1944, 1000 hours: Many bombers and fighter planes were in the air. The MOERDYK Bridge and the railway station at LAGE-ZWALWE were bombed and the heavy bombardment of last night destroyed WILLEMSDORF completely. There must be something happening very soon. 1300 hours: The first transport planes of the huge Allied Force appeared over the villages soon to be followed by hundreds of gliders towed by transport planes. Very impressive (counted 1500). . . . At about 1330 hours one plane was afire and we could see 16 paratroopers leaving it. The plane fell down in the flooded area near the farm from A. van Sprang. At about 14 hours a glider crashed near DREIHOEK. The Germans took prisoners ten wounded airmen, while the rest of the soldiers hid themselves."

Partisans of the Dutch underground were the first to arrive at the scene of the crash. They treated the badly burned and wounded paratroopers. They assisted two H Company men not requiring medical assistance, Walter Leginski and Everett Ridout, to the house of an underground member, Hendrick Nijhoff, in Fynaart. They were protected and concealed there for forty-four days, then returned to our forces in the area.

The NIF kept and concealed a record of their activities and events. Jan Bose, a member of the NIF, provided a list of the names, ranks, and even serial numbers of the air force crew killed in the crash, and their grave site numbers. From a monthly issued by authorities, an article entitled "Brilliant in Gouden Delta," by Constable van Nispen, details the response by the NIF on the day the C-47 was shot down:

> On September 1, 1944, a part of the 719th German Infantry Division, stationed at Willemstad was sent to Brussels. They never reached Brussels, for the Allies liberated the city on September 3, 1944. On Sunday, September 17, 1944, a huge armada flew over Fijnaart in an

eastern direction. German anti-aircraft guns stationed at Dintelsas shot down one of these planes, a C-47 with serial number 45-15308. The plane dropped 16 paratroopers and came down in the flooded Heijningse Polder near the farm of A. van Sprang. The plane belonged to a formation with paratroopers of H Company, 504th Parachute Infantry Regiment, 82nd Airborne Division, aboard. Its destination was Grave.

In the area where the plane crash-landed lived nobody. The area was flooded and could only be reached via dikes. It was a very dangerous undertaking. Falling flak shrapnel and attack of fighter planes hit the four men, sent to the plane by Dr (M.D.) Schiphorst. Finally we reached the place where the Americans were where armed soldiers stopped us. Their commanding officer was shot in his leg and the Dutch took care of his wounds. One of the Dutchmen was sent to Willemstad to fetch an ambulance. There were more wounded men. Three soldiers were not wounded and stood on guard. In the house were nine very badly burned men. They had no more skin on their faces and hands. Very lucky for them that they fell in the water. The Dutchmen treated the wounds and gave morphine shots. One of the Dutchmen could see the pain and misery of the soldiers and went home. One of the Dutchmen was treating the last soldiers, when the Germans appeared. There was a shooting near the schoolhouse the officer was in. One of the Dutchmen was also there. The fight was fierce but short. When it was over, the German wounded were taken care of by the Dutch. The Germans hit the paratroopers in their faces, if they didn't give away the cigarettes, etc. Doctor Schiphorst arrived with an ambulance and the two most badly wounded soldiers were taken to his hospital. The others were taken prisoners and taken in open trucks to Steenbergen.

In my briefing to the men on my plane just before we took off from England, I indicated, as the jumpmaster, that I would begin the jump command about five minutes from the drop zone. The most difficult time in a parachute jump is the sweating that takes place while the men are standing and ready to go prior to the jump. Accordingly, jumpmasters always tried to minimize the length of time the stick was standing prior to jumping out the door of the plane. However, when I saw one of our company planes burning and then crash, I immediately gave the order to stand up and hook up to the men in my stick. We were standing and ready to go for almost forty-five minutes prior to the actual jump.

The purpose of this command, of course, was to have the stick ready to go and give everyone a chance to get out of the plane if it was hit by antiaircraft fire. This period before jumping was a long and agonizing wait for my stick.

The farther we penetrated into Holland, the more intense the small-arms fire from the ground became. The C-47s leveled off at an altitude of about five hundred feet as we approached the drop zone—easy targets from the ground. From the bridge at Eindhoven, a 101st Airborne Division objective, the enemy fired at us. As I stood in the door of the plane looking out, I could see many tracers. From my vantage point, it seemed that every bullet would hit me between the eyes. A considerable amount of small-arms fire did zip through my C-47. There was nowhere in the fuselage or the cockpit that could provide any kind of cover from the enemy line. Nor was there any way we could return fire.

Shortly before reaching the drop zone, two men in my stick were hit by ground fire and crumpled to the floor still hooked up to the static line. There was nothing that could be done for them. It would be only a matter of minutes before we were over our drop zone. I called back to Sergeant Rice at the rear of the stick to unhook the two wounded men and move them out of the way. It would be important that we all get out as quickly as possible in order to avoid a scattering of the men on the ground. In jump school, we had been trained to exit a stick of sixteen men in thirteen seconds or less and to assemble rapidly once on the ground, ready to fight.

It was a sobering introduction to the Netherlands for us.

First, one of our H Company's planes was hit and shot down in flames; I lost two of my men before we could get out of the plane. At the time I hoped this was not a harbinger of things to come. My platoon was two men short and we had not yet engaged the Germans.

I had given the first two in the sequence of jump commands after the H Company plane was shot down about forty minutes before: "Stand up and hook up." When I spotted the drop zone ahead, I gave the next command in the sequence, "Check your equipment," then "Sound off for equipment check." The final command before jumping was, "Are you ready?" This last command evoked a deafening, almost blood-curdling "Yeah" from the stick, venting all the tension and anxiety that had built up while standing and waiting to jump. It was a tremendous relief to all of us when we were over the drop zone.

About 1315 I gave the final command: "Let's go." The men probably broke all records going out the plane door and hitting the ground. At the time, I guessed that the plane had descended to between 400 and 450 feet when we went out the door. It was the closest to the ground I had jumped in any of the forty-eight parachute drops I'd made overall.

Fortunately, none of the men in my stick suffered any jump injuries, nor were any hit while suspended in chutes. We were not suspended in the air long from the altitude at which we jumped. My chute was barely open when I hit the ground; its opening shock was the most severe I had ever experienced. When I had loaded on the plane in England, I was weighted down with everything but the kitchen sink. I carried a Thompson submachine gun, a sniper's rifle with a telescopic sight, a Colt .45 pistol, extra clips and .45 ammo for my tommy gun, three bandoliers of .30-caliber ammo for my sniper's rifle, six hand grenades hanging on my jumpsuit, two antitank mines strapped off my belt, a combat knife, two first-aid packets, all my personal equipment, and two days' worth of rations. In addition, I had three D-Bar rations. A D-Bar weighed four ounces and contained sugar, chocolate, skim milk powder, cocoa fat, oat flour, and vanilla. One bar contained 1,770 calories and was designed to sustain a man for a short time only. All of the above was on top of my combat clothing and two parachutes. The main chute was on my back and the reserve chute on my chest. I also packed a musette bag, which normally was on my back but in the jump was hanging below my reserve chute. In it I carried my field glasses, maps of the area, compass, extra socks, toothbrush, and candy bars and cans of tuna that I had scrounged and saved in England.

My normal weight at the time was 180 pounds, but with the load I was carrying it had to be more than 300 pounds. The landing jarred every bone in my body and broke the chin strap on my helmet, with the tip hitting hard on my nose but not breaking it. The landing shock was so severe that my musette bag broke loose, came free, and unfortunately flew away. I never saw it again. So much for canned tuna and candy bars in combat.

In September 1994, I spoke to the fifth-grade history class at Evans Elementary School in my hometown of Fond du Lac, Wisconsin. The arrangements were made by one of the students, my nephew, Matthew Wuest. The occasion was the fiftieth anniversary of the airborne invasion of Holland. During the presentation, I narrated my experience in jumping behind enemy lines, describing the equipment and guns and ammunition with which I had jumped. Then I paused and asked the class a question, "Why do you think I jumped carrying these weapons?" There was a large display of hands and an offering of intelligent answers. "To protect yourself," "to kill the enemy." One boy gave the most succinct answer: "The side that kills the other side's soldiers wins." Reduced to its simplest terms, that's how combat and war are defined. The army uses the term "military occupational specialty" (MOS) to identify and specify a man's job. It could range from cook to clerk to truck driver, but the MOS for my platoon and me was "killing Germans"—nothing more, nothing less. It was the only thing that mattered. As the war progressed, we became increasingly proficient in our MOS.

The relief I felt from being out of that flying boxcar

tempered any discomfort I felt from my hard landing. Except for losing my musette bag, my jump into Holland was successful. As we used to say, "Any jump you can walk away from is a good jump."

While lying on the ground, I was still vulnerable. I hurried to unstrap my parachute and reserve chute. I quickly freed up my tommy gun, took it off safety, inserted a clip of ammo, and put a round in the chamber. I saw many tracers being fired at the planes heading for drop zones farther north. I believe that every fifth bullet fired from automatic weapons by the Germans was a tracer; if so, there was a lot of lead being fired at our C-47s. As they were passing over us, I saw several go up in flames. However, the casualties suffered by U.S. airborne forces in the air were considered light and well within the limits of calculated losses. The highly successful landings justified the decision to accept the risks involved in flying over enemy-held territory and jumping in daylight hours.

My stick quickly assembled and unpacked equipment, retrieved crew-served weapons, and headed for the H Company rendezvous point. There I was reunited with the rest of my platoon, which had jumped from another plane. They did not suffer any casualties. We were assembled, equipped, armed, and ready to move out on our initial objectives. Now it was our turn to hunt Germans. We were determined to make them pay dearly for our casualties.

The 3d Battalion moved out of the wooded area where it had assembled, and three rifle companies deployed to clear the Germans out of our sector. The 2d Battalion had the objective of seizing the bridge over the Maas River at Grave. E Company, 2d Battalion, jumped on the south side of the river and quickly moved toward the bridge while the remainder of the battalion attacked the bridge from the north. Although there were German company-sized units on and around the bridge, they were surprised by this rapid action and were unable to organize a coordinated defense. After several sharp engagements, the Maas River bridge at Grave, a principal objective of the 504th, was securely in our control. It had been attacked simultaneously from both ends and seized before the Germans could react. By dropping rifle companies on landing zones near both ends of the bridge, we had achieved a tactical surprise.

Unfortunately, this was not the case with the Waal River bridge at Nijmegen for which we would pay dearly three days later. By 1800, less than five hours after landing on the drop zone, the 504th had achieved all of its objectives, establishing some kind of record for airborne units. The 3d Battalion had seized one of the two bridges over the Maas-Waal canal similar to those at Grave, but the Germans blew the second bridge. With all of its initial objectives firmly in our control, the 3d Battalion held up, strengthened its defensive perimeter, and aggressively patrolled the immediate area.

VII

Linkup with British Armor

Shortly after our drop into Holland and the securing of our initial objective, I was ordered to take a patrol to clear adjoining small villages in the division area. I took about twenty men and several small vehicles. The division had little organic transportation, and I had barely enough for the patrol. We entered six or seven villages and were received by the Dutch in every instance as liberators. We were the first Allied troops they saw. I remember the first village we secured. Not knowing whether or not the enemy occupied it, we dismounted about a thousand yards from the edge of the village and proceeded cautiously on foot.

As we approached the center of the village, the Dutch turned out en masse and with great jubilation. My men were showered with flowers and other tokens of affection. Young damsels surrounded my men and overwhelmed them with attention. I felt uneasy while this was going on, because we had not yet cleared and secured the village and I had a difficult time maintaining a semblance of combat formation. Fortunately we were able to clear the village and determine that the Germans had departed, less than twenty-four hours before. One wounded German soldier was left behind, and we took him prisoner. After securing the village I placed lookouts, and the rest of the patrol returned to the center of the village. At this point the Dutch underground rallied to our side.

Out of hiding they brought weapons and in several instances vehicles in running condition. They insisted they accompany my patrol and me on our mission, and I permitted them to do so. In the meantime, hidden stocks of whiskey, cognac, and beer soon were brought out and served to us. It would have been delightful if we could have spent the rest of our day with these wildly jubilant people, but we had work to do. In every village we entered, our experience was the same. The Dutch underground, wearing orange armbands, insisted on joining with us in fighting the enemy. When I eventually returned to our battalion area, my patrol of three vehicles had increased to twenty-five, plus some forty motorcycles, all carrying armed members of the Dutch underground wanting to get into the fight.

I remember the Dutch people for their hospitality and friendliness, and their picturesque dress, particularly the wooden shoes. However, I had no contact with civilians after the first few days of the invasion. Thereafter, we were in frontline positions, from which civilians were evacuated to safe havens.

The contributions of the Dutch underground to not only the operations of the 504th but those of other Allied units as well cannot be overlooked. The NIF was probably the best organized and most efficient resistance force in all of Nazi-occupied Europe. Countless paratroopers and glider men who were misplaced in their landings owed their rescue and safe return to their units to the NIF. Dutch civilians placed themselves at risk by providing intelligence to the Allied forces on German positions and troop movements, which too often were ignored. Just prior to D day (17 September 1944), the Dutch reported movements of enemy armor in the Arnhem area indicating the presence of major panzer units. Lower echelon officers and British intelligence picked this up and sounded the alarm. But planning for the mission was well under way and would not be deterred by Dutch civilian intelligence reports. Arnhem was supposedly a quiet, lightly defended area that posed no threat to the success of Market Garden. Not only were the warnings disregarded, but the bearers of the bad news were sacked. There was a mind-set in the British command that Montgomery's hastily devised plan would permit the British Second Army to turn the corner at Arnhem and sweep across Germany. Optimistically, the war would be over by Christmas and Montgomery and the British would have delivered the knockout blow. When Dutch underground intelligence reported German movement prior to 17 September, Montgomery believed only what he wanted to believe. Market Garden was a "go," no matter what.

Having seized our initial objectives, the 504th now waited to link up with the British Second Army, which launched an offensive against a thinly held German line fifty-seven miles to the south. However, the British XXX Corps, spearheading the Second Army drive, encountered stronger than expected German resistance in the breakout. The British had expected that the lead tanks of XXX Corps would reach Eindhoven (held by the U.S. 101st Airborne Division), thirteen miles away, within several hours, but the German crust proved to be a lot tougher than the British had anticipated. Market Garden got a delayed start and was now more than thirty hours behind schedule. A blown bridge over the Wilhelmina Canal at Son, about five miles north of Eindhoven, caused further delays in the linkup force. It was not until 0820 on 19 September that the lead elements of British Second Army crossed the bridge at Grave, linking up with the 504th.

That morning, British armor began passing over the road adjacent to my platoon position en route to the bridge at Nijmegen over the Waal River. For at least twenty-four hours, British armor passed bumper to bumper over the Grave bridge in an awesome display of the sinews of war. I couldn't conceive how any German force could stand up to it. For the first time since I'd been in combat, I felt that the end of the war was in sight. Tanks, armored vehicles, half-tracks, mounted artillery pieces, mechanized vehicles of all types and sizes, and accompanying infantry paraded by in a steady stream, all heading toward Nijmegen, about ten miles farther north. As General Horrocks, the corps commander, had stated in a briefing conference prior to D day, he intended to pass 20,000 vehicles advancing two abreast over the single highway from Eindhoven to Arnheim in sixty hours.

XXX Corps was the lead element of the British Second army, which followed in its wake. The steady, unrelenting rumble of tanks and the accompanying clanking of teakettles hanging over the sides of the tanks were earsplitting. However, when the lead elements of the force reached the outskirts of Nijmegen, the column came to a halt. The two bridges over the Waal River, objectives of the division, were still under control of the German Wehrmacht. The paratroopers of the 82d had encountered strong enemy resistance in Nijmegen and were fighting to gain control of the southern approaches to the railroad and the main highway bridges. Either was capable of supporting armor. Casualties were running heavy on both sides.

The Germans, meanwhile, having captured a copy of the Allies' tactical plans, rushed up reinforcements to fortify the north side of the highway bridge. There were no friendly forces on the north side that could dislodge them from the bridge positions. At this point, the drive to Arnhem and relief for the beleaguered British 1st Parachute Division was stalled. It was a critical moment in the Market Garden operation. The bridge had to be captured intact if Second Army was to move on to Arnhem and capture the final highway bridge. The success or failure of Market Garden hung in the balance. British tanks would not attempt a crossing of the highway bridge at Nijmegen until they were certain that both ends were secure and firmly in our hands. Still, the armor kept coming in a constant stream, all jamming into Nijmegen. There was a further concern that if we did not successfully engage the forces holding the north end of the bridge, the Germans might blow it up, thus denying the Allied forces its use and halting the entire operation. Something had to be done, and done quickly, or Montgomery's grandiose scheme to end the war by Christmas would go up in flames.

News began to trickle down through the ranks of the dire straits the British division was in at Arnhem. Radio contact with the Red Devils (as they were known) was lost; it was only through the efforts of the Dutch underground that any communication link was established. The news was bad, and there was concern not only for the success of the mission but for the fate of the British paratroopers. Two factors contributed to the difficulties at Nijmegen: the failures of British intelligence at first and a flaw in the drop zone planning. In the Arnhem area, just a few miles east of the vital highway bridge over the lower Rhine River, the German II SS Panzer Corps, consisting of two divisions, had relocated to resupply and refit. Montgomery and his staff had ignored Dutch underground warnings of significant German armored presence there. British planners selected drop zones from six to eight miles away from their main objective, the bridge at Arnhem. By the time British paratroopers could assemble and move, valuable time was lost, and with that any tactical surprise that they hoped to achieve. One valiant battalion did succeed in reaching the north end of the bridge, but the men paid a heavy price in blood and were quickly surrounded and isolated. The rest of the division was unable to reach them and suffered great losses in the attempt. The surrounded battalion held on precariously, anticipating that the XXX Corps would soon make contact with them. If they could hold out a while longer, their heroic efforts might not be in vain. However, due to the lack of communications with the corps, they were unaware of the difficulties at the bridges in Nijmegen, ten miles to the south. Communications from Arnhem to the corps could not be established because their radios lacked sufficient range, another glitch in Montgomery's plan.

This was the situation in Market Garden as the paratroopers of the 82d were encountering heavier than expected German resistance while attempting to seize the southern approaches to the 1,500-foot-long highway bridge and the railroad bridge across the Waal River in Nijmegen.

In the meantime, men and armor of the corps kept streaming into Nijmegen over the corridor of roads and bridges that had been secured by the two U.S. airborne divisions. Once the tactical linkup was effected, the 82d Division came under operational control of the British First Allied Airborne Army.

Elements of the two regiments of the 82d were still engaged with the enemy controlling the southern side of the highway bridge in Nijmegen. Major General James Gavin proposed a hastily devised plan to seize both the highway and railroad bridges. The units presently engaged in Nijmegen, reinforced by British armor, would accelerate their attacks to seize the southern end of the highway bridge, which was heavily defended, while a third regiment attempted to cross the Waal River one mile downstream and circle around to capture the north end of both bridges. The plan, crossing the Waal in broad daylight, was risky, bordering on suicidal. The chances of failure appeared great, and heavy casualties could be expected. But some course of action had to be taken; in the absence of an alternate plan, the British commander quickly approved Gavin's plan. Although XXX Corps had three assigned infantry divisions—Irish, Scot, and Grenadiers—it would be the Americans who would undertake a mission that many thought impossible. General Gavin selected the 504th for this daring venture. This would be the 504th's Omaha Beach.

The first problem to be worked out was how we would navigate the river. Boats had to be found, but none—civilian or military—were available in the Nijmegen area. British engineers reported that the corps carried some thirty-three small boats capable of transporting men across the river; however, the units were strung out for miles over a narrow road, and no one was certain how far back the boats were or how long it would take to bring them up. But if they could be made available that night, the assault could begin early on the morning of 20 September, D+3.

A hastily contrived plan was set in motion. In the meantime, my platoon and I speculated about everything related to and affecting a river crossing. It was not standard fare in a paratrooper's repertoire of tactical missions. It would be, as one commander noted, "on-the-job training."

Sometime after the river crossing, Chaplain Delbert Kuehl recalled: "I went to a wooded area in the evening and overheard several of the 3rd Battalion officers talking about how we were going to cross the river and take the bridges from the rear. While I heard all this they mentioned that we were going to be using British boats. At the time I thought the boats would have some kind of armor and power since we had to cross a wide river with a strong current, heavily defended on the other side. . . . They decided to make the river crossing the next day. I thought we would do it at night, under the cover of darkness but they said we had to reach the British airborne troopers who were being decimated by armor in Arnhem."

That evening the 3d Battalion set its plan in motion. There would not be enough boats for us to cross in one wave. Two companies, H and I, would go in the first wave along with two engineers from C Company, 307th Engineer Battalion, in each boat. Once across the river, the engineers would return (there were also two engineers in Lieutenant Sims's boat) to bring the remainder of the 3d Battalion, G and Headquarters Companies. Beyond that we would have to deal with the situation as it developed. The Germans had not yet been cleared from the southern approaches to the two bridges, so no reconnaissance had been made of the area. Nor did we know the extent of enemy strength on the north side of the highway bridge, our principal objective. The situation was confused, to say the least. No one knew when we could expect the boats. The main road from Eindhoven to Nijmegen was jammed with British vehicles, and it would be difficult for the three trucks carrying the boats to get around them. We were hoping that the boats would arrive in time to enable us to cross the river at night. We never expected to cross the river in daylight in full view of enemy gunners. As the situation at Arnhem grew more desperate, the urgency to capture the highway bridge intensified. We would go as soon as the boats arrived, whenever that might be.

Early the next morning, the 3d Battalion moved out of the wooded assembly area and started for the south bank of the river. We were to establish a position there from which we would launch our assault. The boats still had not arrived, although they couldn't have been more than thirty-five to forty miles to the rear. Because no one in this mass of confusion seemed to know when they would arrive, it was difficult to set a precise time for the assault. Initially, H hour was planned for 0800, then advanced to 1100, then to 1400.

The area selected for the jumping-off point was one mile downstream (west) of the two bridges. The assault site was just east of a tall, modern stone building that housed the Nijmegen power plant. Private James Musa remembered the power plant as the "glass factory" because it had many windows, not because it was made of glass.

When we arrived in the southern outskirts of Nijmegen, the 3d Battalion deployed in a column of twos, one on each side of the road. Our march to the assault site was often delayed when German snipers, who had not yet been cleared from the city, fired on the columns.

Sergeant Albert Tarbell recalled that morning of 20 September: "We were moved by trucks early in the morning closer to Nijmegen. I remember the people lined up on each side of the street greeting us as we marched to our area. At one time a call went out for a sniper to be taken care of. I saw Sgt. Daun Rice running by with a sniper's rifle. While we were stopped for a short while, a little girl offered me an orange. At first, I did not want to accept it, but a lady standing next to her spoke in perfect English, 'Please accept the orange from the little girl.' I never forgot that incident."

By noon the 3d Battalion had arrived at the assault site, with H and I Companies in the lead. Some units took their positions in and around the factory while Rivers and I took up defilade positions behind the high embankment to the west. The embankment was tall enough to conceal us from enemy gunners on the north side. From the top of the embankment, I got my first look at the river. It was wide and swift. On the north shore was a flat, open expanse that in places extended up to eight hundred yards back from the shore to another dike embankment that rose to more than fifteen feet.

Any of us fortunate enough to survive the blanket of fire the Germans could lay across the river would face enemy automatic fire from entrenched positions on the dike. About eight hundred yards beyond the dike was another formidable obstacle to the river assault and advance on the bridges, Fort Hof van Holland. In addition, enemy forces were in position on the north end of both bridges, and still more were ensconced in the bridge wells. The 82d Airborne Division's revised estimates of German strength were that 500 German top-quality SS troops held the highway bridge alone. Against that array of men and German artillery and mortar fire, H and I Companies would send about 250 men in the initial wave to capture the bridges.

Wishful thinking soon gave way to reality. When the river-crossing plan was first proposed, many of those involved believed it would be humanly impossible to carry out. After a first look at the river and what lay beyond, the paratroopers of H and I Companies were in accord with the doomsayers. Yet as improbable as it seemed, the determination of the men to "get on with it" did not diminish.

As we grouped behind the protected dike along the river prior to the assault, we prepared in our own way to meet our maker. It did not seem militarily or humanly possible to accomplish such a mission. I remember asking Rivers to contact my mother if he survived and I did not. His request to me was similar. First Lieutenant Harry Busby, of I Company, whom we called "Pappy," said he had a premonition that he would "get it today." He was killed that day.

His death premonition was not the only one related to me during the course of the war. Often when we were preparing for a dangerous mission, the threat of death loomed large. Usually it was accompanied by a strange feeling that the men associated with death. Whether it was due to a combination of circumstances surrounding the battlefield or some divine sign from above would be difficult to ascertain.

As we waited for the boats to arrive, some of the men gathered in small groups; others did what a combat soldier does when waiting: take off his pack, assume the prone position, and catch a few winks. Sergeant Clement Haas was with a small group of his buddies and recalled that moment: "I remember Louie Holt saying, 'This is suicide, we will all get killed.' We could see that it would be a very dangerous crossing. The river was very wide. The Germans were well entrenched and the bridges well protected. . . . Allen, Dixon and I kept trying to assure Holt that we would be okay, as we would have plenty of support in the form of artillery, tanks, and aircraft firing on the Germans before and during our attack. In addition a smoke screen was to be laid just prior to our attack. . . ."

Chaplain Kuehl wrote: "I remember that we all looked at each other and said that this was a suicide mission if we had ever seen one. It was then that I decided to go with H and I Companies in the first wave, thinking that if there ever was a time when the men may need a Chaplain, it was now. . . . One of the officers I was with said, 'I have no chance of getting across' so he threw away his pack of cigarettes and Zippo lighter. . . . I didn't have to go on the mission since I was the Regimental Chaplain, but I thought this was going to be very difficult for the men, so I decided I was going to go. The Regimental Commander, Col. Reuben Tucker, didn't know about it at the time. When he found out, it was after he went across [in the second wave] and he was really upset with me."

As we waited anxiously for the boats to arrive and the assault to begin, speculation among those who would have to do the dirty work was vocal. How many enemy gunners would be looking down our throats from the other side of the river? What friendly support could we expect? Would any of us make it across the river? Capt. Carl Kappel, H Company, doubled the initial estimate of enemy strength from 500 to 1,000 when he briefed us platoon leaders. "Anything less," said Kappel, "would be pure gravy." As it turned out, Kappel's estimate was nearer the mark than the estimates from higher headquarters.

Just before the boats arrived, we got our first indication of enemy strength on the north side of the river. Thirty minutes before H hour, British Typhoons flew across the river, strafing the entire north bank with bombs, rockets, and automatic fire. German gunners responded with a devastating barrage of antiaircraft fire. Rivers and I watched in awe from our concealed front-row seats as the planes attempted to neutralize enemy resistance. More awesome, however, was the amount of fire the enemy threw up. The sky was black from puffs of exploding shells. The "ack-ack" was so thick that you could have walked on it. Paddling across the river was going to be a bloodier venture than anticipated. In spite of Kappel's estimate, no one on the Allied side knew what strength the Germans had on the north bank.

Several hours before H hour, the 2d Battalion was in position around the factory area, where it could support us with overhead fire. The 2d Battalion was also assigned the objective of clearing the area in front of the embankment leading to the edge of the river. First Lieutenant Edward T. Wisniewski of D Company was ordered to take a patrol to clear the approaches up to seventy-five yards or more. Wisniewski, or "Pollock," as he was nicknamed, was one of my closest friends. We had gone through jump school and Fort Benning together, sailed to Oran, Africa, and fought through Italy and Anzio. He was an outstanding officer and combat leader, highly respected by officers and enlisted men alike.

Shortly after his patrol moved, the Germans fired on them from the railroad bridge and from the north bank of the river. Wisniewski was badly hit by enemy small-arms fire, and his patrol was pinned down. Medics from the 3d Battalion tried to reach him, but they too came under enemy fire.

Wisniewski lay in a flat, open area crying out for help for a good while before anyone could get to him. He died in a field hospital six days later. Hearing of his fate and his patrol had a chilling effect on us, but it prepared us for the worst.

Meanwhile a plan was devised for H and I Companies. Upon crossing the river and reaching the opposite shore, we would attack across the flat terrain and dislodge the Germans from their defensive positions. We would then regroup with whatever strength we had and complete assigned objectives. H Company would first neutralize, then bypass Fort van Holland, seize the juncture of the railroad and the Nijmegen-Arnhem highway, then drive southeast down the highway to take the north end of the highway bridge. I Company was to defend against a German counterattack from the north and northwest and, if possible, help take the north end of the railroad bridge.

Finally, three British lorries carrying twenty-six boats (thirty-three had been expected) reached the glass factory area and pulled up behind the embankment. I stood behind one of the trucks when its canvas curtain was raised and the unloading began. For the first time I got a glimpse of the boats that would transport us across the Waal. The boats, stacked up like playing cards, were dealt off the top of the pile to the men assigned to each boat. Nineteen feet long, the craft were flimsy and collapsible, with canvas sides and a flat plywood bottom. The canvas sides were to be pulled up and held in place by wooden staves measuring thirty inches from the floor to the gunwales. Watching the unloading, Chaplain Kuehl asked, "How are they propelled?" The answer: "Canoe paddles." Each boat was supposed to contain eight wooden paddles, four feet long, but some boats had only two paddles. Other means would have to be devised to negotiate the eight-mile-per-hour current.

As I watched the boats being unloaded, my thoughts flashed back to my earlier years in Wisconsin. I had been an avid sportsman and fished in many lakes. The boat I was accustomed to was only a few feet shorter than these boats but was sturdy, wooden, and seaworthy and had a gas-powered outboard motor. Only three people could fish out of it; four was somewhat crowded and five or more made it over-crowded. Yet here we were, thirteen paratroopers with our individual weapons, crew-served weapons, ammunition, and packs, along with two engineers—fifteen of us all told—preparing to squeeze into a nineteen-foot canvas boat pro-pelled by an armful of paddles. By any standard, the boats would be dangerously overloaded. I wondered if we could stay afloat even without enemy resistance.

Sergeant Clement Haas remembered his thoughts after seeing the boats: "This didn't do much for our confidence. In addition, I couldn't swim and I didn't have a Mae West; however as paratroopers we were expected to tackle any dangerous and hazardous mission and fulfill it successfully."

The tension to get going intensified as the men of H and I Companies lined up by their boats. War correspondents com-pared the river crossing to Tarawa. Major Julian Aaron Cook, 3d Battalion commander, was quoted as saying, "We were being asked to make an Omaha Beach landing all by our-selves."

Fifteen minutes before H hour, Allied artillery began to pound the north bank to soften up the enemy. After about ten minutes, the artillery changed from high explosive to white phosphorus to lay down a smoke screen over the river. An er-ratic wind quickly dissipated the smoke, however, denying the boats any semblance of cover and leaving us as naked as jaybirds.

At 1500 on 20 September, Major Cook blew a whistle sig-naling the start of the assault. Shrill cries of "let's go" fol-lowed as the paratroopers released pent-up emotions. We grabbed the boats by the gunwales, charged up the embank-ment, crossed the open, flat top of the dike, and made a mad dash for the river. The boats, loaded with our gear and weapons, were heavy, and the going was tough in the loose sand.

We caught the Germans by surprise. For the first hundred yards they hadn't fired a shot, but when they realized what was happening, all hell broke loose. They opened up with everything they had: small arms, machine guns, 20mm flak wagons, mortars, and artillery. As we frantically scurried for the river's edge, chaos and confusion reigned. With shells exploding all around us, we kept charging forward. At that point we were all driven by instinct and running on adrenaline with but a single purpose: to get our boats in the water and across the river.

VIII
Assault Across the Waal

The twenty-six boats were spread out for about a hundred yards. The water was shallow in most places along the river's edge, so it was difficult for the men to debark. Those who had climbed aboard soon found they had to jump overboard and try to push the boat to deeper water. Some found themselves stuck in mud. One boat moved out, leaving behind a man unable to extricate himself from the muddy bottom.

Other boats encountered deeper water near shore, making it difficult for the men and their equipment to get aboard. Trying to coordinate the efforts of men getting in the boats and crossing a river with a fast-moving current was next to impossible. Under ordinary circumstances it would have been difficult enough; with the Germans raining fire on us, it became a living nightmare. The hail of small-arms fire and shrapnel stirring up the waters around us reminded me of a school of piranha in a feeding frenzy.

Sergeant Albert Tarbell, H Company radio operator, was with the company commander, Carl Kappel, as they tried to launch their boat. Here is Tarbell's account of that hectic moment:

I was assigned to the same boat as Capt. Kappel and was walking behind him. We each took hold of the side of the boat. When we got word to go, we ran down to the riverbank and then all hell broke loose. I saw Capt. Kappel remove his web belt with pistol, canteen etc. and throw them into the boat. I unconsciously did the same thing. . . . It was then that I saw him dive into the river and pull out one of our men who was drowning. We reached out to help them out of the water, which was very deep there at the bank. Right after that incident, I got into the first boat available and everything seemed so crazy. We were receiving machine gun fire, small arms fire, and it seemed as though rain was hitting the water. Our boats were going in every direction because the current was a lot stronger than was first thought and most of the men had never paddled before. I tried to count cadence so that we could straighten out our boat. We started receiving artillery or mortar fire. . . . The boat to my right took a direct hit, turning the boat around. To this day I can still see the look on Private Lewis Holt's face as our eyes met. The boat went down and out of sight. We finally did make the other side after having lost all but 13 of the boats which we started out with.

Sergeant Clement Haas added: "We charged over the embankment with our boats. Lt. Megellas, Dixon, Zimmerman, and myself got into one boat. I didn't know the names of the other nine men. Louis Holt tried to get into our boat, but there was no room. He jumped into another boat and was killed when he was hit shortly after starting across the river."

The man whom Kappel pulled to safety was Private Legacie, assistant machine gunner, H Company. In the confusion, Kappel's boat moved out without him, and he had to hitch a ride with another boat still floundering near shore. Some boats were overturned as men were trying to hoist themselves aboard to be with a buddy. They were willing to take their chances on the river rather than being left on the south bank.

Private John Schultz, H Company, was in a boat that managed to shove off intact. This is his account of the river crossing: "I was with the 60 mm mortar squad with Sgt. Wilford Dixon who was right beside me. About halfway across, he was hit in the head and died immediately. When we hit the other side, we flushed out the Krauts directly in front of us, then turned right and headed for the bridge. It was then that we discovered we didn't have the barrel for the mortar. I was sent back to get it. Our boat was still there. I removed [the barrel] from Sgt. Dixon's body and headed back to our squad. We set up and began firing. We got to the bridge just in time to see a couple of our tanks coming across the bridge. We spent the night in the town and waited for the British to arrive. Of course, they never arrived."

Sergeant Jimmy Shields, H Company, was in a boat with fewer than eight paddles. He was in the same boat with Sgt. Daun Rice, one of two brothers in H Company, who was killed six days later by a German patrol. Shields recalled: "I was paddling with the butt of my Browning Automatic Rifle, while others were using the butts of their rifles. Some without paddles used their hands, anything to keep the boat on a northward course."

Captain Henry B. Keep, 3d Battalion S3, along with the rest of the staff (1st Lt. Virgil F. Carmichael, 1st Lt. Thomas F. Pitt, 1st Lt. T. E. Otterbach, and the battalion commander), were in the first wave with H and I Companies. Keep wrote the following account shortly after our return to France in November 1944:

> At last we reached the drop. We let the boat slide down to the beach and ourselves slid alongside of them. We pulled our boat quickly across a short beach and everyone piled in. By this time, the situation was horrible. The automatic and flat trajectory fire had increased and the artillery was deadly. Men were falling right and left. In everyone's ears was the constant roar of bursting artillery shells, the dull wham of a 20-mm, or the disconcerting ping of rifle bullets.
>
> After a false start we got stuck in a mud bar and several of us were forced to get out and go through the extremely uncomfortable process of pushing off again. We found ourselves floating in the wrong direction. Everyone grabbed a paddle and frantically started to work. Most of the men had never paddled before and, had it not

been for the gruesomeness [*sic*] of the situation, the sight might have been rather ludicrous.

Every movement in excess of the essential paddling was extremely dangerous since the bullets were flying so thick and fast that they gave a reasonable facsimile of a steel curtain. By now the broad surface of the Waal was covered with our small canvas crafts and crammed with frantically paddling men. Defenseless, frail, canvas boats jammed to overflowing with humanity, all striving desperately to get across the Waal as quickly as possible. Large numbers of men were being hit in all boats and the bottoms of these crafts were littered with the wounded and dead. Here and there on the surface of the water was a paddle dropped by some poor unfortunate before the man taking his place had been able to retrieve it from his lifeless fingers.

Somehow or other we were three-quarters of the way across. Everyone was yelling to keep it up, but there was very little strength left in anyone. But at last we reached the other side. We climbed over the wounded and dead in the bottom of the boat and up to our knees in water waded to shore where behind a small embankment we flopped down gasping for breath, safe for the moment from the incessant firing. All along the beach what was left of our flimsy boats were reaching shore. Men more dead than alive were stumbling up the beach to get momentary protection behind the unexpected but welcome embankment before pushing across the broad flat plain in front of us.

At 1500, when Major Cook blew the whistle to go, my men and I charged over the embankment toward the river's edge clutching the boat. Those of us without paddles used the butts of our guns to help keep the boat moving in a straight direction. I had a miserable time trying to paddle with my short-stocked Thompson submachine gun while keeping low in the boat. Private Simon Renner, seated in the middle of my boat, was holding guns so others could row. I was also concerned about my weapon. It had to be ready for business if we made it across the river.

Fear gave way to hysteria. The fear of making it never entered my mind. I was one of about 250 fanatical men driven by rage to do what had been asked of us: capture the two bridges at Nijmegen, intact if possible. In the early going I was aware of Chaplain Kuehl, Major Cook, and Captain Shapiro in the boat next to me valiantly trying to hold a steady course.

I could distinctly hear Major Cook, a devout Catholic, in a loud, quivering voice trying to recite the rosary, but "Hail Mary, full of grace," continuously repeated, was all he could utter. Then the "Hail Mary, full of grace" became just "Hail Mary," which he kept repeating as a sort of cadence for the rowers just as a coxswain would rhythmically beat on the side of a shell to synchronize the efforts of oarsmen. Chaplain Kuehl kept repeating, "Lord, Thy will be done."

Undoubtedly, the Germans firing at us were praying to the same God: "Thy will be done" and "give us the strength and courage to defeat our enemies." Whose prayers would be heeded? Whose cause would be deemed righteous and whose not? Which side would be favored over the other, and who would live or die?

I ask these questions, but I have no answers for them. I was only a combat platoon leader whose MOS was to kill Germans. I had been endowed with physical strength, courage, and an instinct for survival, as undoubtedly were our enemies. My creed was, God helps those who help themselves and does not take sides in human conflicts.

Lead was flying at us from all directions. In other boats, bullets opened gaping holes in the canvas sides. The men were frantically trying to keep their boats afloat, bailing with their helmets. Some boats didn't make it. Others unable to navigate the strong current floated aimlessly down the river. Of the twenty-six boats that took off from the south bank, only thirteen made it across; eleven were able to return for the rest of the 3d Battalion. The rest had been sunk in the crossing or their engineers killed, leaving the boats to float downstream carrying the dead and wounded with them. In some respects, this was the most horrifying scene of all, because nothing could be done for them. One I Company boat, badly riddled by bullets, floundered in the current and drifted back to our side farther down the river. Two Dutch civilians retrieved the boat and found one man in the bottom, Pvt. Leonard G. Trimble, still alive but badly wounded.

Halfway across the river, an artillery shell or perhaps a 20mm round crashed into the overloaded boat near me that was carrying the other half of my platoon. The boat capsized and sank, spilling all its occupants—two engineers and thirteen paratroopers—into the river. They splashed frantically to keep from submerging or being swept downstream. There was nothing we could do to help them; the strong current made it impossible to maneuver our boat toward them, and there were no other boats near enough to provide aid. Nor were there any Mae Wests or other type of inflatable life jackets of the type we wore when we jumped near water. There were simply no life preservers in the boats. There had not been time to be concerned about such matters.

Lieutenant Ernest P. Murphy, H Company, recalled the river crossing: "We were the lead boat nearing the north bank and suddenly an enemy 20-mm shell tore through the canvas sides of the boat opening two gaping holes. The boat started taking on water and we had to swim for shore. On shore I took count of my men and all but one had made it. Then I noticed a helmet pop out of water and the missing man, Private Joseph Jedlicka, walked out of the water to safety. Jedlicka, who could not swim, had sunk in about eight feet of water. He was still carrying his BAR and two boxes of ammo when he emerged. Drenched and shaken by his ordeal, he rejoined my platoon thankful to be alive. We had our boat shot out from under us, but fortunately, I had no casualties."

Chaplain Kuehl recalled reaching the opposite shore: "There were dead and wounded in each boat. I remember one boat reached the bank and had four dead troopers draped across each other. There were dead and wounded all over the place. . . . I carried a first-aid kit and immediately began working on the wounded. While I was leaning over a trooper who had three bullet holes in the stomach, a mortar shell exploded behind me. I was hit in the back by shrapnel, knocking me down. Despite being critically wounded, the man cried out, 'Chaplain, they got you too.' The men who made it bayoneted the German machine gunners that were dug in all along the riverbank. They didn't pause, they bayoneted and bayoneted and took off for the bridge. I had never seen such bravery. It was pretty gruesome. I was proud to be the Chaplain of such brave troopers."

Captain Shapiro made it across safely. With his limited medical resources, he aided the most severely wounded while still under enemy fire. When my boat reached the other side, we jumped into the shallow water and waded ashore. The fact that the other twelve in my platoon and I made it across the river when others failed was due largely to the efforts of the two engineers with us. With a minimum of help from us, and with just four paddles and using our rifle butts as paddles, they managed to navigate the river, albeit on a zigzag course, and reach the shore safely. After we unloaded, the engineers shoved off to return for the rest of the 3d Battalion, having to run the same gauntlet. Of the thirteen boats that made it across in the first wave, eleven returned for a second jaunt, but only five returned for a third trip. All told the remaining boats made six crossings.

The heroic efforts of the engineers, who had a high percentage of casualties, have been largely overlooked in historical accounts of the crossing. Even with their background as engineers, they had never trained for or ever experienced anything like this, although their MOS came closer than ours. Their job was to get the paratroopers across the river. The engineers were the real heroes of the Waal River crossing. They merit a special badge of valor.

When the men jumped out of the boats and waded ashore, they were near complete exhaustion; some were overcome with nausea. With the beach being raked by automatic grazing fire from the embankment, it was not a healthy place to remain for long. The first objective had been reached; now we had to dislodge the Germans in the embankment that blocked our way to the bridges. There was no time to reorganize, to move out in units of squads or platoons. It was every man for himself, and "the devil take the hindmost."

Men soon found themselves separated from their squads and platoons and devoid of any unit organization. As they charged toward the embankment, they looked for familiar faces, their noncoms or officers or closest buddies. They formed in a line of skirmishers firing their weapons from the hip as they charged wildly toward the enemy. In his letter of 20 November 1944, just two months after this epic occasion, Captain Keep wrote: "After getting my breath, the men and I moved out across the open field into the face of fire. In many ways, this was the most remarkable scene of the whole operation. You have seen in movies, pictures of infantry troops attacking across open terrain employing fire and movement. Well, this made any Hollywood version pale into insignificance. All along the shoreline now our troops were appearing deployed as skirmishers. They were running into murderous fire from the embankment 800 yards away. They cursed and yelled at each other as they advanced, non-coms and officers giving directions, the men firing from the hip their BARs, rifles and machine guns and steadily they moved forward."

After moving away from the shore, I headed for the embankment, with several men from my platoon in close pursuit. Machine guns opened up on us and small-arms fire crackled all around us. It was utter chaos. There were so many bullets in the air that it was difficult to tell who was firing at you and from what direction. Instinctively we attacked in the direction from which most of the fire appeared to be coming, the fifteen-foot-high embankment in front of us. Trying to find cover from the hail of bullets was impossible, and retreating back to the river would have been insane. It was kill or be killed. Men driven by rage were cursing the Germans as they charged forward, running low and firing their weapons as they advanced. In the midst of the confusion, I noticed a small indentation in the flat area about fifty yards to my left. A shallow channel ran from the embankment to the river, undoubtedly used to drain the area of runoff water. Running low, I charged up that ditch toward the enemy, firing my tommy gun in their direction as bullets whistled close to my head.

Sergeant John J. Toman, H Company, crossed the river in the same boat with me in the first wave. As soon as we reached the opposite shore, he and several men from his squad instinctively charged toward the entrenched Germans with his M1 rifle blazing. He didn't make it to the embankment. An enemy bullet pierced his skull just above his ear. The war was over for him. He was evacuated and hospitalized in the States. I never saw him again. From his wife and daughter, I learned that he had lost his hearing and the use of his facial muscles and was confined to a wheelchair. He was in a nursing home for six years, then was transferred to a VA hospital, where he died in January 1999.

Sergeant John M. Fowler, H Company, one of the original members of the 504th, reached the north bank of the river safely. He quickly organized the men around him and charged toward the railroad bridge in the face of withering fire. For his gallantry, he was awarded the Silver Star.

Lieutenant Sims, then an H Company platoon leader, recalled reaching the north shore of the river: "My boat landed some distance west of the railroad bridge and we disembarked rapidly forming a skirmish line. Another boat landed nearby with many casualties. Those who had not been wounded joined with me and I led this combined group on a frontal assault that was several hundred yards further north. I was armed with an M1 rifle as I directed the assault by bounds with our guns at rapid fire. Enemy fire from the dike was heavy but no one faltered. I will never forget the courageous determination of those men with me."

Sergeant Tarbell was charging toward the dike road when he met up with Pfc. John Rigapoulos, from my platoon. A Greek-American like myself, Rigapoulos had joined my platoon at Anzio. Tarbell recalled: "I met PFC Rigapoulos. He showed me his left thumb, which had been shot off. He said, 'Well here's another Purple Heart.' John Rigapoulos and I came from jump school together and joined as replacements in Anzio, Italy. He was also one of the volunteers for pathfinders in Normandy. He was killed shortly afterwards that afternoon, two purple hearts in one day."

Braving intense small-arms and automatic fire, the group of men I was with managed to reach our first objective, the fifteen-foot embankment about eight hundred yards to our front. We were among the first to reach the embankment, which also served as a dike and was wide enough at the top to form an all-weather road. We pulled up behind it to catch our breath and await the arrival of the remainder of my platoon. Two men in my boat had been wounded by small-arms fire. One of them was my platoon sergeant, Marvin Hirsch; he had been shot in the arm just above the wrist but not seriously enough to keep him from charging forward with us to the embankment. I bandaged his wound with gauze that I had strapped to the sides of my boots. There were still no aid stations established on the beach, so for the time being the wounded had to manage for themselves. In the meantime the men from H and I Companies who had survived the river crossing were reaching the embankment and holding up.

According to the original plan, H and I Companies, after reaching the embankment, were to reassemble, then attempt to seize the two bridges over the river. There was only a scattering of men at the dike, where I was dressing Sergeant Hirsch's arm, when just to the right of me I saw SSgt. William White, I Company, run to the top of the dike.

White hollered out, "There go those sons of bitches. After them, men." With that, he and a few men went in hot pursuit of the fleeing enemy. As others arrived at the dike, they did likewise. Our plan to reassemble at this point had obviously gone astray, but I believe that White's ingenuity served to our advantage, because the enemy was not given an opportunity to regroup at alternative defensive positions. White was killed ten days later in a minefield.

Upon seeing White and his small group of men moving

down the embankment after the retreating Germans, the few
men with me and I charged over the top of the dike and followed him. The same thing happened all along the embankment. Without hesitation, men charged over the top, yelling
and cursing, not giving the Germans a chance to regroup.
The attack on the north bank developed into a series of daring, small-unit actions of individuals from different squads
and platoons. The hectic, frantic crossing of the Waal had
scattered the survivors, leaving little semblance of unit co-
hesion.

Although the situation remained confused and chaotic,
we were now in pursuit and on the offensive. The Germans
had blown their opportunity to stop us when they had us in
their crosshairs on the Waal. We were no longer sitting ducks
but moving targets coming at them. H and I Companies had
lost half their men getting to this point, but for the 125 or so
survivors, it was now their turn to hunt Germans. It was payback time.

Ahead of my men and me were open fields, orchards, and
a scattering of farmhouses and barns. Beyond that was the
ominous specter of Fort Hof van Holland. From the fort, the
Germans had rained fire on the boats crossing the Waal. To
our right (east) were the two bridges, first the railroad
bridge, then the highway bridge about a mile farther.

As we charged through the open fields, it was difficult to
tell who was firing at us. Most of the fire seemed to be coming from the fort. So we veered to our left and charged in
that direction, realizing that, although the fort was not a
principal objective, it had to be neutralized if we were to
capture the bridges.

The retreating Germans were trying to stop our advance
while they fell back to defensive positions. Immediately to
our front, we drew small-arms fire from a farmhouse. We
surrounded the house, calling for the enemy to come out.
When there was no response, I charged up next to the house.
In a small shedlike attachment, I detected some movement.
I threw a hand grenade into the structure and fell back. After
the explosion, the front door of the house opened and an

elderly Dutch couple came out with their hands extended over their heads. Earlier, the Germans had escaped out the back door. In the shed there was a dead horse, an innocent victim of my grenade.

In all the confusion, I did not see Rivers until after the highway bridge was captured. Sims recalled seeing him shortly after the river crossing as he was moving east to flush out a sniper who had shot and killed one of his men. Privates Musa and Young, who had taken off from the shore together, met Rivers in a wooded area and remained in his small group all the way to the highway bridge. Musa recalled that they received small-arms fire from a farmhouse: "We charged towards the house and someone threw a Gammon grenade through a window. We came around the back and stormed into the badly shattered house. All we found in the house was one somewhat elderly, unarmed, German soldier shouting 'Komrad.' He was a prisoner, but we could not take him with us or leave anyone to guard him, so we tied him to a chair and, as Lt. Rivers said, 'We will let someone else worry about him.' On our way to the bridge, we spotted a German patrol but we avoided them in our haste to get to the bridge. We were among the first if not the first to reach the north end of the highway bridge."

Our small group of men, which included SSgt. Marvin Hirsch, Sgt. Leroy Richmond, Pvt. Simon Renner, and me, fought our way across fields, through orchards, and around houses to within assault distance of Fort Hof van Holland. Although the fort had been one of H Company's objectives, we had no idea of its layout or structure. It was ancient and moat encircled with a drawbridge on the north side. It resembled an inverted bowl, with sides sloping at about a forty-five-degree incline from the edge of the moat to the top of the fort, a distance of about fifty feet. The sloping sides were earthen and sodded. There was a parapet ringing the top from where the Germans had been firing at us.

I saw an opportunity to silence the 20mm antiaircraft guns and machine guns that had rained so much havoc on us when we were sitting ducks. I directed all the fire we could mass at those targets, forcing the Germans to seek cover. When the enemy fire ceased, we charged forward and reached the moat, which surrounded the fort. At the time we were not aware of the drawbridge over the moat on the opposite side.

Sergeant Leroy Richmond, one of my platoon squad leaders, without hesitation and on his own initiative, pulled off his harness and gear, jumped into the water, and swam across the moat to the edge of the incline. In the face of the concentrated fire we had laid on the parapet, the Germans withdrew to bunkers inside the fort—bunkers sturdy enough to withstand an aerial attack.

Richmond scaled the incline, reached the parapet, and peered down into the fort. He began frantically waving his arms, pointing to the Germans inside and motioning us to circle around to the opposite side to a drawbridge, the only entrance into the fort. As he was looking down into the fort, the sound of a German Mauser rifle broke the silence. Sergeant Richmond must have been carrying a rabbit's foot. The bullet grazed the side of his neck but did not seriously wound him. He started back down the incline, swam the moat, and rejoined us.

From our position on the edge of the moat, we lobbed hand grenades over the parapet and inside the fort. That kept the Germans in the bunkers while we circled around the back to the drawbridge.

At the drawbridge we met up with three more troopers from H Company: Privates Dunlop, Legacie, and Davis. In all the commotion and confusion, we had not been aware of one another's presence at the fort. They had crossed the river in the same boat as part of a machine-gun section. Fifty to sixty yards from shore, they had set up their gun and fired at an entrenched German position. They then picked up their gun and headed east for the railroad bridge. Dunlop distinctly remembered: "There was a tunnel wide enough for a wagon and cows to go through the side banks of the railroad. I looked south toward the Waal River and saw 20–30 Germans at the railroad banking. The three of us crawling on our bellies set up the machine gun. I fired a burst at the Jerries and then the damn gun jammed and it just wouldn't fire. I could see the Germans rolling off the bank and heading for the river. I said to Larkin and Davis, 'Let's get the hell out of here.' So we moved east again and came to an old fort with a wooden bridge across the moat. . . . Then a trooper appeared soaking wet. He says, 'Where the hell have you guys been?' He must have swum across the moat on the other side. I said to him, 'Buddy, we were here before you.'"

Joining up with Dunlop and his two assistant machine gunners, my small group grew by 50 percent, plus the added fire of a light machine gun. Although we were close to the fort, the Germans did not come out of their bunkers to engage us. I wanted to be certain they stayed there and the situation did not change. I didn't know how many Germans were inside the fort, but as long as they didn't constitute a threat to our forces still crossing the river or impede our attack on the bridges, I was not concerned. We could move out to help seize the bridges, our principal objective, and let the men of the 1st Battalion coming up behind us take care of them. Before leaving and heading for the highway bridge, I wanted to make certain the Germans stayed buttoned up in the bunkers. I had Dunlop set up his machine gun at the head of the drawbridge and fire a number of bursts into the fort while the rest of us lobbed grenades over the top.

After we left for the highway bridge, Sergeant Finkbeiner and two men from his squad arrived at Fort Hof van Holland: "The most resistance we had met was from a medieval type fort. It had a moat and a wooden drawbridge. I took a 35mm camera from a dead German soldier. At the foot of the drawbridge we were not fired on nor did we see any Germans in the fort. The camera had an exposed film in it which I later had developed. It had pictures of the construction and repair of the fort. From there we headed for a railroad embankment."

After overcoming enemy resistance near the river, Lieutenant Murphy with several of his men veered right and headed for the highway bridge. Approaching the edge of a

wooded area, he spotted one of our paratroopers. It was
Capt. W. Stanford Burkholder, commander, Headquarters
Company, 3d Battalion. Murphy recalled: "I found Captain
Burkholder propped up under a tree. He had been shot in the
leg or perhaps the hip by a German sniper. I talked with him
to determine if he was all right and told him we were hurry-
ing to get to the highway bridge. I left my platoon medic
with him with instructions to get him to one of the returning
boats and back to an aid station."

Firefights were taking place over the entire area. The situation was still chaotic and confused. We were in the dark
concerning the status of the two bridges or the whereabouts
of the rest of H Company or I Company. Satisfied that we
had neutralized enemy resistance at Fort Hof van Holland,
my small group and I headed east for the prize, the highway
bridge, but we would not get there without a fight. We had to
overcome determined German resistance from small groups
that had fallen back from the embankment.

Men from H Company, led by Captain Kappel and Lieutenants Sims and Rivers, reached the approaches to the north
side of the railroad bridge. Sergeant Tarbell managed to
reach the railroad embankment and recalled: "After fighting
with different groups from H Company, I was trying to rejoin Captain Kappel. I finally met up with him at the railroad
bridge. We had quite a fight there also. At one point we were
passing Gammon grenades to Captain Kappel who was
throwing them at German soldiers through an opening in the
north bridge tower entrance."

Sergeant Finkbeiner, not encountering any resistance
from within the fort, bypassed it and headed for a railroad
embankment about a thousand yards from the bridge.
Reaching the embankment, he stuck his head over the top
and found himself looking into the muzzle of a German machine gun. He recalled:

 I think that he was as surprised as I was. I ducked but
 the muzzle blast blew the little wool liner cap off my
 head. My two companions and I tossed hand grenades

over the embankment and the Germans tossed some over at us. I heard what I assumed was a command and several Germans charged at us. We repulsed the charge, killing a couple and wounding another. I had to restrain the engineer who had stayed with us from going to the aid of the wounded German.

We then left for the highway bridge, which was our objective. Following a road we went through a pass under a dike. Here one of our men was killed by a shot that must have severed a femoral artery in his hip and he lived only a few minutes.

One of the enemy on the other side behind the machine gun started waving a white flag. The same engineer who wanted to go to the aid of a wounded enemy stood up to go capture prisoners, and was immediately shot and killed. We were yelling at him to stay down. The white flag was an obvious ruse. An experienced paratrooper would have known better.

Kappel's party converged on the northern end of the railroad bridge just as a force of German soldiers, about company strength, was starting to cross from the southern end. Their apparent objective was to reach the northern end of the bridge and defend it before the soldiers crossing the river could reach it. They were unaware that the men of H Company were in position and looking down their throats.

Sims recalled that hectic moment: "We let them come within range and then opened fire. After we ceased our firing we allowed those still alive to either withdraw or surrender. At the time, my men and I were tense and angry because of the strenuous fighting and loss of many of our own men during the crossing. We had little concern about destroying the large enemy force opposing us."

Caught on the bridge between H and I Company paratroopers on the north end and paratroopers and British armor arrayed on the south end, the Germans had nowhere to go. Some turned around and headed back south, apparently intending to surrender, but instead they ran into a hail of fire.

Others jumped into the river; still others sought cover in the girders. By any account it was a slaughter. For the German commanders, it was a horrible sight. For the vengeful dog-faces, it was payback. These were the same Germans who had been taking potshots at us in the river. When the fury subsided and the smoke of battle cleared, 267 dead Germans were counted on the bridge. Many others were wounded and many more were taken prisoner. At 1700, just two hours after the start of the river assault, the railroad bridge was securely in Allied hands.

A quick search at the north end of the bridge for mines or demolition charges revealed nothing, but in the confusion we were uncertain as to whether the bridge was mined and the Germans could still blow it. Captain Kappel radioed Major Cook that we had control of the bridge. Kappel and Capt. Moffatt Burriss, I Company, urged Major Cook to get tanks across the bridge immediately. They would be needed to support the drive to the highway bridge. In the midst of all the confusion, the British thought we had taken the highway bridge. Still others thought they saw men waving from the railroad bridge; someone else thought they saw an American flag on that bridge.

With the railroad bridge now in our hands, attention turned to the east toward the main highway bridge, less than a mile away. Captain Kappel and some men from H Company, and Captain Burris and I Company, moved out toward the highway bridge, where they would meet my small group and me.

Sims, with a few men from H Company, remained at the railroad bridge to eliminate a number of Germans still holding out in girders. They took defensive positions in anticipation of a German counterattack. Sims received the Silver Star.

The race to seize the highway bridge was on. Paratroopers from H and I Companies, having seized the railroad bridge, were encountering German resistance in orchards, on dikes, and in houses. But the enraged paratroopers would not be deterred from the grand prize that lay ahead.

On the Nijmegen side of the bridge, the 2d Battalion of the 505 battling house to house to seize the southern approaches to the bridge, were encountering stiff resistance from about five hundred Germans. Supported by antitank guns, the enemy was desperately trying to defend their position south of the highway bridge.

Under intense pressure, the Germans started dropping back. British tanks supporting the 2d Battalion knocked out a line of antitank guns holding up the advance. An all-out paratrooper and tank attack on the remaining German self-propelled guns collapsed the German perimeter defense. The German bridgehead split wide open, and the enemy broke ranks and fled in panic across the bridge. Some sought cover in the girders.

A number of other retreating Germans fled across the bridge and set their sights on reaching Fort Hof van Holland. But before they could reach there, they ran into my men. The troopers from H and I Companies joined us. Disorganized and panic stricken, the Germans suffered further casualties. After a bitter fight, they withdrew and headed north in the direction of Arnhem. Having eliminated an obstacle to our advance, my men and I regrouped and continued moving toward the highway bridge.

In the meantime, the engineers—with the few remaining boats—succeeded in ferrying the 1st and 2d Battalions, and G Company, across the river. The men of the 1st Battalion moved out quickly, heading for the railroad bridge and the fort. At the railroad bridge they relieved Sims and his men and assumed defensive positions. Others from the 1st Battalion advanced on the fort; after a pitched battle, the men there surrendered.

With the German bridgehead routed on the south side of the highway bridge and the confusion over which bridge H Company had reported captured, four British tanks from the Guards Armored Division started across the Nijmegen highway bridge. In later historical accounts, it is unclear whether the British felt that the bridge was secure or the tanks crossed on their own initiative. When we were just reaching the northern end of the bridge and farther, it was uncertain whether the bridge was cleared of demolitions. In the aftermath, those of us who had made it to the bridge believed that the British thought it was safe to cross. The British, ever cautious and deliberate, would not have risked sending tanks across the bridge if they felt it unsafe.

We were never sure why the Germans failed to blow the bridge once they realized they could not defend it. Accounts we heard varied from failure of the detonating mechanism to the Dutch underground cutting the wires. But to us, on the north side of the bridge, the only thing that mattered was that the bridge was still intact. At 1900, just four hours after setting our canvas boats in the Waal River, the badly battered 3d Battalion had achieved all its objectives. But the cost in blood had been high, and a lot of hard fighting still remained.

After Rivers and his men left the railroad bridge and raced for the highway bridge, he met Privates Musa and Young. Musa recalled they were among the first to reach the bridge: "We deployed on both sides of the bridge. The Germans were firing at us from the girders and there were more on the bridge. Some Germans tried to escape the advance of the Allied Forces on the south and ran toward us. We held our fire until they were within close range and then opened fire. Some turned around and started back towards the south end trying to surrender. Other Germans were still holding out in the girders on the bridge. We called for them to come down and surrender. I remember one of our men climbing a girder when an SS officer shot him in the chest. We retaliated with a hail of bullets, knocking him out of the girder and into the river below. About 40 Germans surrendered to us. Lt. Rivers told Private Young and me to take them back to the north side of the bridge and look for H Company. We met Capt. Kappel and he said they would take control of the prisoners."

Small groups of H and I Company men were arriving to join their buddies in the fight at the bridge. Sergeants Shields and Rice reached the bridge after overcoming two

German 88mm gun emplacements. Shields related: "We were being fired at by Germans from the girders above the bridge. I returned fire with my BAR and hit one of them. On the way down, the helmet fell off the German revealing long, flowing hair. To my surprise it was a woman who had been firing at me."

That was the only time I had heard of German women in combat.

After being delayed in a pitched battle with retreating Germans, I reached the north end of the bridge with a small group of men. Firing at the bridge had subsided, and prisoners were being rounded up. The highway bridge was littered with German bodies, evidence of the fierce fighting that had taken place.

The ever-present Dunlop, with Legacie and his machine gun, made it to the bridge from Fort Hof van Holland. Dunlop recalled: "There was still some firing going on as we came up to the end of the bridge. There were only about 15 or 20 guys there at that time. I remember Lt. Rivers, Lt. Megellas, Sgt. Finkbeiner, Legacie, Sgt. Rosenkrantz and myself, all of H Company; Capt. Kappel, H Company; and Capt. Burriss of I Company. It was now getting darker and the shooting was sporadic. Many SS troopers were killed and wounded on the bridge. They were hanging from the girders where they had tied themselves. An officer told me and Legacie to keep our eyes open, to spot any German skin-divers who might swim down and try to blow the bridge. The river was very dark now and it would be very difficult to see anyone in the water."

With H and I Companies in control of the north end of the bridge, British tanks started for the bridge; three made it across. Everyone held their breath, expecting that the Germans would blow the bridge at any minute, but it did not happen. At 1915 on 20 December, both bridges were securely under Allied control.

In recognition of this effort in the face of great odds, the 3d Battalion was awarded the Presidential Unit Citation, the second awarded to us. The first was for our stand at the Anzio beachhead in February 1944. For H Company, it was the third Presidential Unit Citation, the first having been awarded for action near Miori, Italy, for the period 10 to 18 September 1943.

Captain Kappel set up an H Company command post, and as men arrived they pushed farther north, extending the perimeter defense of the bridge. The way was now clear for British tankers to continue north to Arnhem to relieve their beleaguered comrades, the Red Devils.

Much to our surprise, the British tanks, after crossing the bridge, held up instead of continuing on to Arnhem. Lieutenant Murphy, who had been busy setting up a perimeter defense, hurried back to tell the British tankers that the road ahead to Arnhem was open. He recalled telling a British tank commander, "We've got the road ahead cleared for about quarter of a mile. Now it is up to you to rescue your comrades." Murphy was told, however, that the tankers had been ordered to stay put and to control the road and the bridge.

I was furious. I could not understand the hesitancy to continue on to Arnhem, where German SS panzer units were decimating the British 1st Parachute Division. The bridge at Arnhem was the key to success for the entire Market Garden operation and Montgomery's grandiose scheme to end the war by Christmas 1944. Understandably, the ten-mile drive to Arnhem would be difficult, and the British tankers could expect to suffer losses, but suffering casualties was never a deterrent to combat planning. Casualties were expected and accepted and weighed against the importance of the objectives. Even the British commanders, their cautious and deliberate style notwithstanding, understood that casualties and combat were synonymous. Certainly we understood that point when we were ordered to cross the Waal River in broad daylight.

I wasn't the only one furious at the British indecision to move north. From the 82d Airborne Division commander down to the lowest dogfaces in H and I Companies, we couldn't believe what was happening.

Dunlop was with me on the north end of the bridge when

the British tanks started to cross. He wrote: "Legacie and I were holding our breath expecting the bridge to blow. The tanks kept coming toward us, and as they went by, we excitedly waved at them. We pointed to the north . . . to Arnhem. . . . The tanks had about 10 miles to go to rescue about 3000 British and Polish airborne men, who were all that was left of about 9000 or 10,000. . . . The tanks went by us and to our amazement they stopped. The next thing we knew the tank crews were brewing tea. We couldn't believe it. Even with a murderous crossing in canvas boats and many of our guys KIA, WIA, and drowned, they are brewing tea. I can still hear Lt. Rivers, Lt. Megellas, and Capt. Burriss swearing like hell at them. . . ."

With the north end of the bridge securely in our control, we expected the British would push north to expand and secure the bridgehead preparatory to the drive on Arnhem. Instead, British tanks assumed only the close-in defense of the bridge while we were ordered to push north to expand and widen the salient. It was after dark on the night of 20 September (D+3) when the badly battered remnants of the 3d Battalion, dead tired, pushed north on the Nijmegen-Arnhem road to expand the bridgehead. The going was rough. We had to overcome stiff German resistance intent on recapturing the north end of the bridge. It was after midnight when we reached the final phase line. Then at daylight we pushed north another thousand yards to consolidate our perimeter while British artillery provided overhead fire. In the meantime, British tanks behind us had settled in for the night, refusing to move unless so ordered by higher command.

At Arnhem, the situation for the British 1st Parachute Division was deteriorating rapidly. The Germans had squeezed them into a perimeter of about three-quarters of a mile square. They overran the Red Devils' hospital and blew up their ammo dump. The Red Devils, having lost almost three-quarters of their strength, were hanging on by their fingernails awaiting relief from XXX Corps. The sand in the hourglass was about to run out.

The situation between Nijmegen and Arnhem was still fluid and confused. The delay by the British tankers to push north gave the Germans time to regroup and strengthen their defenses. If the remaining Red Devils were to be rescued, the tanks had to move and move quickly. With each passing hour, the anger level of the men and officers of the 504th grew, but none more so than Rivers. Sergeant Jimmy Shields, who was with Rivers, recalled his reaction: "Rivers told the lead British tanker to get going or 'I'll blow your head off and take the tanks myself.' "

The British tanks eventually did move toward Arnhem, but it was more than twenty-four hours later. They had gone about two miles over the narrow road when a German 88mm gun hit the lead tank. It started burning and spun around, blocking the road. The rest of the British tank column, instead of pushing the disabled tank off the road and continuing the attack, turned around and headed back to the safety of Nijmegen. I personally witnessed this action.

About noon on 21 September, we were alerted to prepare to pull back. We were being relieved of our defensive positions north of the Nijmegen bridge. The British were positioned behind us and would provide close-in security of the bridge. At 0530 the next day, G and I Companies started moving out, but the withdrawal would not be without risk. The Germans were bringing up reinforcements and would be nipping at our heels as soon as they realized what was happening. The withdrawal had to be carefully orchestrated. G and I Companies fought a rear-guard action and leapfrogged H Company, which was providing cover. Then H Company, fighting a rear-guard action, passed through I Company. It was touch-and-go, but by 0945 the battalion had reached the British defenders at the bridge. Sergeant Tarbell recalled: "When we got to the bridge entrance, we saw some British troops there. They did not seem too concerned about the situation and we remarked to them why it was they were still milling around. . . . We let them know our feelings, that we would not leave our men stranded like that. It was not a very cordial meeting."

We walked across the highway bridge, many stories high and 1,800 feet long; it was the prize we had fought for and where we had paid such a terrible price. There was still battle debris scattered over the bridge, and the stench of death was everywhere. More than two hundred Germans had been killed attempting to defend the bridge. We walked on into Nijmegen, and at 1100 we were transported to the 82d Division assembly area; we arrived at about 1230. That afternoon, supply brought up our bedrolls, which had been left behind when we crossed the river, and some dry clothing. What was left of our K rations was supplemented by captured German rations.

Later that afternoon, we moved south about a mile and dug in behind the 2d Battalion of the 508th Parachute Regiment. The following day, back to the power plant where we had jumped off for the river crossing, we were able to take showers. It was my first encounter with soap and water for almost a week. It felt great to get cleaned up, but it was greater still to be alive.

The following day, 24 September (D+7), we moved out to relieve the 2d Battalion, 508th Parachute Regiment, and by dark we occupied high ground somewhere near Beek, Holland. We would now be defending the eastern side of the perimeter around Nijmegen, making certain that the mass of the British forces packed into Nijmegen were secure in their new quarters.

In the planning of Market Garden, the British 1st Parachute Division, assigned the mission of capturing the bridge at Arnhem, was promised relief within twenty-four hours. Under the worst of circumstances, it was expected that the Red Devils could hold out for a maximum of ninety-six hours without relief. But at 0605 on 25 September (D+8), when relief from XXX Corps still had not arrived, the Red Devils received orders to withdraw. Of the 10,000 British paratroopers who had jumped at Arnhem on 17 September, only 2,500 remained on the night of 26 September (D+9), when they began withdrawing south across the Rhine. Only about 2,100 men made it back safely to our lines.

The bitter defeat and the withdrawal of the remaining British forces signaled the failure of Market Garden. Field Marshal Montgomery's plans to end the war by Christmas 1944 smoldered in the ashes of Arnhem. The airborne phase of the Holland campaign, which involved three airborne divisions, was now over. The campaign would become one of attrition reminiscent of the trench warfare of World War I. For some of us in the 504th, this was not an unfamiliar situation. After the fierce fighting of the first few weeks at the Anzio beachhead, the battlefield became static for the next several months, with the men of both sides looking at one another.

In my almost eighteen months as a combat platoon leader, the crossing of the Waal River was the bloodiest battle I experienced. Yet the casualties within the two lead assault companies, H and I, were forty killed and another hundred wounded. Insignificant in terms of the broader picture, it hardly made an impact on overall U.S. casualties, but it made a lasting impression on me and those of us who survived the river crossing. Replacements for the men lost would be forthcoming. Parachute jump schools in England and the replacement depots were more than meeting our needs.

In retrospect, I consider the successful crossing of the Waal River and the capture of the bridges at Nijmegen the finest hour in the history of the 3d Battalion, particularly H and I Companies, and perhaps the finest in the history of the 82d Airborne Division. In daring and heroics, it was a feat perhaps unequaled by American forces anywhere in World War II.

Bill Downs, a CBS war correspondent, had this to say about the crossing in the *Saga of the All-American*: "A single isolated battle that ranks in magnificence and courage with Guam, Tarawa, Omaha Beach. A story that should be told to the blowing of bugles and the beating of drums for the men whose bravery made the capture of the crossing over the Waal possible."

But in the midst of all the bravado expressed by the senior

U.S. airborne commanders, no one had the foresight to ask the British, "What happens if we capture the bridges intact?" No one asked the British, "How quickly will you move on Arnhem?" and "What British units will lead the attack?"

In the aftermath of this great debacle, British field marshal Sir Bernard Law Montgomery lavished praise on the Arnhem defenders and portrayed Arnhem as a great victory. If there is any such thing as a great victory in defeat, then Market Garden must surely be a prime example.

In his book *Triumph and Tragedy*, published in 1953, Prime Minister Winston S. Churchill, in a telegram to Field Marshal Smuts on 9 October 1944, commented on the battle at Arnhem: "I like the situation of the Western Front, especially as enormous American reinforcements are pouring in and we hope to take Antwerp before long. As regards Arnhem, I think you have got the position a little out of focus. The battle was a decided victory, but the leading division, asking quite rightly for more, was given a chop. I have not been afflicted by any feeling of disappointment over this and am glad our Commanders are capable of running this kind of risk."

Churchill was correct in saying that Arnhem was a decided victory, but he should have qualified for whom. I am inclined to agree with Prince Bernard of the Netherlands: "My country can never again afford the luxury of another Montgomery success."

With the withdrawal of the battered remnants of the British 1st Parachute Division and the delegation of the two U.S. airborne divisions to the perimeter defense of the salient, the airborne phase of Market Garden was over. Both sides licked their wounds, buried their dead, and dug in for protracted warfare.

In the book *A Bridge Too Far*, Cornelius Ryan noted that Allied forces suffered more casualties in Market Garden than in the invasion of Normandy. In the first nine days of Market Garden, the Allied forces' killed, wounded, and missing amounted to more than 17,000. British losses were the heaviest, with 8,000. German losses were unknown, but estimates ranged up to 13,000. Although casualty figures may be imprecise, one fact emerges: Market Garden was a bloody campaign in which both sides suffered heavy losses. When measured in the cold, hard realities of war, the debacle at Arnhem didn't necessarily delay Allied efforts to end the war quickly. The Germans more so than the British and Americans lost quality troops they could ill afford to lose. Given their limitations on manpower resources, their capability to fight an extended war suffered in Market Garden.

IX

Holland: Defensive Phase

24 September to 13 November 1944

The airborne phase of Market Garden may have ended, but the fighting did not. In the initial planning stages, it was anticipated that the two U.S. airborne divisions would be replaced by regular infantry divisions at the termination of the airborne phase. That was a stipulation under which Eisenhower approved the participation of the two divisions. Doctrine dictated that paratroopers be relieved as soon as possible after completion of airborne operations. This would be in keeping with the most efficient tactical use of airborne forces, given the specialized training, combat capability, and difficulty in replacing casualties.

My battalion was badly battered and understrength. We had completed all our assigned missions and could have been relieved from frontline duty and returned to the rear to refit, receive replacements, and prepare for a new mission appropriate for airborne forces. But Montgomery, citing strengthened German resistance and increasing counterattacks against the Second Army salient, refused to release us. The salient created by Market Garden had added 130 miles of front, which had to be defended. Arnhem so severely depleted the British 1st Parachute Division and the 1st Polish Parachute Brigade that they no longer were viable combat units and were withdrawn from the combat zone. Eisenhower, faced with a decision on the continued use of airborne forces in the defensive phase, donned his political hat and came down on Montgomery's side.

The controversy over the continued use of airborne forces for defensive purposes was of no consequence to the men in

H Company or to me at the time. Our MOS had not changed. If the tactics we were to use to "kill Germans" changed, so be it. We had our orders, and we would undertake missions of a defensive nature. How long we would continue fighting as frontline troops was not ours to determine. We were combat troops and would do whatever was asked of us.

The German victory at Arnhem demonstrated that there was still a lot of fight left in the enemy. They would not fold their tents and go away quietly. The war would not end by Christmas 1944. For the combat soldier, the situation was unchanged. We were in for the duration.

In the meantime, the Germans brought up reinforcements to contain and drive back the Allied forces defending the salient. Marshaling scarce resources, the Luftwaffe attempted to destroy the bridges at Nijmegen and deny their use to British armor. On successive days up to forty airplanes bombed the bridges, causing problems, however temporary. Unsuccessful attempts were also made by German demolition personnel to place charges on the bridge buttresses.

Obviously, the loss of the two bridges over the Waal River at Nijmegen was a tactical defeat, but it was also an embarrassment to the German high command. In reality, the bridges were of little value to the British XXX Corps after the remnants of the 1st British Parachute Division had withdrawn from Arnhem.

To the south of us, our comrades in the 101st Airborne Division would not be relieved from frontline duty until 25 November, sixty-nine days after D day. Casualties during the airborne phase had been high, as they would be in the defensive phase. The Germans would see to that.

For the next fifty days, until we were relieved from Market Garden, and for another four months thereafter, the front lines in Holland stabilized, with neither side able to mount a major offensive. The British did not make another attempt to reach Arnhem or to break out of the salient the Allies had established and attack east into Germany.

For their part, the Germans appeared content to contain

the salient. Although Hitler had vowed to wipe out the Allied penetration, the Germans did not mount a major attack against it. The war in Holland settled down to one of attrition, with the combat soldiers on both sides looking at one another down the barrels of their guns.

The 504th established defensive positions on a line from the Waal River near Erlecom to the Wyler Meer, extending south to the Den Heuvel Woods (Dutch for Den of the Devil). During this period we were subjected to constant and often determined attacks by the German Wehrmacht supported by tanks and artillery. However, all the attacks were repulsed and beaten back, which inflicted heavy casualties on German units. During this time frame, we did not launch a major attack on enemy positions. A static situation developed, with both sides strengthening their defensive positions supplemented by minefields and barbed-wire entanglements. Combat actions initiated by my battalion were confined largely to probing of enemy positions and small-unit attacks. As was always the case when we found ourselves in a defensive position for protracted periods, extensive use was made of patrols operating behind enemy lines. Patrols were undertaken mostly at night and seldom involved more than a platoon and often less. Both combat and reconnaissance patrols were sent out regularly every night along the entire regimental front. Combat patrols were sent out to engage the enemy and capture prisoners; recon patrols generally tried to avoid contact while probing enemy positions.

In a defensive position, commanders at every level, from battalion to division, were constantly ordering patrols, some on successive nights to the same locations. There seemed to be an obsession with patrols. Most often the objective was to secure prisoners who supposedly could provide information about the enemy that would be of value to us. However, the German privates we managed to pull out of foxholes were not privy to any information of value. They could not tell us anything about their unit that we did not already know.

James Megellas after graduation from jump school at Fort Benning, June 1943.

After debarking in Africa on September 25, 1943, we boarded the "African Express" in Oran and headed south for Oujda, the site of the airborne training center in northeast French Morocco. The boxcars could hold forty men or eight horses.

Mount Sammucro in the Apennine Mountains of Italy. The 504 occupied positions on Hills 950 and 1205. I spent my first of three Christmases overseas on a forward mountain we called the "pimple."

(left) Sitting behind a large rock on the "pimple," which served as the platoon CP and protection against incoming fire, Lieutenant Megellas and Sergeant Kogut clean their weapons. December 1943.

(above, right) Pugliano, Italy, January 1944. Lieutenants Aldridge, LaRiviere, Megellas, and Kappel in a tent area located in an olive grove in a valley behind the Apennine mountains after being relieved of front-line duty on December 27, 1943, and prior to our landing on the Anzio beachhead about three weeks later.

Bagnoli, Italy, April 1944. General Mark Clark decorates the H Company guidon with the Presidential Unit Citation for action at Anzio.

Lieutenant Megellas and his platoon at the guidon decoration ceremony, Bagnoli, Italy, April 1944.

H Company officers, Leicester, England, 1944. Captain Kappel, Lieutenants Sims, Rogers, Megellas, LaRiviere, Rynkiewicz, and Murphy.

Leicester, England, September 1944. Lieutenant Megellas and Captain Kappel in the H Company bivouac area prior to our taking off for Holland on September 17, 1944.

Leicester, England, September 1944, just prior to our jump in Holland, Lieutenants LaRiviere and Megellas, known to their peers as Maggie and Rivers, developed a bond in combat closer than brotherhood. Both were wounded in combat (Megellas twice) but survived as platoon leaders fighting side by side until the end of the war.

England, 1944. Sergeants Gonzalez, Tague, and Toman. Gonzalez and Tague were killed in the Battle of the Bulge, Toman was wounded in the Waal River crossing.

I posed for this picture with Lieutenant Sims (back row) shortly after our jump in Holland on September 17, 1944, with an extended Dutch family. Their home, which was ten miles away from Nijmegen, survived the initial fury of our invasion to retake Holland.

View of the Waal River taken from the north side of the river behind the dike, east of Nijmegan on the road to Arnhem. The bunker was built by the Dutch prior to 1940 and used later by the Germans. The 504th Regiment captured it on September 20th.

This photo taken with Sgt. Leroy Richmond was taken on September 1944, shortly after our assault across the Waal River and the capture of the north ends of the rail-road and highway bridges across the river in Nijmegen.

Brothers Bill and Daun Rice, both sergeants in H Company. Daun was later killed when a German patrol penetrated H Company lines at night in the Den Huevel Woods area. Bill continued with H Company and survived the war.

Photo of Sgt. Jack Fowler was taken in Holland before he was wounded on a night patrol behind enemy lines. With a bullet lodged near his spine, I carried him to safety behind our lines. He survived his wound after spending three months in hospitals in Europe.

Bra, Belgium, December 25, 1944. Fuselage of downed and booby-trapped B-17 in front of H Company defensive position. German SS troops stormed out of the woods in the background; they were turned back with heavy losses.

Houfalize, Belgium, December 1944. This snow-capped area was the scene of bitter fighting in the Battle of the Bulge.

Men of H Company posed for this picture on January 7, 1945, after seizing Petit Halleaux during the Battle of the Bulge. I am standing in the first row far left with Lt. Sims, H Company Commander, standing next to me.

Remouchamps, Belgium, January 1945. A few days' rest behind the front lines. Lieutenant Rivers, Captain Keep, 3d Battalion, S-3, and Lieutenant Megellas enjoy a brief stay in the rest area.

In pursuit of the retreating Germans we passed through villages and towns that had been reduced to rubble during the bitter fighting in the Battle of the Bulge.

Germany, February 1945. Pillboxes such as this one blown by our big guns were veritable fortresses covering roads that went through the dragon's teeth. The dwindling German forces retreating into Germany were poorly manned and offered little resistance.

Germany 1945. General Gavin with 3d Battalion, 504th officers: standing, Lieutenant Reeves, Gavin, Lieutenant Colonel Cook, Lieutenant Megellas; kneeling, Lieutenants Blankenship and Pickard.

General Gavin awards the Silver Star with Oak Leaf Cluster to Lieutenant Megellas for gallantry during the Battle of the Bulge.

H Company overruns the Wobbelin concentration camp. Bodies of inmates stacked in door of a house.

Ludwigslust, Germany. The local citizens of Wobbelin were forced to dig graves and markers for the dead. U.S. engineers made a precise alignment for the graves.

The Russian sector bordered on the right of H Company's location, Berlin, Germany, 1945.

Berlin. Few buildings were left unscathed by allied bombs.

Our contacts with our Allies the Russian soldiers were frequent and friendly in the occupation of Berlin. The Russian sector in the divided city bordered on H Company. Here H Company men pose for a photo with a Russian Cossack. Sergeant Tarbell, standing, is fourth from the left.

General Lee congratulates Lieutenant Megellas on the award of the Distinguished Service Cross.

Nijmegen, Holland. The bridge over the Waal River captured by the men of the 504 on September 20, 1944. (This picture was taken in 1936.)

Margraten, Holland. A recent photo of the U.S. cemetery neatly kept and arranged.

If there was one thing a dogface hated, it was going on night patrols behind enemy lines to capture prisoners. Killing Germans was one thing, but trying to disarm them and take prisoners was another. One who has never been on a combat patrol at night behind enemy lines could not possibly understand the eerie feeling the men had. The only light that would penetrate the darkness was an occasional enemy muzzle flash. The patrol leader led by instinct and the mental picture he had formed of the terrain in daylight. Every strange noise gave rise to concern that an enemy gunner was lurking behind it. Every possible approach to enemy defensive positions had to be considered mined. Movement was careful and deliberate, for with every step, the explosion of a German mine seemed probable.

Once past friendly lines, there was no turning back, no communications with friendly forces, and no fire support of any kind. We were on our own in hostile territory. If we suffered casualties, killed, wounded, or missing behind enemy lines, it became the responsibility of the patrol leader to determine what could be done for them.

The elements were never a deterrent to patrols. Rain, mud, snow, cold, and terrain had to be dealt with in carrying out a mission. Sometimes it was so dark that there was a constant fear of the patrol getting lost or disoriented and thus not able to find its way back. Through all this, the patrol leader had to keep his men closed up and accounted for. Strict noise and light discipline was essential if the patrol was to achieve surprise.

When the patrol completed its mission, it still faced the hazard of returning through friendly units. A forgotten password or a trigger-happy soldier on an outpost who hadn't gotten the word that a friendly patrol was in the area posed a distinct risk to the patrol. The more often a soldier went on a patrol, the more probable the next one would be his last. Many men felt that the law of averages would eventually catch up with them.

To spread the risks fairly and evenly along units on the

line, patrols were rotated among the rifle companies. There were occasions, however, when a mission was of such urgency or import that a particular squad or platoon was singled out for a patrol because of its experienced leaders with a record of successful missions. If a patrol leader was worth his salt and expected the respect and support of his men, he led the patrol from the front, not from the rear.

Who were the patrol leaders? If the patrol consisted of a squad or less, an NCO—a sergeant or a corporal—led it. If it was a platoon, a lieutenant led, or a sergeant if officers were unavailable. Beyond the platoon level, from company headquarters through the chain of command to division and beyond, nobody was charged with patrol duty. Commanders and staffs at higher levels were engaged in what they thought were the important aspects of war: planning and commanding. Their MOS was entirely different from ours.

It is interesting to note that in World War II, the chain of command was like a pyramid, descending from the president to the Pentagon, to Gen. Dwight D. Eisenhower (Commander, Supreme Headquarters, Allied Expeditionary Force), to U.S. Army groups, armies, and finally to platoons and squads at its base. At every level, the unit head was called a commander, except for platoons and squads, which were headed by "leaders." Platoons and squads fought the war; they consisted mostly of men still in their teens led by young lieutenants and NCOs. They carried the heaviest burden and paid the highest price.

In his book *On to Berlin,* General Gavin commented about the defensive phase of the Holland campaign: "As the battle developed, thanks particularly to the skill of the individual troopers, the NCOs and Junior Officers, we were able to beat off major German counterattacks by patrolling effectively the large gaps around our perimeter."

E. J. Sims, who commanded H Company the majority of the time, echoed similar thoughts: "In my unit, Company grade officers were the real leaders in combat. Non-coms, who stepped in when their leaders became casualties, performed this function well. However, in normal day-to-day activities non-coms were the leaders. . . . Except for initial combat jumps behind enemy lines, senior commanders seldom visited my Company when on the front lines or during an attack."

Contrary to how historians have portrayed World War II, General Eisenhower and his top army commanders did not fight the war; the fighting was left to soldiers in squads and platoons and the young lieutenants and NCOs who led them. I am proud to say that I was one of those platoon leaders. Moreover, in retrospect, I would not have traded places with those who never led a patrol or an attack against the enemy or never heard a shot fired in anger. Although we were in the same army, we were light years apart in the jobs we had to do.

It should come as no surprise that the casualty list of the 82d Airborne Division in the defensive phase of Market Garden, 24 September to 13 November 1944, indicates that squad and platoon leaders suffered the highest percentage of casualties, with hardly any at higher echelons. I have no misgivings about this fact. Commanders were doing their jobs and doing them well, just as those of us on the "business end" of a gun were doing ours. The point is that this fact is seldom understood or appreciated by historians whose primary focus is on the so-called "big picture" of the war. Their portrayal of who the heroes were in World War II frequently varies dramatically.

When we took defensive positions on 24 September, we dug in on high ground, so looking east we could see German soil. We had observations on suspected enemy positions, which restricted their daylight movement, but they were active with patrols at night. During the day, German artillery shelled our positions with 20mm rockets, 50mm mortars, and *nebelwerfers* (screaming meemies), which kept us confined to our foxholes. H Company occupied positions near Groesbeek; G and I Companies of our battalion moved out to the Den Heuvel Woods. The following day, a large German force supported by tanks attacked I Company. The battle in Den Heuvel Woods, the most intensive single engagement of the defensive phase of Market Garden involving my battalion, ensued for several days. Casualties were high on both sides.

Operating from our defensive positions, H Company patrolled actively at night in the vicinity of Den Heuvel Woods. Sergeant Theodore Finkbeiner, or "T," as he was called, led several reconnaissance patrols. Here is his account of one of them: "I went on a few night reconnaissance patrols, with usually 3 to 8 men, to find out what I could about enemy positions and capture enemy prisoners if possible. On one night patrol, we went into a farmhouse entering from the rear through a sort of livestock or garage addition. Evidently we made some noise, because a German officer opened the door, issuing orders, I assumed to us. (We found out later he was expecting replacements.) We took him prisoner. Someone reopened the door and slammed it closed. We fired a number of rounds through the door. We heard groans and cries of pain, then a lot of German voices inside. We took our prisoner and returned to our lines. The German officer had an 82nd Airborne patch in his pocket."

Private Dunlop was in Finkbeiner's patrol that went out that night. Dunlop remembered: "We crossed some railroad tracks, crossed the German border and came to a farmhouse. We opened up with our weapons and captured the German officer. Our mission completed, we got the hell out of there and returned to H Company CP."

The following morning a German force of about two hundred men, supported by tanks, launched an attack from three sides on G and I Companies in Den Heuvel Woods. To support and protect the right flank of I Company, Lt. Joseph Forrestal, H Company, was ordered to take his platoon and seize the farmhouse where Finkbeiner's patrol had captured the German officer, and establish an outpost.

At the same time, I was ordered to take my platoon and

establish defensive positions to the right of I Company. In addition to the German attack on G and I Companies, we expected that the enemy would attack along the entire front line of the 3d Battalion.

It seemed strange to Finkbeiner and his men that they would be sent to the same farmhouse they had attacked the previous night, but they didn't question the order. It had been about 0530 when the last man from Finkbeiner's patrol returned to H Company.

Forrestal's platoon captured the farmhouse and dug in, but not before a furious fight forced the Germans to withdraw into the wooded area. Finkbeiner recalled that Forrestal set up the platoon CP in the farmhouse and the rest of the platoon dug in around it. Finkbeiner continued: "The next day the Germans counterattacked the platoon position. I was being called from one side of the house to the other to help out. I was known to be a good combat rifleman. At one point we were being attacked from one side and platoon Sgt. David Rosenkrantz stood up behind a tree to fire when he was killed by enemy fire from another direction. I was calling for him to get down when machine gun fire killed him."

Dunlop was dug in outside the farmhouse in a low fog at daybreak when he spotted four German tanks with about two hundred infantrymen heading north out of the woods, then toward G and I Companies:

The battle started, and we figured, this is it—we'll all be killed or captured. A little later, I saw a tank turret start turning toward us and firing, hitting the barn behind us and setting it on fire. The Lieutenant was frantically cranking on the field phone, but I was certain lines were cut or blown up.

By now artillery was firing at the Germans and driving them back, along with troopers from G and I Company. I remember Finkbeiner saying, "We will try to get back to our own lines when it gets dark."

Just around four o'clock, I decided to try and get back

to our lines. I crouched down low and started out the path that we had originally come from the night before. I hadn't gone 100 yards and there staring at me 50 feet in front of me were two big Germans. I turned around and was gone in a flash before the two Germans could move. I made it back to the house and took cover, looking in the direction of the Germans, when suddenly Sgt. Rosenkrantz goes by me. I hollered out at him, "Rosie, Rosie, don't go out there. Jerries are out there," but I guess he didn't hear me. I heard the burp of a German Schweitzer machine pistol that got Rosie 50 yards in front of me. I could see him when he went down and I was pretty sure he was killed. If I tried to get anywhere near him I would be a goner too.

The heavy German shelling around the house occupied by Forrestal's platoon knocked out the telephone line back to H Company. Captain Kappel sent Tarbell out to trace and repair the line; it was essential that communications be restored. Tarbell recalled: "In going out to repair the telephone line, I had to follow it to the platoon CP in the farmhouse. It was very dark, but I found the break near the CP and was able to repair it. I started drawing fire from the German side, which seemed to be on my right. Then the men from Sgt. Rosenkrantz's position returned fire, and after a brief exchange, the firing stopped. I heard Rosie calling out to me to come to the farmhouse. He met me outside and told me communications to the Company were now restored. I talked with Rosie a short while and started back for H Company. I did not see or talk to Rosie again."

Finkbeiner recalled: "After dark, I got word that Lt. Forrestal had given orders to 'fall back to our lines as best we could.' " The platoon left the farmhouse two at a time. Privates Dunlop and Kancir were the last two to go, covering the rest of the platoon as they withdrew. It was early on the morning of 28 September when they got back to H Company.

Sergeant William Hannigan recalled: "When the platoon got the order to pull back, I could see Rosie's body not far from the farmhouse, but there was nothing I or anyone else could do about it. Sgt. Finkbeiner led the platoon out of the woods and back to our lines. I will never forget Finkbeiner; he was fearless."

In addition to Sergeant Rosenkrantz, listed as missing in action because his body was not retrieved, the platoon suffered two more casualties, both new replacements who had just recently reported to H Company. They were Pvts. John J. Baldassar and Gerald W. Knight; like Rosenkrantz, their bodies were not retrieved when the platoon withdrew.

Sergeant Dominic "Dick" R. Moecia, H Company, had been one of the Pathfinders, along with Hannigan, who had volunteered to jump ahead of us in Holland. Moecia returned to H Company when we were on the line after the Waal River crossing. He remembered being with Finkbeiner, who he said was "one helluva sergeant," when the patrol captured the German officer. He recalled returning to the same farmhouse with Forrestal's patrol:

> I remember Sgt. Rosenkrantz being killed. . . . Rosie was a great guy and I considered him as one of my best friends. I first met him when I joined H Company at Anzio and I remember how helpful he was to me.
>
> I had dug a foxhole out in front of the farmhouse and I was not aware of the order to pull back in the morning. I guess I just didn't get the word. I looked up out of our foxhole and I didn't see anyone, they were all gone.
>
> Shortly after that, the Germans moved in and retook the farmhouse; several were standing next to my foxhole. I could hear them talking, so I lay motionless in my hole with a piece of camouflage cloth over my head. They must have thought I was dead.
>
> I stayed in my foxhole all day, too frightened to move until dark when the Germans moved out. Several hours after darkness fell, I decided to try and make it back to

our lines. I must have walked about a mile when I was stopped and challenged in English. I didn't know the countersign for the new password, so I responded with the one from the previous day. I then shouted out, 'Don't shoot, I'm lost.' I was taken back to the unit's CP. I didn't know what outfit it was, but it wasn't H Company and they were friendly forces. I stayed with them for several days before I could find the H Company CP [which] had moved during that time.

Lieutenant William H. Preston had just joined H Company and had been assigned as executive officer. With all the activity going on in Den Huevel Woods and the entire H Company front, he decided to check the line positions and CP security. It was late on a dark, miserable night when, disregarding warnings from 1st Sgt. Mike Kogut, H Company, that security guards would be trigger-happy on a night when the Germans seemed to be everywhere, Preston left the CP. No one saw him alive again. On his return to the company's CP, he was shot and killed by one of our own men in a foxhole on CP security. The man who shot him challenged him first, but when he didn't receive the countersign, he shot him. When checking on our men at night or returning to our lines from a night patrol behind enemy lines, I always approached our outposts cautiously, taking care not to surprise or startle our guards. The men in my platoon had come to expect me on the nights we were on the line and took extra precautions when a single soldier approached. If they had not, I wouldn't be here to write about it.

While the 3d Battalion was beating back attacks in Den Heuvel Woods and along the entire battalion front, the Germans were also sending out patrols probing our positions. On the night of 26 September, around 0130, a German patrol penetrated H Company lines, attacking a platoon CP. Sergeant Tarbell accompanied Captain Kappel to the platoon after the German patrol had withdrawn and returned to their lines. This is Tarbell's account: "There was a grenade fight in one of the buildings that Sgt. Daun Rice and Pvt.

John A. Beyer were in. What Beyer told us was that when the Germans threw in a grenade, they would quickly toss them back out. Somehow a grenade landed between Rice and the wall and went off. When Captain Kappel and I arrived at the house, the body of Sgt. Rice was on a litter by the door. (Private Beyer was killed later in Holland, on November 1.)"

Acceptance of tragedy became a reality of life during combat. Death was accepted philosophically and without remorse. The general reaction to tragedy was one of revenge with the vow to make the enemy pay. I saw this reaction throughout my entire combat experience. But the death of Daun Rice cast a pall over H Company. Daun was one of two brothers, both sergeants, in H Company; both were veteran, fearless combat leaders. First Lieutenant Virgil F. Carmichael, 3d Battalion S2, stated: "On the night Daun was killed, his brother Bill was on patrol behind enemy lines. Ironically, the German officer Finkbeiner's patrol had captured was reportedly the officer that had ordered the patrol."

Early the following morning, I Company, still holding defensive positions, reported that a strong enemy force, supported by tanks, was attacking in Den Heuvel Woods, forcing G and I Companies to withdraw to the main line of resistance. My platoon was dug in behind an embankment just to the right of I Company when the attack started.

The enemy opened with a heavy artillery barrage; then German infantry, supported by tanks, came charging out of a wooded area heading straight for us. When they cleared the wooded area, they advanced across level terrain covered by a smattering of tall grass, bushes, and trees. When they came within range, we opened fire while their artillery was still pounding our positions and shells were impacting all around us. Occasionally a shell would hit a tree and burst, sending shrapnel down on men in the foxholes. Private Jim Musa was firing at the advancing Germans when a shell hit a tree above him and burst, sending shrapnel down on him, hitting him in the left leg. Although badly wounded, he kept firing at the Germans until they began to withdraw to the cover of the woods. Musa then crawled down from the embankment into a foxhole he had dug. He tore open the pants of his jumpsuit and saw that the flesh had been torn from the bone. He remembered: "I had a pack of sulfa with me and I tried to pour it on the open wound."

Musa had been with me all the way from Africa, through Italy and Anzio, and was in my plane in the Holland jump and the Waal River crossing. We had come this far together. I was some distance from him on the firing line when someone hollered, "Musa's been hit."

I jumped out of my hole, running low behind the embankment for cover from enemy fire, and made it to him. He recalled: "I looked up from my foxhole and there was my platoon leader, Lt. Megellas, next to me." Musa remembered his leg went numb and had lost all feeling. It was bleeding, and he could not put any weight on it. I called for a medic, but no one was within range of my voice. I remember trying to console him, saying, "It's not bad, you'll be okay, son. [I was eight years older than Musa.] We will just have to get you back to the aid station." The aid station was located next to the H Company CP, about two hundred yards to the rear and across flat, open terrain. My platoon was still engaged in a firefight, and there was a lot of lead in the air, but fortunately we made it to the station without being hit. Musa recalled that I set him down in a shed next to a pile of potatoes. There were two other wounded paratroopers from H Company with him in the shed, one of whom Musa remembered as "Frenchy"; he had a hole in his chest. I left the aid station as quickly as I could—my rain parka covered with blood—and made a beeline back to my platoon, which was still engaged with the enemy.

For Jim Musa the war was over, but not his ordeal. The shrapnel that cut his leg open had cut his sciatic nerve in half. He and the other wounded were taken back to a field hospital, then sent to a hospital in Brussels and from there to England. After two months in hospitals in the ETO, he was evacuated to Kennedy General Hospital in Memphis,

Tennessee, where he was confined for about ten months before being released. I hadn't seen or heard from him again and wasn't even aware of what happened to him until I tried locating some of my old H Company buddies to contribute to this book.

Now, some fifty-five years later, Musa and I have been able to relive some of our war experiences, including the battle of Den Heuvel Woods. Certain combat memories remain vivid.

Musa wrote: "It was so good to hear from you after all these years. I've thought of you often. I remember you as an officer whom we all liked and respected. I also remember you as being on the line with the men, and would not ask anyone to do something you would not do yourself. I . . . remember you as the one who carried me off the line when I was wounded in Holland. Many, many thanks for that. . . . When I came back home, I wanted to forget the horror and memories of things I had seen, done, and participated in. So, I very rarely discussed or thought about it. I do recall my sister telling me in later years that after I came home, in my sleep I would yell and talk aloud. . . . I have a paralyzed left leg and walk with a limp but at least I'm alive and get along well. . . ."

Under intense enemy pressure and suffering heavy casualties in Den Heuvel Woods, I Company was forced to withdraw to the MLR. Four British tanks had moved up to support the I Company withdrawal as well as antitank guns. A gun crew had moved up across from the H Company CP on a dirt road leading into Den Heuvel Woods. Tarbell could see the antitank gun being set up: "First Sgt. Mike Kogut and I were watching them set up, and as soon as they got their gun set up, they got one round off. They received return fire immediately and it was a direct hit. A few minutes later we went over to see if anyone was alive. Everyone was killed, and as I recall, there were three men. After we found that all were dead, we started back to our CP. The Germans started shooting at us with an 88 gun. We ran like hell for a haystack and dove into a deep foxhole behind it. The Germans must have thought we had another gun position there. When I dove into the hole, Sgt. Kogut was already curled up in it, all six feet plus of him. The Germans blasted that haystack apart. It was one helluva feeling getting shot at by an 88 SP gun."

Later that night the 3d Battalion, 504th, was relieved from positions on the MLR by the 2d Battalion, 508th. The relief was accomplished just before midnight, and at 0130 on the morning of 29 September, the 3d Battalion closed in on an area near Bad Wyler. We dug in on high ground overlooking the Wyler Meer and the border of Germany. For my battalion the battle of Den Heuvel Woods was over. Both sides suffered heavy casualties, with I Company being hit hardest; G and H Companies were not far behind in the casualty count. An unusually large number of casualties were listed as MIA, some still to this day.

It had been only eleven days since we jumped in Holland, and it would be another forty-six days on the line before we would be relieved and could return to the rear. Continuing friendly and enemy patrol actions and smaller-unit attacks were taking a heavy toll on my battalion. We would need a steady infusion of replacements if we were to continue as viable fighting units. The Germans had absorbed heavy casualties as well, but they continued to challenge Montgomery's salient in Holland. For the next six months, the British Second Army was unable to break out of the approximately fifty-seven-mile salient that the airborne phase of Market Garden had established.

On 28 September, after the battle at Den Heuvel Woods ended and the battlefield had quieted down, I was recommended for a Bronze Star. I was cited for carrying a wounded man back to the aid station while under enemy fire and returning to my platoon to successfully repel an enemy attack. The recommendation was made by Captain Kappel, endorsed by the 3d Battalion commander, and forwarded to the 504th Regiment for approval. Bronze Star awards were approved at regimental level; Silver Stars went to division.

Later I learned that the recommendation was not approved and was returned to H Company. The executive officer, 504th Regiment, noted that although my actions were heroic, my place should have been with my platoon and not back at the aid station. At the time I didn't think much about not receiving a Bronze Star. Actions in combat were never motivated by the thought of receiving a medal; actions were spontaneous and instinctive by soldiers just doing their job without concern for personal risk. In combat, in the struggle for life or death, heroic actions by individual soldiers are commonplace. I did what any combat platoon leader in the 504th would have done whose primary concern was for the well-being of his men.

Further, it was a reflection of the bond that develops in combat between squads and platoon leaders and the men in their units, a bond so strong that the men would follow their leaders "to the gates of hell." It was a relationship that combat leaders sensed and felt, unlike their commanders to the rear who had never led a patrol or an attack. This also explains why casualties in the defensive phase of Market Garden were heaviest among junior officers.

Shortly after the Waal River crossing, the 504th captured a truckload of German *panzerfausts*, an antitank weapon, along with instructions. It was an effective weapon, especially suited for airborne forces that lacked means of combating armored tanks and vehicles. I was one of several officers pulled out of the line to test and try the weapons somewhere to the rear of our positions. The *panzerfaust*, something like our bazooka, contained a six-inch warhead on a wooden stem to be fired from a tube about three inches in diameter. Only the stem was inserted into the tube. Unlike our bazooka, the tubes were disposable, and the *panzerfaust* was manned and fired by a single soldier. It was accurate up to fifty yards and could penetrate the front plate of any known tank; it also had a multiplicity of other uses. It was a much better weapon for a lightly armed soldier against armor than anything we had in our arsenal. We issued a limited number to the frontline troops, but unfortunately our only source of supply was relieving the Germans of them.

On the morning of 30 September, word came to the rifle companies that the Germans were planning a major attack against the division. It seemed that Allied intelligence had received reports that we would be attacked that evening by three divisions of German infantry and two of armor. The Germans supposedly intended to wipe out our position and all our forces. This was boastfully decreed over a German radiocast. The entire division was alerted for a major German attack. We were told to stay in our foxholes and let the leading tanks pass over us, then engage the accompanying infantry.

Later that day I received a call from H Company saying that I should report to Colonel Tucker at regiment without delay. It was unusual for a platoon officer on the line to be summoned directly like this, bypassing both company and battalion headquarters. I had no idea what he wanted with me, but I surmised it was a matter of some emergency. I sensed there was anxiety among the men in my platoon about my going to regiment. With the division alerted for a major enemy attack, it seemed ominous to them. Could it be another patrol so soon after we were just on one? It wasn't our turn to go behind enemy lines again, but something was up and it looked as though we were it.

When I arrived at the regiment, Tucker and the staff were gathered around a large map of the division area. In his usual somber and serious tone, Tucker said, "Maggie, division needs some prisoners, and soon. We have to know where and when the Germans plan to strike. Take a patrol as soon as it is dark and come back with some prisoners." That was it, a five-paragraph field order wrapped up in a couple of sentences. How large a patrol and where we would go was left to me. We gathered around the map, and suspected enemy positions were identified. All regimental units on the line were alerted to be on the lookout for my patrol shortly after dark. The password for the night would be "Hey Greek."

I proceeded directly back to my platoon CP. There would

be time enough to inform our battalion and company of my meeting at regiment. But first we had to get the platoon ready for another night mission. We had suffered heavy casualties in the Waal River crossing and in the battle of Den Heuvel Woods, but replacements had brought the platoon strength up to twenty-four men. The medic, Pvt. Robert T. Koeller, who had been killed in the river crossing, was replaced by Pvt. Richard Van Ort.

I decided to take the entire platoon with me, including the unarmed medic; if division intelligence was correct, we had to be prepared to fight. I called together the platoon sergeant, Marvin Hirsch, and the three squad leaders—Sgts. Leroy Richmond, Jack Fowler, and John Foley—to discuss our mission. On the high ground we occupied, we could look out over no-man's-land and for some distance beyond. We could detect fresh dirt at intervals on an embankment about a thousand yards to our front, which generally indicated digging new foxholes. On top of the embankment were several small blockhouses about the size of the shanty I used for ice fishing in Wisconsin. What the Germans might be using them for was uncertain. From our visual reconnaissance, it appeared that the embankment was the enemy main line of resistance, or perhaps the final protective line. Most likely this was where we would get our prisoners. To get there we would have to cross what appeared on the map as Wyler Meer. It was a large body of water, more like a lagoon— shallow and boggy. On the south end of Wyler Meer was a small bridge, not large enough to accommodate vehicles; it was most likely used for pedestrian traffic. If Wyler Meer were fordable, we would wade through it; otherwise, we would have to use the footbridge to cross it. We would move out as soon as it was dark enough to conceal our movement. The squad leaders returned to brief their men on the mission and check on their equipment, weapons, and ammo.

Shortly after dark, we pulled back from our frontline position, passed through I Company on the left, and proceeded into no-man's-land on our way to Wyler Meer. As was always the case, I was the point man leading the patrol; the

platoon sergeant brought up the rear and kept the patrol
closed up. There was always a concern at night that the patrol might become separated or some men might get lost if a
close interval was not maintained. We exercised noise and
light discipline, so the patrol was directed by arm and hand
signals relayed through the ranks or in muted voices.

I led the patrol on a course parallel to Wyler Meer for
some distance before checking the depth and the bottom to
determine if it was fordable. After checking several times, I
decided that the best avenue of approach to the German
MLR would be to cross Wyler Meer at the footbridge. I realized that the Germans would also know this avenue of approach and might be prepared to deny its use as a crossing.

We moved cautiously, expecting an outburst of enemy fire
as we neared the bridge. When we were about forty to fifty
yards from it, we halted and hit the ground. I approached the
bridge alone, and when I was within fifteen feet I hit the dirt
and started crawling on my stomach. Using the index and
second finger of my right hand in a scissorlike action, I
probed for trip wires that might lead to mines. I was surprised to find that the bridge approach was not mined. The
Germans had strung barbed accordion wire across the
bridge.

I decided to cross over and reconnoiter the other side, but
I became tangled in the wire and ripped my trousers. I was
so disgusted that I used profane language, causing a couple
of Germans to pop their heads out of their foxhole, making
it evident that the enemy was entrenched on the other side of
the bridge. I freed myself quickly and hit the ground.

I was alone confronting a German outpost line guarding
the footbridge. It was dark and I was separated from my platoon by fifty yards. I crawled to the foxhole where I saw the
first German helmet pop up and in my broken German called
for the German to come out: *"Kommen sie hier mit der
hands hoch."*

When I didn't get a response, I pulled the pin on a hand
grenade and tossed it into the foxhole. The sound created by
the concussion caused two more Germans to rise up from

their hole to see what was going on. They were manning a light machine gun. I crawled next to their hole and repeated my previous command in German. When they didn't come out, I rolled another grenade in on them and their machine gun. I spotted another head popping out of a hole a short distance away. I crawled to that hole and repeated my German command. This man also chose to remain in his hole, so I raised up on one knee and fired a quick burst from my gun into the hole.

To this day I do not know why the Germans did not fire on me when I was hung up on the barbed wire, or why they remained in their foxholes while I was rolling grenades in on them. Apparently they were waiting to be relieved by another squad and I caught them by surprise. It was one of those incidents that happen in combat where you can never rationalize the behavior of the enemy. This was also true sometimes of our own forces.

On my solitary quest I killed four Germans and knocked out a machine gun, but I was still without a prisoner. The burst from my tommy gun must have gotten some attention, because it brought one German out of his foxhole with his hands held high. All this while I had been on my stomach crawling from one hole to the next without exposing myself. But when the German came out, I jumped up behind him and put my left arm around his neck and my tommy gun in his back, using him as a shield. My adrenaline was flowing at a record pace in that hectic moment. I wasn't certain that one of the Germans wouldn't rise up and shoot us both.

Although the prisoner I now held was the fifth German I had accounted for, I had no way of knowing how many more there were in that outpost. So I tightened my hold around his neck, dug my tommy gun deeper into his back, and in my broken German asked: *"Wieviel Deutsch soldat hier?"* (How many German soldiers here?) The response was, *"Ich verstehe nicht."* (I don't understand.)

I didn't think my German was that bad, so other more persuasive means had to be used to make him talk. This was not a time for German arrogance. In the heat of battle I was

locked in mortal combat and in a struggle for my life. I
would just as soon have slit his throat except for the fact that
I needed information, and division wanted him for the same
purpose. I knocked him to the ground and, lying next to him,
began choking him. Then I repeated my question. I got the
same response. I'd about had it with him. If he wouldn't co-
operate, there was no way he'd make it back to a prison
camp. I got so exasperated that I whacked him across the
mouth with the butt of my tommy gun. I hit him so hard that
I broke some teeth and probably his jaw. I then asked again,
"*Wieviel Deutsch soldat hier?*" This time I get a positive response. Spitting out blood and teeth, he said in English,
"There are ten German soldiers here."

I stood him up and, with my tommy gun still dug in his
back, said, "Call your comrades to come out and surrender."
With that he began calling his buddies by their first names.
One more surrendered, raising the count to four dead and
two prisoners.

At that point I called out for the platoon sergeant to bring
up the patrol, which had been waiting for my order to move
out. They covered the entire length of what appeared to be
the outpost position. Four more Germans were accounted
for, two prisoners and two KIA. The prisoner was correct;
there were ten German soldiers in that outpost. Now all were
accounted for. The score on our first encounter was "bad
guys," six dead, four prisoners; "good guys," no casualties.

With four prisoners in hand, the patrol completed the purpose of the mission, but we were only halfway through carrying out the original plan to attack the enemy's main line of
resistance, about five hundred yards ahead.

The patrol had overcome an unexpected obstacle and the
men were in high spirits. We had momentum going for us.
Our MOS was still "kill Germans," and there were a lot
more ahead of us. I called the squad leaders together and discussed the original plan to attack. We would deploy in two
columns and head for the MLR.

Realizing that division intelligence was expecting prisoners, I called two of my new men out of the patrol and in-

structed them to escort the four prisoners back to our lines alive and without delay. By retracing our course, they would enter I Company's line, where a vehicle would take them back to division.

The daily log kept at 3d Battalion headquarters recorded the activities of my platoon that night in the following two entries: "30 September 1944, 2100 hours [actually it was much earlier]. Lt. Megellas and 24 men left on combat patrol to (778163). 1 October 1944, 0100 hours. Report of Lt. Megellas' patrol. Had light firefight. Killed 17 Krauts, captured 6. One man wounded. Contacted enemy in vicinity (778613). Enemy strong point at RJ (778613)."

The platoon reached the German line on the embankment without being detected or fired upon. We then deployed into three squads in front of the position: Sergeant Fowler's squad on the right, Sergeant Richmond's squad on the left, and Sergeant Foley and his squad with me in the center. At the signal to go, we charged over the embankment where, as we had expected from our reconnaissance, the enemy was dug in. Fowler and his squad were quickly engaged in a firefight, killing a number of Germans; Richmond's squad captured two more prisoners. We apparently had caught the Germans off guard and were exacting a heavy price. Suddenly a call for "medic" came from Fowler's squad. In a situation such as this behind enemy lines, the call for a medic was something we dreaded. Private Richard (Doc) Van Ort called for me: "Lieutenant, Fowler's been hit." I charged over to Fowler's side. He was lying on the ground, alive and groaning. It was difficult to detect the extent of his wound, but the medic said, "He's been hit bad in the stomach and will need help soon."

A German had risen up out of his foxhole and shot Fowler at close range. The bullet pierced the wrist on his right arm, penetrated the stock of his tommy gun, and lodged near his spine. At the time he was hit, my platoon was busily engaged in carrying out our MOS. Germans were everywhere, but with Fowler lying there with a bullet in him, killing Germans suddenly became a matter of secondary importance. The war had a long way to go, and it was certain we would have other opportunities. One of our squad leaders was more important to us than all the Germans in the Wehrmacht, even more than Hitler's scalp.

To a man, the platoon was concerned about one thing: getting Fowler back to our lines and to a doctor as quickly as possible and without further casualties.

I hefted Fowler over my left shoulder and charged down the embankment while his squad covered us. I started back toward our lines while the rest of the platoon was behind me laying down heavy fire on the German position. I called for Sergeant Richmond's two prisoners. They could be useful in leading us back to our lines, avoiding German mines and any further German contacts. With Fowler over my left shoulder, the tommy gun in my right hand pointing at the two captives, I hollered at the Germans, *"Macht Schnell!"* (Get going.) A swift kick in the butt got their attention. One squad positioned itself on my left, another on my right; the 3d brought up the rear, providing cover. With two prisoners leading us, we headed for home.

We had not gone fifty yards before the Germans sent up flares in an attempt to locate us. Enemy flares, like our own, were used extensively during night combat. A flare could be detected in its vertical trajectory just before igniting and casting light over the area. It lasted only a minute or so before it burned out. When we detected one going up, we would hit the dirt and lie motionless to avoid detection. Then when the flare had run its course, we would get up and continue our movement. After numerous flares were shot up, the Germans opened up with mortars, firing at our suspected location; fortunately none hit us.

After hitting the ground every twenty yards or so with Fowler draped over me, I was becoming concerned that he might not be able to withstand the ordeal. I made certain that the two Germans also hit the ground so they didn't expose us. Actually the two prisoners were too frightened to cause me a problem, particularly with a tommy gun trained on their backs. I don't believe that either of them expected to make it to our lines alive. Had they attempted to make a break, they would have been dead meat. Fortunately for all of us, the Germans stopped shooting up flares and the mortar barrage ended.

I was uncertain of the terrain we had to cross in no-man's-land on a dark night, not knowing what obstacles we might encounter. I was greatly relieved when I sighted the foot-bridge we had crossed earlier. From that point, it was all "downhill" back to I Company. The route we had taken following Wyler Meer was etched in my mind. We were home free, suffering no further casualties; and Fowler, although breathing hard, was still alive.

My final concern in returning to our own lines was the possibility that some jittery, trigger-happy outpost guard might open fire as we approached. It was less than a week ago that Lieutenant Preston was killed by one of our own men at night as he was returning to the H Company CP. I didn't hesitate throwing out the password "Hey Greek" loud and clear.

I Company medics laid Fowler on a stretcher and drove him to the battalion aid station. I Company also relieved me of the two prisoners; they were sent to division, where they were joined with the four we had sent back earlier. My platoon and I reported back to H Company, then returned to our positions on the line. Tomorrow would be another day. But one thing was certain: Not all days would be as epic and hectic as the one we had just finished.

During the encounter with the Germans at the embankment, before Sergeant Fowler was shot, the platoon and I had killed eleven more Germans and captured two additional, raising the total number of German casualties, as noted in the daily log, to seventeen killed and six captured. We suffered one casualty; Sergeant Fowler was wounded but survived.

All mail from the front was censored. As an officer, I could censor and sign my own mail, but I also read and censored the outgoing mail from men in the platoon. The purpose of mail censorship was to ensure that letters did not contain information of value to the enemy. However, reading and censoring mail also gave me an insight into the feelings and morale of the men in my platoon. For example, in 1967 I wrote the following: "The mail from my platoon after the successful patrol carried notes of jubilation. My men were elated over the fact that their patrol carried them onto German soil for the first time. I was pleased with the effect the successful patrol had upon the morale of the men. It was as though the Alma Mater had just gone ahead of the Arch Rival by fifty to zero."

About a week later, during an infrequent lull in the battle, Sergeant Hirsch and I visited Sergeant Fowler. He was being cared for in a temporary hospital in Nijmegen. An operation removed the bullet that had lodged near his spine and luckily had caused no damage to his vital organs. When he looked up at me, he managed a smile and a cheery, "Hi, Dad." He wore a chain around his neck fastened to the bullet they had dug out of him. He held it to be a badge of honor.

I never saw Fowler again. Like thousands of others, he became a statistic in the numbers game; but to his comrades he was a good friend and a soldier who would be missed. I never tried locating him until I began writing this book. With Pittsburgh the only address I had to go on, I was able to locate his family. Jack Fowler had died in 1975. His son, John, remembered the bullet on the chain that Jack wore. Whenever he displayed the 9mm slug, he would jokingly say, "This is how I lost my appendix." From his wife, Elizabeth, I learned that he had spent three months in hospitals in the ETO. He had recovered in England, then was assigned to another combat unit and fought in the Battle of the Bulge. He was a veteran of the 504th, having jumped in Sicily and fought in the Italian campaign at the Anzio beachhead. For gallantry in action in the Waal River crossing, just eleven days before being wounded, he was awarded the Silver Star.

The anticipated attack against the 82d Airborne Division by five divisions never materialized. As usual, high-level Allied intelligence had it all wrong, but it did not detract from the urgency of securing prisoners for additional information.

For my part of that patrol, I was cited for "extraordinary heroism in connection with military operations against an armed enemy" in Holland on 30 September 1944. I was awarded the Distinguished Service Cross, the second-highest U.S. Army award for valor, second only to the Congressional Medal of Honor.

The following day, 1 October 1944, I received a call from Lt. Charles A. "Hoss" Drew, G Company, saying he wanted to see me. Generally, when we were on the front line, I seldom saw or heard from platoon leaders outside my own company. In England, prior to the jump in Holland, we had a regimental officers' club where junior officers could while away the evenings. It was during this time that Hoss and I became steadfast friends. When I got his call, I was sure it concerned an urgent matter.

The usual number of patrols was planned for that night, and Hoss's number to lead one of them had come up. I was astonished when he told me he had been ordered to take a combat patrol behind enemy lines to secure enemy prisoners in the same general area I had just been with my platoon. Apparently the six prisoners I had sent back to division less than twenty-four hours earlier had not satisfied them. I couldn't understand what more Germans dug out of the same foxholes could tell us that the previous six could not.

When I saw Hoss he was visibly shaken, not so much by the fact that his number had come up, for that was the lot of the junior combat officer, but because he had a premonition that he was "going to get it tonight." Only eleven days earlier, Lt. Pappy Busby had told me the same thing just before the Waal River crossing, and he was killed that day.

I remember trying to allay Hoss's fear, telling him it was "only natural to feel this way when you've made it this far while many of your buddies have not, but that doesn't mean tonight will be it for you." I took him to the same vantage point on the high ground overlooking Wyler Meer and no-man's-land where I had taken my squad leaders the previous night. I pointed out the path my patrol had taken along Wyler Meer and across the footbridge to attack the enemy's MLR. I strongly emphasized not crossing Wyler Meer on the bridge. I may have caught the Germans off guard, waiting to be relieved, but it wouldn't happen again. The Germans undoubtedly would have replaced and fortified the outpost line at the bridge. The replacements, knowing full well what had happened to their comrades the night before, would be alert and trigger-happy. I emphasized that Hoss should find a place to wade across Wyler Meer "even if it's up to your armpits." With our field glasses trained on the area, I pointed out where I thought Wyler Meer might be fordable.

Nothing I said, however, seemed to ease his mind. His premonition was so strong that he was having a hard time focusing on anything else. I offered to go with him to help find a way across Wyler Meer without resorting to the footbridge. Hoss appreciated the offer, but in reality there was no way he could accept. Major Cook later learned of my offer and didn't think it was a very bright idea.

Lieutenant Virgil "Hoagie" Carmichael, 3d Battalion S2, recalled that Drew had come to battalion headquarters after he was ordered to take a patrol out that night to bring back prisoners: "Lt. Drew was terribly upset. He told Major Cook, 3d Battalion CO, that he had a strong feeling about leading a patrol on this particular night and asked not be sent out. Another night would be okay. There was nothing Major Cook could do about it. Division had ordered patrols out along the entire front. In the 3rd Battalion and H Company, it was Drew's turn. Division G-2 had an insatiable demand for prisoners." Carmichael further recalled Major Cook telling Drew to talk to me.

Shortly after dark, the following entry was made in the 3d Battalion log: "1 October 44—2015. Lt. Drew and 25 men left on a combat patrol to ZYFFLICH. Capt. Ferguson, Battalion Executive Officer, goes to I Company to observe actions of patrol."

Drew and his platoon passed through I Company and

proceeded along the edge of Wyler Meer, just as I had the previous night. Following my advice they tested several possible crossing sites over Wyler Meer but probably found them too deep to ford. Disregarding my advice, Drew and his men proceeded in the direction of the bridge I had warned them to avoid. What happened to the patrol was recorded in the battalion log that night: "1 October 1944—2115. Capt. Ferguson reports that patrol hit by heavy machine gun fire at (765606) and are pinned down. 2300. Capt. Ferguson reports that patrol withdrew to I Company. Lt. Drew and four men wounded."

The Germans had reoccupied and fortified the outpost line defending the bridge, as I had predicted. They needed and valued their combat soldiers as much as we did ours. They realized from their costly experience the previous night that the footbridge was an avenue of approach to their MLR and it had to be defended.

Drew was out in front when the Germans opened fire. He was probably the first to drop, the victim of multiple gunshot wounds. His patrol was pinned down, unable to move, with four men wounded. It was unable to continue and withdrew. Eventually the patrol made it back to I Company lines.

Lieutenant Roy Hanna, a platoon leader, G Company, recalled: "A sergeant had carried Lt. Drew back to our lines. When I saw Hoss, he was laying on a stretcher at I Company. A bullet had creased his skull and taken off part of his ear. There was a wide gash in his head, but it wasn't bleeding. I believe he was also hit in several other places. He was unconscious or dazed and incoherent."

The war would grind on, but for Hoss Drew it was over. He had fallen victim to a mission that served no tactical purpose. He was ordered to lead a patrol that wasn't necessary. Another junior officer would be sent to G Company to lead his platoon. None of us saw Hoss again until one day in August 1970. Lieutenant Carmichael recalled that day: "What happened to Hoss was a real tragedy. He was not the robust, outgoing, daring Hoss I had previously known. The bullet that pierced his skull had damaged his brain affecting its full use. As a result, he was left with the capacity to function at a level equivalent to that of a young child." Hoss died in 1975.

The fighting continued unabated. Patrols were sent out regularly at night, and casualty figures continued to mount. Wyler Meer remained a menacing obstacle, but we kept sending patrols into the area. The Germans fortified their positions on their side; then on 3 October, as reported in the log, they blew the bridge.

The front lines stabilized, with both sides resorting to night patrols to probe enemy positions. On 6 October the log recorded: "1930. Lt. Hanna's platoon plus one section of light machine guns and demolitions move to outpost line. 2145. Lt. Hanna reports, am pinned down by enemy fire (4 machine guns). 2150. Major Cook orders Lt. Hanna to withdraw to safe distance so 60-mm mortars can lay on them."

The 7 October log recorded: "0115. Lt. Hanna's platoon still pinned down. Major Cook orders Lt. Hanna to withdraw when it is safe. 0800. Capt. Thomas, G Company, reports two men slightly wounded and one missing from Lt. Hanna's platoon."

On the following night, 8 October, Hanna's number came up again as noted: "2145. Lt. Hanna and six men left on recon patrol to dike in vicinity (767607). 2350. Lt. Hanna's patrol returned; did not cross canal. Kraut machine gun and riflemen on bank of blown bridge."

We kept trying to find avenues around or through Wyler Meer, but without success. On the night of 10 October, Rivers led a combat patrol to secure prisoners, but, as was noted in the log, "The patrol returned, could not cross canal as water was too deep."

Apparently, Wyler Meer was not fordable, as Drew must have determined before advancing toward the footbridge and into a barrage of enemy fire.

On the night of 11 October (D+24), a battalion of the 505th Parachute Regiment relieved us. On 12 October the regimental front line was shortened by three miles. With the many casualties suffered at Den Heuvel Woods and on night patrols, we did not have sufficient troops to cover and defend such a wide area.

Once again we dug in and established defensive positions. Each day saw the strengthening of our positions, as well as those of the enemy. The Germans brought up reinforcements and strengthened their defenses with extensive use of mines and barbed wire. It became increasingly difficult for combat patrols to capture German prisoners. We not only met increasing resistance, we were losing men daily in enemy minefields. Artillery on both sides intensified, but the front lines barely moved.

I was unaware at the time, although it would have mattered little had I known, that the 82d Airborne Division was transferred to the command of General Horrocks, XXX Corps, Second British Army. Nor was I ever aware that we had been under command of General Browning's British Airborne Corps. During the course of the war, the 504th Parachute Regiment would fight under nine Allied armies: five U.S., three British, and one Canadian.

As a platoon leader during the entire course of my war experience, it never made one iota of difference to me or the men in my platoon in which army we were. Army headquarters was so far to our rear that it seldom appeared on the map or the radar screens of the combat areas. I always said, when in combat, my unit was the 3d Platoon, H Company. Most important to the men laying their lives on the line were their buddies with them and on their flanks. Who was behind us and how many was of little comfort when engaged in an attack against the enemy or on a night patrol. The soldiers in the squads and platoons were on the cutting edge of the battlefield. To us, "higher headquarters" was located off in some mystical land. We were never concerned which army's chain of command provided us with rations and the means of killing the enemy. We knew someone was doing it, because for every one of us fighting on the front lines there were many others behind us. This is not a cynical view of a soldier with a "foxhole mentality"; we were simply doing our jobs, just as they were doing theirs.

Coming under XXX Corps hardly caused a ripple in our ranks, except when we received British rations. I was never overly fond of our C and K rations, but they sustained us and were better than the British menu. I disliked their bully beef, and British tea was never my beverage of choice. Coffee was never offered, so I opted for water.

In my association with British forces at Anzio and now in Holland, I noticed that tea was more than a drink at mealtime. To them, teatime was a tradition, almost a way of life. At the allotted time they would stop, no matter what they were doing, and have their "spot of tea."

In my mind, tea and the British deliberate, cautious approach in combat became synonymous. Just as I swore that if I made it home alive I would never look another bean in the eye, I vowed I would never drink tea, but for a different reason. In time the bean returned to its prewar status in my menu, but British tea never did.

The weather in Holland in October and the first part of November turned cold and wet. It was not unlike "sunny" Italy in January 1944, where we faced similar conditions on the Anzio beachhead. It was a period of being dirty, cold, and wet, of being alert at night for enemy patrols, and of seldom being able to take off our boots at night. Casualties from enemy action continued to mount, and the changes in weather took a further toll. Burrowing like a groundhog in wet foxholes was sending men back to the field hospitals with an ailment familiar to the combat soldier—trench foot.

When not on guard at night or on patrol, the men caught a few winks whenever and wherever they had a chance. At times it rained profusely, and keeping dry was next to impossible in a wet, muddy foxhole. It was of little consolation that the elements and battlefield conditions were the same for our enemies as they were for us.

Summer had come and gone and fall would soon be giving way to winter, but the lot of the combat soldier did not change. We were in for the duration, although we did not expect the duration would all be in Holland. This was hardly the type of warfare that airborne troops were trained to fight.

Yet the combat veterans of Sicily, the mountains of Italy, and the Anzio beachhead took it all in stride, and the stream of new paratroopers arriving to keep us near combat strength would fit in. Although the time, place, and conditions under which we would fight and die were never of our choosing, we did whatever our commanders ordered us to do.

The battlefield had quieted down and the level of activity had been reduced to night patrols, probing enemy positions, and the never-ending exchange of artillery fire. As the prospects for a prolonged, stalemated situation in Holland increased, efforts intensified to fortify our bunkers and make them livable in the most rudimentary sense. Lieutenant Ernest P. Murphy and I dug and fortified such a foxhole, which we shared as a platoon CP. It was more than just a shallow, quickly dug hole that would shield us from enemy mortars and machine-gun fire. It was wider and deeper, and the top was fortified with logs and mounds of dirt that could withstand a direct hit from a mortar shell. The interior, illuminated by two candles, was lined with camouflage parachutes; our blankets served as carpets. The entrance was covered to seal any light that might give away our location. We could smoke without being detected by enemy gunners. It wasn't exactly the Ritz, but for a combat soldier it was first class.

Telephone lines were strung laterally among platoons on the line and vertically to company headquarters. Lieutenant Rivers's platoon was on our left, and we communicated frequently on enemy activity and dispositions. At night our rations for the following day and a resupply of ammunition as needed were sent down to us, or we sent men back to the H Company CP for them. We were back on U.S. rations again, with K or C rations the daily fare of the combat soldier. In my entire combat experience, I never saw a hot meal while on the line, and it was absurd to expect it. Any reports to the contrary were as accurate as the tooth fairy and conjured by our rear echelon for consumption on the home front.

A situation such as the one we found ourselves in seldom lasted for more than a few days before one side or the other attempted to gain an advantage. During those infrequent lulls on the battlefield, a backlog of mail would catch up with us and also give the men an opportunity to write to family and loved ones. Letters, however, seldom reflected the brutality and totality of what we faced. Censorship of mail and the media shielded our families from the realities faced by a combat soldier. Good news from the front was trumpeted; bad news was suppressed. Optimistic reports of when the boys would be coming home were in evidence but seldom substantiated. The combat soldier himself rarely wrote home about anything that would raise his family's level of concern or anxiety; rather he tried to assure them that he was well.

It was on one of those quiet nights on the front when a batch of long-delayed letters and newspapers were brought to us on the line. As Murphy and I browsed through them in our deluxe foxhole, I ran across some articles in the Fond du Lac newspaper that left me in a state of disbelief. I read them to Murphy and he reacted just as I did.

The articles concerned the internment of German prisoners of war at the Fond du Lac County Fairgrounds, on the southern edge of town. I could hardly believe that German POWs were shipped to Wisconsin, given the cost and logistics involved. The greater disbelief, however, related to the favorable treatment they were receiving.

The group who arrived in Fond du Lac was part of a larger group, as Gen. Henry G. Arnaud, commander, Sixth Service Command, noted: "There are about 16,000 German prisoners in Michigan, Illinois, and Wisconsin. About 5,000 [have] permanent year-round jobs at military posts while about 11,000 are working at crop harvesting."

The following was extracted from the Fond du Lac *Commonwealth Reporter,* part of it under the title "Foreign troops given plenty of privileges under system adopted by U.S."

On the day the camp was visited, the mess hall crews were baking huge pans of appetizing spare ribs while kitchen crews were opening large cans of sauerkraut especially purchased for the prisoners. Other German mess attendants were dicing a good grade of bacon for tomorrow's soup. . . . The work gangs that are marched into the surrounding woods are provided with plenty of food and hot coffee for their noon lunches. . . . Rumors concerning the laxity in the guarding of prisoners in the Green Lake Camp were investigated by members of the American Legion. . . . The officers stated that though there had been a certain amount of fraternizing between civilians and the prisoners at first, the practice had been ordered to cease. . . . Although Army security regulations permitted little publicity as to the manner in which the local camp was conducted, it was apparent to the casual observer that the prisoners led a comparatively pleasant existence while in the community. They were granted cash allowances of 90 cents a day for their work, much of which was spent in their own canteen. . . . One Fond du Lac beer dealer was reported to have delivered twenty-five cases of beer shortly after the prisoners arrived and had made regular deliveries every other day during their stay.

Another article in the Fond du Lac paper at the time concerned a German POW missing from camp. He was located in a downtown bar just having "a few beers with the boys."

The fairground camp was within walking distance for most Fond du Lac residents. Many watched the Germans in camp when they were out for recreational activities or close order drill. Teenage girls would line up around the fairground fences to catch a glimpse of the young German soldiers. The most galling for Murphy and me were reports that the girls were entranced with the German POWs. Nothing I had read or heard in almost two years of combat in World War II disgusted me more than these articles.

Certainly, prisoners of war should be treated humanely. We were not barbarians. This is something we believed in even though our enemies had a different definition of "humane treatment" for prisoners. Murphy had this to say about the Germans: "They were treating our boys, their prisoners, like dogs, while back home we were treating them as guests. A German POW camp was a living hell."

How Murphy and I, two combat-hardened platoon leaders in H Company, felt about the news from back home must be viewed in the broader context of the situation we found ourselves in at that time. We had lost almost half of H Company in an hour or less while crossing the Waal River in broad daylight under intense enemy fire and had continued to suffer heavy casualties. The Germans fortified their defensive positions, and their minefields and artillery were exacting a daily toll. And we had been in continuous combat since we jumped into Holland about thirty days before and saw no relief in sight.

Yet the disturbing news was nothing we could dwell on for long with artillery shells whistling overhead and impacting around us. There were more serious matters of survival occupying our attention. We had no control or influence over events occurring behind us, which extended all the way to Fond du Lac, but we did have the resources and capability to contend with the Germans in front of us who threatened our existence. That was our job.

For the next thirty days, until we were released from frontline positions in Holland, the war of attrition ground on. Front lines barely moved, with men on both sides looking down their gun barrels at one another across no-man's-land. Small-unit skirmishes, the dreaded night patrols behind enemy lines, and the constant terrifying artillery duels were leaving the men on edge.

Yet life in combat was not always grisly and contentious. In quieter times on the front lines, we found humor in otherwise morbid situations. One evening a white domestic rabbit strayed near our foxhole. Murphy and I duly captured him, and for the next several days he enjoyed a preferred pet status, staying close to us. The following day, Rivers, on a visit to our foxhole, glanced at our newfound friend and offered to make stew out of him. But there was no way

Murphy and I would allow our Dutch rabbit to become *hasenpfeffer*.

The following night a big tomcat strayed into our position, and it too was captured. We decided to skin the cat and delivered it to Rivers. He thought it was our rabbit and proceeded to cook it. He later commented that he had never eaten better rabbit. Several months later I corrected his misconception.

With little movement in the frontline positions, regiment deployed two battalions on line and one in reserve. My battalion was relieved on 20 October. On 27 October we relieved the 1st Battalion, which replaced us as the reserve. H and I Companies were now on line, with G Company in reserve. This generally was the order in which units were deployed until the division was relieved from frontline duty on 13 November.

When assuming our defensive position, I put my three squads on line along an unimproved road leading to a small village. To the rear and center of the squads, I established my platoon CP in a small abandoned farmhouse. It was well scarred by German artillery but had a deep, accessible cellar that could serve as a bomb shelter. The farmers of Holland had been victimized by previous wars, and almost without exception their homes were fortified with shelters. When using a building for a CP that at every level could be reached by artillery, especially in a platoon this close to no-man's-land, a deep cellar was essential.

The Dutch occupants had left in a hurry, leaving the inside intact. Chickens were scrounging for food, and there were eggs in the henhouse. I wrung one chicken's neck and told my platoon runner, "This is our supper tonight. Clean it up, find a kettle and we'll have chicken soup." I envisioned making my favorite soup, Greek egg and lemon. We had the eggs, but lemons would be a problem and we also needed rice.

One of the men volunteered to reconnoiter the abandoned village just to the left of our position to see what he could find. But the cupboard was bare: no lemons or rice. All we had was the chicken and eggs. I found lemonade powder, which was often included in the dinner K rations, hoping that it could substitute for lemon juice. The rice we would have to do without.

Later that afternoon, with the chicken boiling in a pot on top of a woodstove, the Germans started shelling my platoon and the CP. Several rounds impacted near the farmhouse, forcing us to seek cover in the cellar. The enemy had a peculiar way of welcoming us back on the line. The farmhouse shook from the concussion of the impacting shells but did not take a direct hit. When the shelling stopped we crawled out of the cellar to assess the damages. It was catastrophic. The concussion had shaken the plaster off the kitchen ceiling, which fell into our dinner on the stove. "You Krauts will pay for this!" I screamed. I don't know if this can be called a humorous incident or a tragedy of great proportions.

For the next several weeks before we were relieved, the stalemate on the battlefield continued. In the log kept at battalion, there were no entries of any unit action larger than a platoon. Activity was mostly at night, except for the artillery barrages, which went on around the clock.

Men were sent out at night to forward outposts to warn of enemy movement and return before daylight. Patrol activity intensified, ranging from small reconnaissance patrols of up to five men to probe enemy positions, to combat parties of up to platoon size to inflict casualties and capture prisoners. It was becoming increasingly difficult to penetrate enemy positions, the Germans not being cooperative and strongly resisting POW status.

Casualties continued to mount, with the German mine-fields exacting a gruesome toll. On 3 October, 1st Lt. Edward W. Kennedy, I Company, led a night patrol to locate the enemy lines and, if possible, secure a prisoner. He stepped on a German mine. The explosion shattered part of his leg.

Staff Sergeant William H. White was with Kennedy on the patrol and was killed that night, probably also from a mine. I can still see him climbing on top of the embankment on the north side of the Waal River, thirty-two years ago, as he cried out, "There go those SOBs. After them, men!" He was an outstanding combat leader.

Kennedy made it back to the field hospital but did not survive the operation on his mangled leg. The word we got was that he died of shock on 1 November. After the victory parade in New York in January 1946, Rivers and I went to Kennedy's home in Massachusetts and paid our respects to his grieving family.

On 2 November another of our junior officers of the 3d Battalion, 2d Lt. Robert G. Wright, G Company, led a night patrol to secure German prisoners. The following entry was extracted from the battalion log: "Nov. Second 1944. 1930— G Co. patrol returned—just before reaching the objective the patrol was mortared and while seeking cover Lt. Wright stepped on a mine and was killed. Patrol returned. No prisoners."

I did not know Wright, but I counted Kennedy as one of my close friends. In those two officers and in Staff Sergeant White, we lost not only good friends but also gallant combat leaders.

On 11 November 1944, we were alerted that we were being relieved on the line on 13 November by elements of the 8th Canadian Brigade, 3d Canadian Infantry Division. After fifty-seven days of continuous combat, Market Garden was over for me and my platoon. We would look back on these days of combat with mixed feelings, grateful that we had survived the bloody ordeal but saddened by the loss of close friends and by the failure of the mission.

The ordeal did not end for our paratrooper comrades in the 101st Airborne Division, to the south of us, until 25 November 1944, sixty-nine days after D day. The Canadians who relieved us and Field Marshal Montgomery's British Second Army would remain bottled up in the salient for another three months before breaking out.

On 13 November, the last units of the 82d Airborne Division climbed aboard British lorries, passed through the British-held salient before crowds of Dutch flag-waving civilians, and headed for France. The destination was

Sissonne and Suippes, both about twenty-five miles from Rheims, where the division would be quartered in old French army cantonments that had been used by the Germans when they occupied France. There we would refit, receive and train replacements, and prepare for the next combat mission or, as General Eisenhower referred to it in England, "greater things in store for us."

Our mission in Holland was over, but the recriminations, finger pointing, postmortems, and questions as to what went wrong were just beginning.

X

Holland: Postmortem

The campaign in Holland had been long, arduous, and bloody. My Company, H, of the 504th Parachute Regiment, had been in the eye of the storm for almost all of the fifty-seven continuous days in combat, without relief. We had suffered heavy casualties and were able to continue fighting as a viable unit only through the steady infusion of replacements.

The campaign will forever be remembered in the annals of military history for the daring, almost suicidal, crossing of the Waal River at Nijmegen in the face of intense, withering fire from a determined enemy force that outnumbered us at least five to one.

In spite of the heroic actions of the greatly outnumbered paratroopers in capturing the bridges intact, the overall objective of Market Garden was not realized because British tanks of XXX Corps failed to seize the moment and lost an opportunity to reach Arnhem, just ten miles to the north.

After the incredible crossing of the Waal River and the seizing of the bridges, the failure at Arnhem relegated us to a war of attrition. The 82d and the 101st Airborne Divisions were deployed to defend the fifty-seven-mile penetration into Holland that had been gained in the first three days of Market Garden. For the next fifty days, we became bogged down in a defensive struggle, with neither side able to mount an offensive. The front lines stabilized and barely moved. Night patrols behind German lines, small-unit actions, and constant enemy artillery continued to exact a heavy toll on our forces. Paratroopers were fighting a war to which they were not accustomed.

To their credit, the Wehrmacht fought stubbornly and valiantly, particularly at Arnhem, where they annihilated the British 1st Parachute Division and prevented the Allies from turning the corner and sweeping across Germany and on to Berlin. They achieved a badly needed victory, which raised the sagging morale of their troops. They fought hard to keep us from entering Germany. By any measurement, Market Garden was a stinging defeat for Allied forces.

In analyzing the failure of Market Garden, the question is asked, did incompetent commanders, ignoring Dutch underground intelligence reports, sacrifice thousands of young British and American lives on the altar of inflated egos and incompetence?

In ordering a suicidal crossing of the Waal River to seize the Nijmegen bridges, which proved to have no tactical value, were lives needlessly lost? A further question is raised about the hastily devised plan to seize the two bridges at Nijmegen seventy-two hours after D day. Because the highway and railroad bridges had to be secured from both ends, why were none of us dropped on the north end of the bridges on D day, when we could have quickly attacked the enemy with the element of surprise on our side? Instead, we attempted to capture the bridges by paddling across the Waal River in flimsy canvas boats in broad daylight, three days after our initial jump. By that time, the Germans obviously knew that British armor would not attempt to cross the bridges if they controlled the northern approaches. The element of surprise was lost, permitting the Germans to react to the threat.

None of these questions was of concern to the soldiers and junior officers who made up the initial river assault force at the time. It was a case of them or us. How it was seen by commanders many miles to the rear, standing in front of large situation maps dotted with pins, and holding pointers in their hands, was of no concern to us. Wars are not fought on maps by moving pins designated as armies and corps. They are fought on the ground by squads and platoons of young soldiers.

A number of reasons for the failure of Market Garden have been advanced. Field Marshal Montgomery, overlooking any shortcomings in his grandiose plan, blamed the weather. Certainly the weather was a factor, and always was in combat operations, but the vagaries of weather must be factored into any military plan. Montgomery wrote: "Had good weather been obtained, there was no doubt we should have attained full success." To ascribe everything to weather overlooks the failure of British intelligence to detect movement of German tanks at Arnhem. Single-minded commanders are not easily deterred by reports they do not want to hear, yet military history has taught us not to kill the bearer of bad news.

In spite of all the difficulties attributed to weather conditions, and delays in the arrival of a Polish brigade, a glider infantry regiment, and a battalion of airborne artillery, Market Garden could have succeeded if the British XXX Corps had moved aggressively on Arnhem after we opened the way for them.

After fifty-seven days in combat, we were relieved of frontline duty. Holland would become someone else's concern. It was good-bye Holland; France here we come. Hopefully we would find hot, decent food, a real bed, hot showers, clean clothes, and possibly—but only possibly—the favor of French mademoiselles, provided that our rear-echelon, noncombatant comrades did not have them all corralled. In any case, it would be great to sleep in a dry bed for a full eight hours without the constant interruptions, in one form or another, prevalent in combat.

But alas for me, France and all the niceties that were dancing through my head were not to be. I would not be returning with my regiment to Sissonne. Instead I was given another assignment back in Leicester, England, and would not rejoin the regiment until 17 December 1944, a night that will forever live in my memory.

I was ordered along with three sergeants to return to the regimental rear headquarters in Leicester, where about 250 paratrooper replacements were waiting to join us. My mission: organize and train them based on combat experience and generally prepare them for assignment to combat squads and platoons. When they were ready, we would move to France.

The replacements consisted almost entirely of enlisted men with a sprinkling of noncommissioned officers but no officers. Their average age was about twenty. I was an old man to them. All had volunteered for parachute training school, had made the requisite five jumps, and were proudly wearing jump boots and paratrooper wings.

One replacement was Pvt. Robert E. DeVinney, who would eventually be assigned to H Company and continue with me in the Battle of the Bulge, the occupation of Berlin, and the victory parade in New York. He had volunteered for combat as an infantry replacement and was sent overseas on 17 September 1944 after having just turned twenty.

In late September he had volunteered for parachute training. Most of the men in this group qualified as paratroopers in newly established schools in England. The course was an abbreviated two weeks, including the required five jumps. DeVinney recalled: "I was on the high seas on September 17 bound for England when I learned that the 82nd and the 101st Airborne Divisions had jumped in Holland. When I arrived at the Infantry Replacement Depot in England, I learned that the Airborne Divisions had suffered heavy casualties and were in need of replacements. The parachute training school at Fort Benning, Georgia was hard pressed to meet the demand for replacements. So training schools were established in England, qualifying Paratroopers in just two weeks. I decided to volunteer. The war was grinding down and I wanted to get a crack at the Germans before it was over. I felt that I would get my chance quicker in the paratroopers than waiting around in a

Repo depot for an assignment to an Infantry Division. Also as a qualified paratrooper, I would earn an additional $50 per month. . . ."

The young replacements were a diverse group representing a widespread area of the United States, although a majority was from south of the Mason-Dixon Line.

I could not help but recall my own experience as a replacement in September 1943 in Oujda, French Morocco, Africa. Although the situation was different from the one my 250 replacements were facing, the thought of what combat would be like was just as stark.

There was uncertainty as to how long the war would last and whether or not the replacements would experience their baptism of fire. DeVinney continued: "I fully expected to find myself in combat. I was apprehensive as to how I would react under fire and concerned about letting my comrades down. The thought of combat scared me. It was an unnatural feeling but I had to do it not only for my country but for myself. After the war was over, and if I survived, I would be able to live with my conscience knowing that I had done my share while other young Americans were dying."

In these men I also saw a mirror image of myself. When the war broke out, young men from poor families like mine saw an opportunity to gain some measure of recognition that might not have been available in their existing environments. We reasoned that recognition could best be accomplished in combat. Volunteering for the paratroopers presented the quickest and surest means of getting there. Although the chance of surviving was slim compared to service in other branches, and the possibility of being crippled or maimed was great, those were risks we were willing to take.

The motive of each trooper was personal and closely held. Yes, love of country was a motive, but that same love could have been expressed sitting behind an army desk and not looking down a gun barrel at our enemies. The lure of combat had a greater calling. Being decorated for bravery in the face of the enemy would lend some modicum of recognition. This more than anything else was the motivation to volunteer for dangerous assignments and protracted combat.

If in a few weeks I could prepare these men mentally for the brutality of what they could expect in combat and how to survive, I would do them a major service. These men were not dogfaces, government issues, or the dregs of society, but the best our nation had to offer.

In the horror of war and combat, these young men would look to one another when the going was roughest, and in the process develop a lasting bond. Whatever the circumstances that led them to volunteer for the paratroopers and certain combat, up to now they had all been peaceful, loving, law abiding, and too young to have experienced the kind of violence they would encounter. If they survived their first fight and observed the killing of both friend and foe, they would in due course become hardened killers. I had experienced this transformation and so would they.

Our journey from England to France was uneventful. Getting these men fed and under cover at night presented some logistics problems, which were eased by the fact that our meals consisted of three boxes of K rations daily. Our bedroll was a canvas shelter half and two blankets (two blankets because the weather in England in December is not very hospitable). We crossed the English Channel in a troop carrier and in France were loaded onto boxcars—the 40 & 8 boxcars so well remembered by veterans.

It was dusk on the evening of 17 December when we arrived at Sissonne. The town was dotted with three-story barracks. We eagerly stormed out of our cramped boxcars, lined up and counted noses to ensure we had lost no one, and prepared to board the trucks awaiting our arrival. We were not met by a welcoming committee, only an air of business as usual for replacements to help fill our ranks.

In many cases we hardly had time to know the replacements; some quickly became causalities. On the night they came to H Company at Anzio, Rivers was preparing to lead a combat patrol behind enemy lines. I talked to one of the new men in the patrol. He had not yet reached his nineteenth birthday. He had graduated from high school, then enlisted in the army and volunteered for the paratroopers. I asked him if he had fired an M1 rifle before, and he responded with an air of confidence, "Sir, I'm a good shot and qualified on the firing range."

The patrol ran into an ambush and suffered three casualties: two wounded, who were helped back to our lines, and one KIA, the young replacement I had just talked to. I never knew his name, nor was he with us long enough for anyone else to know him.

As I walked across the railroad station toward the trucks awaiting our arrival, the first friendly face I saw was that of 1st Lt. Richard "Dick" Owens from regimental headquarters. Dick, "a good ole boy" from Alabama, had been a great friend since I'd joined the 504th in Italy. He had an outgoing personality and infectious smile, and he could be counted on when the going got tough.

Dick was ordered to meet our train and bring "Maggie" and his replacements back to the 3d Battalion. I hadn't seen Dick since the Holland campaign, about two months ago, so we had a lot to talk about as we rode together in the front seat of the lead truck: the rehash of the Holland jump, who made it back and who didn't, and the regiment's overall shape. I was astonished when Dick abruptly changed the subject: "Maggie, we're moving out in the morning." He said that the word at regiment was that the Germans had made a major breakthrough "somewhere in Belgium." Our mission would be to find them, make contact, stop them, and drive them back.

At first I dismissed this as just another rumor circulating through the ranks. Rumors in combat units either actively engaged or in a rest area somewhere to the rear of the front were a way of life. Regardless of how ridiculous they might appear on the surface, rumors often gained a degree of credibility and a life of their own. After all, we were a hardened, experienced combat force, and any type of mission was possible for paratroopers. Up to this point, we had jumped into battle, fought as mountain troops in Italy, stormed ashore as assault forces on the beachhead at Anzio, and paddled across the Waal River in Holland to capture the bridges at Nijmegen. We were a combat unit always in a state of readiness and committed for the duration.

Any doubts I had about the authenticity of Owens's comment about moving out in the morning were quickly dispelled when we reached our units. I found a bedlam of activity generally associated with breaking camp on short notice and the urgency of immediately undertaking another combat mission. Rivers said this latest order caught us by surprise. There wasn't the slightest advance indication of the events that were unfolding on the Belgian front. We were all looking forward to spending a quiet Christmas in France, away from frontline duty. We had already experienced Christmas 1943 in combat in the mountains of Italy without a break from pounding artillery. Not to mention the cold K rations and the eerie conditions on Mount Sammucro on that Christmas Day. We thought this year would be different. But for us, death would not take a holiday on Christmas, which was only days away.

We were far removed from the front and out of range of the Germans' most powerful artillery. All was quiet on our western front. No one throughout the chain of command expected that would change, least of all on the Ardennes front, which was referred to as a "ghost front." It ran eighty-five miles through the Ardennes forest from Echternach, in the Grand Duchy of Luxembourg, to just above the Luxembourg border north of Monschau, a German border town.

The Ardennes front was manned by four U.S. infantry divisions: the 4th and the 28th, both worn out and exhausted, and two untested divisions, the 99th and the 106th. The 106th, the Green Lions, was the newest division on the Continent; the 99th, almost as green, had been in the Ardennes for a month but had seen little action. It was a quiet area where the 4th and 28th Divisions could recuperate and the

99th and the 106th could gain experience. In the meantime, the Germans were planning and amassing forces for a major assault on what would turn out to be one of the greatest battles ever fought by the U.S. Army.

By moving divisions from other fronts and committing reserve units, the Germans had amassed, behind the Siegfried Line, an army of twenty divisions (250,000 men) and about a thousand tanks supported by 1,900 pieces of artillery. American commanders dismissed intelligence reports from friendly civilian sources of the movement and buildup of large forces and tanks "twice the size of the Sherman."

The operations division of Supreme Headquarters, Allied Expeditionary Force (SHAEF), reported that the Germans were all but finished. General Bradley's intelligence officer said, "It is now certain that attrition is steadily sapping the strength of the German forces on the western front." There was a mind-set among American commanders that the Germans were beaten. Any suggestion that the Germans might launch a winter offensive in the Ardennes was deemed preposterous. Like Montgomery's dismissing Dutch underground reports of large panzer units around Arnhem, American commanders believed what they wanted to believe. German intelligence had correctly identified the soft spots in the American lines and the location of the new, green U.S. divisions. On the night of 15 December 1944, while the Germans were preparing to launch an early-morning attack, there was not an inkling of the impending disaster that would soon befall American troops.

The most surprised of all were the American commanders. General Gavin first learned of the breakthrough on the evening news on 17 December as he was dressing for dinner. Shortly thereafter, he received a call from the chief of staff, XVIII Airborne Corps, that General Ridgway was in England and that the corps, consisting of the 82d and the 101st, was designated as the SHAEF reserve force. Acting in his capacity as corps commander, Gavin alerted the two divisions to be ready to move within twenty-four hours.

First Lieutenant Rufus K. Broadaway, Gavin's junior aide, was a witness to history that night. He was at the general's quarters when the news of the breakthrough was received. He recalled taking a phone call from an excited, almost incoherent officer from a higher headquarters asking for the division chief of staff. The news stunned the chain of command.

General Maxwell Taylor, 101st Airborne Division commander, was in Washington, D.C., which left Brigadier General McAuliffe in command of the 101st. Taylor returned to his division on 27 December in Bastogne.

On 16 December, at 0530, the Germans launched a massive attack along the entire Ardennes front. American casualties were extremely heavy on that first day. Two regiments of the 106th Division, surrounded and low on ammunition, surrendered. About 8,000 American soldiers were taken prisoner, which next to Bataan was the greatest mass surrender in the history of the American army.

Many more, panic stricken, dropped their weapons and fled, clogging the roads to the rear. In the headquarters, there was confusion and chaos. Staff officers were burning classified papers and maps. There was a complete breakdown in order and discipline. A rout was under way, and it was every man for himself.

In my brief army training, I learned one fact: A commander may be excused for defeat but never for surprise. Whenever we were dug in defensive positions, I never rested at night until I checked my platoon positions and made certain that security was adequate so that the men who did the fighting could get some rest.

What I saw that December were two divisions of young paratroopers committed to battle with little notice, poorly equipped and scantily clad to endure the snow and frigid weather of a bitter Belgian winter. What I saw were countless men streaming back to aid stations and hospitals with swollen, frozen feet barely able to walk, surviving on cold, often frozen rations and enduring hardships they had no warning of or time to prepare for. By any criteria, it was a failure of commanders to look after their fighting men.

On that night in Sissonne, 2d Lt. Ernest Murphy was watching a movie when senior regimental officers were being called out to return to their units. Murphy remarked to the officer seated next to him that something extraordinary must be going on, and indeed it was. A short time later, all men and officers were told to return to their units.

When I returned to H Company and my platoon, no one had the slightest notion of what was happening in the Ardennes or that another combat mission was imminent. As was always the case when we were in a new area refitting after several months on the line, a certain percentage of the men were on leave. On this occasion, more than a quarter of my company was elsewhere, and there was no way to contact them. Also, as was the case when we were relieved of front-line duty and sent to the rear, our crew-served weapons (machine guns and mortars) had been picked up by ordnance for general maintenance and repair. Although the 82d was a highly mobile, rapid-strike division that maintained a high degree of readiness, we were hardly up to the state of readiness of former well-planned operations. On 17 December, the men and officers were generally in good spirits. It had been a sunny and mild winter day by Belgian standards, and men who had not left on R and R in the first quota were lining up for passes. There had been nothing startling announced that day on Armed Forces Radio. There was a generally festive mood in the rifle companies. It was Sunday, and plans were being made for Christmas celebrations. Live Christmas trees were being cut in the surrounding area, and mess halls were decorated for the upcoming holidays.

Mike Kogut, our first sergeant, had gone to Rheims for a night on the town. When he returned late that night, all the lights in the CP were on, in violation of light discipline procedures. Company equipment was being packed, and confusion and chaos reigned. It first appeared to be some kind of joke, until he realized we were heading east in the morning to meet the Germans who had broken through. Barracks

bags had to be collected and stored, company records safe-
guarded, and ammunition and rations accounted for. It was a
sleepless night for H Company. Sergeant Albert Tarbell remembered it this way:

> I was on chute patrol duty with the MPs in the city of
> Rheims. Our job was to intervene on behalf of the troop-
> ers should they get rowdy or drunk and get arrested by
> the regular MPs. They would listen to us. We were usu-
> ally able to reason with them and bring them back to the
> truck pick-up point and avoid serious charges. As we es-
> corted the fellows to the MP station, we noticed a line of
> trucks behind the building. As the men were processed,
> they were put right on the trucks and taken back to camp.
> When I arrived late that night, there was a lot of activity
> going on. There were replacements all over the place. As
> I walked by the orderly room, I heard one of the replace-
> ments talking to Mike Kogut. He was telling Kogut that
> he had never fired an M-1 before. Sgt. Kogut told him,
> "That's okay, son; you'll learn soon enough." When I ar-
> rived back at my quarters, it was then that I first found out
> about a German counterattack somewhere in Belgium.
> We didn't get much sleep that night. We were trying to
> help in the orderly room getting the replacements squared
> away, getting supplies, ammo, etc.

Later that evening, all officers of the 3d Battalion were
called to the CP for a briefing and an estimate of the situation. Although it was fluid, and intelligence was vague as to
the extent of the breakthrough and strength of the German
forces, our best estimate was that the Germans would attempt to split the U.S. and British forces and drive on to
Antwerp to seize the major port there.

We were up early on 18 December, and the lights were on
in the barracks before daylight. Armed Forces Radio on the
early-morning news was chronicling the events that were
taking place over a wide area of the Ardennes front. German
panzer units were on the move and gaining momentum. Ger-

man paratroopers were committed, and the Allies were cautioned about the movement of Germans dressed as U.S. officers and traveling in American jeeps. The company area was a beehive of activity. Two days of K rations and two D rations (hard chocolate) sent down from division were distributed. Weapons were checked and a basic load of ammunition was passed out. For the tommy gun I carried, I packed a double load of 45mm ammo in an ammo bag, which hung off my belt, and I stuffed all the grenades that the side pockets of my combat pants could hold. Meanwhile, semi-trucks pulling stake-bed trailers sent down from XVIII Airborne Corps had been arriving in a steady stream in the regimental area.

XI
Battle of the Bulge

17 December 1944 to 19 February 1945

Shortly after 0800, we began loading into the trailers. They looked a lot like the cattle trucks I remembered from back home. There were no seats, and we were packed in like sardines, about fifty men per truck. Most of the men stood; some sat huddled on the floor of the trailer. I recall sitting next to Carl Kappel, H Company commander, as we left the regimental area at around 0900 and headed in a northeasterly direction for what for us was destination unknown.

We passed through numerous small towns in Belgium and a beautiful countryside covered with a heavy blanket of snow. Most of the men found little to talk about in an atmosphere of uncertainty. How far we would travel, how long we would be in these cattle trucks, and what would happen when we detrucked were questions on everyone's mind, but they were not issues of open speculation.

Earlier radio reports indicated that the badly mauled German Luftwaffe had been active in support of the breakthrough. Kappel and I wondered if we would see planes on our long ride into the combat area, because we certainly were tempting targets. We were in a long column of trucks loaded with combat troops but with no antiaircraft guns or antiaircraft units accompanying us. The only defense we could have put up was in the mass firing of our individual weapons.

Fortunately for us, although the weather was favorable for enemy air activity, we did not encounter any German planes. Later the weather closed in, limiting the support of the U.S. Air Force, which was particularly true for the beleaguered 101st surrounded at Bastogne. However, for us, close-in air support was not a factor. To a soldier in a foxhole dug in on the front lines, airplanes of all types flying overhead were almost a daily occurrence. In time, we paid little attention to them, our preoccupation being on what lay in front of us on the ground. All planes we spotted overhead were identified as B-2s: "Be too bad if they're not ours." If they were not ours, we took cover. If they came in low, we would rise out of our foxholes and unload our weapons on them, mostly from a sense of frustration.

We passed through a number of small towns whose names were of no importance to me or of little tactical significance. However, later that day we passed through Bastogne, which was destined to be a major battleground in the Battle of the Bulge. The town was quiet, and lead elements of German panzer units were still some distance away. Some townspeople lined the street to wave, unaware of the impending disaster. The panzers were far enough away that the sound of German 88s and the rumble of tanks were muted and the muzzle flashes of German artillery were not yet visible. This serene scene would soon change, and the people lining the streets now would soon be jamming the roads heading west carrying with them only a few meager possessions. Elsewhere up and down the front, Belgian families were vacating towns and cities en masse as the Germans advanced, often creating problems on the road for advancing U.S. forces.

When we had departed Sissonne, our destination was Bastogne, but while en route we were ordered to proceed to Werbomont. The 101st Division was committed there instead. Their column was, however, several miles behind us, so they arrived in Bastogne just ahead of the Germans.

We arrived in Werbomont at 1730, unloaded, and quickly moved out to set up a perimeter defense northeast of the city. From the sound of German artillery and the muzzle flashes of their big guns, it was apparent that the German forces were not far away. Werbomont had some tactical significance as a vital communications junction between Bastogne and Liège. It would be only a matter of hours before the inevitable head-on collision between the two forces would occur.

General Gavin wrote the following in his after-action report: "I arrived at Werbomont at approximately mid-afternoon and immediately made a reconnaissance of the entire area. It offered excellent defensive possibilities, being the dominant terrain for many miles from the crossroads at Werbomont. At about 1600 hours I contacted an engineer platoon at the bridge at Werbomont. The bridge was prepared for demolition and they reported the Germans were in the immediate vicinity, coming over the main highway from Trois Ponts. At that time, a number of civilians were very excitedly moving west on the Trois Ponts–Werbomont road. They all stated that the Germans had passed Trois Ponts and were 'coming this way.' I made a reconnaissance down the valley from Hablemont to the Ambleve River but encountered no enemy or any indication of his whereabouts."

On the evening of 19 December, my battalion moved forward (east) toward the town of Rahier, where we contacted and relieved elements of the U.S. 119th Infantry. Advancing northwest to seize the high ground, we made contact with German lead elements, which we quickly routed. On the way, we passed a number of abandoned U.S. artillery pieces, as well as soldiers who were, as we would put it, "advancing to the rear." We tried to get some account of what had happened from a retreating NCO, but he was no help.

On the morning of 20 December, Col. Reuben Tucker, the regimental commander, received word from Belgian civilians that approximately 125 German vehicles, including about thirty tanks, were moving toward Cheneux. If this was true, the seizure of the bridge over the Ambleve River was imperative if the vehicles were to be stopped. The scenario was set for the first major confrontation between our lightly armed paratroopers and elements of the 1st SS Panzer Division.

On the afternoon of 20 December, the 1st Battalion, less A Company, but reinforced by G Company of the 3d Battalion, was ordered to seize and occupy the village of Cheneux. The attack began at 1400, departing from Rahier with B Company, commanded by Capt. Thomas Helgeson. The units were deployed on both sides of the road from Rahier leading to Cheneux. About five hundred yards east of Rahier, the leading platoon of B Company met enemy resistance in the form of a rear guard, which inflicted numerous casualties. The attack pressed forward for about a thousand yards until the lead elements contacted the enemy. The main attack on the enemy main line of resistance jumped off from a wooded area about forty yards from the MLR. The lead elements were soon pinned down by devastating cross fire from two 20mm cannons supported by two machine guns and enemy mortar fire, killing six men and knocking out the company radio.

The company found itself in an untenable position unable to advance in the face of withering fire. A decision was made to withdraw to the cover of a wooded area about two hundred yards to the rear. There it reorganized and set up a perimeter defense along the edge of the woods. Although B and C Companies had suffered heavy casualties in the initial assault, a night attack was ordered to seize Cheneux. At 1930, preceded by a ten-minute artillery barrage, B and C Companies attacked astride the road leading into the town with two M36 tank destroyers in support. They moved through barbed wire and across four hundred yards of flat terrain that was subject to intense grazing machine-gun fire. Casualties were heavy.

This attack was led by squad and platoon leaders, because all officers and NCOs had been either killed or wounded. Only twenty-eight men remained in B Company. Privates took over and continued the attack. With ammunition running low, the men used trench knives and rifle butts as clubs, and grenades to attack 20mm cannon and light machine guns. Company C, attacking in close hand-to-hand fighting, was able to penetrate the German main line of resistance, killing about twenty enemy; the remainder fled into the town. By 2200, C Company had advanced about four hundred yards, suffering about seventy casualties, with a large number KIA. By 2300, the 1st Battalion had fought itself into the outskirts of Cheneux. At 0200 on 21 December, G Company was committed to continue the attack, which commenced at 0245. In the face of enemy fire from 20mm cannon, machine guns, artillery, and mortars, G Company suffered heavy casualties; their attack was repulsed by the German panzers and SS troops.

For the rest of that night, the 1st Battalion dug in, preparing for an enemy counterattack. At 0745 on 21 December the Germans attacked, preceded by a half-hour artillery barrage and supported by 20mm cannons. The 1st Battalion countered with artillery and 81mm mortar fire and beat them back, inflicting heavy casualties. The 1st Battalion then resumed the attack, committing the reserve, G Company, along with two tank destroyers, and pursued the retreating enemy.

Meanwhile, my platoon and H Company moved forward in a series of probing actions, then overran the village of Monceau, lightly held by the enemy. Then we turned to attack Cheneux from the north. Until then, Cheneux had not come into my gun sights. The town was of no consequence to me except that it represented the enemy's advanced point of penetration in the Battle of the Bulge. We had broken camp hurriedly at Sissonne and had come a long way to meet the Germans head-on.

The battle began with the 1st Battalion and elements of the 1st SS Panzer Division in deadly combat, often hand to hand, for control of the town. Cheneux now became more than just a spot on the map. It will forever be remembered by both friend and foe as a place where many gallant young men died in fierce combat. As we proceeded to attack the town from the north, I was aware that German resistance had been fierce and the purpose of our flanking movement was to relieve some of the pressure on the 1st Battalion.

Corporal George Graves, 504th Regimental S1, recorded the following in his diary on 21 December:

Company B had lost all eight of its officers and the 1st Sergeant. A Staff Sergeant was commanding the remnants of the Company they believed to be about 30 men. Company C had lost five officers, about 55 men wounded, and a rough estimate of 15 killed. HQ 1st Bn had two officers killed, two or three enlisted men killed, and about 30 wounded. Company G, which had come up to reinforce them, had had its 1st Sergeant killed and some 25 men wounded. In reality, no one knew exactly who was killed and who was alive. Lt. Col. Harrison, 1st Bn Commander, said the assault across the top of the hill crossed with many barbed wire fences was far worse than any nightmare he had ever imagined as a solid sheet of 20mm flak and machine gun fire raked the assault wave from three sides. That morning they had beaten off one strong counterattack and they were wondering if they had the strength to beat off any more. Some houses in the town were occupied, but the whole town was not yet cleared. We took a rough estimate at what was thought to be the remaining strength of each Company and left for our S-1 headquarters. On the way back, I looked at some of the bodies in the ditches to see if I knew any of them—the same boys who were laughingly shouting "four more shopping days until Xmas" only the day before. I didn't recognize any personally, but I could recognize what they must have gone through. At least there was one place in this German drive where the rampaging Huns had been stopped, perhaps only temporarily, only time would tell.

On 22 December, Graves wrote the following:

About noon the 2nd Bn left their entrenched positions to relieve the 1st Bn in the town of Cheneux, now completely occupied. The shattered remnants of the 1st Bn came straggling listlessly down the road, a terrible contrast to the happy Battalion which had only two days before gone up the same road wisecracking and full of fight. They were bearded, red-eyed, covered with mud from head to foot, and staring blank-faced straight to the front. No one spoke. What few officers there were in the columns, half of what had started for Cheneux, were indistinguishable from the men except for the markings on their helmets. They carried their rifles any way that seemed comfortable, some in Daniel Boone fashion. They had written a page in history that few would ever know about. Already there was talk of a Presidential Citation to record for posterity what was plainly written on their faces that morning. To millions of Americans at home, the name Cheneux was meaningless. In the swirling holocaust of fire and fury which descended on the peaceful valley of the Ambleve River in Belgium, it might not even be mentioned in the newspapers, such was the confusion of places, units, and deeds being churned around in the "witch's brew" which was the present battle of the Ardennes.

This was the situation at Cheneux as the 3d Battalion, less G Company, approached Cheneux from the north. The terrain around the town was hilly, and as we approached in two columns, with H and I Companies abreast, we were careful to take advantage of available cover to avoid detection from enemy gunners. Behind the crest of a hill just outside Cheneux and the Ambleve River, H Company deployed as skirmishers.

Rivers and I were leading our platoons down the barren hill when we were fired upon by enemy 20mm flak wagons and machine guns. When the Germans opened fire, I was about halfway down the hill heading for the Ambleve River. The shrapnel from the exploding 20mm shells initially took a heavy toll in wounded men, forcing those who had just started down the forward crest to seek cover behind the hill. I was at least halfway down the forward slope, so instinctively I charged down the hill in the direction of enemy fire rather than retreating for cover behind the hill. In my combat experience, I learned that in a situation such as this, the best course of action was to charge in the direction of the enemy fire. The enemy certainly had to be confronted if we were to achieve our objective. I reached the bottom of the hill along with five other men, including Lieutenant Murphy and Pvt. Donald Herndon. We took cover along the bank of the Ambleve River in a growth of brush and saplings hidden from the view of the flak wagons. Meanwhile, the remnants of the battalion picked up the wounded and took cover behind the hill. The battle site suddenly became quiet. Sergeant Tarbell recalled:

As we charged down the hill, the flak wagons turned their weapons on us. We had many casualties from that encounter. There was a captain with us from Service Company who was severely wounded and eventually died. Another of our men was wounded in the leg and was yelling like a stuck pig. The officer told him to quiet down, that he was not hit that bad. I helped with the wounded by getting them out of the line of fire and onto the trucks which were parked nearby to get them to a medical station. We were pinned down awhile from the 20mm shrapnel. The trucks with wounded were unable to move for quite a while. Just before dark, I walked over to see some of the wounded, as they had not moved out yet. All of our casualties were wounded, except for the one captain from Service Company. There again a lot of the casualties were unknown to us, having just joined us as replacements for losses in Holland. The same thing always enters your mind after things cool down a little: When is my time coming? Men are being hit all around you and you are not hit, but you worry about the law of averages.

Some soldiers felt that when their time comes, the delivery will be made by a bullet with their name on it. Others, such as Tarbell, believed in the law of averages. If we lost 50 percent and upward of our combat strength on missions with extended days on the line, such as Anzio, it would be only a matter of time until the arithmetic would catch up with us.

I believed that the bullets fired in my direction carried the caption "to whom it may concern." The bullets did not differentiate among Catholics, Protestants, and Jews; between blacks and whites; between officers and enlisted men; between young and old. These bullets did not distinguish between armed soldiers and unarmed medical corpsmen, between doctors wearing Red Cross patches and chaplains armed only with a cross. Anyone who came face-to-face with the enemy and within range of enemy fire became the target of "to whom it may concern." Those "it did not concern" included the millions of servicemen in the States, the millions more in the rear echelons overseas, and the tens of thousands out of range in the higher commands. The Germans had yet to perfect a weapon that could reach them.

From our covered positions along the riverbank, we were able to view much enemy armor: Mark VI tanks, 77mm self-propelled guns, half-tracks, 105mm howitzers, and 20mm (SP) cannons, all part of the 1st SS Panzer Division. If we had had the weapons to engage them, they would have been tempting targets, but our small arms would not have fazed them.

We were in a precarious position. For the time being, our most logical course of action was to do nothing and remain concealed. A short time later, eight German soldiers approached the other side of the river from us and proceeded to dig an emplacement for an antitank gun that could cover the approach to the bridge. They were probably the squad responsible for that particular gun and were most likely expecting another assault on Cheneux from the north. They were not laboring with any urgency; they went about their task with an air of casualness, completely unaware of our presence fewer than two hundred yards away. We watched them carefully and trained our sights on them, but we took no immediate action. One of them walked down to the bridge, crossed it, then returned. He probably was the squad leader, but he was indistinguishable from the rest.

While this was going on, I weighed our alternatives. We were separated from the rest of the battalion, with no means of communicating with them and uncertain of their location and disposition. We had been in this concealed position for what seemed like an eternity but was really only several hours. I concluded that we could do nothing and remain in our present concealed position until darkness fell, then make a mad dash along the Ambleve River, wind around the hill, and come back to our starting point. We would then rejoin H Company, if they were still there. Or we could attempt to crawl or move quietly, taking advantage of what cover and concealment the riverbank offered to try to get around the hill before the enemy could fire at us. Or we could carry out the second alternative after exacting a toll on the enemy. The eight men with their heavy weapons were within easy killing range for the small arms we were carrying, although this would expose our position to the enemy and bring a hail of fire on us.

The prospect of killing eight German soldiers was the deciding factor for us. Five of us were combat-hardened veterans, and the rules of the game were clear. Whenever a man had a German soldier in his sight, he would pull the trigger and take his chances.

Often when I wrote home, I would say, "I'm out hunting Germans again." Too often, we were the hunted and they the predators, but here we were looking down their throats. Given this situation, we should choose the third alternative: Unload the clips in our weapons and drop the Germans in the hole they were digging, then run along the river to the rear of the hill.

Quietly, I passed the word along: "Fire on my order, unload your guns, then make a mad dash for it." In rapid order, we unloaded on those eight unsuspecting Germans. Although a body count was not possible, I am certain they all ended up in the hole.

The 20mm flak wagon gunners almost immediately opened fire. The six of us, now running as low to the ground as we could, tried to get around the bend of the river and behind the hill, where we would be safe from fire. Enemy artillery was chopping down leaves and branches, and shrapnel was pouring down on us. We had about seventy-five yards to traverse through heavy brush and foliage before we would reach a safe position.

Just ahead of me, and about halfway to safety, one of the men was hit in the leg, and his paced slowed. I hefted him over my shoulder and continued our frantic dash. Fortunately, no one else was hit, and we were able to reach safe cover around the hill. The wounded man was Pvt. Donald Herndon, who had been in my platoon since he came to H Company in Holland as a replacement.

In short order, we were reunited with H Company, which remained under cover behind the hill. Captain Kappel was certain that we were casualties, either killed or missing. This was not the first time I had become separated from the company during the war and was assumed to have been either dead or missing in action.

Herndon was sent back to the regimental aid station and from there eventually to an army hospital in Liège, somewhere along the line getting gangrene in his leg that he recalled was due to dirty or unchanged bandages. From the hospital in Liège, he was evacuated to a hospital in Bath, England. Fortunately he recovered and, after three months, returned to H Company at the Rhine River. He remained with us through the end of the war, the occupation of Berlin, and the victory parade in New York in January 1946. He then mustered out of the army and, within a week after donning civilian clothes, returned to finish high school; then he headed to the University of Georgia. It was only since my research of the action at Cheneux that Herndon and I were able to confirm the narrative in the citation for the Silver Star I received. Prior to that I did not recall the name of the wounded man, nor did Herndon recall who had picked him up and carried him to safety.

When I rejoined the battalion, G and H Companies were preparing to resume the attack and enter Cheneux. During the time we were in position along the banks of the Ambleve, we noted the locations of enemy gun positions and 20mm flak wagons. From a map of the immediate area, I was able to determine the coordinates of the enemy positions. Lieutenant Allen F. McClain of Headquarters Company brought up the 81mm mortars and, before resuming our attack on Cheneux, was able to bring fire on enemy positions from the coordinates I had marked on the map.

At the same time, 1st Battalion, after beating back a counterattack, pushed forward into Cheneux, and H and I Companies, 3d Battalion, advanced into the city from the north. At 1700 Cheneux was firmly in our control. The remaining elements of the badly battered 1st German SS Panzer Division were able to withdraw and move to another area to resume their attack. We would meet elements of that division again.

By nightfall on 21 December, the bloody battle for Cheneux was history, with losses heavy on both sides. A captured German stated that five companies of SS infantry had been annihilated. When we entered Cheneux, I saw burning vehicles, half-tracks, SP guns, and a Mark VI tank littering the main road through the town. The enemy's 20mm flak wagons had been particularly effective against our attacking infantry. B Company, 1st Battalion, bore the brunt of the battle. H Company had one officer killed, one officer wounded, and ten enlisted men wounded. Lieutenant E. J. Sims recalled that when we entered Cheneux, he felt a wetness on his left hip; when he reached back, he discovered that his canteen had been penetrated by a slug.

The men and officers of the 504th fought with courage and determination in the face of great odds, pushing forward in spite of heavy casualties. In his after-action report on Cheneux, General Gavin wrote: "The fighting at Cheneux was increasing in bitterness and in a final, all-out assault on the Germans in the town and in close, hand-to-hand fighting, many of the parachute troops jumped aboard the German half-tracks and knifed the Germans at their posts. The Germans were driven back across the Ambleve River and our troops seized the bridge. In this attack we destroyed a considerable amount of armor and killed and captured many Germans from First SS Panzer Division."

Cheneux was only a blip on the map of Belgium—a city of no consequence in the path of the German advance—but for the fact that this was where the German blitzkrieg was first turned back. It blunted the German offensive, although it did not stop it. German units were still attacking along a broad front; momentum, at least for the time being, was on their side. Cheneux was the first town taken back from the Germans in the Battle of the Bulge. All up and down the Belgian front, men were being led by NCOs and junior officers, often against heavily armed forces, to thwart and drive back the juggernaut the Germans had assembled. The actions of small units, taken together, made up the big picture being reported in terms of divisions and corps. While we were engaged at Cheneux, other units were also engaged with the elements of the same panzer division in a line through Trois Ponts, Ottre, and Regne. The story there was much like ours: lightly armed troops battling a heavily armed German division.

We spent the night of 21 December in Cheneux, moving the platoons in H Company to a perimeter defense of the city. It was the first time since leaving Sissonne that we were not on the move in trucks or plowing through deep snow in our hunt for Germans. The story of the 101st Airborne Division is similar to ours. They left the base camp several hours after we did and had combat elements in place in Bastogne at about the same time.

It must have been comforting to our supreme commander's senior staff members, who were caught unaware of the massive German buildup and counterattack on two green American divisions, to have two tested, combat-hardened divisions in reserve, ready to move on short notice. Sometimes, lady luck or fate can smile on errant senior commanders. Such was the case here with General Eisenhower, who had been asleep at the switch.

Cheneux was now history. It was firmly in our control as we pondered our next move. The Germans were still on the offensive and had to be stopped and turned back. We had been in action for less than a week, and a long, arduous campaign lay ahead. After Cheneux, there would be other cities to fight for, rivers to cross, and high ground to seize. The regiment had suffered heavy casualties thus far in the Battle of the Bulge. Replacements would soon be arriving to keep our combat units at or near combat strength. The pipeline of young replacements, many just out of high school and still in their teens, was reinforcing the airborne divisions in Europe and one airborne division in the Pacific as fast as paratroopers could be qualified.

One of these replacements was my brother Louis, nine years my junior. He had graduated from high school, volunteered for the paratroopers, and shipped out to the Pacific theater as a replacement in the 11th Airborne Division. When I first heard that he had volunteered for the paratroopers, I was at the same time concerned and proud: concerned because he was certain to see combat, but proud because he had the guts to do it. He certainly could have chosen an easier and safer place to serve. On 27 March 1944, I received a letter from home saying he had been wounded in action. In his short military career, he had risen to the rank of platoon sergeant and was leading his platoon against entrenched Japanese in the battle for Manila when he was shot in the shoulder.

But how about our enemy, the Germans? They too were absorbing heavy casualties on four fronts at the time they were being mauled at Cheneux. Where would their replacements come from? Could they measure up to the Germans whom they were replacing? Were they the caliber of our young replacements? Other than the SS panzer units we confronted in the Battle of the Bulge, the Wehrmacht was scraping the bottom of the barrel in order to man their combat units. Younger Germans, some barely sixteen years old, were being drafted, and men older than fifty with families were filling the depleted ranks of their units.

On 23 December the situation along the division front was still confused. Germans were reported to be wearing American uniforms and using American armor. They were well equipped and fighting with unusual spirit. Heavy fighting was being reported over a wide area. It was time for us to move out and start hunting Germans again, but first we had to find them. On 24 December we moved out early in the morning and headed in a southerly direction to Lierneux, about twelve miles away, with orders to seize and occupy the high ground southwest of the city. The weather was bitterly cold, with fresh snow blanketing hills and valleys. The going was slow and rugged, and the delays in our march were frequent as we attempted to discern our location. Unused roads heavily covered with snow made it difficult to follow a map. I was with the point leading the battalion column and had to go entirely by compass, taking frequent azimuth readings to maintain our direction. Occasionally, when I halted the battalion, Lt. Col. Julian Cook, the battalion commander, would come up to the point and check with me. It was an eerie feeling, not being able to identify any roads or terrain features. The day was clear, although cold, and visibility was good—for us as well as the enemy. The clear weather brought out the U.S. Air Force, and they were active along our entire front, bombing and strafing enemy armor and personnel. There was no doubt that the planes were ours, and a welcome sight.

The elements were hard on the men. We paused frequently for short breaks and to get our bearings. At every break, we would get off our feet and shed our packs and some of the weight we were carrying. A big concern was the effect that the bitter cold was having on our hands and feet. During several delays en route to Lierneux, word would pass through the column that "this is it, men," as was frequently the case in forced marches. Few men in the battalion column knew where we were with respect to our final destination, and any of the stops could have been "it." After the men fell out of the column, the word would go out to "smoke if you got them," and almost everyone did. One word we did not have to pass along to combat veterans during a rest stop was "dig in." Whenever we were approaching an enemy position and within range of their artillery, the entrenching tool car-

ried on our belts automatically came out and went to work.
A hole in the ground can be a welcome place when enemy
artillery is nearby. But because on this march, digging a hole
in the frozen tundra was out of the question, the men would
look for anything in the terrain that might shield them from
incoming shrapnel. Then the word would go out "on your
feet," and we would move out. I recall this particular forced
march because it was Christmas Eve, a somber, stoic occasion, no complaints, no questions, no one asking why us, no
wondering what was happening back home. We were doing
what combat soldiers do: trying to make contact with the
enemy.

It was late afternoon on 24 December when we reached
our objective, the high ground southwest of Lierneux, and
began to dig in. We had barely established a defensive position when units of the 2d SS Panzer Division attempted to
dislodge us and seize the high ground. We were able to repulse a determined effort by the Germans, suffering a minimum number of casualties and inflicting disproportionate
casualties on them. Having beaten back the enemy attack,
we continued digging in and strengthening our defensive positions in anticipation of another attack by the enemy the following morning, Christmas Day. As darkness fell, the battle
area became quiet except for the staccato of German machine pistols, and the artillery shells penetrating the air
above our heads.

We had just settled in for the night when orders came
down that we were to withdraw to a new defensive position
along the line of Bergival-Bra-Vaux-Chavanne, about five
miles to the north. The corps commander had issued an
order to all units to withdraw to a more defensible position
along a line of Trois Ponts–Erria–Manhay. The withdrawal
order did not set well with my platoon or me. General Gavin
in his after-action report was concerned with the attitude of
the troops toward the withdrawal, the division never having
made a withdrawal in its history. Gavin noted: "In all the operations in which we have participated in our two years of
combat, and there have been many of multitudinous types, I

have never seen a better executed operation than the withdrawal on Christmas Eve. The troops willingly and promptly carried into execution all the withdrawal plans, although they openly and frankly criticized it and failed to understand the necessity for it."

Christmas Eve 1944 was cold, bright, and moonlit. Although the Germans were closely engaged with us, the withdrawal went smoothly. Sergeant Tarbell recalled: "It seemed as though we would just get set up, then we would receive orders to move out again. We had to move back to another line of defense; in other words, we were making a strategic withdrawal to consolidate our defenses. We started moving out at approximately 2000 hours, and what a walk that was! We walked across fields, roads, and whatever. I ended up in front of the column quite a few times. Whenever we came to a fence that had to be cut, I would use a pair of TL29 pliers to cut the wire. As we were moving along, the engineers were blowing down the trees onto the road for blocking, anything to place obstacles in the path of German tanks and infantry. We could hear armor behind us. Whether they were ours or the enemy's, we did not know. It was past midnight when we reached our destination (BRA). What a Christmas Eve it was!"

By that time, the German offensive through the Ardennes penetrated almost sixty miles behind Allied front lines, creating a salient six miles wide.

The 307th Airborne Engineer Battalion, the same unit that had helped us across the Waal, was supporting the division withdrawal by blowing bridges over the Salm River, laying minefields, and establishing roadblocks.

We reached the southern edge of Bra around midnight or shortly thereafter on Christmas Day. My platoon and I dug in on the high ground with a field of fire to the south. My foxhole, the platoon CP, was just behind and central to my three squads. The H Company CP was about two hundred yards to the rear in a house occupied by a Belgian family: husband, wife, and two small children. I felt the Germans would be in hot pursuit and hunting us. They were still on the offensive over a wide area of the Belgian front, and we were in their way. Another head-on collision was imminent; but unlike the battle for Cheneux only several days ago, we were in a defensive position.

It was several hours before we were in place. I made the rounds to ascertain that sufficient security was present to permit the men to get badly needed rest. It had been a long, grueling day of forced marches and contact with the enemy. It did not seem that only one week ago we had spent the night in the relative calm of Sissonne. Actually, the first week of the Battle of the Bulge seemed more like an eternity ago.

We were now in combat within a confused, fluid situation, and Germans had yet to be repelled. There were no Christmas services behind us, no Christmas revelers, no carols being sung, just weary, bedraggled young men preparing for an enemy attack certain to hit us. As we grabbed a couple of hours of badly needed sleep, the question of "when" remained.

On 25 December I awoke to another cold, wintry day in Belgium, and a K-ration breakfast. Although the ration had a packet of soluble coffee, I had no water-heating device. I was wearing the same combat suit I had on when we left Sissonne and had not had my boots off or changed socks during that entire time. I made a quick check of my squad positions, then proceeded to check with Rivers, whose platoon was dug in and on line on our right. It had been a quiet night, with no enemy patrols or incoming artillery. We knew that would not last. As I ate my K ration that morning, I imagined that the rear echelon would be feasting on turkey.

It was no different for our enemy, the German soldier. What he saw through the sights of his gun were American paratroopers standing in the way of his objective. Nothing else mattered: the calendar, his family back home, his own personal comforts, what the German high command was doing, what his rear echelon would be eating on that particular Christmas Day. He had his orders as we had ours, and successfully completing his mission was his only concern.

In the meantime, elements of the German 9th SS Panzer Division had moved up and taken positions opposite us in a wooded area that offered them a degree of concealment from friendly planes. They began probing our defensive positions with combat patrols operating all along the 3d Battalion front. Later that Christmas morning, one of those patrols came within range of my platoon's weapons. From our entrenched position, we opened fire, killing several men and scattering the rest. Most of the patrol retreated for cover, but three of them huddled under a wing of a downed but still intact B-17 airplane about three hundred yards in front of my platoon's position. We poured a lot of small-arms fire in their direction, but when I went out to check the plane after dark, I found no bodies. No other enemy soldiers had attempted to probe or penetrate my platoon's positions on that Christmas Day, nor did we see any in our gun sights. Apparently, the German patrol had returned to its lines with the information it sought.

The specter of that downed B-17 and the elements of the German patrol that used it as a cover haunted me. When the enemy made his major frontal attack on us, he could use the B-17 for cover as he advanced. Something had to be done about it. I got word back to battalion that I wanted to booby-trap the plane and blow it up in the event that Germans approached it and used it for cover. I was certain that two hundred pounds of composition C with primer cord leading to my foxhole and a detonating device would do it.

There was no hesitation in acceding to my request; it seemed like a great idea, worthy of the effort. Shortly after dark, the engineers reported to my platoon position, ready to proceed. I took several men with me to accompany the engineers and provide security. In short order, the explosive was placed in the plane and wired up, ready for detonation. All that night and into the next day, that wired plane was the center of my attention. If there was any way I could have enticed the Germans to head for it, I would have done it.

That night, when I checked on my three squads, they were alert and ready. They recounted the action with the

German patrol and how they had unloaded on them, except for the light machine gun I had placed in the center of the platoon. It was manned by two new replacements, one of whom I remember because he was of Greek descent. They did not fire a round; either their gun jammed or they didn't react quickly enough to the brief engagement. I took pains to ensure that did not happen again, because the next German attack would be in greater force.

After the German patrol was beaten back early on Christmas Day, the enemy made no further attempts to probe our defensive positions or attack in force. The battlefield quieted down, enabling us to strengthen our defensive line in the expectation that the Germans were preparing for an attack in force—and soon. They had come a long way since 16 December and, although they had encountered stiff resistance and been driven back, they still were on the attack. The tide of battle had not yet turned. The next several days would be crucial if they were to achieve their ambitious objectives.

On Christmas Day, the 504th Regiment occupied positions along the line Bergival-Bra-Vaux-Chavanne, with the 2d and 3d Battalions on line and the 1st Battalion in reserve. All elements of the 82d Airborne Division were in position, with the 7th Armored Division defending on our right and the 30th Division on our left.

All along the front men were digging in and stringing barbed wire; engineers were laying minefields to cover avenues of approach to our defensive positions. Signal units were laying communication lines between units in rough terrain and under great difficulties. We were ready for whatever the 9th SS Panzer and the 62d Volks Grenadier Divisions would throw at us.

Taking advantage of the lull on Christmas afternoon, the three platoon leaders were called back to the H Company CP for a briefing. A Belgian family of four, including two small children, was still occupying the house. They ignored warnings to evacuate and were planning to observe Christmas there, regardless of the impending threat to their safety. The Christmas dinner, a pot roast, was cooking on a wood-burning stove. Most Belgians in Bra and the surrounding area had already left. For days, the roads leading out of the path of the advancing panzers had been clogged with refugees trying to escape. In most cases, they did not have to be ordered to leave.

Corporal George Graves wrote the following in his diary: "Christmas 1944 was a tragic day for the citizens of the tiny village of BRA-SUR-LIENNE. The village was in danger of being overrun if we were unable to hold our present position, which was not too secure, to say nothing of the positive certainty of its being heavily shelled by the enemy. The orders were given early in the morning for the evacuation of all civilians. All but the very old and sick would go on foot. Trucks were supposed to be provided for the tiniest children, the aged, and the sick. They never came. I was impressed with the fact that we were so much better off than these Belgian civilians. It was just another day, and a sad one at that, to them. . . . An old lady with two infants in her arms said bravely, 'We went through all this in 1940 and now once more. When will it all end?' There was little we could do or say to comfort them as they snatched up a few bare essentials for the trip on foot. It was a tragic sight to see them shuffling off down the dirt road out of reach of the German guns."

Captain Carl Kappel, H Company commander, and Lt. E. J. Sims, executive officer, urged the Belgian family of four to pack and leave before all hell broke loose at Bra. But the family insisted on observing Christmas, not knowing whether the house would remain intact for any more holiday celebrations.

When Rivers arrived at the H Company CP, he refused to accept the presence of the Belgian family or a delay in their departure. Not only might they be in imminent danger when the Germans attacked, but they could be a problem for us. He soon lost his patience with them, demanding they leave immediately and threatening to oust them forcibly if they did not. There would be other Christmases and family observances if they survived, but that might not be the case if they attempted to ride it out in their cellar.

Apparently, they understood. They bundled up to face the frigid Belgian winter, gathering up what personal belongings they could carry and leaving to join the mass of refugees heading west. Their destination, how they would travel and be cared for, and how soon they might be able to return were not our concern. Elements of our rear echelon would be charged with those matters.

In their hurry to leave, the family left Christmas dinner boiling on the stove. I remember Rivers saying, "There's no reason to let a perfectly good pot roast go to waste." So we sat down and enjoyed a home-cooked Christmas dinner. I joined in eating their dinner; however, given the circumstances and the fact that it was the holiest of days, I had a sick feeling in my stomach.

On 26 December, the Germans renewed their patrol activity along the entire 3d Battalion front, probing to find a weak spot in our lines. In H Company, we continued to strengthen our defenses, enlarge our foxholes, string concertina wire, and lay mines. That afternoon, we set up eight-man outposts ahead of our lines to observe and report on enemy activity. Extra ammunition was issued to the men with instructions to keep low during the artillery barrage that most certainly would precede an enemy attack. Regardless of what the Germans would throw at us, the men were told to stay in their foxholes and, when the enemy approached, open fire on them until they were overcome.

If the enemy came out of the wooded area, charging at us as we anticipated, we would be looking down their throats and they would pay a terrible price. Since 18 December we had been on the attack. Now the tables would be turned: They would be attacking us.

That night, Sgt. Robert A. Tague, a squad leader in Rivers's platoon, called the H Company CP from an outpost. He reported that the woods in front of us were full of German soldiers. It would be only a matter of time before they came storming out of the woods in a full frontal attack.

That same night, Rivers and I were at the Company CP when we received a call from one of our forward outposts that they were bringing in a German prisoner. A young SS trooper—wounded, incoherent, and disoriented—had wandered into our outpost carrying a Mauser rifle and a box of machine-gun ammunition. When he arrived at the CP, he was still carrying the box of ammo, which, Sergeant Tarbell recalled, also contained a small slab of bacon. He had been shot in the head and had been lying on the battlefield for some time, yet somehow managed to get up and walk. A bullet had entered the front left side of his head, leaving a wide, deep gash that exposed his brain. He was a horrible sight; it was a miracle that he was still alive. His eyes were glassy. Other than an occasional groan, he was unable to utter a sound or communicate. I saw many Germans, dead and wounded, during the course of the war, but no one quite as grotesque as he.

Sergeant Tarbell recalled: "We were able to take him back to the Aid Station, but not without some difficulty. How a man with his head split wide open can walk at all was beyond my ability to comprehend. Our medics had their hands full with our own wounded, but they sat him down to look at him. The medics didn't hold out much hope for him, but said if he were still alive in the morning they would send him back to the hospital with the other wounded. I inquired about him the next day and was told that he was still alive when they put him in the ambulance going to the hospital. We inquired about him later. We were told that he would survive, but that he would not be a whole person."

The following morning, Lieutenant Sims, the executive officer, while checking the company's defensive positions, noted a hidden road on the right flank of Rivers's platoon that could be used by the enemy in an attack. Sims sent word to Rivers that he wanted to go over our company's defensive position with him. Sims recalled:

There was a photographer from the U.S. Army newspaper, *Stars & Stripes,* at the H Company CP. His purpose was to take pictures of the men on the front lines at the Battle of the Bulge. Instead of providing him an escort, I invited him to accompany me on an inspection of our company lines. On our way to Rivers' CP, I talked to Lt. Megellas, whose platoon was dug in on the left and tied in with Rivers' platoon. After I explained that I was concerned about the company's right flank, Megellas decided to accompany us.

While I was pointing out the hidden road to Rivers that the Germans might use in attacking H Company, we spotted a German patrol heading towards our lines. The four of us—Megellas, Rivers, the photographer, and I—started for cover, and engaged in a firefight with the German patrol. Lt. Megellas tossed a fragmentation grenade that exploded in the midst of them, causing some casualties and forcing the patrol to scatter. Several of the men from Rivers' platoon joined us in the firefight.

When the shooting stopped, we went into the area where we had spotted the patrol. We took one SS trooper prisoner and noted several dead Germans who were left behind when the patrol withdrew. After this action, we shifted our right flank to cover this hidden road that was used by the patrol.

The *Stars & Stripes* photographer got more than he had bargained for, and the scare of his life, but he also got close-up shots of paratroopers in action. One of his photographs, depicting Rivers hunkered down, leading the SS trooper back to our lines, appeared on the front page of an edition of *Stars & Stripes*. That same picture eventually found its way into the 82d Airborne Division Museum, where it was prominently displayed for a number of years.

We interrogated the prisoner at company headquarters, then sent him back to battalion. Like other privates we had captured, there was little he knew or could tell us that we did not already know. Later that afternoon, Sergeant Tague's eight-man outpost came under attack from a superior force. They were pinned down and were unable to move or withdraw to our lines. They returned fire, but their thinly held outpost was in danger of being overrun.

A call came back to Rivers's platoon CP. I was with Rivers when he got the call. Without hesitation, he took several of his men and headed for his outpost like a man shot out of a cannon. It was his outpost, his squad, his sergeant, and his men who needed help. Charging low and taking advantage of available cover, he was able to reach his beleaguered outpost.

I waited anxiously for my closest buddy to return to our lines, not knowing the situation and concerned that he might not make it back. After an agonizing period, he returned with the six men from his outpost, bringing with them the bodies of Tague and Pfc. Clarence C. Smith, both killed in action.

Corporal George D. Graves had known Tague for several years. He wrote the following in his diary: "I got up at 0630. Upon going outside I looked in the death trailer of 'Judge' Vance's Grave Registration Jeep. To my horror, I recognized that carrot top of Red Tague along with three other corpses. He had just come back to duty the day before after having been wounded in the Waal River crossing in Holland. The last time I had seen him was in the aid station on the south bank of the river when he had weakly called my name and asked for a cigarette. He had been my squad Sgt. for nine months in Fort Bragg. I stood staring at him for a full 3 minutes before I turned away with a bad frog in my throat. Somehow, the frozen bodies looked miserable even in death."

Because of his immediate, heroic action, and after a fierce firefight, Rivers was able to rescue the six survivors and returned to our lines at the risk of his own life. He could have sent one of his other squads to their rescue, but this was a job for a leader, not a commander.

It was cold and miserable in Bra on 28 December, so cold that the water in our canteens froze. A light snow had fallen during the night, adding to the accumulation that already blanketed the countryside.

The men in the foxholes got little uninterrupted sleep that night. There were not enough blankets, and the threat of an enemy patrol sneaking up on us kept the men in a constant state of alert. They strained to listen for strange sounds and look for shadowy figures moving in the dark.

Nights on the line were eerie and lonely, and a man's imagination could run wild. In the solitude of a dark, quiet night on the line, a teenage soldier could relive his entire life. There was no talking among the men in the holes for fear of revealing our position; voices could be heard a long way. There was no lighting of cigarettes, because the flame from a match could be seen for a great distance. The men were always hungry at night, for frozen K rations did not ease their hunger. A hot meal when we were on the front was out of the question and was never expected.

Leaving the foxholes to move around to restore circulation and freezing feet could leave us vulnerable to incoming mortars and artillery. If it was clear, we could look up at the stars and find serenity and companionship in the sky. Spending one night in a frozen foxhole on the line looking in the direction of an enemy intent on killing you was unforgettable. Spending sixty continuous days on the line without relief was hell.

We had been in Belgium for ten days battling the elements and the advancing German army. During the night, the Germans intensified their artillery barrage, pounding the front line, the village of Bra, and the roads leading into it. All around us, the ground seemed to tremble.

Early on 28 December, every man was alert, ready, and waiting for the expected attack. For three days, the Germans had been pounding us with artillery and probing our position with patrols. I checked my platoon defenses early that morning to see if the men were in good shape and our weapons in firing condition with plenty of ammunition. To each man I passed words of encouragement.

At about 0900, the Germans opened up with mortar fire on our entrenched positions, then followed with heavy artillery. Behind the artillery barrage, the infantry charged out of their concealed positions. They came at us waving their arms and weapons and letting out blood-curdling yells. Behind them, German machine guns opened up, providing overhead fire for the advancing troops, while their artillery kept pounding our positions. We kept low in our deep foxholes until they got into range; then we opened up with everything we had.

Our first volley dropped a number of the enemy, but a second wave soon followed, screaming and yelling and charging past their fallen comrades. Repeatedly they kept streaming out of the woods, still employing the same tactics. But in the face of our withering small-arms fire, they were unable to penetrate our positions.

In this action, I laid aside my trusted submachine gun. The tommy gun was an excellent weapon for close infighting and patrols, but it was not accurate at long range. On this occasion, with a barren and open field of fire, I relied on a sniper rifle, which was more accurate and had much greater range. All the while I kept my eye on the booby-trapped B-17 sitting out in no-man's-land, hoping that the charging men would take cover behind the fuselage. But they never gave me an opportunity to pull the cord and set it off.

Suddenly the Germans withdrew to the cover of their concealed positions in the woods, leaving the battlefield littered with their dead. Their attack was at a terrible price. The remnants of what must have been a battalion withdrew with their wounded to regroup. After that beating, I doubted whether they had the resources to launch another attack. But we stayed on the alert and were ready for them if they did.

After the action was over, I checked my platoon line and found the men in good spirits. Each man had fired his weapon in rapid fire. The two new men on the machine gun had not frozen, as they had earlier. This time, their holes and the ground around them were littered with spent cartridges and empty boxes of ammo. We did not have a casualty—a testimony to the effort we had made to prepare defensive positions, and to the squad leaders who had the men prepared, ready, and determined.

To varying degrees, all units of the 504th had similar experiences. A battalion from another regiment of the 82d on our left, defending the village of Erria, counted sixty-two dead Germans in one field in front of their machine guns. All along the line, the Germans had used the same tactics: yelling and screaming like fanatics and charging into intense small-arms fire.

A captured SS officer told me they had used that tactic to break through American lines on 16 December and in attacks since then. He said we were the first troops they faced who hadn't broken ranks and run. I knew that the difference was that we were well-led, combat-hardened troops, whereas the soldiers who had broken ranks and fled were green troops. In combat, there is no substitute for experience and leadership.

That night, Rivers and I left our foxholes and went out to check on the enemy carnage. We found no wounded soldiers, but the Germans had made no attempt to retrieve their dead. We kicked over some of the bodies and made a cursory search to relieve them of any valuables they had with them. They, like us, seldom carried anything of value or any personal identification into combat. The pickings were slim: a few pocket watches, SS skull and crossbones, rings, and some wallets. The most prized possessions, P38 and Luger pistols, were seldom found on low-ranking men. The wallets contained little of value, usually no IDs, but they were generally bulging with family pictures, which revealed a lot about the German psyche. Most photos were of school-age boys wearing uniforms. In the early, heady days of the war when the blitzkrieg was sweeping across Europe, patriotism was rampant. Serving the Fatherland and wearing a uniform was a national honor, a privilege. Boys were joining patriotic groups, goose-stepping in precise formation, and extending their right arm forward and upward in a salute to the Führer.

Searching dead bodies lying on the battlefield may appear to be ghoulish; although it was not advocated, it was not an uncommon practice. When the name of the game is killing your enemy, relieving him of any possessions of value pales into insignificance by comparison. As Rivers said, "Where they are going, they won't need them."

For the next several days, we kept a vigil while the enemy remained in the general area. Though they continued to pose a threat, they did not attack us again in force. They did, however, continue their artillery barrages, targeting Bra and our supply routes. On 29 December they bombarded Bra with white phosphorus, setting houses on fire. It was the first time we'd seen the Germans using incendiaries in the Battle of the Bulge. On that day, several German planes came in low, strafing and bombing our positions, but we kept concealed in our holes and suffered no casualties.

XII

The Tide of Battle Turns

By the end of 1944, the first phase of the Battle of the Bulge was over. We had met and confronted the Germans at Cheneux on 20 December and Bra on 28 December. We stopped their momentum, and now, in our sector, the tide of the battle turned. For the next six weeks, we would be attacking and advancing.

On 31 December, a call came from division that the 504th had been given a quota of one officer and nine enlisted men to go back to the States on a thirty-day "rest and recuperation" leave. The regiment was to select men based on length of time overseas and combat and other factors deserving of consideration. In the 504th, the officer selected was Capt. Thomas C. Helgeson, B Company. He had led his company in the attack against SS panzer units at Cheneux, Belgium, on 20 December.

Helgeson was a close personal friend. His hometown, Ripon, Wisconsin, was only twenty miles from mine. I was elated to see him leave for R and R; in my mind, no one was more deserving. I contacted him to wish him well and Godspeed home. I had one request of him: If it was possible, would he visit my mother and family in Fond du Lac and assure them that I was well. He promised that he would, and he did.

For the second consecutive year, I celebrated the advent of a New Year on the line. I had been in the cold, dreary mountains just beyond Venafro, Italy, on 31 December 1943; this year I was on the line in Bra, Belgium. Just as we had come out of our tents precisely at midnight to fire weapons in the air in Italy, we ushered in the New Year in similar fashion in Bra.

Our heavy artillery behind us as though in concert with us opened up with a barrage exactly at midnight, sending New Year's greetings to the Germans. That was the extent of our New Year's Eve celebration, but we could not help but wonder how people were celebrating back home. I was more optimistic at the end of 1944 than I had been in Italy a year earlier that this would be my last New Year's Eve in combat. Everything considered, we had much more to be thankful for. We were still alive.

On 1 January 1945, I wrote the first letter of the new year home to my sister Catherine: "We rung in the New Year last night with artillery and guns but, of course, not a drink to celebrate—but maybe next year. I'm sitting in the cellar of the house I am using for a CP and I've got a little candle burning. The rest of the house is pretty well knocked down by the 88s but so far they haven't gotten the cellar—here's hoping."

On 4 January we were relieved in the Bra sector by the 329th Infantry, 83d Division, with orders to move on Fosse, Belgium, about fifteen miles southeast. Our objective: seize the high ground overlooking the Salm River and Grand Halleaux.

That morning we were pelted by a hard snowfall, wet and sticky, which added to almost eight hours of snow already on the ground. During the forced march, we were breaking trail through snowdrifts waist deep in some places.

As was generally the case in a march over difficult terrain and in the adverse weather conditions, we left our packs and bedrolls at the takeoff point so as not to impede our pace. In Belgium, the bedroll we generally carried—draped over our backpack like a horseshoe—consisted of two army blankets and a canvas shelter half. We were told that once we reached our objective, the bedrolls and packs would be brought up to us. Our rations for the entire day (three K rations) were stuffed into the side pockets of our trousers. In the freezing weather we were facing, they would have to be eaten cold or perhaps even frozen.

It was dark when we reached our objective, the high ground in a heavily wooded area just outside Fosse. We would resume our advance to Petit Halleaux in the morning. After I had positioned my three squads for the night and had sentries posted, I looked for a spot for my platoon CP. It was impossible to dig a foxhole in the frozen ground. I remember clearing the snow behind the trunk of a large tree. This was where I would spend most of the night, without blankets or shelter of any kind. Attempting to sleep or even lie down on the frozen ground in temperatures that dropped below zero that night was out of the question.

For supper, we ate the last of our three K rations. There was no way we could heat them. A flame of any kind would expose our positions and bring artillery fire in on us. Sergeant Tarbell remembered that cold night and what reportedly was the coldest winter in Belgium in twenty years: "We were on top of a mountain or a high hill and were getting casualties. Everyone was perspiring from the climbing and the adrenaline rush. We found a Company CP area around some trees and put our casualties there. There was only one blanket among us so we used that to cover our wounded. I found a small tree that I could put my hands on and started to walk around it to keep from freezing during the night. After awhile, three others joined me. A person can sleep and walk like that. We told the newer men not to fall asleep because they could freeze. That had to be one of the longest nights I ever spent."

Our bedrolls never caught up with us, so to keep warm and get a little rest, a man would cuddle up with a buddy on the frozen ground. We welcomed the dawn of the new day tired, cold, and hungry but still alive. Some of the men were sent back to the aid station with frozen feet, but fortunately most of us made it through the night unscathed.

That morning, several hundred yards below us on a narrow road, we saw the Germans moving horse-drawn caissons. It was the first time I'd ever seen horses used in combat.

It was also a sign that the Germans were running short of fuel and had to rely on other means to move equipment and artillery. They vanished in the heavily wooded area before we could bring fire down on them.

We ran several patrols ahead of our position trying to contact the Germans, but we encountered only light and scattered resistance. A single unarmed German soldier came out of the woods and surrendered to me. I was not in a position to care for a prisoner or escort him to the rear. About that time I saw my battalion commander, Lieutenant Colonel Cook, behind me heading to his CP. He agreed to relieve me of the prisoner, but I noticed he was unarmed, so I offered him my Colt .45. He replied, "Maggie, I don't need a weapon. You've got him so scared he isn't about to cause a problem."

Later that morning, we moved out of the high ground where we had spent the night and headed for our objective. Corporal Graves made the following entry in his diary: "Just outside Fosse, we passed the 3rd Battalion stumbling along in columns on either side of the road. . . . They looked like creatures from another world with 10 days grimy beards plus a blue tinge in their faces from the extreme cold . . . yet their ordeal was just beginning."

About two weeks earlier, German SS panzer units had rolled through Fosse, leaving behind a path of death and destruction. German bodies littered the streets, stark testimony to the fighting that had taken place. The town had been reduced to rubble, with few homes left intact. These were the same SS units we had met, bloodied, and turned back at Bra, twenty-five miles to the northwest.

The enemy we were encountering now offered only sporadic resistance, bearing little resemblance to the elite SS units we had faced earlier. What we saw now were poorly trained and led German soldiers, a hodgepodge of service troops, conscripts from satellite countries, and young and old recruits scraped from the bottom of the manpower barrel. They did little more than slow our advance and certainly posed no serious threat to our reaching our objectives. However, German artillery was having an effect and continued to be a factor to contend with. Our commander, Capt. Carl Kappel, was seriously wounded by shrapnel and had to be evacuated. Sergeant Tarbell had spent the night in a hayloft above the battalion aid station where he had been treated for frozen feet. He recalled: "That morning there was a lot of commotion on the barn floor. I got up and looked down rows of stretchers and ambulances pulling in and out of the yard. On one of the stretchers I saw what looked like my Company Commander, Captain Kappel. I went down the ladder and headed for the ambulance where they had placed the stretcher. It was Captain Kappel. He was badly wounded and told me what had happened. PFC Philip Foley, who had taken my place as Company radioman, was killed. Phil Foley had been in Paris on leave when we left for the Bulge. He had just returned to the company from the rear echelon."

Once again, Lieutenant Sims assumed command and continued the attack on Petit Halleaux. Kappel was sent to a hospital in the rear. Shrapnel had entered his stomach, causing intestinal damage, but he recovered and returned to command H Company again in May 1945.

In addition to the casualties from German artillery and snipers, the severe Belgian winter was taking a toll on our ranks. Men were being sent to the medics with swollen feet, barely able to walk. Some of the least affected were kept overnight, treated at the aid station, and returned to their units. The more serious cases were hospitalized. Many men lost toes; in some cases amputation of feet was necessary. If frostbite was not quickly and properly treated, gangrene set in, requiring amputation. During the Battle of the Bulge, about 45,000 U.S. combat soldiers most susceptible to the cold were removed from the line because of trench foot.

Yet, despite the seriousness of trench foot, care and treatment of feet by frontline soldiers was next to impossible. I, like most men in my platoon, went into combat and to the front lines with just the clothes on my back. Brushing my teeth or taking a bath were luxuries I hardly ever knew in combat. I seldom found an opportunity to remove my boots or use other means to dry or change socks. When we were on the line in a fluid situation, such as we experienced in the snow and cold of Belgium, we had to be ready for action with only the slightest notice.

On 7 January, we, accompanied by two supporting tank destroyers (TDs), moved out to seize Petit Halleaux and control of the high ground overlooking the Salm River. Along our entire front line, only a few enemy units made a determined effort to impede our advance.

Sergeant Charles Crowder recalled: "We had walked about four or five miles through two feet of snow and had taken up positions on the high ground overlooking Grand Halleaux. . . . At daybreak, I left with three men—Albert Tarbell, Andy Kendrot, and Joe Ludwig—to return to our starting point and escort a Jeep carrying ammunition and rations to our lines. On the way back, we encountered no opposition; but about halfway back to the Company, we ran into small arms fire. We dispersed and returned fire, and in about 10 minutes, it was over. Five enemy were killed and one who was talking in a language I did not understand was badly wounded. Someone said he was speaking Polish and wanted help, that he was in terrible pain. One of our men said, 'I'll help him,' pulled out his pistol, shot him in the head, and said, 'Now he's not in pain.' Four of these men were wearing American fatigue clothes underneath a German overcoat and cap. I believe now that these were Polish men we found on this patrol with two Germans behind them. They opened fire on us but hit no one. I believe they would have surrendered if they had a chance."

The attack progressed well for about 1,500 yards, until we encountered stiff resistance at Petit Halleaux. The Germans would not give it up without a fight. In the ensuing action, Lt. Ernest P. Murphy, a platoon leader, was cited for gallantry in action and awarded the Silver Star to go with a Bronze Star and Purple Heart he had received previously.

Technical Sergeant Eddie C. Heibert, H Company, was a rifleman in Murphy's platoon. The following is his account of that action: "One of our two supporting TDs struck a

Teller mine and was knocked out about 800 yards from the town. Six of our men were killed or wounded. At this point, enemy machine guns opened up on us and we were pinned to the ground. I saw Lieutenant Murphy crawl forward for about 50 yards under a curtain of murderous machine gun fire and call for the remaining TD to come up to him. The TD silenced two of the enemy machine guns."

Private First Class David E. Ward Jr., a rifleman in Murphy's platoon, added the following to Heibert's statement: "Lieutenant Murphy then returned to us and organized us into two squads and led our attack on the town. When we reached the town, Lieutenant Murphy ran from house to house, under heavy enemy fire, firing his Thompson submachine gun and throwing hand grenades, forcing many of the enemy to surrender."

After an intense firefight, we overcame the enemy resistance and occupied Petit Halleaux, having inflicted heavy casualties on the Germans and capturing about two hundred prisoners. The remainder of the Germans fled across the Salm River into Grand Halleaux. Our casualties were light by comparison, with the exception of Lieutenant Murphy's platoon, which lost six men when one of the TDs hit a mine.

Ward was also decorated for heroic action; his citation reads: "While pinned down in a shell hole by heavy small arms fire, one of our men was seriously wounded through the neck and was losing a considerable amount of blood. Private First-Class Ward, in the face of murderous fire, dragged the wounded man from the hole and by crawling and carrying him, started to the rear and medical aid. Under complete enemy observation and heavy fire, and even though he had been wounded in the right leg, PFC Ward refused to take cover and continued until he found medical aid for the wounded man."

On 8 January we occupied Petit Halleaux and controlled the west bank of the Salm River overlooking Grand Halleaux. As the Belgian name implies, Grand Halleaux was the larger of the two cities; they were connected by a bridge, which had not been blown. We maintained a close watch on the Salm and Grand Halleaux for signs of enemy activity.

Early the next morning, Rivers and I stood on the high ground overlooking the river looking for any sign of activity in Grand Halleaux. We did not detect anything that would suggest the town had any life, civilian or enemy. There was no telltale smoke pouring out of chimneys and houses indicating that the Germans might be preparing breakfast or trying to keep warm in freezing weather. In the center of Grand Halleaux rose a towering steeple above a large church; from there the enemy could direct artillery fire on us.

Rivers and I decided to check it out; six men from our platoons, just as curious as we were, volunteered to go with us. We went into Grand Halleaux, uncertain whether any Germans were in the town. We had informed the company commander of our intention, and he thought it was a good idea. We seldom if ever saw senior commanders on the front line and in combat. At squad and platoon level where the war was being fought, we used our best judgment, relying on one another. If anything significant happened, our commanders would learn of it in their briefings and would not hesitate to identify with favorable results.

We proceeded cautiously into Grand Halleaux, covering one another's advance from empty building to empty building. We reached the end of town; as far as we could determine, no one was there. We now felt it was safe to return and check out the church steeple. A sergeant made it to the top and found that it was unoccupied, although it was evident that the Germans had used it earlier as an observation post (OP).

While we were in the church, I decided to search it for anything we could use, such as candles. The altar in the Catholic Church resembled the one at the Greek Orthodox Church where I had served as an altar boy. I remembered the priest always having a supply of wine on hand for communion. With that in mind, I took a closer look. In the back was a sliding panel leading to a narrow passageway. Near the opening, I found a stack of candles. Not satisfied with my search, I crawled to the opposite end. My instincts were correct. At the most remote corner of the passageway, I found four bottles of wine.

I crawled back out with a firm grip on the spoils of war, possessing something we only dreamed about on the front lines: alcoholic beverages. Never mind that it was communion wine. Finding it didn't bother my conscience one bit; I was proud of the fact. Rivers, a Catholic, felt it was sacrilegious to steal wine from a church and thought I should put it back. It was a rare occasion when we were not of one mind. I kept the wine, certain that Rivers would drink his share.

It was a quiet night on the front lines, and there was no sign of the enemy, so I decided to go to the company CP and share my bonanza with Lieutenant Sims and his men. I had called Lieutenant Rivers, told him of my intention, and suggested he meet me there. Unknown to me, and as fate would have it, Father Edwin Kozak, regimental Catholic chaplain, was making the rounds and was at the CP when I arrived. Chaplain Kozak was not averse to taking a little drink now and then. As I had done in a watering hole in prewar days, I called out, "When Maggie drinks, everyone drinks," and with that I poured wine for everyone.

In a situation such as this, you don't look a gift horse in the mouth, so no one questioned the source except for Kozak. I may have done some unethical and immoral things in my days in combat, but lying to a priest was not one of them. So I related how Rivers and I had found the wine and candles. Rivers was quick to respond by pointing the finger of guilt at me. Kozak told Rivers he shouldn't have let me steal the wine. Although none of this bothered me, I didn't enter another church in my remaining years in the combat zone.

Rumors began making the rounds that we were going to be relieved on the line and sent to the rear for a period of rest and recuperation. We were in need of replacements and a respite from combat to refit and thaw out. The thought of hot food, clean clothes, and warm, soft beds danced through our heads.

Several miles behind our frontline positions, General Gavin observed the movement of the 75th Division to relieve us. In his book *On to Berlin*, he wrote: "I felt sorry for them in many ways. It was such a fine looking division, but so green. They had proceeded according to the textbooks, and trucks were unloaded about 10 miles behind the lines, because of the danger of enemy artillery fire. From then on they walked, wearing long overcoats, black rubber overshoes, carrying full field packs and all the equipment, weapons, and impedimenta they believed a combat soldier should have. Some of them placed some of this burden in ration boxes, which they pulled along the icy road with a short rope. By comparison, the 82nd was still in its old, faded jump suits, wearing long johns, to be sure, but carrying only essentials for fighting. However, the 75th went into the line, got its first blooding on the Salm River, and developed into a good division."

It was just after dark when the platoons and companies came up to take over our positions. One of the most precarious moments on the line occurs when units are being relieved in place. That is why it usually happens at night. Unless the changeover is executed quietly, cautiously, and in a timely manner, the enemy can detect the confusion and bring in his artillery.

That is precisely what occurred this night. The company-grade officers of the 75th Division lost control of their men and failed to exercise light and noise discipline. The men were lighting cigarettes, clanking mess kits, yelling at one another, and generally making a lot of racket. It didn't take long for the enemy to realize what was happening and to call for artillery, creating a hazardous situation for all of us.

Fortunately my platoon and I were able to take cover in our entrenched positions and ride out the barrage, but the exposed men of the 75th didn't fare as well. I am certain they learned a valuable lesson.

The following morning we boarded trucks and headed for

Remouchamps, a picturesque village located on the Ambleve River about twenty-five miles northwest to our rear.

Corporal Graves had arrived there earlier with the S1, seeking quarters for us. He recorded: "Our problem of finding billets and administrative installations for the regiment and approximately 1300 men was complicated by the fact that although we had been allotted the town by the First Army, various communications zone troops were billeted in the best hotels and civilian houses. They were reluctant to leave their luxurious quarters, which enabled them to have private hotel rooms and beds. In our present frame of mind, we had no sympathy for these men who had been 'roughing it' in soft feather beds for the past month or so."

After Rivers and I helped settle the men from our two platoons into civilian homes, we located the H Company CP, where the company officers—I and Lieutenants Sims, Rivers, and Murphy—would be housed. On 14 January I wrote the first letter home from Remouchamps to my sister Mary: "We're several miles off the front lines, getting a well-deserved rest and thawing out. The weather has been very cold and with a lot of snow, that makes fighting even more miserable. We are now billeted in a small Belgium village. The men are living in small groups in civilian houses. The people are very friendly and there isn't anything they won't do for us within their means. We have our CP in an ex-barroom and I sleep in one of the rooms upstairs in a bed with sheets. The lady puts warm bricks in it every night to heat it up before I go to bed. She's a swell old lady. Her two sons are prisoners in Germany."

Sims was also impressed by Belgian hospitality: "I will always remember the little lady who . . . painstakingly tailored our white mattress covers so they could be worn to camouflage our combat suits when fighting in the snow. . . ."

While we were in Remouchamps, Capt. John Gray arrived to assume command of H Company, replacing Captain Kappel. Gray continued as our commander through the remainder of the time we fought in the Battle of the Bulge. After the Bulge, when we returned to a rest area near Laon,

France, Gray broke his leg and was hospitalized. Sims once again assumed command of H Company and continued until the end of the war. During my time with H Company, he commanded the company longer than any of the three assigned captains. However, because Kappel remained on our roster filling the CO slot, there was no vacancy to promote Sims. I always have thought this was a great injustice to Sims.

I have frequently recalled the day that mail arrived in the barroom of our CP in Remouchamps. I received what appeared to be a quart jar of maraschino cherries, well protected and carefully packed. I could not imagine why anyone would go to all the trouble of sending a jar of cherries overseas. I did not bother to open the jar, setting it aside in disgust. The following day, a boy about ten years old was in the barroom. I treated him to several cherries, and to my surprise he nearly gagged on them. The jar had only a few cherries floating on top; the rest was bourbon.

I suddenly remembered a letter I had received from my older brother, George, saying he was sending me a bottle of cherries for Christmas, noting that the juice was the best part. After George had been discharged from the army, he bought a tavern in our hometown. He knew that the best present he could send me was whiskey. Therefore, he devised a means of circumventing postal restrictions to mail me a quart of Old Granddad.

On 26 January our brief period of rest ended. We thanked our Belgian friends for their hospitality and wished them well. There was a certain air of sadness in our departure. The Belgians regretted our leaving, knowing that we faced an uncertain future. Sergeant Tarbell, one of a group of eight men who had been housed in a Belgian home, recalled the day we left: "We pulled out of Remouchamps and, as we were leaving, the whole family lined up to bid us goodbye. It was a tearful farewell, because I guessed they figured we would never meet again. The old lady had prayer cards of St. Ann for Brett and me. I still carry that card on my person all the time. Before that the older sister had asked me if I could get a used sleeping bag. I obtained one from the Supply Sergeant and now the big surprise was at hand. She had gotten an old fur coat and used it to line the insides of the head part of the sleeping bag. She had cut the bag off and attached [the lined head] onto my combat fatigue jacket. What a going away present! It was big enough to fit over my helmet. I used that headpiece throughout the war and what a Godsend it was."

We loaded onto trucks and started toward Saint-Vith, Wallerode, and Hunnange. We had another mission: attack the vaunted Siegfried Line, anchoring the right flank of the U.S. First Army.

Following a winding course through the Ambleve Valley, we got a close-up look at the terrible destruction suffered by a number of small towns: Stoumont, La Gleize, Stavelot, Beaumont, and Recht. A few houses stood intact; dead cows and horses lay in the fields where they had fallen, and trees were sheared and uprooted. The stench of death permeated the air. Debris and wreckage littered the road; burned-out German tanks, trucks, artillery pieces, and guns were stark evidence of the ferocity of the battle that had descended on this once peaceful valley.

After more than thirty-five miles of difficult, winding roads, we reached our destination at Hunnange, a small village north of Saint-Vith. We took up positions outside the village, our line of departure for the attack on 28 January. What few houses still stood had been taken over by units of the 7th Armored Division and by our own unit commanders and their staffs. For the rest of us in the squads and platoons, it would be another miserable night in the bitter cold and snow.

We stayed pretty much in place that day, preparing for an early-morning departure. Our initial objective would be the village of Herresbach, about ten miles east of Hunnange. The forced march in deep snow through a heavily wooded area would be another test of our durability. We expected to encounter enemy artillery fire, but there was only slight resistance from enemy outposts and scattered units until we reached our objective.

That night, special services made arrangements to have a movie from the States shown to the troops in an improvised theater in one of the buildings that remained intact. Movies were frequently shown when we were far enough off the line and circumstances permitted. It was a form of relaxation enjoyed by the men, and tended to take their minds off the gruesome tasks that lay ahead. For lack of anything better to do, Rivers and I decided to attend.

It was a night at the movies I never forgot. I do not have the faintest recollection of what was showing. It was inconsequential, but the news we received was not. About midway through the movie, Father Kozak tapped me on the shoulder and quietly asked me to step outside.

"Maggie," he said, "we've just gotten word through the Red Cross that Rivers's brother, Roland, has been killed. We don't know any of the details, only that he was KIA. You're the closest to him. I think you should be the one to tell him."

I returned to the theater, mulling over how I would break the news. I was uncertain how he would take it. We were scheduled to leave early in the morning and resume the attack. How would he feel about that? If the opportunity arose, would he want to return home?

I tapped Rivers on the shoulder and motioned him to follow me. When we were outside, I said, "We have just received some awful news from the Red Cross. Your brother, Roland, has been killed."

That was all. I said nothing more as we started walking back to the H Company CP. He was sullen as the news began to sink in. He showed no outward sign of remorse, although I knew that deep inside he was suffering. In combat, death was commonplace. Rivers had seen many of his buddies killed around him, and he had cut down countless Germans. That was our lot as combat soldiers. But his only brother—that was something else. Rather than brooding about the shock he had just received, he said: "Maggie, we will make them pay for it tomorrow. There will be no prisoners taken."

Just before we reached the Company CP, Rivers stopped in the middle of the road and turned to me. "Maggie, you and Roland were all I had, and now he's gone, but I still have you." Then he looked me in the eye and said something I've never forgotten: "Between you and Roland, if I had to lose one of you, then I guess it had to be Roland."

His comment took me aback for a moment, but, actually, it was a true reflection of our relationship. We had fought side by side up to this point in the war, had experienced the hell and fury of combat, had overcome adversity, had witnessed death and destruction, had twice bade each other farewell when chances of survival seemed bleak, and had come through it together. In the process, we had developed a bond stronger than brotherhood. I wondered, if the situation were reversed—if it had been my youngest brother, Louis, a paratrooper, killed in action in the battle for Manila rather than wounded in action—how I would have reacted. On reflection, under similar circumstances, I might not have used his exact words, but I would have felt the same way.

Rivers was not the only one in H Company to receive the tragic news of a brother killed in action. Sergeant Sus J. Gonzalez, H Company, had been notified earlier that his brother, Lt. Frank Gonzalez, had been killed in action at Saint-Lô shortly after D day. Gonzalez was a veteran of H Company, having jumped in Sicily and fought in every campaign since. In the Battle of the Bulge, he was assigned to H Company headquarters. After he learned of his brother's death, he asked Captain Gray to assign him to my platoon. He wanted to be on the cutting edge of the battlefield, where he could avenge his brother's death. He too was determined to make the Germans pay.

With two supporting TDs, before daylight on 28 January we set out on an eastward course toward the village of Herresbach, about ten miles away. To reach our objective, we would have to contend not only with German opposition, which we expected to be light, but with the unfriendly weather and difficult terrain. That morning the thermometer hovered around zero and would stay there; the snowdrifts were two feet deep and more in places.

The battalion crossed the line of departure in single file strung out over a quarter of a mile. Breaking trail in the snow was slow and exhausting. Men breaking trail had to be relieved every thirty to forty yards, with the column following in their tracks. The three companies leapfrogged one another, taking turns in setting the course. The snow made it tough for the two TDs, but, surprisingly, they were able to keep pace. I was amazed at their ability to maneuver.

During the twelve-hour march to our destination, Rivers and I took turns leading the point platoon. The German soldiers were clad in white hooded coats and pants, which made it difficult to spot them in the snowy, wooded landscape. As we overcame enemy resistance, our men relieved the Germans of their white suits, often sending prisoners to the rear, some in just their underclothing. As the day wore on, we began to see a sprinkling of white suits in our ranks. I was one of those wearing a white jacket taken off a German prisoner.

Trudging through waist-deep snow, we must have looked like "Cox's Army." With three cold K rations stuffed into our pants pockets, we hardly qualified as the best-fed, best-clothed soldiers in the world. That was a distinction that probably applied to the rear-echelon troops. A spit-and-polish type of general would probably have been mortified to see us. As unkempt, dirty, and unshaven as we appeared, we still could fight.

As with the previous forced marches, we were told to leave behind our bedrolls. The long, grueling march would be exhausting, and we had to be prepared to fight on short notice. Backpacks would only delay and hinder our movement. We were assured that our bedrolls would be brought up when we reached our objective and held up for the night. As on previous occasions, however, that was only wishful thinking. Given the deep snow and difficult terrain, it was unrealistic to expect them to follow.

In addition to the three boxes of K rations we were issued

for the day, each man received one canteen of water. There would be no resupply during the long march. The men would have to melt snow to replenish canteens, and the three K rations would have to suffice.

More important to me and my chances for survival were the instruments of enemy destruction: weapons and ammunition. As usual, I was armed with a Thompson submachine gun. It served me well as a platoon leader, leading attacks and patrols. At night I used it as a pillow, but above all I maintained it in good firing condition, and it never failed me when I needed it. I generally carried a toothbrush when we were on the line, but as to priority, my tommy gun came first. Clean teeth and general cleanliness were desirable, but my survival depended on my gun.

I also holstered a Colt .45 pistol, which used the same caliber ammunition as the tommy gun. I could have done without it. Worn by commanders and by platoon and squad leaders, it had a certain prestige, but as a weapon it had limited value. I never fired it in combat, nor did I ever see anyone else rely on it; we had better and more accurate means of engaging the enemy. Only in Hollywood movies is a pistol portrayed as an important combat weapon. I also carried four hand grenades, my usual load, which hung off loops in my harness. More importantly, I carried a triple load of .45-caliber ammunition, six magazines of thirty rounds each. I had two magazines welded together, so that, in changing magazines, I needed only to invert the second welded magazine. The rest I carried in a specially designed bag.

In the pockets of my jumpsuit, I carried two Gammon grenades. This grenade was relatively new in our arsenal and was ideally suited for lightly armed paratroopers as an antitank weapon. Made of C-4, it was four times more powerful than dynamite. It was so soft it could be molded like putty, and by itself it was harmless. It could burn and cast a blue flame; in fact, the men would ignite pieces the size of a golf ball to heat rations and water. One to three pounds of the plastic could be molded into the size of a softball and fitted into a specially designed elasticized black cloth pouch. The cloth contained a cap, housing a detonator. Because of C-4's weight, its range was somewhat less than a man could throw a softball. It detonated on impact and produced a flash like an artillery shell. It was powerful enough to demolish a small house, as I once learned when I used C-4 to blow up an iron safe in Germany. It was a great weapon for paratroopers fighting tanks, provided you could get close.

Enemy resistance encountered by the battalion was scattered and sporadic, mainly from snipers and outposts, causing a minimum of casualties. Sergeant Tarbell recalled one of those brief encounters: "We noticed a German soldier sitting by a tree facing in our direction. Just then, we saw some movement on our left and just below us. There was a bunch of German soldiers moving parallel to us, and we could see their heads. We rushed over with Lt. Megellas and he started barking orders to his men to fan out. There was not much of a fight. I believe they were just as happy to give up. I had the opportunity of observing a combat officer in action right up close for the first time. He was just like a cat that had a bunch of rats in a corner and he knew every step to take next. I never forgot that because I was next to his right side as we looked at the German soldiers. I mentioned that to him years later."

XIII
Herresbach, Belgium

28 January 1945

After twelve hours of fighting our way through light enemy resistance and battling deep snowdrifts, we arrived at our destination, a wooded area about half to three-fourths of a mile from the outskirts of the village of Herresbach. Squad leaders were trying to get the squad settled and were posting guards while the men were clearing the snow for a place to relax and eat their evening K rations.

According to the tactical plan, we would occupy positions in the woods for the night, then attack Herresbach at daybreak with another battalion of the 504th. The 3d would attack from the south, where we were now located, and the 2d Battalion would come from the west. With two companies in the attack and one in reserve in each battalion, the regiment would commit about four hundred men in the initial attack on Herresbach. Our battalion would be supported by the two TDs that had been with us since we crossed the line of departure twelve hours earlier. Herresbach was an important German supply center, and our intelligence estimated it was defended by about a battalion of infantry.

That was the plan as I knew it, but first we would have to endure another restless night in the frigid Belgian winter without any blankets or shelter. I checked on my three squads to make certain they were settled and secure.

Suddenly, a small vehicle coming out of Herresbach started moving down the road in our direction. We took cover and let it continue. It was an American jeep carrying four German soldiers. Sims clearly recalled the occasion: "When the jeep got close enough so we could identify the soldiers as Germans, Lt. Rivers shot the driver with a round from his M1 rifle. The three others jumped out with their hands raised high and shouted *'Nicht Schiessen, Nicht Schiessen.'* I never understood what they were up to but apparently we surprised them. From the prisoners we learned that a large force on foot was following them."

With an obsolete plan, we would come face-to-face with the enemy sooner than we had expected. The Germans were still some distance away, heading toward us, and not with a welcoming committee.

Out of the still of the night came a resonating call in a deep familiar voice, "Greek, Rivers." The call did not come from H Company or 3d Battalion headquarters but directly from the regimental commander, Col. Reuben Tucker. He and his staff had crossed the line of departure with us.

Rivers and I hastened back to find Colonel Tucker. Without hesitation, he compacted what is taught in the Infantry School as a five-paragraph field order, "Take those two cans and get into that town."

That was it: no hows, whats, whens, wheres, whys, or anything else. Just do it, and do it now. Suddenly the town that had been a two-battalion objective was reduced to a force of two understrength platoons supported by two tank destroyers. I hurried back to my platoon and called my three squad leaders: "Get the men up. We're going to take that town."

I got the two TDs cranked up and started heading toward the Germans coming out of Herresbach. It was only a matter of minutes before Rivers had his platoon on the road. With our two TDs we started moving toward the enemy, with my platoon in the lead. I had twenty-seven men in my platoon, a number of whom had just arrived as replacements and were about to get their baptism of fire. Rivers's platoon numbered about the same.

Sergeant James Ward recalled that moment: "On January 28, 1945, I remember the trek through the Ardennes Forest, when at dusk we encountered a German force of what I estimated to be over 300 men. They were leaving the town of

Herresbach heading in our direction. They apparently were unaware the enemy was near. I observed Lt. James Megellas, H Company rifle platoon leader, engaging this force with his platoon and the support of two tank destroyers."

Private First Class Robert Breland was in my platoon on 18 December 1945 when we were committed to the Battle of the Bulge. He recalled Herresbach: "After crossing into Germany we met a battalion of German troops in the town of Herresbach. We captured a good number of men; many of their men were killed and one Mark V tank and crew also disposed of (Maggie's tank)."

As we advanced toward the oncoming Germans, most of us took cover behind the two TDs. Sergeant Fred Andrews and several others climbed aboard and were riding on the turret. I was behind the lead tank, and Private Brewer took cover behind the second TD. Privates Harold Sullivan and John Schultz, riflemen in Rivers's platoon, took cover initially behind the second TD, then moved to the side of the tank when we neared the Germans. Sergeant Donald Zimmerman was in my platoon when we started out. He remembered: "I jumped on the back of the lead TD. Then when we neared the two columns of Germans, I jumped off and fanned out."

We were in the middle of the road and suddenly found ourselves between two columns of German soldiers, one on each side of the road. I estimated that the German force consisted of two rifle companies of about 125 men each.

The Germans had come out of Herresbach hunting Americans, German style, just as we had plowed through two feet of snow hunting Germans. We had come a long way in search of them, and suddenly they were all around us. They had not dropped their weapons or approached with the thought of surrendering.

The attack had not been planned. It was a spontaneous reaction to a combat situation that in retrospect seems incredible and unbelievable. Nothing that I had learned about infantry tactics in ROTC in Ripon College, the Parachute Training School, or the airborne training center in Oujda,

Africa, or anything the men in my platoon had learned in basic training, applied. In the midst of the Germans, all hell broke loose.

There was no science or tactics involved, just combat-hardened paratroopers seizing an opportunity to kill many Germans. Before they could react, the Germans found two platoons of American paratroopers and two menacing TDs in their ranks, and we attacked in all directions.

We were firing at almost point-blank range. The enemy was so close that I did not have to put my gun to my shoulder to aim it; I just pointed and fired in their direction. My tommy gun was red hot, rapid-firing clip after clip. It was a killing frenzy unlike any other I experienced in the war; we were shooting everything in sight. As I later wrote home to my sister Catherine about that night, "It was a slaughter beyond anything you could imagine."

Private Gordon Brewer told me he used two bandoliers of .30-caliber ammo: "It was like a shooting gallery, the biggest battle of the war." Private Harold Sullivan wrote: "We met the Germans who came down the same road to attack us. I don't know who was more surprised. But I know who had the best firepower. I was on the left-hand side of a tank and everybody was firing to the side and out front. Clips seemed to pop out of the M1 very fast. A lot of dead Germans were on the road and alongside the road."

I remember my platoon runner, Pfc. Julian Romero, attempting to disarm a German soldier when I raced around the house and hollered, "Get out of the way." Before the German could get his hands up and the word "Komrad" out of his mouth, I cut him down with my tommy gun. As I raced back on the road in search of more victims, I spotted Rivers and cried out, "Rivers, there's one more for Roland."

Sergeant Crowder recalled: "The situation was chaotic. We were all firing at a rapid clip. I remember Lieutenant Megellas calling out 'here are two more for your brother.' They never had a chance to surrender."

In the heat of battle, when two opposing forces out hunting each other met head-on and the air was bristling with flying lead, a recalcitrant German who suddenly changed his mind about killing Americans soon found he had no alternative: kill or be killed. Although both sides were opposed to shooting unarmed soldiers, especially after they had been taken prisoner, this was not a time to read anyone's rights or to cite the Geneva Convention or the rules of land warfare. For Lieutenant Rivers and Sergeant Gonzalez, it was payback time for the brothers they had lost to the Germans in France. For the rest of us in H Company that night, it was payback time for the buddies we had lost earlier.

We worked our way methodically through the two lines of Germans who had broken ranks and tried to take cover. A few escaped, but the great majority did not, the bodies lying in grotesque positions near one another in the snow. Within fifteen to twenty minutes, we had fought our way through the panic-stricken Germans and reached the edge of the city. What originally had been a two-battalion objective was now ours for the taking.

We held up to count noses and regroup. Miraculously, in all the carnage strewn on both sides of the road, not one body was ours and we had no wounded. We had expended almost all our ammunition, killing between 180 and 200 Germans and taking 280 prisoners, almost all of whom surrendered after we entered the town.

Unlike the Vietnam War, efforts to determine precise body counts in World War II were never made, so accounts of German dead varied, depending on the distance from the actual battle. The most accurate count with the best credibility came from those who did the actual killing. My estimate of 180 to 200 Germans killed is supported by the men there. Counts of prisoners taken were generally more precise.

We stood on the outskirts of Herresbach, our two platoons intact, poised to seize the town. But to do so, we first needed a resupply of ammunition. I was down to my last clip for my tommy gun. Private Brewer had used up his two bandoliers of .30 caliber, and almost everyone else in the two platoons was dangerously low. We would not be able to engage the enemy again in a sustained firefight with what we had. I summoned my platoon radio operator, Cpl. Oscar Smith, to hightail it back to H Company. I gave Captain Gray this message: "We're going to clear the town. Urgently need ammunition or men who have ammo."

While we were waiting for resupply preparatory to a move into the town, a German Mark V came out of Herresbach toward us, firing its machine gun. The men quickly took cover. Our two TDs were behind us and not in position to engage the enemy tank. Instinctively I charged toward the oncoming tank. Taking advantage of available cover along the side of the road, I was able to get close enough to throw a Gammon grenade; it hit the side of the tank, knocking out its tracking mechanism and stopping it cold. With the tank disabled, I charged up to its side and dropped a fragmentation grenade down the open hatch of the turret.

We now had removed the last obstacle to our entrance into Herresbach, but we still had not received more ammunition. I brought up the two TDs and lined them up side by side. Darkness had fallen and the night was pitch black. I told the gunners I wanted an incendiary or high-explosive round fired into the silhouette of every building that appeared in their sights. "We are going into the town," I said, "and I want to be able to see what I'm doing." A number of high-explosive shells found their mark, illuminating the town.

Normally, when battling house to house to capture a city, the action takes place in daylight, but we could not wait for morning. I did not want to give the Germans time to regroup or organize a counterattack. We would have to make do with what we had.

I had the machine gun dismounted from one of the TDs and handed down to me. I called for Sgt. James Wright, one of my squad leaders, and asked, "Have you ever fired a machine gun from the hip?" The answer: "Negative." "Okay," I said, "you are about to get a thirty-second demonstration." I took a belt of ammunition, wrapped it around my neck, draped it over my shoulder, fed it into the breech, pulled back the bolt, and fired a burst. The gun, dismounted, was difficult to hold, spraying lead in all directions, but it created the desired effect; the staccato of the burping machine gun scattered lead at everything in its path. Accuracy was of secondary importance. Wright took the gun and fired a short burst; we were ready to move out and clear the town. I told him to stay by my side and fire a burst in the direction of every building we approached.

Together, with one TD in support and a squad of men, we moved out. I called out to Rivers, "We're going through this town. See you later." We proceeded down a street in the center of Herresbach that appeared to be the main artery, Wright spewing out lead in bursts, our individual weapons on the ready, and the menacing presence of the tank destroyer ready for action. While we were moving through the town, Murphy and Rivers and their two platoons, Gray, Sims, and the rest of H Company were going house to house rounding up prisoners. The Germans forced out of the houses had no fight left in them and offered little resistance. For them the war was over. They were not about to give their lives for the Fatherland, the Führer, or any other cause.

The following are accounts of that night from four of the H Company men going house to house taking prisoners:

Private Harold Sullivan: "Twenty-five Germans came out of one house and they gave up quickly. We lined them up on the road and headed them toward the rear. Private Rufus Sampson hollered at them to get going. Losing patience, he fired a burst behind them to get their attention. One of the rounds hit a prisoner in the heel which upset our medics who had to take care of him."

Private John Schultz: "A group of prisoners streamed out of a house leaving their uneaten dinner on the table."

Sergeant Albert Tarbell: "I noted a German soldier coming out of the shadows with his hands up. I hollered to our men, 'Don't shoot, there may be more.' A few minutes later, several more came out of the shadows and surrendered. For the rest of the night, we were busy clearing the buildings of soldiers, taking prisoners and placing them in a large barn guarded by troopers."

Sergeant H. Donald Zimmerman: "Every man was fighting his own war. I was busy rounding up prisoners going house to house."

My small force and the supporting TD fought its way to the outer limits of Herresbach with only a minimum of resistance. We had cleared the town without incurring any casualties. Now that we controlled the town, we had to be prepared to secure and defend it against a possible counterattack. That was always the tactical scenario after a city was captured. I placed Wright and the few men we had with us in defensive positions extending on both sides of the road. The rest of H Company was also deploying, forming a perimeter defense around the town. Private Sullivan wrote: "I don't know what happened to the night I was supposed to spend inside. After a brief warm up and rest, Sgt. Jimmy Shields, my squad leader, came and said, 'My guy's outside—another night in the snow watching to make sure we wouldn't be surprised."

The men moved out on a defensive perimeter, dug foxholes, ate cold rations, kept watch for any sign of the enemy, and prepared to defend whatever it was they had just seized. To suggest that they fought to take a town so they could sleep in a bed and prepare warm food did not apply to fighting men. The quarters they slept in consisted of the hole they could dig with an entrenching tool. They would be awake most of the night taking turns on guard.

To the victors do not always belong the spoils. As soon as Herresbach was captured and secured and the Germans driven out or captured and a perimeter defense established, our rear-echelon comrades would follow, taking over the best buildings. Houses made good command posts, especially if they had fortified basements that could provide shelter from enemy artillery. In the morning, the men who seized the town would be moved out in pursuit of the enemy.

I was annoyed to read a First Army press report filed by Associated Press war correspondent Tom Yarbrough on 29 January about the battle for Herresbach: "A famous infantry unit has performed the remarkable feat of capturing the town of Herresbach by killing 138 Germans and capturing 180 without losing a single man, killed, wounded or missing. . . . The best explanation was given by Capt. Fordyce Gorham, Coudersport, PA (504th Regiment S-2): 'The guys had been walking in the snow for 12 hours and when it got dark, they were in sight of the town. They wanted some buildings to sleep in, so they took the town. Those beds,' said Capt. Gorham, 'were all right.'"

For those of us who attacked and captured Herresbach, it did not make any difference who slept inside in warm beds or who took credit for what we had achieved. We had just done our job. Tomorrow would be another day, another objective to take, and more Germans to kill. We would be battling the elements and the enemy for another twenty-one days before we would be relieved of frontline duty in the Battle of the Bulge.

It was late in the evening when I left Wright and his squad on the outskirts of the town and started back in search of H Company and the rest of my platoon. Sims was the first person I met when I arrived at the CP. He was euphoric about what had happened. "Maggie, you and the men with you are the last to be accounted for. We didn't lose a man."

It was the first time I became fully aware of what had happened in Herresbach that night. The streets were cluttered with some two hundred German prisoners lining up to be escorted to the rear. Whatever the actual number, it was the largest bag of prisoners we had taken in a single engagement in the Battle of the Bulge. Added to the number of Germans killed and the fact that we had lost no one, Herresbach was a victory of major proportions.

Captain John Gray was overwhelmed. Sims told me, "We're going to recommend you for the Congressional Medal of Honor." I was never certain how far up the chain of command it progressed, but it was eventually downgraded to a Silver Star. Some of the most important aspects of the action were either misplaced or inadvertently overlooked.

Fifty-two years later at a small reunion of the 3d Battalion's company-grade officers, E. J. Sims (colonel, retired) inquired about my citation for the battle of Herresbach. He was aware that I had been the recipient of the Distinguished Service Cross and assumed it was for the action at Herresbach. When he learned that I had received a Silver Star instead, he asked for a copy of the citation. He then realized that important individual acts were not included in the award. He asked if I would object to resubmitting the recommendation to upgrade the Silver Star to the Medal of Honor, as originally intended.

On 18 May 1999, he directed his request to the president of the United States to upgrade the Silver Star to the Medal of Honor. He described the entire action in detail and wrote, "This request, long delayed, is an attempt to rectify an injustice done to James Megellas in 1945." Supporting his recommendation were the two eyewitness statements of Lieutenant Murphy and Sergeant Shields and subsequently five additional statements from men of H Company who were there that night. Colonel Sims's recommendation is currently under review.

I left the CP in Herresbach and returned to my platoon. While my runner, Private Romero, was arranging for a platoon CP, I went out to check on the men. I looked for Pvt. Gordon Brewer and Pvt. Joseph McBurnett, who had been placed on outpost, but all I found was an empty foxhole. They had just been assigned to my platoon as replacements the day before our attack on Herresbach. There was no sign of them, and when they did not appear that night, I had to assume they were casualties, so I reported them as missing in action. After we were relieved of frontline duty in the Battle of the Bulge, I learned that they had been captured and were being held in a prisoner-of-war camp in Germany. In May 1945, when the war was in its final days, American forces overran the camp and freed them.

Returning to my CP, I spotted a six-man German patrol dressed in white camouflage suits. They penetrated our thinly held perimeter defense and headed toward a large barn where one of our TDs was concealed. They did not see me, but I quickly took cover behind the barn. They came around the other side and were about 150 feet from me. I opened fire on them with my tommy gun, taking them by surprise. Evidently uncertain as to what they were up against, they beat a hasty retreat around the barn and quickly vanished. It was a dark evening, and I was unable to determine where they went. I kept hidden and quiet and was ready for them if they returned. I had fired only one burst at them. At night the sound of an automatic weapon, theirs or ours, fired at close range can be terrifying if it's in your direction. Early the next morning, I walked around the barn looking for German bodies but found only blood in the snow where they had been.

Later that evening, a larger German force probing my platoon position was engaged in a firefight by Sergeant Wright's squad. At the sound of gunfire, Wright charged out of a house toward his squad and was met by a hail of enemy bullets. He fell, mortally wounded, and died four days later. Although we had incurred no casualties in the assault on Herresbach, I had three casualties in my platoon later from German patrols: two MIA and one KIA. In some small measure, it was payback time for the Germans. It was also a reminder, lest we became complacent, that the Germans still had resolve left in them and were prepared to fight.

Several days after Herresbach, when the battlefield quieted down, most men in my platoon took advantage of the lull to write letters home. As a rule, most men seldom wrote home from the front for lack of an opportunity or the means. Besides, the news was never pleasant. But Herresbach was different; it was an unforgettable experience and left the men in high spirits, so they felt compelled to sound off to their families. Most of the men were not certain where Herresbach was, and few could spell it, but they knew they had accomplished a remarkable feat.

Given the total number of Germans killed and captured in Herresbach (almost five hundred) while we did not suffer a single casualty begs the question, How could this have happened to the once mighty German Wehrmacht?

One of the reasons for the Germans' demise at Herresbach

was leadership. We had it and they didn't. Undoubtedly, their squad and platoon leaders had never addressed the situation and did not lead by example. They may have commanded and ordered their men into battle, but they did not lead. The sight of those two TDs in our midst must certainly have unnerved them, and when we started rapid-firing our weapons on them, they panicked and lost all semblance of order. They obviously were not of the caliber of SS troopers we had found earlier in the Battle of the Bulge at Cheneux and Bra. Finally, we were in a killing frenzy, shooting everything in sight.

On 25 March 1945, from somewhere in France, I wrote, "A few days ago I received a Silver Star from the general. I will send it home in a few days. I'm enclosing a copy of the citation. I wish you'd save it for me. P.S.: There's one correction in the citation—I killed 25 Germans that night. I had 27 men in the attack and lost on one. It was a slaughter beyond anything I've ever heard of. P.P.S: I have now killed more Krauts than anyone in the regiment who is still alive."

Early the following morning, 20 January, the 32d Cavalry Reconnaissance Squadron moved in behind us in Herresbach and relieved us in place. H Company was ordered to attack and seize the high ground that the Germans had occupied overlooking Herresbach. The Germans commanding the high ground could observe the town, making it difficult to assemble and organize for the attack. Enemy-direct artillery and mortar fire sent the men in H Company scurrying for cover. German machine guns were raking the road on which we were trying to launch the attack. Rivers's platoon was designated to lead the attack, but in the face of intense small-arms fire, it was difficult to get started. The men in his platoon took cover behind the tank destroyer. A new officer recently assigned as Rivers's assistant platoon leader actually crawled under the tank and refused to come out or lead the attack. In all my experience in World War II, it was the only time I saw a paratrooper in the 504th, officer or enlisted man, display signs of cowardice. Rivers was furious and inclined to shoot him on the spot, but Sims persuaded him otherwise.

Instead, Rivers relieved the man and sent him to the rear. His act had been demeaning to all of us.

I had taken cover behind one of the buildings next to the road waiting for the lead platoon to move out. My platoon would be next, and the rest of H Company would follow. I edged out just beyond the building so I might be able to observe where the gunfire was coming from. Private First Class Romero, the platoon runner, and Sgt. Sus J. Gonzalez were standing behind me. We moved about a foot outside the building next to the road looking in the direction of the enemy automatic fire. A German machine gun opened up. The trajectory of the bullets followed along the side of the building. Gonzalez, Romero, and I were within an arm's length of one another when fire hit Romero and Gonzalez, standing on both sides of me, but missed me completely. Both dropped at my feet on the edge of the road. I pulled Gonzalez behind the house and called for a medic. Then I dragged Romero from the edge of the road to behind the house. He had been shot through the neck, and his carotid artery was severed. Blood was spurting out of his neck like a fountain, and his entire body was quivering. I placed my hand over the jugular, applying pressure. It was an instinctive reaction but a futile gesture; the blood just kept spurting out, covering both of us. In a matter of minutes, he stopped quivering; his body drained of blood, he died in my arms. Gonzalez had been shot in the chest. The medics placed him on a stretcher and evacuated him to a field hospital. The following day he died of his wounds. Gonzalez and Romero became faceless statistics, adding two more KIAs to the growing total kept at higher headquarters. But for their buddies in H Company, they were cherished friends lost.

I brought up my platoon and deployed them in a small gully ahead of the tank destroyer. We laid down a curtain of fire on enemy gun positions on the high ground in front of us. This action gave Lieutenant Rivers and his platoon cover and a brief respite from enemy small-arms fire to get organized and move out. As they progressed toward the enemy positions, my platoon and the rest of H Company fell in behind them and closed up. In the face of a determined frontal attack, the Germans withdrew and fell back. We cleared the area of Germans and rounded up a few prisoners. We had several men wounded, but overall our casualties were light. We occupied the high ground, prepared to defend it from a possible counterattack, and dug in to spend another miserable night in the frigid Belgian winter.

The next morning, 30 January, we noticed enemy activity about five hundred yards to our front. Small vehicles were moving in and out with some frequency, but we saw no evidence of German combat forces. The battlefield was quiet, so Rivers and I decided to satisfy our curiosity and check out the situation. Taking a few volunteers from our two platoons with us, we proceeded cautiously in the direction of a house, not knowing what we would encounter. We approached the back of the house without being fired on. We tossed several hand grenades into the basement, then charged around to the front. For the first time, we realized that the Germans were using the house as an aid station, clearly marked from the front but not visible from the back. We took no further action. Our curiosity satisfied, we decided to withdraw and return to our lines.

On 31 January we moved off line to prepare for an attack on Germany's vaunted Siegfried Line. The Germans had begun construction of the west wall, as they called it, in 1936 and intensified their efforts in 1938 before invading Czechoslovakia. By the end of 1938, more than 500,000 men were employed to build it, consuming about one-third of Germany's annual production of cement. Hitler touted the west wall as impregnable, but in reality it was intended to delay an enemy advance until mobile reserves could stop any penetration.

In many places, the Siegfried Line consisted of tank obstacles called "dragon's teeth," laid in five staggered rows. Roads leading through the dragon's teeth were covered by fire from large concrete structures resembling pillboxes, and so named. About half of each pillbox was underground, fortified by walls and a roof constructed of three- to eight-foot-thick reinforced concrete. A pillbox was generally twenty to thirty feet wide, forty to fifty feet deep, and twenty to twenty-five feet high. It provided quarters for defenders and was built as a small fortress, including bunks, kitchen, showers, toilets, telephone, electricity, and generator.

If properly armed and adequately manned, the pillboxes could have been a strong deterrent to an advancing army, but in the waning months of the war, the Germans lacked the manpower to fully staff them. Also, the west wall had fallen into disrepair and neglect, and the caliber of defending troops had deteriorated. Even though the structures had become outdated and the defenders were being scraped from the bottom of the German manpower barrel, the pillboxes still had to be fought for and the wall breached.

On 2 February, H Company, along with other units of the 504th, jumped off on the attack and moved east through the Mertesrott Heights/Forest Gerolstein area south of Neuhof, Germany. On our advance, we were delayed by extensive minefields and booby traps laid as a first line of defense for the west wall. Fortunately, many of the mines we encountered did not detonate. Exposed to years of snow, ice, and rain, some were inoperable. For the first time we encountered *Schue* mines, antipersonnel mines composed of about a quarter pound of TNT in a small wooden box. They were simple, inexpensive to make, and effective. If stepped on, they could demolish a foot or a leg, or worse.

The weather began to change. From the deep snow and frigid temperatures we had had to endure, we were now sloshing through mud. Snow turned to incessant rain and, although the weather was still cold, it was no longer freezing. Life was still miserable. The cold, wet boots and clothes, mud, damp foxholes, and constant gnawing pangs of hunger were the order of a soldier's day.

Small-arms and machine-gun fire were of limited value in attacking a concrete pillbox, but our Gammon grenades and captured German *panzerfausts* proved effective. Fortunately, not all pillboxes were manned, but those that were engaged us with machine-gun and small-arms fire. As formidable as the Siegfried Line appeared, it was not matched by the resolve of its defenders. Once we had surrounded a pillbox, the Germans chose to heed the call *"Komen Sie hier"* and surrender rather than lose their lives. Our casualties were light from enemy action, but the toll from trench foot remained high.

On 5 February we were replaced on the line by units of the U.S. 99th Infantry Division and pulled back near Schmithof, Germany, for a brief rest and to receive an infusion of replacements. On 9 February, H Company, along with other units of the 504th, attacked eastward to seize the high ground overlooking the Roer River, then dug in. Enemy resistance was light, with delays caused by washed-out roads, artillery, and minefields.

With American troops now on German soil, General Eisenhower ordered a policy of no fraternization. It was an ill-advised order that contradicted human nature and was difficult to enforce. Most soldiers were young and in their sexually active years. On the front lines far removed from Europe's most alluring cities and enticing damsels, they didn't see girls or have sex for months at a time. Combat soldiers dreamed and talked about two things—girls and booze, in that order. The new policy, which applied only to German civilians, would affect the rear-echelon soldiers who would be cavorting with the fräuleins. The men looked forward to being relieved on the front lines and getting a pass to places such as Paris and Brussels, where girls and booze were available and affordable.

When units were pulled back for a rest, they generally bivouacked in the countryside away from urban centers, where the rear-echelon soldiers were engaged in what they considered to be the important matters of war. Combat troops had a way of messing things up for the noncombatants who had worked hard to set up officers' and NCO clubs, Red Cross, and USO facilities. To the rear echelon, combat troops were vulgar, dirty, uncouth, and even barbaric. Their place was in the front lines. In the rear, they caused nothing but trouble for the support troops. Fraternization with the enemy when we entered Germany was not a matter of concern to our commanders and staffs; they were not near any enemy. In the capitals of Europe, mistresses went with the territory.

Later, when the 504th became occupation troops, enforcing the no fraternization policy became a problem. Personally, I was for it. I detested all Germans and held them responsible for the deaths of many of my comrades. I felt no compassion, sympathy, kindness, or forgiveness toward them. They would be dealt with humanely, but firmly. I made it equally tough on those men who fraternized and the German girls who enticed them.

On 11 February the fortunes of war smiled on me. My number was called for a weekend pass to Brussels, one of Europe's most glamorous cities, where women and wine were abundant. It was the first and only time I received a weekend pass to anyplace while we were on the front lines. After checking into a hotel, my first visit was to a Turkish bath, then to a barber. When I came out, I was clean-shaven, sporting a handlebar mustache, and ready to hit the nightspots. It was great to be part of the human race again.

For the combat soldier, Brussels was more than just another R and R center. It embodied everything he dreamed about. Although it was not far from our present position, it was far removed from the misery and deprivation of combat. It was a beautiful, bustling city unscarred by the violence and fury that engulfed much of the rest of Europe.

Like other cities in Belgium designated as rest areas, Brussels was conspicuous by its absence of young men. They had gone off to war when the Germans invaded, and few had returned. Many languished in German POW camps. The young German soldiers—when they occupied Brussels—and now the young British and American soldiers filled the void in the lonely hearts of the mademoiselles.

Brussels was deep in the British sector and they kept a tight rein on the city. Unlike Paris, Brussels did not have a large, flourishing black market or underground activity. Quartermaster supplies intended for British troops did not end up in the black market at the rate they did in Paris or other U.S.-controlled centers. Brussels was a cosmopolitan city that welcomed military men from all Allied nations. The nightclubs did a flourishing business, and the many first-rate hotels seldom posted vacancy signs. It was a mecca of merriment that was perfect for the combat soldier on a weekend pass.

After forty-eight hours in Brussels, I was happy to return to my platoon and H Company, which were preparing to cross the Roer River and attack into Germany. It was like returning to family. My buddies were my family, mattering more to me than material pleasures.

In preparing to cross the Roer River, small-unit patrols were used to secure the river's west bank. We were alerted for the crossing several times, but each time it was postponed. The melting snow and heavy rains raised the river from a stream to a torrent. We waited for the water to recede before attempting a crossing. On 18 February word came that we were being relieved. At first we dismissed the news as just another rumor, but this time it was true. We would be relieved in place by the 99th Infantry Division.

The next morning we boarded trucks headed for Laon, France, about two hundred miles to our rear. The route back took us north into German farming country through Aachen and across the Belgian border and into Liège. Aachen was the scene of fierce fighting, with much of the city reduced to rubble.

Liège, about thirty-five miles southwest of Aachen, presented a contrasting picture. Except for occasional buzz bombs, the city was not targeted by German or Allied bombing. Shops were open and appeared to be well stocked. The bars were lined with imbibing customers. We headed south and crossed the French border. It was late in the afternoon when we arrived in Laon, our home for the next six weeks before returning to combat in Germany.

XIV
Return to France

Our stay in Laon gave us an opportunity to recuperate, receive and train replacements, and prepare for our next mission. After Hitler's big gamble backfired in Belgium, the Wehrmacht was relegated to fighting a delaying action on German soil. Even the most pessimistic among us felt that the war was in its final stages. But none of us wanted to be killed on the last day of the war.

For a combat soldier, garrison life can be boring. I expressed as much in a letter home on 29 March: "Things are awful quiet and unexciting here. When coming back from the front, a warm, dry place to sleep and eating warm food again seems heavenly but after a month or so I find myself becoming very restless. . . . I sometimes wonder if I'll ever be able to sit still again. I don't know how long I will be here but when I go hunting Krauts again I am sure you will know it from the papers."

Fortunately Laon was not Leicester, England: no parading for the lord mayor, no pep talks from the supreme commander about greater things still to come, and, above all, no close order drills for combat-hardened paratroopers.

We stayed in good physical condition and kept training, however, because both were essential. Our training included parachute jumps—exiting the plane quickly and assembling on the ground as a cohesive unit. For the first time, I jumped out of a plane with two sticks of men using two side doors (C-46). Jumping out a left side door was a new experience for me. Instead of turning to the left after exiting the plane, we turned to the right.

One of the great pleasures of returning to France was getting to see our three lady friends and their Red Cross clubmobile. Mary, Charlotte, and Marianne had been with us in England about six months ago. It was always a treat to see pretty American girls, but these were special. Not only did they serve good coffee and doughnuts, they did a lot for our morale and gave us a reason for fighting.

Since we had last seen them in England, they were attached to the U.S. First Army on the Continent. They had a lot to tell us about their travels, but more importantly their travails. They said that the Red Cross had assigned them to one of the new American divisions on the Ardennes front in Belgium. On the morning of 16 December 1944, they drove their clubmobile to a regimental headquarters. They set up as usual, and the men from the rifle companies rotated back for coffee and doughnuts.

Although the headquarters of the regiment was on a front so quiet that it was referred to as "R and R," it was actually an area where 250,000 German soldiers and 1,000 tanks were poised to launch a major offensive. American intelligence, caught by surprise, failed to notify the Red Cross girls. They were preparing coffee and getting ready for the soldiers when they noticed commotion outside the CP. Staff and command cars and other military vehicles were jamming the roads leading away from the front. The girls didn't know what was happening, so they continued with their preparations.

They became concerned when they saw officers packing their personal belongings, cleaning out files, and burning papers and maps. Concern gave way to anxiety when the officers made a hurried departure, leaving the girls alone in the CP. An MP finally told them what was going on.

A similar situation occurred on the Holland front. The Red Cross had a greeting postcard that the girls would help the men send home to their families. The girls had sent one such postcard of the Clubmobile "Oregon" to my mother with the message: "We have just served your son, James, with coffee and doughnuts from the Red Cross Clubmobile.

He is looking well. With sincere best wishes from the Club-mobile Crew."

One might assume that they had served us somewhere far to the rear. But that was not the case. The clubmobile had been in Nijmegen, Holland, on 22 September 1944, just two days after my battalion made the bloody crossing of the Waal River. To reach us, the girls had to drive through the fifty-seven-mile salient, established by the two airborne divisions, through enemy territory. It took a lot of guts on the part of those girls to go into the battle area. But they always tried to reach frontline troops to give them a feeling of being appreciated and a touch of "back home." The United Service Organizations (USO) sent movie stars and celebrities overseas to entertain the servicemen, but they never got as close to the action as did the Red Cross "donut dollies," as we called them.

The six weeks we spent in Laon were to prepare us for our next assignment. We brought our units to near authorized strength. In addition to replacements, we welcomed back men from hospitals, many of whom had been evacuated with frozen feet.

With Allied troops now advancing on German soil, any type of mission was possible for us. General Gavin spoke to the entire division while we were in France. He referred to the training we were undergoing and how it related to a possible mission. He specifically mentioned Berlin and indicated that redeployment to the Pacific theater might occur. Our possible missions confirmed the belief most of us had that the training in France was not routine. Gavin's talk about probable missions generated excitement among the combat units, but otherwise life in Laon was boring.

With the Germans falling back along the entire western front and with Allied troops in hot pursuit, some fanatic SS and Hitler youth units were still resisting. Elsewhere, fuzzy-cheeked German youths and older graybeards were surrendering en masse without much of a fight.

With the inevitable in Europe approaching, divisions were being identified for future redeployment to the Pacific.

A point system was devised for demobilization of individuals based on length of service, time overseas, combat decorations, and dependent children. Still others were being selected for thirty days' leave back in the States. Two officers of the regiment, both close friends—Capt. Thomas Helgeson and Lt. Roy Hanna—were selected; when their leaves were completed, they returned to the regiment. Off the front and in a rest area to the rear, the division had a liberal leave policy. As many men as could be spared were given weekend passes to Paris and Brussels and even some seven-day leaves to the French Riviera and London. Before our stay in Laon was over, I received another forty-eight-hour pass, this time to Paris, my first visit there. My buddies talked about the city as if it was another world; for the combat soldier it was. I was awestruck by the history it embraced, the Champs-Élysées, the Arc de Triomphe, Napoleon's tomb, the Cathedral of Notre Dame, and the city itself. But with only a short pass, I was attracted to creature pleasures, such as the nightclubs and the Folies-Bergère. Because, in the push into Germany, the city had become an important supply center in the chain flowing from the beaches of France to the front lines, it was a beehive of military activity. American service troops by the thousands had moved in and taken it over. The streets and sidewalk cafes were crowded with uniformed Americans. I was astonished by the number of men who were assigned to the services of supply and other support units. I made a mental comparison between the relatively few men in the rifle companies on the front lines and the thousands strung out for miles behind us in support. I couldn't think of a single instance while we were on the front line of being at authorized strength. I asked myself the same question that other combat soldiers asked when in Paris on leave: "Where were all these guys when we needed them?" The answer was simple: They were doing their jobs, just as we were doing ours. What I have never been able to understand is why it took so many of them and so few of us.

By late March 1945, Allied forces had crossed the last natural obstacle to the advance into Germany and to Berlin.

Three bridgeheads were established across the Rhine as attacking troops moved rapidly east. American forces encircled the Ruhr, Germany's industrial heartland, closing the loop on an estimated 350,000 Germans. With the Ninth Army pushing from the north, and the First Army coming from the south, then attacking west toward the Rhine, the Wehrmacht was trapped in the Ruhr pocket. It started from Frankfurt and Kassel and was bordered on the west by the Rhine River.

Supporting the advance across the Rhine was an air assault by two airborne divisions, the U.S. 17th and the British 6th, a combined force of more than 20,000 troops. The 17th was the newest American airborne division in the ETO, having arrived on the Continent in December. The men experienced their baptism of fire in the Battle of the Bulge and gave a good account of themselves. They, like those in my division, made practice jumps in France for a possible airborne mission.

On 24 March the 17th took off from marshaling areas in France and landed in Germany behind enemy lines at 1010. They encountered unexpectedly strong enemy resistance. On the first day, they suffered more than 900 casualties: 159 killed in action, 522 wounded, and 250 missing. Many troop carrier planes and gliders were also destroyed or damaged. Given the tactical situation and the status of German forces, the question was asked, Was the airborne assault necessary? And was it worth the casualties the airborne forces suffered?

In April 1945 our intelligence gurus could have confidently predicted that it was now only a matter of time. The nearest Allied forces were within 250 miles of Berlin; the Russians, moving rapidly from the east, had reached the Oder River about thirty miles east of Berlin. This was the tactical situation when the 504th received warning orders to depart Laon and take up defensive positions on the west bank of the Rhine facing the encircled Germans in the Ruhr pocket.

XV
Watch on the Rhine

16 April 1945

On 4 April we moved out of Laon and went about 250 miles to the east. The division was assigned a sector extending about ten miles, with the 505th deployed south of Cologne, Germany, and the 504th deployed north of Cologne.

Unlike the last time we left France for Belgium, the snow and ice of winter had given way to spring and flowers. It felt good to be alive. More importantly, we had sufficient notice to prepare for what lay ahead. Furthermore, the tactical situation when we departed for the Rhine was drastically different from what it had been on 19 December. Instead of being on the offensive, the Wehrmacht was now retreating into Germany, fighting a delaying action. Our mission when we left France was to keep the Germans contained in the Ruhr pocket and prevent them from escaping across the Rhine while U.S. forces were tightening the noose.

The likelihood of the Germans attacking us was remote. However, American commanders took nothing for granted. They would not be surprised again by what the Germans might do as they had been on the morning of 16 December, nor would they be accused of lack of imagination. Our mission was unlike any we had been given up to now, not a demanding assignment but more a reflection of the rapidly deteriorating situation for the Germans.

We assumed defensive positions previously occupied by the U.S. 86th Infantry Division. During daylight, we looked for signs of enemy activity. After dark, we sent listening posts from each platoon in H Company to take positions along the Rhine where they could detect enemy movement.

If the Germans tried to attack across the river, we would be ready for them.

However, our commanders were not content to occupy defensive positions to guard against a threat that did not exist. They ordered patrols—rotated among the rifle companies—across the river at night to make contact with the trapped Germans and attempt to capture prisoners. Without exception, whenever we were in a defensive position for even a brief period, night patrols behind enemy lines were ordered.

On 5 April it was H Company's turn. To cross the river we were given two wooden boats capable of carrying a platoon. The boats were propelled by oars, not paddles. Lieutenant Rufus K. Broadaway was selected to take his platoon into enemy-held territory to seize prisoners.

It was late at night when his patrol reached the river and the boats. The men began rowing across, maintaining a true course against the rapid current. It was a quiet, calm night with little activity on either side of the river. Albert Tarbell accompanied Broadaway: "I was ordered to go with the patrol as the radio man. I took along an SCR-300 radio. I had to have a man for protection because I could not carry a weapon [such as a tommy gun] other than my .45 pistol. I never realized how swift the river was. We got over OK without being shot at. I believe the Germans may have thought we were their men coming back."

The patrol disembarked without being fired on, then moved out in the direction of the suspected enemy location. The men secured the boats but felt no need to leave a guard with them. A letter written by Broadaway shortly after the patrol gives some details:

> The patrol had both a radioman and a demolitions man; the latter was to de-mine the landing area, if necessary. We landed 600 yards north; that is, downstream, of our objective. Part of the patrol's mission was to explore the Bayer factory at Leverkusen.

> After we had checked out the Bayer factory, we

proceeded north again toward the boats. I had two choices in returning to the boats: One was to return on top of the dike—a faster route, but it would silhouette us against the sky for any enemy that may be in the vicinity. The other was to proceed between the dike and the river, and that is the one I chose.

Soon, we saw a line of men moving on the dike towards us, estimated at platoon strength. I recalled the warning that other American patrols might be active in our sector. It would have been unforgivable to fire on and wound or kill American soldiers. I went with my BAR [Browning automatic rifle] man on the right flank to apprehend them. He quickly identified them as German. I heard the bolt of the BAR slam forward and misfire. Immediately, everyone began firing at once.

The situation was not good. The enemy was on high ground, and we were with our backs to the river. I had to presume they had backup with other enemy troops behind them. The chance of overwhelming them was not good.

I chose to disengage and get my men to the boats as quickly as possible, hoping that the boats had not been discovered. This was my responsibility and my decision. In addition, I had been hit in my left eye. There was a lot of blood, which clotted and closed the eye. I assumed my eye was gone. This, however, was a minor element in deciding our course.

When I arrived at the boats, three men were missing. I started back to find them, but the enemy again engaged us from the dike near the boats. We returned fire, loaded in the boats, and began rowing across the river, meanwhile returning fire until we were out of range.

I did not lose my eye. That wound accounted for my only Purple Heart in a year of almost constant combat.

It was nearing daybreak when Broadaway and his patrol returned to H Company. Although the Germans were hopelessly trapped in a rapidly shrinking pocket, they demon-

strated that night and again at Hitdorf the following day that
they would not go away quietly. By the same token, the actions of those two days made it clear that the Germans could
not possibly storm across the river to attack H Company and
the 3d Battalion. Still, we continued to send patrols nightly
across the river to engage the enemy and attempt to secure
prisoners.

Sending patrols at night across the Rhine River involved
a high degree of risk, and casualties could be expected.
Whether all the patrols were essential and the risk to the men
involved was justified was of secondary concern to the commanders, who would not have to lead them.

To avoid the perils of crossing the river at night, a plan
was devised to send a larger force of company size to seize
and occupy a town on the east side of the river to be used as
a base of operations for our patrols. This would negate the
need to take boats across the river every night. On the situation map, it looked like a good idea; it proved to be otherwise.

On 6 April, at about 0230, shortly after Broadaway and
his patrol had returned, A Company, 1st Battalion, started an
assault across the river to implement the plan. The objective
was the village of Hitdorf. Overcoming heavy enemy fire
and working its way through minefields, the first wave of
A Company entered the village. By 0830 the company had
deployed the platoons in a perimeter defense and established
a command post in the village. In the battle for Hitdorf, sixty
German soldiers surrendered. Everything proceeded according to plan. Hitdorf was seized and occupied, and the base
for further patrol action was in place. The situation seemed
to be under control, but that would soon change. To the Germans, an American beachhead across the Rhine and the occupation of Hitdorf were bones in their throat they couldn't
swallow. They would not retreat quietly.

At 0845 that morning, they launched the first counterattack on Hitdorf, from the south, in company strength. They
hit A Company's outposts and forced them back into the village. When the enemy reached the edge of the village, they

ran into a heavy barrage of small-arms and automatic weapons fire. The attacking force was quickly routed, with heavy casualties. Another thirty-eight Germans surrendered. During the morning, A Company began ferrying prisoners back across the Rhine.

But the Germans were not through. About noon they zeroed in on Hitdorf with all the guns at their disposal, sending A Company scurrying for cover. The heavy barrage knocked out the company's lines of communication with the platoons and an artillery observation post in a church steeple. The company radioed back for artillery support; the 376th Field Artillery Battalion responded, scattering the Germans.

But the Germans attacked Hitdorf again, from the south and east with another two hundred men supported by two tanks. This time the Germans did not use second-rate soldiers; they sent their first team, paratroopers from their 3d Paradivision. They soon overran the 3d Platoon, defending to the south of Hitdorf, and fought their way into the village. At about the same time, another force of approximately two hundred Germans attacked from the north. They soon overran A Company's 2d Platoon and also entered Hitdorf. Greatly outnumbered by the enveloping Germans and having lost contact with the 3d Platoon, A Company was forced to drop back. With its two remaining platoons, it fought its way through the surrounding Germans and pulled back to the beach, where it established a defensive position.

I Company of the 3d Battalion was alerted to cross the river to support A Company. I Company crossed the Rhine at 0930 on 7 April with two platoons and joined up with A Company on the beachhead. Together, they beat back another attack of about two hundred Germans supported by a platoon of tanks. In the attack, the lightly armed paratroopers engaged the tanks with Gammon grenades, knocking out one tank, presumably a Mark IV.

While maintaining their position on the beachhead, the companies came under artillery fire, but they held their ground. In the morning, isolated groups, using boats undamaged by German artillery, infiltrated back across the river, taking advantage of an early-morning mist over the water. I Company launched a counterattack and cleared the beachhead area, permitting additional men to cross. I Company then withdrew from the beachhead, taking with them their wounded and another thirteen German prisoners. Shortly thereafter, A Company was able to withdraw with their wounded. The thirty-eight remaining prisoners under A Company control, having been disarmed, were released.

This engagement was one of the bloodiest battles of the war for small units. Casualties were high. A Company with attachments numbered about 150 men. They reported 112 casualties: nine KIA, twenty-four WIA, and another seventy-nine MIA. With all the confusion prevalent at night and the breakdown in communications, the KIA figure was probably higher. For A Company, having to withdraw after seizing and occupying Hitdorf was a demoralizing setback. To their credit, the men fought courageously against a superior force. Before they withdrew from the east bank, they had killed or wounded an estimated 350 Germans and taken another eighty prisoners.

From the vantage point of planners at higher headquarters, the mission at Hitdorf was a success. Enemy troops and armor were diverted from other areas of the Ruhr pocket to counterattack the forces occupying Hitdorf. They believed it hastened the collapse of German resistance and shortened the battle of the Ruhr pocket by weeks, but not everyone was in agreement on that point. The 504th's regimental book *Those Devils in Baggy Pants* concludes the account of the battle of Hitdorf with the following notation: "Whether or not A and I Companies served their purpose in diverting enemy troops from a more important sector is impossible to say."

When we had taken up positions on the Rhine, I had two weapons: a Thompson submachine gun and a .30-caliber sniper's rifle. A rifle with a telescopic sight could be more effective than a tommy gun with limited range. In the early-morning hours, I remember climbing a church steeple overlooking the river. From there, I had a clear view of the river and the approaches on both sides. When the early mist over the river cleared, I could spot smoke coming out of chimneys, a telltale sign that Germans, probably cooking breakfast, occupied the house in question. Occasionally I would observe a German soldier out in the open. With a telescopic sight on the sniper's rifle, I could fire on targets at a thousand yards and more, although hitting a moving target at that range would have been a lucky shot. I don't believe I hit anyone across the river at that distance, but I probably came close enough to scare my quarry and make him think twice about being exposed.

Several days after the battle for Hitdorf, H Company men spotted a boat crossing the Rhine coming toward our company sector under a white flag of truce. On 11 April I wrote a letter to my sister Catherine describing that incident: "Several days ago a German Colonel and a sergeant crossed the Rhine River in a small boat carrying a white flag. When they reached our side of the river, they were escorted by one of our men to the H Company CP located in the cellar of the house. The Colonel was a medical officer, and I thought they had come in to surrender; but, instead, the Colonel had come across to our side to tell us we had been shelling their hospital and asked us to stop. I relayed their message to Battalion. [The German officers] were detained and spent the night in our CP as our guests. However, the Colonel objected to having to spend the night in the same corner of the basement with his sergeant. I ran across a lot of Krauts in this war and have done business with them from the other end of a Tommy gun, but this was the first time I ever had to be nice to them. I had an interesting and unusual talk with them about the war, after the war, and conditions in Germany. The Colonel was an arrogant Nazi, slickly dressed, medals all over his chest and wearing a monocle—Hollywood style."

The colonel spent the night in our custody. The following day he returned to his lines. His message and the location of his hospital were dispatched to higher headquarters. I never knew whether the shelling of his hospital stopped, but I assumed that it did. Less than a week after the Germans returned to their lines, patrols from the 504th made contact

with the 97th Infantry Division, sweeping north on the east
bank of the river. The Ruhr pocket was eliminated, and the
Germans were surrendering by the thousands. The hospital
was now under our control and secure from artillery from either side.

The morning the colonel departed, we received a call
from battalion saying that the assistant division commander
(ADC) could be expected at our CP soon. A newly promoted
brigadier general, the ADC had recently been assigned to the
82d. I reported to him when he arrived. "Sir, I am Lieutenant
Megellas. Welcome to H Company." I had never met or seen
him before, nor was I aware that the 82d had an ADC, but
that was of no import. I was wearing dirty clothes, was unshaven, and wore no insignia. Although I had reported that I
was a lieutenant, the ADC asked, after noting my appearance, "Are you an officer?" I replied in the affirmative. The
next question he asked he could have answered himself just
by looking at me: "When was the last time you shaved?"
Once again, I sucked it up. "Sir, when we left Laon, I didn't
bring a razor with me." His most galling comment was, "I
expect officers to set a good example for the enlisted men."
To me that was more than just an offhand expression. I took
it as a personal insult. After the general finished expressing
his displeasure with my appearance, he indicated he wanted
to inspect our defensive positions. I pointed out that we had
all three platoons on the line dug in behind an embankment
about two hundred yards from the river. Just behind our lines
we manned an observation post during the day in the highest point in our area, a church steeple. I pointed out that at
dusk each platoon sent a listening post to the edge of the
river to provide an early warning of enemy movement. I re-
iterated that the likelihood of the Germans, trapped in the
pocket, attempting to escape the closing pincers by crossing
the river in the H Company front was not within the realm
of possibility. In the unlikely event they did attempt to navigate the river in force or with patrols, we were ready for
them, even welcomed an attempt. We would be looking
down their throats and would have them lined up in our gun

sights before they could get started. Both Lieutenant Sims, H Company CO, and I felt confident and secure in our defensive preparations.

However, the ADC did not share our confidence. He questioned why we did not have men dug in at the edge of the river during daylight hours. He pointed to an area on the edge of the river where he said we should have men placed twenty-four hours a day. I noted that the area he indicated contained an old minefield. There was no map of the minefield, but because we believed that the mines had been laid indiscriminately, we thought it would be risky to send men there. Yet as a lowly lieutenant, all I could say was, "Yes, sir," even though I believed that his request was foolhardy and unnecessary.

I was fuming and reported back to Sims. Then I called Lt. Col. Julian Cook, 3d Battalion commander. I knew that calling battalion to plead my case against a general's order was an exercise in futility, but I had to vent my feelings. At the very least, I hoped someone at battalion would sympathize with me. Colonel Cook's response was understandable: "Maggie, he's a general. You better do as he says." I remember we used to have a saying in our outfit: "If you're looking for sympathy, you'll find it in the dictionary between suicide and syphilis."

Sergeant Smiley was the one ordered to take a squad to the riverbank and dig in. The men didn't make it to the river. They ran into a minefield and froze in place when one went off. Smiley, leading his squad, stepped on a trip wire and was killed. His body was placed in the back of a jeep. I was waiting in front of the company CP when it arrived.

The U.S. forces encircling the Germans in the Ruhr pocket were tightening the noose. German resistance was collapsing, and the soldiers of the Wehrmacht were surrendering by the thousands. In isolated areas, some fanatics continued to hold out. Elements of the elite SS and Hitler youth groups chose to continue fighting rather than surrender. Hitler had ordered the 350,000 Germans trapped in the pocket to organize into small groups and escape to the east. A few did, but most had lost their will to resist. For them, the handwriting was on the wall.

Yet we continued to maintain our vigilance. The regiment kept ordering patrols across the river at night on tactical missions of questionable purpose. In H Company, we still manned our defensive positions, with men deployed along the river during the day and with listening posts at night. The men were rotated within the platoons to occupy the outposts on the riverbank. A minefield between the company line and the river continued to present a problem, in spite of all the precautions taken to avoid it. On 11 April the hidden mines claimed another victim. On the way to an outpost on the river, Pvt. Clarence E. Willand, a new man, set off a mine, which killed him. Although the war was nearing the end, it would not be over for us until Germany surrendered.

On 12 April we received news of the death of President Franklin Delano Roosevelt. I remember exactly where I was at the time. Many men in my platoon had volunteered just out of high school and were in combat before most were old enough to vote. Franklin Roosevelt was the only president we ever knew or could remember. He was one person in a long chain of command whom I could identify with and respect. The combat-hardened paratroopers with me who had come to accept death stoically and without remorse were stunned by the news. Our president symbolized everything we held dear and were fighting to preserve.

On 13 April patrols from our side of the river made contact with elements of the 97th Infantry Division on the east bank. It signaled the end for the Germans trapped in the Ruhr pocket. Three days later, organized German resistance in the pocket had ended, with most of the remaining 325,000 Germans surrendering. In addition to the German POWs, some 200,000 slave laborers were liberated and 5,639 Allied prisoners of war were freed. With elimination of the pocket, the 504th was relieved from its watch on the Rhine.

XVI
Hitler's Last Gasp

V-E Day, 7 May 1945

With the elimination of the Ruhr pocket, we entered Cologne, where for the next ten days we were engaged in policing an area north of the city. In the wake of advancing U.S. forces into the heart of Germany, military government was installed in the occupied cities. Our job centered around enforcing military government, clearing the area of weapons and ammunition, and assisting in relocating displaced persons. It was a job to which combat-hardened paratroopers were unaccustomed.

It was a far cry from the grueling, demanding days of continuous combat. The war was not over officially, but there was no doubt that it would be soon. Talk revolved around meeting up with our Allies, the Russians, and about the possibility of going on to Berlin.

Cologne, the fourth largest city in Germany and an important commercial and industrial center, had been the target of intensive Allied bombing. The city lay in ruins. Miraculously, its famous Gothic cathedral, towering 529 feet, was still intact. All five bridges across the Rhine were blown. The retreating Germans, unable to get their tanks across the river, left hundreds behind.

The sight of devastated cities became commonplace as we entered the heartland of Germany. Any city capable of producing the sinews for the Nazi war machine had been targeted by wave after wave of Allied bombers. The war had been brought home to the Germans in a way they never envisioned when Hitler sent the Wehrmacht streaking across Europe in all directions.

For the next ten days, H Company continued policing activities in a 360-square-mile area northeast of Cologne. We encountered practically no resistance. The Germans surrendered by the thousands, although some fanatical elements continued to resist. They were dropping back to the next natural barrier, the Elbe River, where they would make their last stand.

In village after village, we encountered white sheets of surrender hanging in the village square and homemade white flags hanging from doors and windows. The few German soldiers we met who had not already surrendered were lined up in the village square, their rifles neatly stacked, waiting to be taken prisoner. I imagined that the populace was relieved that the war was ending and the surrendering soldiers were grateful to be taken alive.

In the towns and villages under H Company control, curfew was imposed from dusk to dawn. I was determined that the Germans, a militaristic nation accustomed to regimentation, would find it no different under our control. They would abide by our rules and orders. I took pains to see that the curfew was strictly enforced.

After dark I patrolled the streets on a captured German motorcycle, with Pvt. George Heib seated behind me. Heib, whose grandparents had migrated from Germany, was fluent in German and was the company interpreter. Like me, he felt no sympathy for the Germans. Heib recalled:

> One night Lt. Megellas and I were cruising down the main street when we heard voices from back of a house. Upon investigation we spotted two young German men. Lt. Megellas commanded them to halt, and I questioned what they were doing out after curfew. They had visited some friends and didn't note the time. They were stammering and visibly shaken. Lt. Megellas had me tell them they could be shot for violating the curfew. Then he told them that he would let them go, but he would count to three. If we could still see them, we would shoot them. At first he and I pointed our Thompsons at them and asked

if they understood. We received a very frightened series of Jawohls! I then started to count to three very slowly. By the time I got to the count of two they were over the fence and away. Lt. Megellas fired a short burst in the air and remarked, "I bet those Krauts won't be breaking any more curfews for a while." In fact, we never again found any German personnel out after curfew. Of course, you had to know how Lt. Megellas looked. He was pretty tall, had very dark eyes, and had a fierce looking black handlebar mustache. He looked and talked tough.

My nightly "bed checks" made believers of any doubters in the towns that H Company controlled. With my tommy gun slung over my shoulder, I looked for any sign of curfew violation. If I found lights on in the house after a reasonable time, I left my calling card—a burst from my tommy gun.

I thought that, from its inception, the SHAEF nonfraternization policy was ill advised, yet I tried to enforce it. I could understand how the men felt but could not accept the willingness of the German girls to sleep with their enemy either for sexual pleasure or to seek favors. I had developed a special bond with the men with whom I had been in combat and could not impose any kind of company punishment on them for doing what came naturally. Scaring off their partners was punishment enough. On one of my nightly "bed checks," I interrupted a love fest in a haymow. I opened a big barn door and lit the area with the spotlight of my motorcycle, breaking up the party. The men quickly scattered, but I rounded up three of the girls. They were not in violation of the nonfraternization policy, because it applied only to the men, but I held them responsible and wanted to make an example of them. At the very least, they were in violation of the curfew restrictions. I brought them back to the company CP and locked them up in the dark cellar of the house. After forty-eight hours in solitude without food or water, they did not resemble the sexy-looking girls who had been with our soldiers. I released them unharmed but terrified by their ordeal.

* * *

On 27 April we moved to an area south of Hamburg and from there continued east, pursuing the enemy to the Elbe River. Those still resisting were falling back all along the front. No matter how old or young the remaining German soldier was, he was still strong enough to pull the trigger of a gun or the lanyard on his artillery piece. Even if there was only one round of ammunition left and only one aging German left to fire it, the war was still very real. Until the last shot was fired, the war was not over for those of us doing the fighting.

On 1 May the 504th reached the west bank of the Elbe and established a CP in the town of Breetze. The 3d Battalion, encountering only minimal resistance, reached the river in the vicinity of Bleckede. Meanwhile, units of the 505th Regiment, using British assault boats similar to those we used at the Waal River, crossed the 1,000-foot-wide Elbe River at Bleckede at 0100. Taking the Germans by surprise, they established and secured a beachhead by dawn. Our engineers constructed a large pontoon bridge. In spite of a heavy enemy artillery barrage, described as the heaviest faced since Normandy, the engineers assembled the bridge in just thirteen hours. The 504th streamed across the river in pursuit of the fleeing Germans. Advancing on our left across the Elbe was the 8th U.S. Infantry Division, to which my brother John was assigned.

In the waning days of the war, the greatest obstacle we encountered was a type of German mine we had not seen before. It was a five-hundred-pound buried explosive that was activated by the magnetic influence of passing vehicles. It was timed to explode after a preset number of vehicles passed over it. It could be offset anywhere in a convoy of trucks or tanks; thus concealed, it was not given to detection. The explosion left a huge crater in the road large enough to accommodate a small house. During the course of the war, I had not seen a crater that big from any type of German weapon. It was something we did not expect, and it took some time to understand what we were up against. Lieutenant Sims recalled seeing a

U.S. tank activating one of these mines: "I was nearby. The explosion lifted one of our tanks about 30 feet in the air, killing the entire crew." With the war so nearly over, it was demoralizing to see men, tanks, and vehicles hurled into the air by mines we were not able to detect. Yet our vehicles and tanks kept coming, taking their chances in order to pursue the enemy.

Sims recalled how the problem of the buried explosives was resolved: "Our engineers somehow or other were able to locate German engineers who had placed and armed these explosives. Together, they were able to locate and disarm the remaining charges."

With the news of Hitler's suicide, the Germans began surrendering in larger numbers—whenever possible to advancing American troops—as they fled from the rapidly advancing Russians from the east. To facilitate their surrender, U.S. planes dropped leaflets on German troop concentrations that would serve as safe conduct passes. They were printed on both sides, English on one and German on the other, over the signature of Dwight D. Eisenhower. The leaflets assured the bearers that they would be treated well and given food and medical attention.

The ever-increasing number of surrendering German soldiers accompanied by camp followers, men and women of all ages, were clogging the roads leading to the rear. The mass of humanity presented enormous logistical problems. The Germans had to be confined, fed, and clothed, and their basic human needs satisfied. Many panic-stricken civilians were fearful of what the rapidly approaching Russians might do to them. They viewed the Russians as barely civilized and their combat soldiers as barbaric. They feared the consequences of surrendering to the Russians or living under their control.

In the meantime, the 3d Battalion was rapidly moving northeast, overcoming only scattered resistance from isolated fanatic Germans who, for whatever reason, refused to give up. Our objective was the city of Ludwigslust, population approximately 10,000. H Company was leading the 3d Battalion advance, and Sgt. Jimmy Shields's squad was leading the point. As H Company neared Ludwigslust, Shields spotted a large enclosed area that appeared to be some type of encampment. On closer examination he noted that it was protected by a chain-link fence with barbed wire on top. When word from the point squad reached H Company, I came forward quickly to see for myself.

When Shields and his squad reached the fence, he saw four or five "skinny looking men" clad in dirty striped clothes peering inquisitively through the chain link. Shields recalled: "One of the prisoners was a boy of no more than 13 years who spoke English. He had been confined for several years. He remembered walking five or six miles when he was placed in the camp. He never knew why he was there." Shields remembered that the front gates were locked, so he took his pistol and blew the locks off. Then they entered the grounds.

I entered the camp at the same time. We proceeded through the camp and found the back gates open; the guards had obviously left in a hurry. The squad proceeded about three hundred yards beyond the gates, looking for any signs of the departed Germans. Shields recalled: "I placed two men, Joe Bernard and Duffey, with two BARs to cover an open field ahead of us. After about 15 minutes, I got word to pull back to H Company. On our way through the camp, I saw bodies stacked up along ditches for burial." Shields lowered the swastika from the flagpole and retained it as a memento of the occasion. In a storeroom, Sgt. Frederick Andrews found two neatly folded swastikas, which he still possesses.

I was not prepared mentally to deal with the horror of the camp. Wobbelin was one of the newer camps in Germany, hastily built to hold the overflow from other camps and to confine the increasing number of political prisoners. It lacked some of the more devious and sophisticated means used in the older camps to exterminate the captives. Here, instead of quick death in a gas chamber, a slow, torturous death through starvation became the principal means of killing. In addition to the Jews marked for elimination,

Wobbelin sounded a death knell for thousands of political prisoners: nationals from Holland, Russia, Poland, Greece, and Czechoslovakia. Most had starved to death before the camp was liberated.

In the early days of the war, when the Wehrmacht was riding roughshod over anything standing in its path, the Nazis had rounded up and sent off to concentration camps anyone who might oppose the regime or became a threat politically. In addition to Jews, civilians who did not measure up to the standards of the super race were sent to their death. The concentration camp at Ludwigslust was one of many that the Nazis had created in Germany and the occupied countries. Sergeant Tarbell recalled the approach to the camp: "You could see the guard towers, and the smell of dead human beings was in the air." The SS had fled in haste, leaving everything intact. Mounds of dead were strewn in the buildings and on the ground. Those barely clinging to life and unable to move were mixed in with the lifeless.

While others moved around the grounds, I headed for a row of buildings that resembled our earlier U.S. Army barracks, poorly constructed tarpaper shacks. In the first I entered were about two hundred twisted, nude bodies of skin and bone, piled four to five feet high. Individual forms were almost indistinguishable. There could not have been a body of more than sixty pounds; most were much less. In one corner of the building was a pile of ragged, filthy striped clothes, apparently taken off the bodies for reissue to the next victims. I proceeded to an adjacent building similar in construction but somewhat larger. Inside were inmates, still alive, some just barely. Most were lying on the dirt floor or propped against the sides of the building too weak to get up. With sunken eyes and skin taut, they looked like living skeletons. In the center of the building were rows of triple bunk beds; barbed wire served as a mattress, without any bedding. I saw no one lying on the wire. I stood motionless looking at the ghastly sight.

I was able to communicate with several of the inmates, one a Greek national. Many were Dutch. From one who spoke English I learned that the Gestapo had rounded up all suspected Allied collaborators and sent them here. This was done either just prior to the Holland invasion or just after our jump there. Many of the Dutch inmates did not know why they were confined, nor were they aware that the invasion and liberation of Holland had taken place. From the inmates I spoke with, I was able to gain some understanding of the inhumane conditions they had endured. Once a day, for dinner, a guard dumped a big bucket of water and turnips on the dirt floor and called for the inmates to come and get it. Those still able rooted through the turnips on the floor like animals. Many had been capable of working when first incarcerated, but it was only a matter of time before their strength gave out. Many suffered from dysentery; too weak to get up, they lay in their filth. Dysentery was commonplace and sanitation nonexistent. On a regular basis the guards loaded the dead on carts and dumped them into pits to be buried in mass graves.

In another building I saw someone I assumed was a doctor tending to an inmate with a large, hideous sore on his back. The doctor appeared to be in better physical condition than anyone else. Apparently, the Germans kept him alive (actually there were two doctors in the camp) to maintain a workforce as long as possible. However, medical care consisted only of advice from the doctors, who had no access to medical supplies.

It was not until our men witnessed this that we fully realized what we had been fighting for. The destruction of the monstrosity the Nazis had created was the cause greater than ourselves that we had often alluded to but never fully understood. It was a defining moment in our lives: who we were, what we believed in, and what we stood for. For Private Herndon, it was a contributing factor to his entering divinity school, then the ministry after the war ended.

We responded quickly to the situation. Inmates on the verge of starvation had to be nourished, dead bodies prepared for decent burial, and decomposed bodies disposed of in a civilized manner. The first concern was for the living.

Bread and canned meat were brought from a German warehouse. The sight of food on the arriving trucks triggered a stampede of frenzied men. They climbed over one another, grabbing for food like animals in the jungle. However, after months of food deprivation, their digestive tracts were unable to process solid food. Distribution had to be stopped almost as quickly as it had started. Ambulances drove those still alive to a nearby hangar set up as a hospital. There, under the supervision of doctors, they were fed intravenously until they could consume solid food. Many inmates survived to tell the story of the horror they had endured. The worst off were not as fortunate.

Attention now turned to the piles of dead bodies. They had to be given proper and reverent burial, honored, and remembered. The citizens of Ludwigslust had to be told of and castigated for the barbarity that had been allowed to take place just four miles from the city. As in most other German cities, the mayor of Ludwigslust had basic food items stored under lock and key. He could have shared some food with the inmates of Wobbelin but had chosen not to. Later I learned that the mayor and his wife and daughter committed suicide.

While we were at Wobbelin, many more concentration camps were being overrun by Allied troops in Germany and the living inmates liberated. The conditions were no different from those we had found; in fact, in the larger, more notorious camps, they were often worse.

General Eisenhower decreed that the remaining bodies of all the victims of the camps be buried in public places and maintained with perpetual care similar to that at military cemeteries. It was further decreed that crosses or stars of David be placed at the head of each grave site and a stone monument erected memorializing the victims.

The public place selected at Ludwigslust was the beautiful and prominently located Palace Plaza. It was a public park that extended outward from the large marbled palace. The town's leading citizens, representing every profession, were ordered to dig burial holes six feet deep, precisely aligned by our engineers, and make markers for each grave. Two hundred bodies—those that could be moved—were brought to the park and laid out, one next to each freshly dug grave. Before the bodies were finally laid to rest, every inhabitant—ten thousand residents, ranging from housewives to city fathers—was required to pass through the plaza and witness the remains. The macabre parade proceeded in an elongated single file. Some, mostly elderly women, seemed mortified by the sight; most residents, with hats in hand, accepted the view stoically. After all the years of sacrifice, deprivation, and lost loved ones, the sight of two hundred bodies, albeit resembling skeletons, changed their outward composure very little.

The entire population was required to attend the burial service. All three 82d Airborne Division chaplains—Catholic, Protestant, and Jewish—participated "in the name of a God who respects no super race but only humanity, regardless of race, creed, or color." Major George P. Woods, division Catholic chaplain, addressed the gathered citizenry, reiterating the horror we had uncovered. He questioned how human beings could be forced to live like animals and allowed to starve to death. He placed the responsibility for the atrocities on the people themselves, even though they claimed no knowledge of what had transpired. They were culpable, he said, "for they were committed by a government elected by yourselves in 1933 and continued in office by your indifference to organized brutality."*

After Wobbelin, we were still in pursuit of the Wehrmacht, although they were offering little resistance. A vehicle carrying four officers entered our line under a flag of truce and proceeded to the Company CP. Sergeant Tarbell recalled their arrival: "The four German officers were all wearing leather coats and dressed to kill. The driver pointed to an officer in the back seat and said he was a General and wanted to meet with

*On 2 May 1995, the survivors of the Wobbelin concentration camp had a fifty-year commemoration in Ludwigslust to recount their ordeal and express gratitude to the liberators.

our General. We told them that just ahead they would find some military police who could direct them. One of the officers told me, Pvt. George Heib, and Sgt. Donald Zimmerman, who were with me, that they wanted to regroup behind our lines and with the Americans fight the Russians."

My platoon and H Company were attacking east of Ludwigslust on 2 May when we learned that the German Twenty-first Army was surrendering. Ironically, the formal surrender of the army by Lt. Gen. Kurt Von Tippelskirch took place in the Palace of Ludwigslust, where General Gavin had established the division CP. The surrender terms were unconditional and accepted by Von Tippelskirch.

The forward element of the 3d Battalion, H Company, set up a roadblock on one of the roads leading into the division sector to disarm the surrendering Germans. On that historic day, an entire army, with a vast array of tanks, trucks, half-tracks, howitzers, vehicles of all types, and motorcycles, began to pass through the division's checkpoints heading to the rear. With Russians not far behind, the convoy of German soldiers and armaments bore little resemblance to the Wehrmacht that had fought so hard against us.

We were witnessing an unprecedented event. First, an entire German army, about 150,000 men, surrendered to a division of about 10,000. Second, their frontline units were combating Russian forces, not American. Third, the Germans passed through our lines in reverse order—army headquarters first, then corps, divisions, and regiments; the combat troops came through last. The general staff included ten generals; the headquarters appeared to be in excellent condition. They seemed to have prepared for the grand finale. Clean-shaven and groomed, uniforms clean and neatly pressed, boots shined, with monocles and medals, they were proud to the very end. They represented some of the top brass of the Wehrmacht. They rode in large, chauffeured staff cars accompanied by their women, wives, or mistresses. The obedient aides, still by their side, took care that the generals were going out in style.

They took approximately one week to pass through our

lines, with vehicles almost bumper to bumper for the first few days. Their rear-echelon troops appeared to be in excellent physical condition, looking much better kept than our own combat forces. All of their equipment and armor was also in good condition. I found it difficult to believe that they were the conquered and we were the conquerors.

On the third day, their frontline units began to pass through our lines. On the fourth and fifth days, their fighting men appeared, not riding but on foot. Varying in age from sixteen to sixty, they were a scraggly looking lot, dirty, unkempt, with shoes held together by rags. They were a far cry from the commanders and staff who had passed through first. There seemed no question that they were a soundly beaten force, with no fight left in them. Although the generals and their staffs were still capable of continuing the war, they no longer had quality frontline troops to command.

As the Germans passed our checkpoints, they were disarmed; in many cases, our troops relieved them of their cameras, watches, and other "souvenirs." Sergeant Charles Crowder recalled: "I obtained a burlap bag, mounted a motorcycle with a sidecar and, as the enemy troops marched by, I told them to throw their pistols in the bag. I started taking watches and rings until the bag was full. I figured this was my chance to get rich. I also took money in German marks. I gave away all the pistols that I gathered to other men in my unit, except four, which I kept for myself. I kept most of the watches." Sergeant Jimmy Shields emptied a barracks bag full of pistols on the table and told his squad, "Help yourself." I picked out several highly prized pieces: a Luger, a P38, and an Italian Beretta. Sergeant Donald Zimmerman traded a Mauser pistol with me for a weekend pass. The Mauser, a semiautomatic that could be fired as a pistol or attached to a wooden holster and fired as a shoulder piece, was carried by general officers and was of World War I vintage. It was the only one I ever saw.

German pistols were highly valued by our rear-echelon noncombatants. With a German pistol, they could spin some tall yarns about the war even though they had never heard or fired a shot in anger. Pistols were relatively small, compact, and easily concealed. There was a lucrative market for the "spoils of war" in our rear echelon.

Although pistols were the most valued, Mauser rifles also drew attention. From a huge pile I claimed one that appeared to be in excellent condition; from another pile I picked out an excellent double-barreled Browning shotgun made in Belgium. I was allowed to bring both guns home with me; I used them for hunting.

Watches and rings were also valued as souvenirs, especially the ring with a crown of skull and crossbones worn by the SS. It was a rare occasion when a German prisoner made it beyond the frontline rifle company still in possession of a ring or watch.

Everything a German army had in its table of equipment that was not needed to move the POWs to the rear was in evidence in large amounts. Two Hungarian cavalry regiments with splendid-looking horses and equipment passed through our lines, offering to join forces to fight the Russians. They were relieved of the horses, which we commandeered for our own use. Sergeant Zimmerman recalled that the men laid out a track and raced horses in what was referred to as "Sauerkraut Downs."

From a large number of motorcycles parked in the H Company area, I commandeered a couple that caught my eye: a single rider bike and one with a side carrier. At the first opportunity I took off on one of the bikes in search of my brother John's unit: the 8th Infantry Division. When I located him, he was perched behind a light machine gun guarding German prisoners inside an enclosed barbed wire POW collecting point. I had not seen him since we were both in England almost a year ago, so it was an unexpected and joyful reunion. John's company commander gave him a pass so he could return with me and spend a few days at H Company. It was a memorable trip of about fifteen miles on a motorcycle capable of speeds up to 150 kilometers per hour.

While the Germans were surrendering, we were expecting to meet the Russians at the Neue Elde Canal, north of

Ludwigslust. On 3 May men from I Company made the first contact in the town of Eldenburg. When they returned to I Company, all they remembered was drinking vodka and toasting leaders of the three Allied countries.

The Neue Elde Canal became the dividing line between H Company and the Russians. A small bridge across the canal connected these combat-experienced forces. With the war practically over, the celebrations began with our Russian Allies. Frequent trips were made across the canal, with both sides visiting each other's command posts. It seemed that the Russians had an unending supply of vodka and were generous in sharing it with us. We did not have access to American whiskey to reciprocate, but it made no difference. They downed vodka by the water glass. Before every drink, we went through the ritual of toasting our leaders: Stalin, Roosevelt, and Churchill. Stalin came first when the Russians proposed the toast; Roosevelt came first when we did the honors. When drinking with the Russians, there was always a toast, but over time the names changed, first to Stalin, Truman, and Churchill, then later to Stalin, Truman, and Atlee. Stalin was a given and Roosevelt had died, but drinking to Atlee was difficult for the Russians. They could not understand what happened to Churchill; nothing like that could happen in the Soviet Union.

The Cossacks were outgoing, raucous, and fearless. They drank hard and fought hard. I was glad they were on our side; despite our differing backgrounds, as combat soldiers we had a lot in common. After we met them, I could understand why the Germans feared them.

Any political differences that may have existed between the United States and Russia were not evident to us. We were celebrating a historical moment, the demise of Hitler's war machine. We had both done our share and survived it. What greater reason could Russians and Americans have for celebrating?

One evening, Rivers, several men from H Company, and I crossed the canal to pay our respects to the Russian commander and, of course, to drink the Russians' vodka. That was a new experience for me, but I found it easy to drink straight. Not to be outdone by our Russian comrades, we went bottoms up with them. That was where we erred. The Russians had the edge on us, and they knew it. After several hours of what turned out to be a boisterous event, they brought food and set it on the table. There were plates of black bread, not sliced but broken off from a large loaf. Another plate contained a ham. Our hosts proceeded to hack off chunks of it from the bone and motioned us to help ourselves. Other than the carving knife, there were no utensils, but no one found that an impediment. After all the vodka I had consumed, I was happy to get some food in my stomach. I found the black bread coarse, dry, and stale, but edible. The ham, however, presented somewhat more of a problem; it was uncooked, and I had difficulty chewing and swallowing it. It didn't seem to bother the Russians. In spite of my difficulties, I managed to express my satisfaction.

After several more glasses of vodka, I passed out. The last thing I remembered that night was drinking to Stalin. I did not know how Rivers and our H Company men were faring and did not remember seeing them again that night. It must have given those Cossacks a great feeling of accomplishment to drink American paratroopers under the table. They dragged me to a corner of the room and threw a blanket over me to sleep it off. I did not come to until after daylight the next morning.

That was unfortunate, because I missed an extraordinary event. Early the next morning, the Russians decided to drive to Berlin. They took Rivers and several of our men with them, and would have taken me as well if they could have aroused me. They viewed the destruction of the city and returned the same day. Rivers and his men were among the first Americans to enter Berlin. Rivers described the scene. The Russians had just eliminated the remaining pockets of resistance. The city was devastated. Between the pounding it had taken from the massive Allied bombings and the shelling it took from the attacking Russians, the city lay in ruins. Dead soldiers still littered the streets, lying in some cases next to dead horses. Berliners were coming out of shelters to find their homes demolished or burning and trying to piece their lives back together.

The traffic across the narrow bridge flowed in both directions, with the Russians coming to pay their respects with bottles of vodka in hand. Lieutenant Rufus Broadaway was visited by a major at his platoon CP. Broadaway remembered the social visit going well until Stalin came on the radio. The major jumped to his feet and stood at attention. Broadaway recalled: "He demanded that all of us do the same. When he became obnoxious about it, I threw him out of my CP bodily."

On the American side, the nonfraternization policy was in effect and, although difficult to enforce, it did constrain our young men from having affairs with the fräuleins. However, the Russians were not subject to any similar restrictions. They openly sought favors from the girls and forced themselves on them when cooperation was lacking. At night we frequently heard the screams of German girls echoing across the canal, expressing not delight but fear. What was happening to them was what most likely happened to Russian girls when the Wehrmacht was sweeping across Russia in the earlier days of the war. When mankind sends their young men off to war to kill one another, the victims extend beyond the battlefield.

After several days across the canal from the Russians, we bade them farewell and moved northeast farther into Germany. At 0241 on 7 May, the Germans signed the surrender document at the Supreme Allied Headquarters in Rheims, France. For the time being, frontline troops were ordered to remain in place and risk no casualties. The surrender of Germany legally took effect at 0001 on 9 May 1945.

After almost two years of bloody fighting from Sicily to Germany, the war was finally over for us. General Gavin noted the occasion in his book *On to Berlin:* "So we had come to the end of the war in Europe. It had been costly. More than 60,000 men had passed through the ranks of the 82nd Airborne Division alone. We had left in our wake thousands of white crosses from Africa to Berlin. And when it came to an end, there was not a man in the ranks of the 82nd Airborne Division who did not believe that it was a war that had to be fought."

The surrender of the Germans and the official announcement of the end of the war did not set off any celebrations in the ranks of H Company. The announcements had been expected and actually were anticlimactic. The question that arose for us in H Company was, What's next? That and any other questions we might have had would soon be answered. It was rumored that our MOS would probably change to "killing Japanese," but there was no basis for it yet. Most speculation centered around when we would be leaving for the States and home. The rumor mills kept grinding away until the official announcement was made of what units or individuals would be eligible to leave the theater. I wrote to my brother George on 23 May about what we were doing:

> At present we are in the northern part of Germany, east of the Elbe. We have been policing up towns, moving slave laborers and refugees and generally keeping things under control and trying to send displaced persons back to their homes. Nobody especially cares for the job, but then we've got to do something while we are here. I don't know how long we will be here, but it's just a matter of lack of transportation.
>
> All the men live in German houses. The civilians were kicked out of their homes we are using. Under the non-fraternization policy which is in effect, we are not allowed to have any relations of any kind with these people, but you probably know all about that. I always thought we'd run across some good beer over here, but so far we haven't found any.
>
> There are a lot of deer up here and we've been doing some hunting. I've gotten two — one four-point buck and the other a doe. Of course, we have no game regulations. Outside of deer, rabbit hunting, and motorcycle riding,

there's not very much to do. I believe if a man stayed here long enough, it would get him down.

We continued occupation duties while awaiting our next assignment. We received official announcement of the establishment of a point system to determine which men would qualify for return. Eighty-five or more points were required based on length of overseas service, days in combat, decorations, and other factors. With 110 points to my credit, I was one of the 50 percent of the regiment qualified to return home, but it was not mandatory. An individual could opt to remain. The point system did not apply to the career, regular army officers. Almost without exception, the company-grade officers were commissioned as reserve officers. What would happen if someone who had sufficient points to leave chose instead to remain was uncertain. The expectation was that the 82d would go on to Berlin as the occupation force.

Lieutenant Sims returned from leave in Paris to learn that he and Lt. Bernard Karnap, G Company, were selected for early return home. Sims recalled: "Lieutenant Karnap and I each had more points under what was called 'Green Project' than anyone else in the entire Division." Sims would be sorely missed. Another seventy men were selected to return to the States. Although I was eligible to return home, I chose to stay and go on to Berlin. When Sims departed, I was named the H Company commander and would continue in that capacity in Berlin, then return with the division to New York in January 1946. We received orders to return to Laon, France, to reorganize, receive replacements, and prepare to move to Berlin to undertake occupation duties. At Laon, an exchange of paratroopers took place between the 504th and the 507th. All the 504th men and officers eligible to leave under the point system were transferred into the 507th. Those men in the 507th with insufficient points were transferred into the 504th. The 507th Regiment would return to the States to be deactivated.

On 2 July 1945, I wrote to my youngest brother, Louis,

from Laon: "I'm sure happy to know that you're home. . . . I volunteered to stay with the 504. We've got all new low point men in the outfit now. All the old men are gone and I don't know a soul anymore. Lt. Rivers is even leaving. He said he was coming to visit the folks when he gets home."

In July 1945 we said farewell to many of the originals and old-timers of the 504th as they departed for the States. It was a sad good-bye, a parting of cherished buddies with whom we had become close. I had mixed feelings about Rivers leaving. He had lost his only brother during the war and felt he should return to his family. Occupation duty in Berlin would not be the same without him, yet I looked forward to going. Although the fighting had ended, there was still some untended business. It was now time for the Germans to be held accountable for the reign of terror they had spread across Europe. I despised Nazis and all they represented, but I did not have a vendetta against the German people. In my area of Berlin, they would not be abused or treated inhumanely.

XVII

Occupation of Berlin: A City Divided

With most of the combat veterans gone from H Company, we now had to reorganize with the cadre of those who remained and the replacements of newer men from the 507th Regiment. The departure from France experienced a number of delays. One reason was that the Soviets who had captured and occupied Berlin were not yet ready for the Allied forces from the United States, Great Britain, and France to join them. Other reasons for the delay related to the availability of transportation to move us from scattered bases in France to the designated area in Berlin. In the meantime, we kept busy intensively training and preparing for a new and unfamiliar role. No one knew what that would entail.

Garrison duty in Laon, France, was boring and uneventful, but it gave us time to regroup, deal with personal matters, and get caught up on letter writing. On 11 July 1945, I wrote to my sister Mary: "I'm feeling swell and in the best of health. We're stranded about 100 miles from nowhere. Nancy is the largest nearest town. About all I have been doing for recreation is playing ball. I play with the men in our Company team and with the Battalion Officers' team. We've been able to get beer now so beer drinking occupies my evenings. . . . In going through my wallet I ran across some bits of foreign money and two German propaganda leaflets that were dropped on us in Italy when the Krauts were still pretty cocky. I'm sending them home."

While we were preparing for our impending move to Berlin, the war was still grinding on in the Pacific, so it was possible that we would deploy there. It was one of the reasons that many of us chose to remain with the division. As Lt. Dick Owens noted: "Rumors had it that the 82nd was destined for transfer to the Pacific, and if that were the case, I would want to be with my Regiment, the 504th."

My youngest brother, Louis, had just returned from the Pacific, where he had been wounded in the battle for Manila. In a letter to him on 2 July 1945, I commented: "If they should send you back and John's outfit [8th Infantry Division] goes, I'm volunteering for the CBI [China, Burma, India theater] myself. There has been some question in my mind if I should volunteer now but I guess I'll wait and see what happens. But if you and John go, I'm not going to sit around in Berlin."

In a letter to my sister Mary, I said that the next time she heard from me I would be in Berlin. It turned out that assumption was correct. Several days later we received orders. Some units of the advance guard had already arrived in the American sector. A week later my company arrived and was in place in our designated area. The division was the first American unit to enter Berlin for occupation duty. The arrival of the 504th was the culmination of two years pursuing the Wehrmacht some 14,000 miles across eleven countries.

The American sector was located between the British 11th Armored Division and the Soviet 5th Cossack Division. My company area was located on the division's right flank and bordered on the Russian sector.

I was in frequent contact with my Soviet counterpart, a captain commanding a Cossack company. Mutual visits to our respective company CPs turned out to be more social than tactical. Drinking water glasses full of vodka, toasting our national leaders, and swapping war stories were the first orders of business. We were, after all, wartime allies still basking in the defeat of the Nazi war machine. Although a number of cultural differences cropped up, there was no evidence in our relationship of the Cold War strains developing between our two countries. We were combat officers who had fought a war and survived. The tension developing in the aftermath of the war between Russia, a Communist state, and its democratic allies had not yet filtered down to our level.

On entering Berlin, we found the city in ruins, almost leveled by the incessant bombing. In the remains of the once proud German capital, the site of the 1936 Olympics, where Hitler had taken the Nazi salute from hordes of wildly cheering Berliners, confusion and chaos now reigned. In the worst damaged sections, rubble and remains of buildings could be seen for miles. The few buildings and apartments still habitable were taken over by the Allied forces for headquarters and billets. Bomb and shell craters in city streets were filled with water. Nearly all the bridges over the Main Canal had been destroyed by bombs or blown up by retreating troops. A few buses and streetcars were the only means of travel available. But the stench of death that Rivers had described when he saw the city about three months before, just days after the Russians had captured it, no longer permeated the air. The Germans had buried the corpses and dead animals. Graves marked by wooden crosses, many without identification, occupied public squares. Everywhere the Germans were removing debris from razed buildings. Bricks and building blocks were being cleaned and stacked in neat piles to be used in reconstruction. The same high level of industry and diligence that had once applied to the development of a war machine was now being directed toward reconstruction. Building materials, in particular steel and cement, were in short supply, so it would be a long time before Berlin again resembled a leading cosmopolitan city, but from what I had come to know of German resilience, perseverance, and the work ethic, it would happen much sooner than anyone expected. Berlin, like the Phoenix, would rise again from the ashes.

In the myriad tasks facing the Allied governing body, public health became a matter of urgency. Dead and decaying bodies still being uncovered in the rubble had to be disposed of and a degree of sanitation restored to avoid the spread of disease and epidemics. In the flooded and destroyed subway system alone there were an estimated 3,000 bodies that had to be removed. Deliveries of food to the city that had been disrupted during the Russian siege had to be restored. Food was in short supply and was strictly rationed; women, children, and older men unable to work barely received a subsistence ration. People were getting only 64 percent of the recommended 1,240-calorie daily allotment. Amid the scarcity of food, a black market soon developed, further complicating the food shortage. Berliners seeking work with Allied forces were not concerned about monetary wages, because there was little they could buy, and markets in the early stage of the occupation were almost nonexistent. What people sought instead for their labors was payment in food. In a letter I wrote from Berlin to my sister Catherine on 9 September, I said: "They would do anything for food in Berlin. I've got some Krauts working for my Company, carpenters, painters, women pressers, tailors and housemaids. We draw rations for them and the German government pays them something like $4.50 per week, which doesn't buy them a package of cigarettes on the black market. So all they work for is what little food we feed them."

German women became a commodity in the black market. When they ran out of things they could barter, they traded themselves. Moral standards in Berlin reached an all-time low. It was impossible to distinguish between good girls and girls of bad character. The number of girls selling or bartering love for goods in Berlin approached a sixth of the population. Because of war casualties, there were nearly three women for every man. Many available men were either too old or too young to support a wife or family, and most men were unemployed with no economic means.

In the American zone of Berlin, about 90 percent of the soldiers ignored the nonfraternization policy until, on 1 October, General Eisenhower rescinded it. An estimated 20,000 to 30,000 illegitimate children had been fathered in the American zone alone. Venereal disease in Berlin was rampant, approaching epidemic proportions. In a spot check, nearly one-third of the girls examined were found to be afflicted. Once a German girl contracted venereal disease, there was nowhere she could turn for help. German doctors had no access to penicillin or sulfa drugs except on the black market at unaffordable prices. Venereal disease spread like the plague in some American troop units.

Winter soon would come, and fuel, like everything else, would be in short supply. Trees from nearby forests were cut down for heating homes and buildings. Basic necessities couldn't be provided until factories were restored and opened. The outlook for a tolerable winter in Berlin in 1945 appeared bleak.

In the midst of the devastation and deprivation, I found it hard to feel compassion for the Germans, even though it was now almost impossible to find a Berliner who professed to be a Nazi or even a Nazi supporter. I expressed my feelings about the Germans in the letter I wrote home on 9 September: "The only trouble I have with Krauts now is to keep them from milling around our chow line with little buckets waiting for leftovers. As far as I'm concerned they can all starve and I have told my cooks to throw any extra chow in the sump hole before they give any to the Krauts."

In retrospect my feelings about the German populace may appear to have been hard-hearted and lacking in civility. But for me and the combat veterans of H Company, forgiving Germans wasn't possible. Our new replacements, who had not experienced combat, harbored no ill feelings toward them, because the new men had no score to settle and occupation duty was just another assignment. This raises the question of why a division such as the 82d, with a long history of combat in the ETO, would be assigned to occupation duties. Militarily the Berliners posed no security threat to the occupying forces, and the possibility of armed riots was nil. The occupying forces of the other three Allied countries were also made up of combat troops. We knew, however, that after taking control and maintaining peace, we would be replaced.

Reports reached us in Berlin of a new type of bomb being used against Japan; it was supposedly more powerful than anything previously conceived. Details were scarce, but we soon learned that an atomic bomb had been detonated on Hiroshima on 7 August, killing approximately 140,000 people and leveling the city. Three days later, a second atomic bomb was dropped on Nagasaki, killing 70,000 people. The devastation was so great that Japan sued for peace. On 14 August, Japan accepted the Allied peace terms, and on the morning of 21 September the Japanese signed the formal instrument of surrender on board the USS Missouri. The war was over and the guns fell silent around the world. Speculation now centered on how long the 82d would continue as occupation troops. The general expectation was that all would soon be returning home.

The surrender of Japan did not trigger wild celebrations in H Company or the regiment. Most men received the news stoically, although they were relieved knowing they would not be fighting another war. Some, such as Lt. Dick Owens, who had enough points to rotate back to the States but had opted to remain with the 504th, decided to leave, now that the possibility of deployment to the Pacific theater no longer existed.

My feelings were expressed in the letter I wrote home on 26 August: "Now that the war is over I understand everyone in the States had a big celebration. To us it was just another date. I have learned to take the good news in the same manner as the bad. I'm disappointed for not getting a crack at them (the Japs)."

I used the word *disappointed* because, as the war had progressed, I found the business of killing and destruction agreeable. I suppose this comes when killers are made out of soldiers. Alexander the Great cried in his tent when he realized there were no more lands to conquer. I didn't cry in my company CP, but I was saddened knowing there would be no more lands to conquer or enemy to kill.

After my regiment was reorganized and I became a company commander, my name was placed on the eligible list for a one-week furlough. Shortly after we arrived in Berlin, my number came up for a furlough to the French Riviera. Lieutenant Robert "Boobytrap" Blankenship, I Company

CO, was also on the list. Together with a C-47 planeload of men from the 3d Battalion, we left for one of Europe's most glamorous vacation spots. It had returned to its prewar status and was bristling with fun-seeking civilians and Allied military personnel.

Boobytrap and I checked into a luxurious hotel just off the beach in Cannes. Our enlisted men were equally well treated in the city of Nice. Cannes was the most beautiful city I had ever seen. I was twenty-eight years old. Every night Boobytrap and I made the rounds of the glitzy nightclubs and spectacular shows featuring scantily clad dancing girls; we didn't return to our hotel until dawn, then spent our daylight hours on the pristine beaches of Cannes in the company of gorgeous girls. We spent several days learning how to navigate a sailboat in the balmy waters, soothed by the refrain of French songs sung by our alluring new friends. The limits of my masculinity were tested in ways never tested on the battlefield. Our one-week stay was a combat soldier's dream of paradise.

Shortly after we returned, Colonel Tucker called Boobytrap and me to his headquarters to discuss a personal matter. The U.S. Army, looking ahead to the postwar configuration, was offering regular army commissions to selected reserve officers. Boobytrap and I had entered military service as reserve officers, having received commissions as second lieutenants from the ROTC. We were the only two officers in the regiment considered and were encouraged to apply by Tucker and our battalion commander. We were led to believe that a regular commission in the U.S. Army would be ours for the asking; all we needed to do was apply.

Although we were both flattered by the proposal, we asked to sleep on it. We had entered military service immediately after graduation from college, so we were uncertain about employment in the private sector. In the army we had found a home and now the possibility of a permanent job and a career. After much soul searching, Boobytrap and I decided to go for it. We submitted the necessary forms with the assurance that our applications with endorsements would be approved as a routine matter.

With my one-week furlough behind me, I returned to the everyday tasks confronting H Company in our role as occupation forces in Berlin. The contacts with the Cossack company bordering on H Company were frequent, mostly for official purposes but also for social get-togethers. The Russians were inquisitive about American paratroopers and the U.S. Army in general. They were particularly interested in what the combat and service medals pinned on my blouse meant. I explained what each one of the decorations was awarded for. While I was relating this to them, they looked at me in awe. They thought that I had it made for life, because Russian army combat decorations equivalent to mine would provide the recipient with a lifetime tax-free pension, free housing, scholarships for children, free public transportation, and more. I was amazed at what they told me, but they were dumbfounded when I responded that none of my decorations entitled me to benefits of any kind, monetary or otherwise. This was before the GI Bill, which the U.S. government approved at the conclusion of the war; to all returning veterans who had served, it authorized benefits for education, housing, health services, and more, which helped not only the veteran but society as a whole.

I was in favor of the GI Bill even though I did not take advantage of it; I had already finished my college education. Shortly after I returned to the States in 1946, I received a "Greetings and welcome back" letter from the Internal Revenue Service advising me that I owed federal income taxes for the years 1943, 1944, and 1945. My taxes had only been deferred while I was overseas; they were now due and payable. The three years added up to a sizable amount. The letter took me aback, because tax on my army pay was the last thing I had in my mind during the years I was in combat, living like a groundhog, just trying to survive. After prolonged periods in combat, we received all our back pay, usually in military scrip. It seemed to be of little value, because there wasn't much I could spend it on, except to squander it on booze and women when they were available off the front lines. Other than that, it served as a medium of exchange at crapshoots and poker games. When we were in combat we called our pay "funny money"; I was now being taxed in real American dollars. With the additional $100 per month jump pay I received for hazardous duty, my total pay exceeded the standard deduction. The irony of the tax due was that if I had been killed I would have avoided paying income taxes, or if I had not volunteered for the paratroopers and certain combat I would not have incurred a tax liability. I had no alternative but to pay my tax bill. It was, after all, the law of the land.

Our mission as occupation troops was to maintain order in our sector of operations. A number of guard posts were established throughout the company area to observe and report any unusual activity. In a letter of 9 September to my sister Catherine, I wrote: "My Company is alert Company tonight so we are restricted to the area. One Company in the regiment is always kept on the alert, in readiness, which can be called out on a minute's notice in case of an emergency or riot. Up until now we have never been called out on such a job but I think as it gets colder we will have some trouble since the fuel and food situation is so acute."

One of the hot spots that concerned me and occupied much of our attention in the area was the Anhalter Bahnhof railway station, the only one then operating in Berlin. Several weeks after I had returned to civilian life, I was interviewed by the Fond du Lac *Commonwealth Reporter* regarding the occupation of Berlin. On 28 January 1946, an article appeared in the paper under the headline "Grim Life-Death Struggles at Berlin Railway Are Recounted by Veteran."

Russian, American troops clashed frequently after the Nazi defeat. Some of the thousands of people trying to leave the ruined city died of starvation outside the station unable to fight their way aboard one of the three trains leaving Berlin. . . . One woman gave birth to a baby on the street adjoining the station.

First priorities on trains leaving the terminal, which was located close to the Russian-American occupation boundary, went to Soviet troops being redeployed, discharged or leaving the German capital on furlough. Next in order were the German wounded and released prisoners of war. The POWs were usually farm owners returned to their homes to raise crops. Last priority was allotted to crippled civilians.

A heavy machine gun, manned by Megellas' men, was set up on a raised platform where the gunner could command all approaches to the trains. When a train came into the station hundreds of people, who often waited for weeks to get a seat would make desperate rushes for the coaches, and age or sex meant nothing if one of them stumbled or fell. The machine gun was necessary to discourage rioting, Megellas said.

The Russians were a rough lot. . . . They were usually armed with pistols and gave us a lot more trouble than the Germans. They were not very cooperative. . . .

When the men were on guard duty, they were armed with M1 rifles, whereas officers carried pistols. When we were off-duty and away from the company area, we were not permitted to carry arms. The restrictions banning arms in Berlin applied only to Americans. The restriction did not apply to the Russians, with whom H Company had the most contact.

An H Company man was arrested by the MPs for carrying a concealed weapon. At his summary court trial he demonstrated that the Colt .45-caliber pistol, which he had been charged with carrying, was not operable. He had removed the firing pin, which he produced as evidence. He did not, therefore, believe he was carrying a real weapon. He intended to deliver the pistol to a friend scheduled to leave soon for the States. The court ruled against him, saying that even though the pistol lacked a firing pin, it could still be looked upon as a weapon.

American units established local government and imposed regulations controlling civilian movement and activities. Those were matters that did not concern me or my men. The civilians in our sector caused us no problems; in fact, we found them cooperative. We employed some twenty civilians as tailors and seamstresses and others for housekeeping and maintenance chores.

The bordering Russian sector was far different. The Soviets, like the Americans, had combat troops deployed in their sector of the occupation. At gunpoint they relieved the Germans of everything of value to them, especially watches and jewelry. We often observed Russian trucks backed up to German houses stripping them of everything not nailed down. I understood that the Russians felt they were due war reparations, seizing what they felt entitled to by virtue of conquest. Russian trucks and railway cars streaming out of Berlin and heading east were laden with the spoils of war.

Russian soldiers were uncompromising in their treatment of women. At night we often heard screams of terrified women from the Russian sector. First Sergeant Bernard Cheney, H Company, stated in an interview: "If we saw a Russian raping somebody on the street or doing something terrible, we had to look the other way. We were supposed to ignore physical abuse of the people if the Russians were doing it in their sector. It was pretty hard. I did not cotton to it. . . . In my Company, men were constantly being arrested and punished because they had gotten into a fight with the Russians trying to stop them from molesting German civilians. I remember it very vividly."

The personal relationship I developed with the Cossack company commander was useful in resolving some problems that arose, but it did not eliminate incidents and conflicts between the men. When they stayed in their own sector, they could do whatever they pleased, but when they crossed over into my sector on a raid, it was another story. Private Simon Renner was on guard duty the night of a Russian foray into our sector. This is his written account: "I was . . . on a guard post near the Russian sector in Berlin when a frightened, screaming German woman came to my post pleading for help. The Russians were looting her house and had attempted to assault her. I immediately called for the Sergeant of the Guard. We loaded onto Jeeps to check it out. When we arrived we found a truck parked at the scene. A Russian officer was standing at the curb talking to a German civilian. The door on the passenger side of the truck was open and the driver was inside. The Sergeant of the Guard ordered me and Private Simmons (H Company) to hold the truck while he took the rest of the men to investigate the building that they had been in. . . . While they were gone the Russian officer told his driver to start the truck. I was standing in front of the truck with Private Simmons behind me. There was a street light to our rear so that I could not see the driver." It was late in the evening and the situation was confused, but Private Renner had his orders. "I pointed my M1 rifle into the driver's general direction and ordered him to shut off the damned engine."

For reasons I was unable to determine, the Russian driver either misunderstood or failed to comply with his order. Renner told me then, and on a number of occasions since, that he believes the Russian not only defied his order but was attempting to put the truck into gear to leave the scene. "Again, I ordered him to shut his engine off," said Renner. "When he did not, I fired and killed him. The German civilian wanted to go for a doctor, so I let him go. When the Sergeant of the Guard returned, I told him we had a dead Russian in the truck. He said, 'Oh, my God.' We loaded the dead soldier into the jeep with me and the Russian officer in another and took them to the Russian sector and gave them to their MPs."

I conducted an investigation into the incident and submitted a report to regiment. Private Renner recounted the outcome: "For this action I was tried and acquitted by a General Court Martial for manslaughter. However, I was not permitted to go near the Russian sector and had to have an armed guard with me wherever I went."

There were other incidents along the border separating

H Company and the Russians where shots were exchanged, but this was the first reported death. The Russians were terribly upset, failing to see any reason why the driver was shot to keep the truck from leaving. Our investigation did not satisfy them. The acquittal verdict further irritated them. My personal relations with my counterpart were severely strained. I tried to soothe his ruffled feelings, pointing out that Renner carried out an order in the only way he knew; he was an enlisted man doing his duty. I told him that Renner had fought the German Wehrmacht all the way from Italy to Berlin and was wounded in the process. He did what he had been trained to do, reacting instinctively on this occasion. Shortly after the incident, Renner, who had sufficient points to rotate home, exercised his option and returned to civilian life with an honorable discharge.

Black markets had sprung up during the war in some of Europe's largest cities. Given the bleak economic conditions at the end of the war, dealing in the black market became a way of life. It involved not only the Berliners but Allied troops flush with money and little of value to spend it on.

The official occupation currency in Berlin was the Allied military mark. The marks for the British, French, and Americans were printed in Washington and controlled. However, the western Allies had given the Russians duplicate plates to print military marks. They printed their own marks without restrictions in quantity.

At the end of the month, the men in H Company lined up at the pay table to receive military marks. Most of the men had had a large portion of their pay deducted and sent home to their families. The balance was spent for personal needs at the post exchange (PX) or at clubs for U.S. military personnel. The PX issued ration cards controlling the quantity of such things as cigarettes. Almost anything available at the PX was highly valued on the black market. Bartering or selling such merchandise was in violation of army regulations. Most soldiers consumed their regular allotment of rationed items, but they were not deterred from bartering or selling excess or unneeded items.

The Russians printed an uncontrolled amount of military marks, identical to the other occupation marks. They then paid off their troops, who in most cases had not been paid for years. For good measure they added a victory bonus. Unlike American soldiers who could convert the marks to dollars, Soviet marks were not convertible. So the Russians had to spend their marks in Berlin or leave them behind when they returned to the Soviet Union. Consequently, they used the black market to buy items of value in Russia. They looked for small, compact, and easily transported items. One such item fitting the bill was something all Americans owned: watches.

Behind the bombed-out Reichstag, a black market flourished in the Tiergarten, where as many as 4,000 people would congregate on an average day. Russians were buying watches from the Americans, and Berliners bartered family valuables for cigarettes, coffee, and candy. For the Germans, money ceased to be a medium of exchange. Barter was the keynote, and ads for everything could be found posted. Russian soldiers carried briefcases full of currency to the black market area; they were on a shopping trip, looking to buy watches. Luxury items in the Soviet Union, watches were beyond the price range of most soldiers, regardless of quality. The soldiers looked for watches with bright, numbered faces, sweep second hands, and loud ticks. Mickey Mouse watches captivated them and sold for as high as $1,000 in marks. During the final days of the war, when the Germans were surrendering en masse, I managed to accumulate a number of watches. I decided to find out how much they were actually worth. Near the Brandenburg Gate a Soviet lieutenant carrying a briefcase approached me. I rolled up my sleeve, exposing ten watches. One by one he examined them, shook them, then placed them next to his ear listening for the tick. The price he offered for each one ranged from $100 to $250 depending on how they met his criteria. He bought half the watches. I ended up with a wallet full of military script, legal tender in the PX and nightclubs of Berlin. To supplement their PX rations, U.S. soldiers wrote home for things to barter, Mickey Mouse watches among them.

On 9 September 1945, I wrote from Berlin to my sister Catherine with a list of things that were unavailable or in short supply and others that were rationed: "There are some things I could use. Two white sheets for my bed, cigarettes and some food; canned seafood, crackers, salami, Kaukauna Club cheese, canned beer, mustard, horseradish, chili sauce, canned chicken, pickles and hot peppers. Well, that's just an idea so you won't make a mistake and send me Spam like you did a couple of times. And don't forget cigarettes. I can use several cartons."

With the war over in the Pacific, war-torn Europe faced an invasion of another kind. As U.S. servicemen were heading for the United States, American celebrities, dignitaries, congressmen, diplomats, and Pentagon brass were streaming east en masse to see firsthand the devastation in Europe. Berlin became a mecca for the travelers. Among the celebrities received by the 82d in Berlin were entertainers Bob Hope, Ingrid Bergman, Jack Benny, Ella Logan, and Martha Tilton. They came to see Berlin and bring a piece of back home to the troops. They were welcomed and appreciated.

American paratroopers, referred to by the Germans at Anzio as "devils in baggy pants," now assumed a new and additional role as "America's Honor Guard." A selective, elite unit of the 82d, made up of combat veterans, all more than six feet tall, became the division honor guard. Resplendent with white gloves, white bootlaces made from parachute shroud lines, white scarves cut from silk parachutes, and chromium-plated bayonets, they were ever present at the Tempelhof Airdrome, meeting celebrities who were arriving in droves. The guard turned out to honor Gen. George S. Patton on V-J Day on the occasion of an Allied victory parade. After reviewing the honor guard, Patton remarked: "In all my years in the Army and all the honor guards I've seen, the 82nd Berlin honor guard is the best."

My company, like the rest of the regiment, spent a considerable amount of time in close order drill, dress rehearsals, and preparing for parades and reviews. To observe V-J Day we paraded with other Allied forces, passing in review before the top commanders. First Sergeant Cheney wrote about that event: "I remember watching Eisenhower and Zhukov in a parade. We had to varnish our rifles, wear white gloves, and make scarves out of our parachutes. After the parade we had to take the varnish off our rifles. [The parade was] quite exciting for the men."

In a letter I wrote to my sister Catherine on 9 September, I mentioned another scheduled review: "The Division is holding a review this Tuesday at which time I will receive my Distinguished Service Cross. The General order came from Washington last week. With the Silver Star And Cluster, the Bronze Star, and the Purple Heart And Cluster I have more higher decorations than anyone in the Regiment. I also have a total of 123 points that are doing me no good as far as getting home is concerned. So don't be building up any false hopes."

When the company left that morning for the review, our German employees were abuzz with the news that the company commander was going to be decorated. When we returned to our area, a group led by an English-speaking tailor requested permission to speak to me. They wished to extend congratulations for the award, which they understood was a high decoration for bravery. They entered my office in single file and lined up at attention facing my desk. The German tailor stepped forward and in perfect English said, "We wish to congratulate the *Herr Kommandant* for receiving a combat award for heroism." Surprised by the gesture and uncertain how to respond, I told them why I was awarded the medal: the action in Holland where we killed seventeen German soldiers and captured six more. My comments prompted an agreeable nodding of heads.

It seemed strange that these Germans felt any compulsion to congratulate an American for killing German soldiers, especially because they now found themselves in the employ of the conquering Americans as a matter of survival. Upon reflection, it seems that these middle-aged Germans, exposed to the reality of war, understood and appreciated awards earned in battle, albeit by an enemy officer.

Berlin was also a center of attraction for high-ranking government officials from countries that Germany overran and occupied during the war. Representatives from Belgium and Holland came to honor the division. The government of Belgium, represented by the minister of national defense, presented the Belgium Fourragère to the 82d as a royal order. I described the award to Catherine: "The Belgium Fourragère . . . is a red twined braid, which is worn over the right shoulder. This is a very distinctive award and a great honor to receive."

The division held a review on 19 October to receive an award from the Netherlands minister of war, Jan Meijnen. In another letter to Catherine, I wrote: "The Dutch are awarding the Division another unit Citation which is an award similar to the Belgian. It is a braided cord that is worn over either the left or right shoulder. I am not certain as to the color. . . . I will know though as I have been notified by Division Headquarters that I have been selected to receive the decoration personally from the Dutch at the formal award ceremony. The Division colors, one officer and one enlisted man will be personally decorated with the award and I am the officer representing the Division. There will be plenty of newsreel photographers and cameramen present and I'll try to get some pictures to send home. . . . I understand that I will also receive a personal award from the Dutch, the Dutch Liberation Medal. I'll know about that soon."

I was selected by General Gavin as the officer, along with a representative of the enlisted men, to receive the Military Order of Wilhelm on the division's behalf. It was the first orange lanyard issued to the division signifying the first award ever presented by the government of Holland to a foreign soldier. This lanyard adorns the colors of the 82d Airborne Division today.

I found the job of commanding a company that was

assigned occupation duties in Berlin completely different from leading a platoon in combat. To be sure I was still responsible for the security and well-being of my men, but, unlike combat, the threat to our existence was not my principal concern. We could look forward to our return to the States with a high degree of certainty. It was no longer a case of being "in for the duration" or being shipped home sooner in a box. I wrote home frequently describing Berlin and my job. On 26 August I wrote: "I am sitting in my desk in the Orderly Room. I've really got a swell office, a beautiful desk, radio, two easy chairs, and a desk for my executive officer and the First Sergeant's room is adjacent. We have apartments for men's quarters. . . ."

Although my company and the rest of the regiment kept busy preparing for reviews and parades, I was grateful that we were not designated as the honor guard unit. H Company had more important matters to be concerned about in Berlin than impressing visiting dignitaries with the sharpness of our drill. I preferred to let the battle streamers and combat decorations hanging from our guidons speak for us. Yet I was strict in enforcing the dress code and personal appearance requirements. I didn't compromise on that aspect of my responsibility. On garrison duty and living in a veritable fishbowl, we were being judged on the manner in which we carried out our new mission. Personal appearance and the ability to excel in close order drill and parades became important.

At night, special police (SP) of the 504th patrolled the downtown streets of Berlin maintaining order and generally trying to keep our soldiers out of trouble. The men on pass often tended to overimbibe, get rowdy, and violate the dress code. One of my men was picked up and charged with being drunk and disorderly, without a pass. He was returned to the company that night and turned over to the charge of quarters. The following day I received a delinquency report from the provost marshal (PM). I chuckled when I read it and shared a laugh with the other company officers. The PM's handwritten comments to "Maggie" are a classic example of the relationship that existed between two veteran officers of the 504th. The report speaks volumes on how we felt about our men. After noting a litany of violations, he recommended "a verbal reprimand only," not serious enough to warrant company punishment.

The air was filled with uncertainty concerning the future of the 82d as a regular division in the peacetime army. In early October, General Gavin received a cable indicating that the division would be deactivated in Europe and be replaced by another division. In November that decision was reversed, so we would not be deactivated but rather returned to the States. However, we were not given a definite date. In the absence of fact, rumors took over. After several letters home stating other dates, I wrote: "Due to a shipping shortage our date of sailing has been set back to about December Fifth." This was still incorrect. All rumors ended when the division received official notification that it would return to New York after the first of the year. Further, it would march up Fifth Avenue commemorating the victory in World War II. In mid-December we began arrangements to move to staging areas in northern France where we would prepare for our return to the States. Private First Class Robert Breland recalled our departure: "When we left Berlin we were sent to Le Havre, France, where we spent several days assigned to Camp Lucky Strike. I remember we had turkey for Christmas. One mess hall served contaminated meat and a bunch of the men got sick. We boarded the *Queen Mary* in Southampton, England, and departed for New York. I believe we docked at Pier 92."

Before arriving in England, I observed my third Christmas overseas but under conditions completely different from the previous two. In England the entire division boarded the *Queen Mary*. I observed my third New Year's Eve overseas in 1946 on the finest liner cruising the high seas.

XVIII
The 82d Returns to New York

Victory Parade, 12 January 1946

My return to the United States in January 1946 was unlike my trip overseas to Oran, Africa, in September 1943 on a 10,000-ton liberty ship. It had taken twenty-three days to cross the German submarine–infested Atlantic; my return trip took only five days. On 3 January the *Queen Mary* docked at New York Harbor. The 82d Airborne Division's long odyssey was over. For the next ten days, Camp Shanks, outside of New York City in Orangeburg, New York, would be our temporary home while we prepared to march a hundred blocks up Fifth Avenue in celebration of our victory over the forces of evil.

Our return to New York was also a happy occasion of reunion with family members and friends. Former H Company buddies who had rotated—including Mike Kogut and my closest friend, Dick LaRiviere (Rivers)—came to New York to welcome us back. Although they had left the army, they were still an important part of the division. Now lost in the midst of cheering throngs, they became anonymous as their places were filled by many who had not experienced a day of combat.

The paratroopers in H Company, marching in class A uniforms neatly groomed and tailored with jump boots and brass highly polished, bore little resemblance to the unit that was surrounded and cut off by the Germans on the Anzio beachhead just two years ago. Nor was it the company that had crossed the Waal River in Holland in the face of murderous fire. It was a far cry from the company that had fought at Cheneux, Bra, Petite Halleaux, and Herresbach and in the Battle of the Bulge only a year ago.

Impatient for a family reunion after almost two and a half years of separation, two of my three brothers, John and Louis (both combat veterans), and two sisters, Catherine and Mary, traveled to New York to observe the parade and be part of the historic moment. Being reunited with my family and seeing my old buddies rank as the highlight of my ten days in New York.

Every night after duty hours I would go into New York, where we all met and celebrated in some of New York's glitziest nightclubs. Luckily, I had accumulated a wallet full of dollars, personal checks, and money orders playing poker on the *Queen Mary*. It was easy come, easy go, and I spent it like water, insisting on paying the tab for everything and everybody in our group.

During the years overseas from Africa to Berlin, I had lost an appreciation for the value of money. In the States it was no longer "funny money" military scrip. Money now had real value and was indispensable in going out on the town. I found that in New York, just as Rivers had said, all those combat ribbons I wore on my chest wouldn't buy me a cup of coffee if I didn't have the dime.

I was amazed at the changes that had taken place in New York in my absence of three and a half years. For the first time I saw a television set transmitting pictures on the screen similar to a Hollywood movie. It was an incredible introduction to American technology and innovation that had developed even while the nation was preoccupied with the conduct of the war. I realized that while we were overseas, technological progress continued unabated, in some cases accelerated by the war effort. And the lights in New York and Broadway were back on in their entire breathtaking splendor. The sidewalks were overflowing with servicemen, sightseers, and people just going about their business. After spending months on end where the slightest flash of light could be detected by enemy gunners, the flashing neon and spectacular lights left me awestruck. It was like another world.

The streets were bustling with all manner of transportation and public conveyance. Production of private automobiles, suspended during the war, was now gearing up to meet the new demand. Cars hastily rolling off the assembly lines reflected shortages in some raw materials; wood was replacing chromium bumpers, and some cars came off the line lacking standard items.

My return revealed a stark contrast between two great cities. Berlin, the capital of the defeated nation, lay in ruins, devastated by the ravages of war. New York, the largest city in the United States, was a thriving, bustling metropolis unscathed by a war fought thousands of miles away. The cities were a study in the difference between winning and losing.

For me and the men of H Company, all was not fun and games. We were in Camp Shanks and New York for a purpose: to prepare for a parade in ten days. Officers and enlisted men arrived from airborne centers to fill the severely depleted ranks of the divisional units. Battalion and regimental staffs also needed additional officers and men to bring them up to strength. I was never certain if these men were on temporary duty (TDY) from their units or were permanently assigned to the division. In H Company the new arrivals were placed in squads and platoons and integrated into the ranks. We then began a week of intensive close order drill, training to prepare for the big event. The division had paraded and passed in review for General Eisenhower in England and again for him and a score of dignitaries in Berlin, but the New York victory parade would be the mother of all parades.

I left most of the daily training to the company officers. Garrison life and close order drills had never been my forte, although as the commander I took my place at the head of H Company when we marched as a unit. Field grade officers, major and above, inspected the companies and observed close order drills. I was happy to see and welcomed visits from officers whom I knew from combat. Comments they made about my company were usually helpful and always respectful.

Several days before the date of the parade, Boobytrap Blankenship and I were called to report to the battalion CP. Lieutenant Colonel Julian Cook, the commander, came right to the point. The applications for a regular army commission that we had submitted in Berlin were on outdated forms. We were handed new, updated forms and asked to resubmit them. According to Cook, nothing had changed; our applications would be quickly endorsed through command channels, then sent to Washington. We were again assured that approval was a certainty and would come soon. Boobytrap and I looked at each other and breathed a sigh of relief. We knew what was on each other's mind, but out of respect for Colonel Cook we asked for time to reconsider it. We were facing the same career fork in the road we had considered about three months before in Berlin. When we had first applied, the prospect of a regular army commission was exciting. Now, after a week's exposure and indoctrination in the peacetime army, we had misgivings. If the nation was still at war, there would have been no hesitation to reapply, but everything had changed. In combat our MOS had been clearly defined; in a peacetime army, we couldn't imagine what it would be. We questioned whether we could make the transition.

It didn't take us long to reach a decision. We decided we would leave the service after the parade and return home. We had done our share when the army was in dire straits and needed us. The future of the peacetime army could be left to others better suited for new roles.

Finally the day of the parade, 12 January, arrived. We were ferried in from Camp Shanks to unit staging areas where we would form up. Newsreels and cameramen were positioned along the route of march to pictorially record this historic moment. With Gen. James Gavin and his staff leading, the 82d Airborne Division smartly marched through the arch in Washington Square and up Fifth Avenue. Every rifle company—nineteen ranks of men and officers, nine abreast—was led by its commander and the guidon bearer. Rifle companies marching in perfect alignment were strung out in precise intervals on Fifth Avenue as far as the eye could see. On the reviewing stand to accept the division salute were Governor Dewey of New York, Mayor O'Dwyer of New York City, and Undersecretary of the Army Royall. General Gavin dropped out after passing the reviewing stand and took his place next to Royall. General Jonathan Wainwright, hero of Corregidor and formerly G3 of the division, joined Gavin on the reviewing stand. General Wainwright was a Medal of Honor recipient.

There had been other parades and celebrations in New York since the war, and in Europe more than eight months ago, and in the Pacific six months ago, but this was the first time an entire division returning from Europe paraded in New York. One after the other, the rifle companies passed by the reviewing stand with an "eyes right," with division commander Gavin taking the salute.

Along the route of march, I would catch a glimpse of a former combat buddy in the crowd. In every case when we passed by, I gave H Company the command "eyes right" or "eyes left," depending on which side of the street our buddies were standing. On numerous occasions I heard "Maggie" called out, twice by my former buddies Rivers and Kogut. They and the other H Company men whom we saluted on the march deserved the honor more than the dignitaries we saluted on the reviewing stand. They were important to the victory we had achieved.

This was a proud moment in the history of the 82d Airborne Division, but personally I was left with mixed emotions. I was always proud of being a paratrooper in the 82d and leading H Company in a ticker-tape parade. But I was also aware that the majority of the 171 officers and men I was leading in the parade had not been in combat with me. I concluded that it was the division that was being honored. Whether or not the men marching in the ranks were a part of that record didn't seem to matter.

The day was topped by an equally eventful night. The

mayor hosted a gala dinner at the luxurious Waldorf Astoria to honor Gen. James Gavin and his officers and men. I was one of the junior officers invited to the banquet. An estimated 350 men attended from the division; we were dispersed and seated at tables with representatives of the city. After dinner we went to a 504th Regiment hospitality room in the hotel. Colonel Reuben Tucker and Lieutenant Colonel Cook were there with their wives. Boobytrap and I received a lot of attention that night. Both Tucker and Cook pleaded with us to change our minds and remain with the regiment; they said it was not too late to receive a regular army commission. I recall Ruth Cook joining the chorus trying to persuade us to change our minds: "Julian needs you, don't leave him." Boobytrap and I realized, however, that if we chose to remain with the division, there was no certainty we would be assigned to the 504th. I had developed a great respect for both commanders, but the likelihood was remote that we would remain with them for long. That night we bade sad farewells to Tucker and Cook, both West Point graduates and career officers. I remember my parting words: "If you should get into trouble again, call us and we'll come back to help you."

The following morning I boarded a westbound train and, after an all-night ride, disembarked at Camp McCoy, in Wisconsin, to be processed for discharge from the army. I had arrived as a lieutenant and was departing as a captain. With the promotion as an inducement, I opted to continue my service in the army reserve. In 1979 I was discharged from the active reserves with the rank of lieutenant colonel.

When I left, my tour of active duty with the U.S. Army was over. I had spent the past two and a half years in combat in the ETO and during the occupation of Berlin in only one unit: H Company. I had amassed almost three hundred days of combat, had been wounded twice, and had seen many men killed all around me, but miraculously I had survived. I returned to my hometown, Fond du Lac, Wisconsin, in one piece to begin a new chapter in my life.

Epilogue

In September 1943 when I and hundreds of other young paratroopers boarded troop carriers bound for Oran, Africa, we had little understanding of what might lie in store for us. We knew that Europe was in a life-or-death struggle and we would soon be part of it. None of us comprehended the brutality of mortal combat and who would survive it.

We were a diverse group with differing backgrounds. But we had more in common than might have separated us. We did not come from a militaristic society. Military service was respected and deemed essential to preserve our way of life, but it was not glorified. We were from a peaceful nation, harboring no ill will toward any other nation or coveting any territory or resources.

We were embarking on a venture for which our short life had not prepared us. None had been exposed to the kind of violence, destruction, and brutality we would soon be experiencing. Many of us were still in our teens; some had not finished high school. Most had not reached the legal age of twenty-one.

Most were not philosophically bent or motivated to fight for a higher cause, but we were reared to distinguish right from wrong. The forces of evil were running rampant across Europe, leaving a path of death and destruction in their wake. If left unchecked, the evil would engulf all freedom-loving people. No place on Earth would be free of Nazi oppression.

In the mountains of Italy, I and many others received our baptism of fire in our first days of combat. Nothing we had experienced could possibly have prepared us for combat. We had to undergo a transformation from peace-loving men to killers. The change would be gut wrenching, but it would happen as night follows day.

The first days were fraught with anxiety and fear—not necessarily of death but of the unknown. How would we react the first time we faced the enemy? Would we stand up to him and not let down our buddies? Once we engaged the enemy in combat, however, and saw both friend and foe killed, any doubts we had soon vanished. Our military occupational specialty (MOS) became clear: kill our enemy, the German soldier; the alternative was to be killed by our enemy. To become successful in our MOS, we had to develop a profound hatred for certain other human beings.

Most seasoned combat soldiers accepted their lot stoically. Death in battle was not unexpected and was accepted without remorse. It only served to strengthen our resolve.

When replacements arrived in my company, they were assigned to one of the three platoons. Those who joined when we were off the front lines quickly found their niches and were welcomed. Generally, however, they joined a unit in combat, replacing men who had fallen in battle. For enlisted replacements, their squad leader, a noncommissioned officer, became the most important man in the army. Sergeants would lead them against the enemy. It was their squad leaders they would look to first. They would then look to their buddies in platoons and companies with whom their fate was linked.

A replacement seldom knew what higher unit he was in, Patton's Third Army or Hodges's First Army. It had no bearing on his chances for survival. This really came from his buddies in his squad and platoon and the squads and platoons on his flanks. His war was being fought there, not at higher headquarters.

Many men knew the particular places or a specific time or battle when they transformed to the role of a killer, when they no longer held fear of death. My personal metamorphosis was on the Anzio beachhead where I killed my first

German. From that day in February 1944 until the end of the war, I had only one purpose in life: lead my platoon in battle and kill Germans.

For a newly assigned replacement, H Company became his home just as it was for me. He fought as part of a team of men that looked out for one another. He followed his squad or platoon leader without hesitation or question. The men who fought with him became more than his buddies or comrades in arms. A relationship beyond brotherhood developed among them.

Combat was a dehumanizing experience. A soldier was not immune to the ravages of nature. Twenty-four hours a day, seven days a week, he absorbed whatever nature threw at him on the front lines: snow, ice, sleet, rain, bitter cold, oppressive heat.

On a broader scale, after an extended period of combat, the same transformation took place within an entire unit. But in reality it was the successful transformation of young soldiers into hardened killers, aged beyond their years. In time, killing Germans became strangely enjoyable. This is difficult to explain in Judeo-Christian terms, but we understood it.

After the tide of battle turned in the winter of 1944–45 and the Wehrmacht began retreating, the end of an endless war finally appeared to be in sight. As we followed the Wehrmacht through Germany, our MOS began to change. Instead of German bodies littering the landscape, hordes of surrendering Germans now clogged roads. Suddenly the war was over.

Another transformation then occurred, from battle-hardened killers back to the peaceful young men and the homes we had left months and years ago. Periods of adjustment would inevitably follow; the transformation would take place sooner for some than others.

In January 1946, I returned to my home. When I left the service my love affair with a Thompson submachine gun and sniper's rifle ended. I had no further need for them. I have not felt insecure since.

The most difficult adjustment I faced was being separated from my combat buddies. I found I had little in common with classmates and prewar friends. They were still my friends, but it would be some time before they could fill the void in my life.

As returning veterans, we were now challenged to display the same level of devotion to become useful, productive members of society. I'm proud to say that my comrades in arms, who are an integral part of this book, and the other returning veterans accepted that challenge and continued serving their community and nation with the same dedication and devotion. Not all my comrades shed their uniforms when the war ended. The regular army officers continued on, helping to reshape the postwar army. Others made the army a career and were in combat again later. Still others, like myself, opted to remain active in the reserve, retiring after achieving twenty or more years of service.

Major General James M. Gavin, our division commander, was the youngest general in the army since Custer; he retired in 1958, after thirty-three years of service, as a lieutenant general. In 1961, President John F. Kennedy appointed him as ambassador to France, a country he helped to liberate from the Nazis. It was a fitting tribute to a distinguished commander. Gavin died in 1990.

Colonel Reuben Tucker was the 504th Regiment commander from December 1942 at Fort Bragg until the end of the war. Gavin referred to him as the best regimental commander in the U.S. Army. Tucker retired as a highly decorated major general. I last saw him in 1956 at The Citadel, in South Carolina, where he was the commandant of cadets under Gen. Mark Clark. Tucker died in 1970.

Lieutenant Colonel Julian A. Cook was promoted to colonel after the war ended. He was portrayed in the epic movie *A Bridge Too Far* by actor Robert Redford, leading the 3d Battalion in the first wave of the Waal River crossing. In 1953 Cook was assigned as a U.S. Army liaison officer to the French forces in Vietnam, where he became ill. He spent eight months in hospitals, which affected his career advancement.

After retiring from the army, he was employed by South Carolina as an appellate claims officer. He died in 1990 in Columbia, SC.

Lieutenant E. J. Sims, a combat veteran of every campaign with the 504th Regiment, from Sicily to the end of the war, returned to Hamilton, OH. After nine months of inactive reserve service, he returned to active duty to resume a career in the U.S. Army. He commanded a rifle company in combat in the Korean War. During his service in the army, he amassed more than 420 days in frontline duty, a record equaled by few officers. He retired from the army in 1968, after twenty-eight years of distinguished service, as a highly decorated colonel. Returning to civilian life, he took advantage of the GI Bill and received a bachelor of science degree from Fairleigh Dickinson University, in New Jersey. He was employed as an executive in a title and guaranty company in New Jersey, where he now resides. He also served as a county probation officer.

Captain Thomas Helgeson commanded B Company, which bore the brunt of the attack on Cheneux, Belgium, during the Battle of the Bulge. He was wounded in the battle, and his company suffered heavy casualties. He was awarded a Silver Star as well as three Purple Hearts. In 1945 he returned to his hometown, Ripon, WI. In 1949 he reentered the army as a captain. In 1950 he was assigned to the 187th Regimental Combat Team in Korea. He retired after thirty years of army service as a lieutenant colonel. He presently resides in Bradenton, FL.

Private George D. Heib entered service at the ripe age of fifteen, volunteered for the paratroopers, and observed his eighteenth birthday during the Battle of the Bulge. After the war, he returned to his home in Detroit, MI, and was employed in law enforcement for a brief period before deciding to rejoin the army. He did two tours in Southeast Asia with the rank of captain. He retired in 1972 after thirty years as a lieutenant colonel. He returned to North Carolina, where he taught leadership courses in high school ROTC for twenty-one years, making a total of more than fifty-one years in the uniform of the U.S. Army. He remains active in special forces and veterans' affairs in Fayetteville, NC.

Sergeant Jimmy Shields chose to make a career in the army. In September 1950 he was wounded in action in the vicinity of the Han River, in Korea, in combat with the 187th Regimental Combat Team. He recovered and returned to duty, retiring in 1968 as a master sergeant. He returned to Stillwater, OK, where he remains active in civic and veterans' affairs.

Private George Willoughby, like George Heib, volunteered for the army at age fifteen. At the end of the war, he returned to Bellville, MI. In February 1947 he reenlisted in the army and rejoined the 82d Airborne Division in Fort Bragg. He again saw combat duty in Korea with the 2d Division. He retired after twenty-five years as a command sergeant major. He resides in Murfreesboro, TN.

Private First Class David E. Ward Jr. joined the army in 1936 at age sixteen. On 7 January 1945 he was in Lieutenant Murphy's platoon in the attack on Petit Halleaux in the Battle of the Bulge; he was awarded the Bronze Star. Ward went on with me to the occupation of Berlin, then decided to make the army a career. He retired as a master sergeant after twenty-seven years of service. He was employed by the city court system of Norfolk, VA, for ten years. He died in 1997.

The majority of my comrades opted to leave the service at the end of the war and return to civilian life to restart their lives. Although few had experience in the workplace, they soon found their niche, many becoming leaders in their chosen fields in business, academics, the ministry, government service, public safety, law enforcement, labor, politics, and community service.

Sergeant Frederic Andrews was a veteran of H Company during the entire war in every campaign from Sicily on. Although he was twice wounded and hospitalized, he recovered and rejoined H Company. At the end of the war he returned to civilian life in Beaverdam, OH. In 1946 he was employed by Sprint Telephone Company and became a supervisor in installation, repair, and maintenance. He retired after thirty-five years of service. He still resides in Beaver-dam.

Lieutenant Robert (Boobytrap) Blankenship and I parted company after the victory parade in New York on 12 January 1946. He returned to DeRitter, LA, and entered private business. The voters of DeRitter elected him their mayor. Every Armed Forces Day, "his honor" jumped with a parachute team; in keeping with tradition, he was first out the door. He died in 1973 from wounds he received in combat.

Private First Class Robert E. Breland returned to his home in Walterboro, SC, and was employed as a civil servant by the U.S. Marine Corps. He worked at Parris Island, SC, for ten years in maintenance, then was transferred to the Marine Air Station in Beaufort, where he was a supervisor of planning, estimating upkeep and repair of mechanical equipment for twenty-three years. He retired after thirty-three years. He resides in Ruffin, SC.

Lieutenant Rufus K. Broadaway returned to Boston in 1945 and took advantage of the GI Bill, earning a B.S. from Tufts College and an M.D. from Harvard Medical School in 1950. Since then he has had a distinguished career as a surgeon, professor of surgery, and delegate and trustee to the American Medical Association. His accomplishments and honors are too numerous to be listed in this brief resume. He currently resides in Highlands, NC, where he remains active as a semiretired consultant in the health-care field and as trustee at the Highlands-Cashiers Hospital.

Captain T. Moffatt Burriss received a reserve commission from Clemson College in 1940. In the daring crossing of the Waal River at Nijmegen, Holland, on 20 September 1944, he led I Company in the first wave. He returned to South Carolina and became a building contractor. He also served fifteen years in the South Carolina House of Representatives, where for nine years he was the minority leader. He recently published his memoirs in a book entitled *Strike and Hold*. He presently resides in Columbia, SC.

Lieutenant Virgil (Hoagie) Carmichael, 3d Battalion S2, was a veteran of every campaign from Sicily to the end of the war. Returning to Cleveland, TN, in September 1945, he resumed prelaw studies. In 1947 he received a law degree from Cumberland University and entered private practice in Cleveland. In 1956 he was appointed assistant attorney general for eastern Tennessee. In 1966 he was elected to an eight-year term as judge of the circuit court of Tennessee. He was reelected in 1974 and served one year of the second term, then returned to private practice. He continued hearing cases in circuit court when needed. He served for forty-nine years as a member of the bar and on the bench. He currently resides in Knoxville, TN.

First Sergeant Bernard Cheney was wounded in the Battle of the Bulge fighting with the 551st Parachute Battalion. He was hospitalized in England, released, and assigned to H Company, 504th Regiment, in April 1945. In December 1945 he left the army and returned to Lubec, ME. He was employed by the state of Maine as a state trooper for ten years. He left the force and became an insurance adjuster, representing insurance companies. He currently resides in Machias, ME.

Staff Sergeant Charles Crowder was in the first wave of the bloody Waal River crossing in Nijmegen and was up front with me in the attack on Herresbach in the Battle of the Bulge. At the conclusion of hostilities, he returned to Harriman, TN. In 1948 he reenlisted in the army as a staff sergeant and was assigned to E Company, 505th Parachute Infantry Regiment. He was injured in a jump and hospitalized for two months. Taken off jump status, he received a medical discharge after almost eight years of service. He returned to Tennessee and was employed as a construction wireman, working for the Tennessee Valley Authority and on several nuclear plants in an area ranging from Atlanta, GA, to the state of New York. He retired after thirty-two years. He presently resides in Clinton, TN.

Private Robert DeVinney left the service after the victory parade and returned to Lansing, MI, where he still resides. He was employed by Abrams Instruments as a draftsman for five years, then by Oldsmobile, from which he retired in 1985 after twenty-five years in design engineering.

Private Lawrence Dunlop, one of the original 504th, was a machine gunner in H Company and fought in every campaign. He was wounded on the Anzio beachhead and hospitalized in Naples, Italy. In May 1945 at the end of the war he returned to Beverly, MA, and was on the Beverly Police Force for more than thirty years before retiring in 1982. He presently resides in Bennington, VT.

Sergeant Theodore Finkbeiner, squad leader and platoon sergeant in H Company, referred to by his men as "one helluva sergeant," jumped in Sicily and, although wounded in Anzio, returned and fought with H Company until the end of the war. He returned to Monroe, LA, and joined the Monroe Fire Department; he retired after thirty-seven years as the deputy fire chief. He resides in Downsville, LA.

Sergeant John (Jack) Fowler, a squad leader in my platoon, was wounded on a night patrol behind enemy lines in Holland on 30 September 1944. He recovered and returned to duty. When the war ended, he returned to Pittsburgh, PA. He entered private business briefly, then was employed by Harmony Dairy as a salesman. He developed a brain tumor and died in 1975 at the age of fifty-three. He is being inducted into the Pittsburgh Hall of Valor.

Corporal John Granado was awarded a Distinguished Service Cross for extraordinary heroism on the Anzio beachhead. In 1945 he returned to Napa, CA (where he still resides), and was employed at the Mare Island Shipyards in Vallejo, CA, for thirty-five years before retiring as a supervisor.

Sergeant Clement A. Haas, another of the original 504th, jumped in Sicily and survived the entire war. Before returning to Riverton, NJ, he married a young lady he met when the 504th was in Leicester, England. Using the GI Bill, he enrolled in the University of Pennsylvania and graduated in 1953 with a B.S. in finance. He was employed as personnel manager for Underwood Typewriter, then by Olivetti. He retired in 1985. Active in civic affairs, he was twice elected president of the local Rotary Club. He still resides in Riverton.

Lieutenant Roy Hanna, I Company, graduated from Pennsylvania State University in 1939 with a B.S. in food science. He volunteered for the army on 21 October 1940, then was selected to attend officers' training school. After completion he volunteered for the paratroopers, was assigned as the machine gun platoon leader, and remained with the 504th until the end of the war. He was wounded on the Anzio beachhead but not before he led I Company to the rescue of H Company, which had been cut off and surrounded. For his part in helping stop the Germans from overriding the beachhead, he was awarded a Distinguished Service Cross in addition to the Purple Heart. In civilian life he was associated with the dairy industry for thirty-nine years. After retiring he volunteered for the International Executive Service Corps, serving in Sri Lanka and North Yemen, where he applied his food service training to help these nations improve their manufacturing and sanitation skills. Roy and Jan live in Southern Pines, NC.

Sergeant William Hannigan returned to St. Paul, MN, in September 1945. Taking advantage of the GI Bill, he entered St. Thomas University and graduated in 1949 with a B.A. He was employed for ten years as a vice president for terminal operations by Merchants Motor Freight, then by two other large freight companies. He retired in 1987 after almost forty years. He resides in Omaha, NE.

Private Donald L. Herndon dropped out of high school to enlist in the army, then volunteered for the paratroopers. I was with him when he was wounded in the Battle of the Bulge at Cheneux on 20 December 1944. Gangrene developed in his leg and he was hospitalized in England. Fortunately he recovered and after three months returned to H Company. After the victory parade he returned to Georgia. He finished high school, then went to the University of Georgia, where he received a B.S. in agriculture and a master's in education counseling. He also received a sixth-year specialist degree in educational psychology. He taught for thirty years in Gwinnett County, GA, fourteen in the classroom and sixteen in district-wide administration. He entered the ministry in 1957 after seminary at Emory University in Decatur, GA. Before retiring he was a pastor for forty years in a rural church in Duluth, GA, where he still resides.

Sergeant Marvin Hirsch, who was wounded in the boat with me in the Waal River crossing, returned to West Hempstead, NY, after the war. He founded and became president of Contemporary Shells. He visited me in Florida in 1981, the last time I saw him. I have not been able to communicate with him since, and his status is uncertain.

Sergeant Michael (Mike) J. Kogut, my platoon sergeant in Italy, then first sergeant, H Company, was a natural leader. At the end of the war, he returned to his hometown of Ludlow, MA, and became active in organized labor. He became a vice president and regional director of the International Brotherhood of Molders and Allied Workers, AFL-CIO, and an international organizer for the union. He was a strong advocate and forceful voice for working men's rights. He died in 1996.

Captain Delbert Kuehl, the venerable 3d Battalion chaplain, seemed to be everywhere he was needed on the front lines from Sicily to the end of the war. In September 1945 he returned to Alexandria, MN, having been awarded a Silver Star, two Bronze Stars, a Purple Heart, and three Presidential Unit Citations. In July 1946 he married Dolores Johnson and together they embarked on foreign missionary service. In March 1951 they arrived in Japan with their ten-month-old son and spent nine years as missionaries. He was called back to the States and assumed worldwide responsibilities for the Evangelical Alliance Mission (Team) as candidate secretary and executive assistant director. He remained active in the army reserve and retired as a colonel. He presently resides in Alexandria.

My buddy Lt. Richard (Rivers) G. LaRiviere, a fearless leader in combat, returned to his hometown of Chicopee Falls, MA, in 1945. He turned his energies into building and creating, earning a bachelor of science degree in industrial engineering; he retired after forty years as a construction engineer. He was a devoted family man, the father of four sons and five daughters. He was as compassionate in peace as he was fearless in combat. He died in 1995.

Lieutenant Allen F. McClain (Mac), 81mm mortar platoon leader, returned to Miami, FL, in 1945, joining his father, a captain in the Miami Fire Department. In 1969 he retired after twenty-four years. He remained active in the army reserve, retiring as major. After retiring, he moved his family to Blue Ridge, GA, where he became the civil defense director. He was also employed as a tax consultant until he suffered a debilitating stroke in 1990. He presently resides in the Bryan Nursing Center in Canton, GA.

Private Richard (Dick) Moecia left the army in December 1945 and returned to Canton, OH. Under the GI Bill he took courses in shoe repairing and in 1947 opened his own shop. He was in private business for thirty-seven years before retiring. He still resides in Canton.

Lieutenant Ernest P. Murphy (Murph) received a battlefield commission at the Anzio beachhead. He returned to Kissimmee, FL, when the war ended and joined the Osceola County sheriff's department. For fourteen years he was the chief deputy, then was elected sheriff for four consecutive terms (sixteen years) in a county that encompasses a large part of Disney World. During that time, the new county administrative building was dedicated as the E. P. Murphy Building. In 1985 he was honored at a retirement ceremony with General Gavin in attendance as a special guest. After retirement he continued as a consultant to the sheriff's department for another four years, making a total of thirty-four years of service to that department. He continued in the U.S. Army Reserves, retiring with the rank of lieutenant colonel. He continues to reside in Kissimmee.

Private James Musa was with me in November 1943 in the mountains of Italy. He was severely wounded in Holland and spent ten months in a hospital in Memphis, TN. He returned to Oswego, NY, and was employed as a district manager for Triangle Shoes for eighteen years. He then owned a private shoe store, which he sold five years later. For the next fifteen years until he retired in 1979, he was employed by the Metropolitan Insurance Company. He resides in Oswego and maintains a winter residence in Sebastian, FL.

Lieutenant L. D. (Dick) Owen returned to Bay Minette, AL, where he still resides. He remained active in the army reserve and was recalled during the Korean War, serving with the 187th RCT. He returned to operate the family hardware business, which he still manages. In 1964 he was appointed a probate judge and was elected to the Alabama state legislature, serving six years in the House of Representatives followed by eight years in the state senate. In 1977 he was voted the most effective member of the senate.

Private Simon Renner joined H Company on the Anzio beachhead and was wounded in action in the Battle of the Bulge. In November 1945 he left the service and returned to Monroe Center, WI. He was employed by the Nekoosa Edwards Paper Company for thirty-six years, the last ten as the senior man on the largest and most modern paper machine. He received a 1,000-hour award for volunteer service in the Wisconsin State Veterans Hospital. On Veterans Day 2000 he was recognized and honored as the most decorated veteran from Adams County, WI. He died in 2001.

Private John Schultz was with H Company during the attack and capture of Herresbach on the night of 28 January 1945. He left the service after the victory parade and returned to his hometown of McKeesport, PA, where he still resides. He was employed by Duquesne Power and Light Company, retiring as a foreman after thirty-seven years.

Captain Hyman D. Shapiro, 3d Battalion medical officer, received his M.D. at the University of Ontario before volunteering for the paratroopers. He returned to the University of Michigan for residency training in ear, nose, and throat, then entered private practice in Lansing, MI, retiring after thirty years. He was with the 504th from Sicily to the end of the war. His decorations include a Silver Star, a Bronze Star, two Purple Hearts, and two Presidential Unit Citations.

Private Walter Souza, H Company headquarters, was one

of the original 504th troopers who jumped in Sicily. He fought in every campaign until the end of the war and miraculously was never wounded. He returned to Mount Vernon, NY, and was employed by a construction company for thirty years as shop steward. For the following five years he worked full time for an asphalt company, finally retiring in 1995 at age seventy-five. He resides in Yonkers, NY.

Private First Class Harold Sullivan was with me in the attack on Herresbach during the Battle of the Bulge. He returned to Watertown, MA. With assistance from the GI Bill, he studied electronics for two years in the Boston Industrial Technical School. He was employed by Boston Gas for five years before leaving to work for a supermarket chain in the field of refrigeration for fifteen years. He was last employed by the Bank of New England as liaison with contractors for five years before retiring in 1990. The Sullivans reared nine children, a close-knit family. Sullivan presently resides in North Reading, MA.

Sergeant Albert A. Tarbell, communications sergeant, entered service from St. Raegis Mohawk Indian Reservation, NY. Miraculously, although often exposed to enemy fire, he was never wounded. He returned to Syracuse, NY, and was employed as an ironworker on large projects, such as the St. Lawrence Seaway and a nuclear power plant. He retired in 1985 as a general foreman after thirty-four years. He presently resides in Syracuse.

Sergeant John J. Toman, a squad leader in my platoon, was wounded twice in action, the second a head wound from which he never fully recovered. After leaving the hospital, he returned to North Tonawanda, NY, where he was employed by the Continental Paper Works for fourteen years. For the next seven years he was employed by the VA hospital in Buffalo, NY, retiring in 1977. From that date until his death in January 1999, he was in and out of VA hospitals and finally confined to a nursing home.

Sergeant James L. Ward returned to McComb, MS. Under the GI Bill he attended a trade school in Baton Rouge, LA, studying refrigeration. In 1950 he founded Ward

Refrigeration Company, which later became Ward Mechanical Contractors Inc. He is still active in the company. He resides in Denham Springs, LA.

Sergeant Donald Zimmerman returned to his native state of Pennsylvania after the war. Taking advantage of the GI Bill, he attended the University of Pittsburgh, then was in private business for nineteen years. He joined a stainless-steel casting firm as a supervisor, retiring after eighteen years. He currently resides in Scottsdale, PA.

I have answered my own question, What manner of men were these? Some have referred to them as the "greatest generation." I do not subscribe to that broad-brush characterization. What I do subscribe to and without fear of contradiction is that the men in the foxholes who fought their country's battles were the best our generation had to offer.

Acknowledgments
and Sources

Reliving war experiences, reading old war letters, and renewing acquaintances with my buddies, some of whom I hadn't seen for more than fifty years, has been a bittersweet experience. For almost three years I dug deep into my memory, restating my innermost feelings that have lain dormant all these years.

Writing this book has been an agonizing exercise as it reopened old wounds, but at the same time I feel a sense of relief in having done it.

In my writing I have recollected events that surrounded me, with a focus on squad and platoon actions. Squads and platoons, on the front line, formed the basis of the combat history of World War II. I rarely saw officers above company grade where the actual fighting took place. In the macro accounts written by historians, battles are expressed in terms of armies, corps, and divisions deployed over wide fronts.

My experience in combat was no different from that of every other platoon leader in the 82d Division. We all endured the same perils and hardships but persevered to meet every challenge we faced.

We were all in this together with a single-minded purpose: defeat the enemy and end the war. It has not been my intention to suggest or imply that any unit in the 82d excelled above the others. I wrote only about what I knew and saw.

Fortunately, after all these years, I was able to locate some of the men I fought with. I have had the pleasure of meeting with about half of those I listed as contributors. I had not seen some of them since the end of the war.

In cases where face-to-face meetings were not feasible, we conversed by phone for endless hours. Individual accounts were checked and verified by several sources. I am indebted deeply to the contributors. They added authenticity and credibility to my own narrative of events.

They are: Frederic Andrews, Robert B. Breland, Gordon Brewer, Rufus K. Broadaway, T. Moffatt Burriss, Virgil Carmichael, Bernard Cheney, Charles Crowder, Robert E. DeVinney, Laurence H. Dunlop, Robert F. Dunn, Theodore Finkbeiner, Jr., Mrs. John Fowler, John C. Granado, Clement A. Haas, Roy Hanna, William Hannigan, Thomas Helgeson, Louis Hauptfleisch, Michael D. Healy, George Heib, Donald L. Herndon, Delbert Kuehl, Allen F. McClain, Dick R. Moecia, Ernest P. Murphy, James Musa, L. D. Owens Jr., Simon Renner, John Schultz, Hyman Shapiro, Jimmie Shields, Edward J. Sims, Walter Souza, Harold J. Sullivan, Albert A. Tarbell, Marnix Versteegh, James L. Ward, George Willoughby, and H. Donald Zimmerman.

I have drawn on more than these oral and written narratives. Notations from unit logs kept in combat, daily journals, and after-action reports helped jog my memory and fill in blank spaces.

I spent many hours at libraries verifying dates, times, and places. In my hometown library I found microfilm copies of the local newspaper printed during the war years.

I have also quoted liberally from a stack of old war letters I found in my attic, including many I had written from the front lines. Excerpts from those letters are really a documentary, accurately reflecting what I felt and thought at the time.

I am especially indebted to Rufus K. Broadaway, whose encouragement and offer of assistance motivated me to finally get started. His advice and suggestions over the past three years have helped maintain my focus. In addition, he computerized my often illegible handwritten accounts into a legible first draft.

A number of retired U.S. Army officers read all or parts of the first draft and made useful comments: Maj. Gen. Michael D. Healy, Col. E. J. Sims, Col. Arvel Hensley, Lt. Col. L. D. Owen, Lt. Col. E. P. Murphy, Chaplain (Col.) Delbert Kuehl, Lt. Col. George Heib, and Maj. Hatcher James. Others, who are contributors to the book, made helpful suggestions after reviewing the first draft: Donald Herndon, Albert Tarbell, James Musa, Lawrence Dunlop, and Bernard Cheney. I am also indebted to our son Jim and his wife, Michelle Megellas, and Robert and Elvira Weiss for their contributions to the final draft.

Finally, I wish to express my gratitude to my wife, Carole, for her understanding. She tolerated my frustrations and disruptions while the book was in process, spending countless hours on her computer trying to locate my World War II buddies and uncovering reliable sources. She devoted as much time and effort in the writing of this book as I did.

*What if Germany invaded
America in . . .*

1901

A thrilling novel of a war that never was

by Robert Conroy

The year is 1901. Germany's navy is the second largest in the world; their army, the most powerful. But with the exception of a small piece of Africa and a few minor islands in the Pacific, Germany is without an empire. Kaiser Wilhelm II demands that the United States surrender its newly acquired territories. President McKinley indignantly refuses, so with the honor and economic future of the Reich at stake, the Kaiser launches an invasion of the United States, striking first on Long Island.

Now the Americans, with their army largely disbanded, must defend the homeland. When McKinley suffers a fatal heart attack, the new commander in chief, Theodore Roosevelt, rallies to the cause, along with Confederate general James Longstreet. From the burning of Manhattan to the climactic Battle of Danbury, American forces face Europe's most potent war machine in a blazing contest of will against strength.

Published by Presidio Press
Available wherever books are sold